PIMLICO

312

# RICHARD BRINSLEY SHERIDAN

Linda Kelly's most recent books are *Juniper Hall* and *Women of the French Revolution*. She is also co-editor of two anthologies, *Feasts* and *Proposals*, and has written for a number of papers, including the *Times Literary Supplement* and the *Washington Post*. She is married, with three children, and lives in London.

# RICHARD BRINSLEY
# SHERIDAN

## A Life

---

# LINDA KELLY

PIMLICO

Published by Pimlico 1998

2 4 6 8 10 9 7 5 3 1

First published by Sinclair-Stevenson 1997
Pimlico edition 1998

Pimlico
Random House, 20 Vauxhall Bridge Road,
London SW1V 2SA

Random House Australia (Pty) Limited
20 Alfred Street, Milsons Point, Sydney,
New South Wales 2061, Australia

Random House New Zealand Limited
18 Poland Road, Glenfield,
Auckland 10, New Zealand

Random House South Africa (Pty) Limited
Endulini, 5A Jubilee Road, Parktown 2193, South Africa

Random House UK Limited Reg. No. 954009

A CIP catalogue record for this book
is available from the British Library

ISBN 0-7126-6693-1

Papers used by Random House UK Limited are natural,
recyclable products made from wood grown in sustainable forests.
The manufacturing processes conform to the environmental
regulations of the country of origin

Printed and bound in Great Britain by
Mackays of Chatham PLC

*To the memory of my parents*

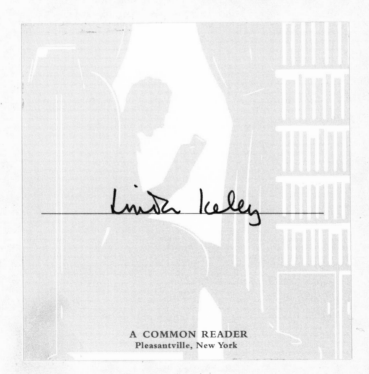

A COMMON READER
Pleasantville, New York

# Contents

# List of Illustrations

———————⟨∾⟩———————

Dr Thomas Sheridan *(Hulton Getty Picture Collection)*

Thomas Linley the Elder by Thomas Gainsborough *(Dulwich Picture Gallery)*

Thomas Sheridan by John Lewis *(National Gallery of Ireland)*

Mrs Frances Sheridan by John Lewis *(National Portrait Gallery)*

*A Portrait of Two Ladies* by Thomas Gainsborough *(Dulwich Picture Gallery)*

*Mrs Sheridan as St Cecilia* by Joshua Reynolds *(The National Trust, Waddesdon Manor, and the Courtauld Institute of Art)*

Mrs Crewe, from a drawing by Downman *(Private collection)*

George IV as Prince of Wales, after the painting by Joshua Reynolds *(Hulton Getty Picture Collection)*

*A Gaming Table at Devonshire House* by Thomas Rowlandson *(Private collection, courtesy of Spink & Son)*

'Ye Falling of the Screen' *(Hulton Getty Picture Collection)*

*A Peep Behind the Curtain at Drury Lane* by James Sayers *(British Museum)*

*Mrs Siddons as the Tragic Muse* by Joshua Reynolds *(Dulwich Picture Gallery)*

Kemble as Rolla in *Pizarro*, after the painting by Thomas Lawrence *(Victoria & Albert Museum)*

Sheridan as Pizarro by James Gillary *(National Portrait Gallery)*

Drury Lane Theatre on fire *(Mander & Mitchenson Theatre Collection)*

ix

Charles James Fox by Karl Anton Hickel *(National Portrait Gallery)*
William Pitt the Younger by Thomas Gainsborough
  *(National Portrait Gallery)*
*Uncorking Old Sherry* by James Gillray *(Hulton Getty Picture Collection)*
Esther Sheridan with her son Charles Francis, from the painting by
  John Hoppner *(National Portrait Gallery)*
Tom Sheridan by Ozias Humphry *(Victoria Art Gallery,
  Bath City Council)*
The Sheridan portrait at Clandeboye by Richard Morton Paye
  *(Dufferin and Ava Collection)*
Sheridan by Joshua Reynolds *(Private collection)*

# Introduction

George III preferred *The Rivals* to *The School for Scandal*; Sheridan liked the first act of *The Critic* best of all his writings for the stage. But in whichever order they are given they mark the high point of eighteenth-century comedy, their wit and brilliance undiminished after more than two hundred years. 'It is such a *nice* play too,' wrote Freya Stark after seeing Laurence Olivier's production of *The School for Scandal* in 1947. 'I mean it has that sort of gaiety and charity which sweetens English literature from Chaucer, Spenser, Shakespeare, Milton, right through, an innate decency.'

The same qualities which have endeared Sheridan's plays to so many generations of audiences run through the story of his life. His wit illumines it at every stage. Who can forget his reply to Dundas in the House of Commons: 'The right honourable gentleman is indebted to his memory for his jests and his imagination for his facts.' Or his answer to the watchman, when taken up drunk in the street: 'My name – hic – is William Wilberforce.' He had the generosity of his own Charles Surface. The painter Joseph Farington records how shortly before his death he was carried off to a sponging house (or debtor's prison):

'He recd. between 4 & £500 to relieve him, but at this period a Man who had been a tenant to him in Surrey, called upon him and stated that He was in the utmost distress, everything he possessed being taken for a debt. Sheridan asked Him what sum would relieve him. The man replied that £300 would restore him to his former state. Sheridan gave him the money.'

From the age of twenty-three, when *The Rivals* was first performed, Sheridan was a celebrity. No Irishman has ever conquered London so completely, or shone in so many different worlds. Reckless, charming and unreliable, his character was full of contradictions. As proprietor and manager of Drury Lane, he presided over one of the most brilliant periods in the history of the English stage. But his carelessness and deviousness about money were a byword; a host of unpaid actors, stagehands and small tradesmen saw the reverse side of his generosity. In Parliament his birth – as the son of an actor – and his lack of connections were inbuilt disadvantages. He rose above them to become one of the greatest parliamentary orators of all time, ranking with Fox, Burke and Pitt and perhaps at times surpassing them. But politically he almost always swam against the stream, whether in his championship of Ireland and Catholic emancipation, or his enthusiasm for the opening stages of the French Revolution. Too independent to be a good party man, he grew to be distrusted even by his opposition colleagues for what they regarded as his double dealing. His fellow Whig Lord Grey once remarked that 'for ability and treachery He might be called the devil on earth'.

The first biography of Sheridan, John Watkins's two-volume *Memoirs of the Public and Private Life of the Right Honourable R. B. Sheridan*, was published in 1817, the year after Sheridan's death. Written from a Tory viewpoint, and hostile to him politically, it was full of inaccuracies where Sheridan's personal life was concerned, but provided an able summary of the main events of his parliamentary career. Thomas Moore, his next biographer, drew so freely from it that he was accused of using Watkins's work to save himself the trouble of reading the Parliamentary Debates. Moore himself gave little credit to his predecessor: 'Worked a little at Sheridan – badly off for materials – almost reduced to Watkins', he wrote in his journal for 30 October 1818.

Moore's journal covering the period when he was writing his life of Sheridan is an invaluable source. Its very first entry reads: 'August 18 [Tuesday], 1818 – Went to Bath on my way to Leamington Spa, for the purpose of consulting Mrs LeFanu, the only surviving sister of Sheridan on the subject of her brother's life.' He met Mrs LeFanu two days later: 'Found Mrs LeFanu – the very image of Sheridan – having all his features without his carbuncles – and all the light of his eyes without the illumination of his nose.'

The journal, edited by Lord John Russell and published between 1852 and 1856 by Longmans under the title *Memoirs, Journal and Correspondence of Thomas Moore*, has recently yielded new treasures. In 1967, Wilfred S. Dowden, Professor of English at Rice University in the USA, discovered the original manuscript of the journal while researching in the Longman archives. It consisted of twelve copy books, a number of them damaged by water and in a poor condition, and with many passages deleted, some in deference to Victorian taste, some simply because the editor found them uninteresting.

The task of restoring Russell's deletions, placing the manuscript under a fluorescent light, with a magnifying glass, to read through the scorings to Moore's writing underneath, was formidable, but eventually 90–95 per cent of the scored-out passages were recovered. The full text was published in six volumes between 1983 and 1991. Some of the most interesting new passages relate to Sheridan, in particular details of his elopement ('There is no coming at the truth of this business, but I fear it was by no means the romantic affair I made it') and the troubled course of his two marriages.

Moore's *Memoirs of the Life of the Right Honourable Richard Brinsley Sheridan*, published in 1825, is probably still the classic biography. He knew Sheridan personally, though only at the end of his life, and was certainly inspired by Sheridan's verses in his own 'Irish Melodies'. He sympathised with him as a Whig and fellow Irishman, though he was perhaps too much in awe of the surviving grandees of the Whig party, Lord Grey and Lord Holland especially, to do justice to his political career. 'Tommy loves a Lord', as Byron remarked.

Of later nineteenth-century biographies, *Sheridan*, in the English Men of Letters series by Mrs Oliphant (1883), and *The Lives of the Sheridans* by Percy Fitzgerald (1886) are both more or less hostile to Sheridan. Mrs Oliphant, as Professor E. H. Mikhail puts it, rises up against her subject 'in all the outraged virtue of a Victorian matron confronted with sin'; Fitzgerald's book, while acknowledging his greatness as an orator and playwright, portrays him as little better than a swindler in financial matters. W. Fraser Rae's *Sheridan*, 1896, on the other hand, goes too far in the opposite direction. Written at the request of Sheridan's great-grandson, the Marquess of Dufferin and Ava, who placed his family papers at his disposal, it included much new material but was 'monotonously laudatory' in its tone. Fitzgerald, predictably, accused it of shamelessly whitewashing Sheridan.

Walter Sichel's monumental *Sheridan* (1909) also included new material, but is so rambling and copious that it almost overwhelms its subject. Sheridan's great-great-grandson Wilfred Sheridan remarked that it would bury Sheridan for a century. There have been a number of shorter biographies since then, of which R. Crompton Rhodes's *Harlequin Sheridan* (1933) is perhaps the most distinguished. Most recently James Morwood's *The Life and Work of Richard Brinsley Sheridan* (1985) examines the various themes in Sheridan's life, as a playwright, theatre manager and politician, and provides a critical discussion of the major plays. Stanley Ayling's *Sheridan: A Portrait*, published the same year, gives an incisive overview.

Moore, Rae, Sichel and, since 1966, the collected edition of Sheridan's letters, edited and annotated by Cecil Price, are still the main authorities on Sheridan's life. But Sheridan was so much a figure in eighteenth- and early nineteenth-century society that there is scarcely a political or theatrical memoir of the time which does not refer to him, and there is an abundance of further information in the newspapers, letters and journals of the day. There seems a place for a more substantial general biography than has appeared in recent years, showing him against this wider background, and making use of the new material now available as well as consulting the Sheridan archives in Belfast, Stafford and elsewhere.

Sheridan's comedies were all written by the time that he was twenty-eight; his political career thereafter spanned more than thirty years. It is a period which has often been given short shrift by his biographers in relation to the more romantic events of his youth, his elopement, his duels, his triumphs as a playwright, but which deserves a fuller coverage. To Sheridan politics were always more important than the theatre. His parliamentary speeches run to five closely printed volumes, and even then stop short of the last four years of his career, from 1808 to 1812. It was an age of long speeches, and Sheridan's were no exception – 'I know I am luxuriant,' says Mr Puff. We have to take accounts of their effect on trust, the tears and enthusiasm aroused by his speech on Warren Hastings, the pitiless invective which made Pitt's eyes start out of their sockets with defiance, as though 'if he advanced an atom further he would have his life'. Many of them, including that on Warren Hastings, have survived only as paraphrases, but in those which are reported verbatim we catch some of Sheridan's true qualities, the vigour of his arguments, the flash of his humour, his humanity and common sense. It is hard to quote from them without falsifying their character, which was cumulative, building up from point to point in a way to which no extract can do justice. I have tried, however, to give something of their flavour and, at the risk of over-simplification, to set them in the context of the eventful years, from the American War of Independence to the Napoleonic War, in which they took place.

I am enormously grateful for the help I have received in writing this book – to Sheridan's descendants, Sir Brinsley Ford, Sir Ian Fraser and Lord Plunket, and to the Marchioness of Dufferin and Ava, whose husband, the late Marquess of Dufferin and Ava, was also a Sheridan descendant; Mary, Duchess of Roxburghe, Colin Crewe and Fionn Morgan, descendants of Mrs Crewe; the late Earl of Bessborough, descendant of Lady Bessborough; Amanda Foreman, who in the course of researching her forthcoming book on Georgiana, Duchess of Devonshire, drew my attention to Esther Sheridan's letters in the Granville Papers; Kate Kavanagh for sharing her discoveries about Quilca, and Alyson and James Spooner for taking me there; Valerie and Thomas Pakenham and the Knight of Glin for their help on Sheridan's Irish background; Katherine Kjellgren for her insights on acting in Sheridan's plays; Douglas Matthews for undertaking the index; Dr Sergei Revyakin for his advice on medical matters; Adrian and Marina Berry for their hospitality while writing this book; my editor Roger Cazalet; His Honour A. J. Blackett-Ord; Eugenie Boyd; George Clive; Miles Gladwyn; Sebastian Grigg; Professor Peter Jupp; Peter Levi; the late Dr Angus Macintyre; Jim McCue; Francis Russell; Mehreen Saigol; Anthony Sheil; Christopher Sinclair-Stevenson; Harriot Tennant; Lola Armstrong, Curator of the Dufferin and Ava Collection,

Clandeboye; Michael Briggs, Chairman of the Bath Preservation Trust, and Isabel Briggs; Alasdair Hawkyard, Librarian of the Vaughan Library, Harrow; Dr Anthony Malcolmson, Deputy Keeper of the Records, Public Record Office of Northern Ireland; Professor Brigitte Mitchell, Chairman of the Bath Museum, Royal Crescent; Dr Jeanne T. Newlin, former Curator of the Harvard Theatre Collection, and Michael Dumas; Victoria Partington, Department of Printed Books and Manuscripts, Sotheby's; the Central Library, Bath; the Birmingham Art Gallery; the British Library; the Chief Herald's Office in Dublin; the Kensington and Chelsea Public Library; the London Library; the Public Record Office; the Theatre Museum Library; the William Salt Library, Stafford. I salute the memory of my aunt, Sheila Birkenhead, whose own plans to write on Sheridan were cut short by ill health, and of my father, Ronald McNair Scott, whose encouragement cheered me in the early stages of this book. My greatest thanks of all are to my husband, Laurence Kelly, whose patience, advice and knowledge of eighteenth-century history have helped me more than I can say.

# I

Mid-eighteenth-century Dublin was a rapidly expanding city, the second largest in the British Isles and said to be the fifth in Europe – surpassed in population only by London, Paris, Rome and Madrid. Its self-confidence and civic pride were reflected in its spacious layout, the sober classicism of its terraces and squares, and the splendour of its monuments and public buildings. The equestrian statue of William III on College Green summed up the triumph of the Protestant ruling classes, the Parliament House, begun in the 1720s, was bigger than that at Westminster, and other public buildings – the Royal Hospital, the Customs House, the library at Trinity – were on an equally ambitious scale. A special commission for 'Making Wide and Convenient Streets' encouraged the creation of the broad main thoroughfares, where sheep and cattle on their way to market jostled with the carriages and sedan chairs of the gentry. For all its grandeur Dublin was still something of a country town, the capital of a country where agriculture remained the chief means of subsistence.

No. 12 Dorset Street, the house where Richard Brinsley Sheridan was born in 1751, was part of a fashionable new development on the north side of the city, its tall sash windows overlooking what was once the main route from the north to Dublin Bridge. It was a substantial four-storey house (now demolished to make way for modern flats) whose size and situation reflected the status of its owner. At the age of thirty-two Thomas Sheridan was at the height of his theatrical career, the manager of the Theatre Royal, Smock Alley, and, in Ireland at least, the leading actor of his day.

Thomas Sheridan came of native Irish stock. The Sheridans, or O'Sheridans as they were originally called, were one of the oldest families in Ireland: the earliest O'Sheridans were said to have arrived from Spain in the fifth or sixth century, founding an abbey on Trinity Island, in the little archipelago of lakes and islands between the towns of Cavan and Killeshandra. A sketchy but more specific family tree, preserved in the Chief Herald's Office in Dublin, begins in 1013 with the marriage of Ostar O'Sheridan, of Togher Castle, owning 'many great possessions in the County Cavan . . . as far as to the borders of the Countys of Meath, Westmeath and Longford, too many and needless to be made mention of', to the daughter of the O'Rourke, Prince of Leitrim. It continues, unhampered by further dates, with the names of other Gaelic chieftains with whom the Sheridans were intermarried: the Princes of Sligo, Longford, Cavan, Tyrone and the O'Conor Don – a remote but glorious roll-call which remained a source of pride to their descendants. In convivial moments Richard Brinsley liked to boast of his family's ancient, indeed princely, origins. 'I have not the least doubt of what you say,' the actor Joseph Munden once replied. '. . . The last time I saw your father, he was the Prince of Denmark.'

By the end of the seventeenth century the Sheridans' estates, like the princedoms, had dwindled away. But, as Sheridan's niece Alicia LeFanu maintained proudly in her life of his mother, Mrs Frances Sheridan, they still held their rank amongst the respectable gentry of Cavan, and, having converted from Catholicism earlier in the century, belonged to what was later called the Protestant Ascendancy. Politically their loyalties were mixed, a few remaining faithful to the Catholic James II at the time of the Glorious Revolution of 1688. One member of the family, Thomas Sheridan, formerly Secretary for Ireland, followed the king into exile as his private secretary; his brother William, Bishop of Kilmore, was deprived of his see for refusing to take the oath of allegiance to William III.

Sheridan's grandfather, Dr Thomas Sheridan, is described as a 'near relation' of these two, probably a first cousin once removed. He was a scholarly, unworldly man, uninterested in politics, but with a strain of quixotry in his character that echoed theirs. 'You cannot make him a greater compliment,' remarked Dean Swift, 'than by

2

telling him before his face ... how careless he was in anything relating to his own interests or fortune.' It was a characteristic his grandson would inherit.

Dr Sheridan is best remembered as Swift's bosom friend. He was a clergyman and schoolmaster, for many years the head of Dublin's leading school – 'doubtless the best instructor of youth in these kingdoms and perhaps in Europe,' in Swift's opinion, 'and as great a master of the Greek and Roman languages'. The classical plays his pupils put on were famous, emptying the professional theatre on the evenings they took place. There were plays in English too and Thomas, his son, made his first stage appearance there as Mark Antony at the age of thirteen.

Swift took lessons for his friend when Dr Sheridan was ill, and he delighted in the doctor's cheerful, witty company. They shared a taste for puns and humorous, often scabrous, verse and once exchanged poems daily for a year, on their honour not to spend more than four minutes writing them. It was at Quilca, Dr Sheridan's small estate in Cavan, that Swift completed *Gulliver's Travels*; he would stay there for months every summer with his beloved Stella, Esther Johnson, and her companion Mrs Dingley.

Quilca House no longer exists but its site by the side of a little reed-fringed lake has an unpretentious charm. Moss-covered stone walls running down to the water's edge are all that remain of the long-vanished garden where Swift once planted the arbour he called Stella's bower; the grassy 'rath' or mound nearby was the scene of outdoor theatricals in the days of Dr Sheridan's son, the actor, with its summit boarded over as a stage. The house itself was little bigger than a cottage – a dilapidated one-storey building backing onto the farmyard and approached by an avenue of chestnut trees. Swift made endless fun of its discomforts, describing them with humorous exaggeration in his poem 'To Quilca, a country house of Dr Sheridan, in no very good repair':

> Let me thy properties explain:
> A rotten cabin dropping rain
> Chimnies with scorn rejecting smoak;
> Stools, tables, chairs, and bedsteads broke ...

Elsewhere, in an occasional piece entitled 'The Blunders, Misfortunes, Distresses and Deficiencies of Quilca', he complained of 'the kitchen perpetually crowded with savages', large chinks in his bedroom door, a chimney so draughty that he had to stuff it with his overcoat, and 'a great hole in the floor of the ladies' chamber, every hour hazarding a broken leg'.

The disorder in his household was reflected in Dr Sheridan's finances. For all his learning he was hopelessly impractical about money. 'He was the greatest dupe in the world,' wrote his son Thomas, 'and a constant prey to all the indigent of his acquaintance, as well as those who were recommended to him by others.' He entertained extravagantly, sometimes forgetting to turn up to his own dinners; he took in promising pupils for nothing; and, a particular sin in the eyes of Swift, he brought up his daughters to be fine ladies and to marry husbands with no money. His school, once the largest in Ireland, was eventually ruined by his carelessness and mismanagement, and he spent his latter years pursued by creditors. 'I pray God,' he wrote to Swift, 'that you may never feel a dun to the end of your life for it is too distressing to an honest heart.'

Swift did his best to help his friend and thanks to his influence Dr Sheridan was appointed chaplain to the Viceroy with a living in Cork. But his absent-minded choice of the text, 'Sufficient unto the day is the evil thereof', for a sermon preached on the anniversary of the Hanoverian succession aroused the memory of his family's Jacobite connections. In the furore that followed, as Swift wrote sardonically, 'such a clamour was raised . . . that we in Dublin could apprehend no less than an invasion by the Pretender, who must be landed in the South'. The unfortunate doctor was dismissed immediately, having shot his preferment, as Swift expressed it, with a single text.

At the time of Stella's last illness, Dr Sheridan was Swift's closest confidant. 'I look upon this as the greatest event that can happen to me,' Swift wrote to him, 'but all my preparations will not suffice to make me bear it like a philosopher, nor altogether like a Christian'; and later, when Stella died, 'The last act of life is always a tragedy at best.' Characteristically Dr Sheridan refused the legacy she wished to leave him.

It is sad to read that towards the end of his life, as his mind grew clouded, Swift turned against his old friend, who, having fallen ill while staying at the Deanery, was cut to the heart when the Dean made it clear that his presence was no longer welcome. He left immediately in great agony of mind and died not long after, having never seen his friend again.

'None of the charges made against him [Swift],' wrote Thomas Sheridan, 'bore more hard than his latter behaviour to Dr Sheridan ... Afterwards when his understanding was gone and his memory had failed, when some former feelings of his heart alone remained, I had a strong instance given me by his servant William, how deep an impression the Doctor had made: who told me that when he was in that state the Dean, every day for a long time constantly asked him the same question: "William, did you know Dr Sheridan?" "Yes, sir, very well" – then with a heavy sigh, "Oh, I lost my right hand when I lost him." '

Thomas Sheridan, Dr Sheridan's third son, was Swift's godson. Even when his manner to others had grown savage and strange Swift was never anything but kind to Thomas Sheridan, who regarded him as the most important influence in his life. It was from Swift that he first acquired his passionate interest in oratory and the correct pronunciation of English – the task of establishing a general standard of pronunciation, along the lines laid down by the French Academy, was one that Swift had always hoped to carry out. Years later when Thomas Sheridan came to compile his pronouncing dictionary of the English language, the work he considered his greatest achievement, he took as his ideal the pronunciation used in Swift's younger days at the court of Queen Anne.

Thomas Sheridan was obviously the cleverest of Dr Sheridan's many children. Impecunious though he was, his father managed to send him to Westminster, where he was awarded a king's scholarship and where he spent his free time, according to his letters home, in visiting the London theatres. Westminster itself had a long theatrical tradition, putting on yearly plays in Greek and Latin and encouraging oratory and public speaking. It was an education designed to bring out Thomas Sheridan's latent talents, but before he could complete his studies to take the entrance to Oxford or Cambridge, the money to make up the shortfall in his scholarship ran out and he was forced to return home. He enrolled instead at Trinity College, Dublin, intending at first to follow his father's career of teaching but increasingly drawn to the stage: a contemporary account describes him as 'frequenting the Playhouses, getting acquainted with the Actors and mixing in their Riots'.

Every summer leading players from London would spend two months at Dublin's Theatre Royal, Smock Alley. In 1742, fresh from his brilliant début in London the previous year, David Garrick made his first appearance there and was greeted with such wild enthusiasm that 'Garrick fever', caused by the crush in trying to get places at the theatre, reached the proportions of an epidemic. For Thomas Sheridan, just down from Trinity, Garrick's success must have been the crowning inspiration. The following January, at the age of twenty-three, he made an anonymous first appearance at Smock Alley as Richard III – the same role that Garrick had chosen for his début. The performance was a triumph and his identity such an open secret that on his next appearance a few days later, in the leading role of Racine's tragedy *Mithridate*, he threw off all disguises. Never in living memory, wrote a historian of the Irish theatre, had a new performer been so well received.

It was still unusual, though not unknown, for a man of Thomas Sheridan's education and background to become an actor. But Garrick's father had been an army officer and Thomas Sheridan's imagination, first fired by the theatrical performances at his father's school, had long been captivated by the stage. Though he would explain later that he had used the theatre as a platform from which to propagate his views on oratory and education, it is unlikely that he needed any further motivation at the time.

At first all went well for Thomas Sheridan. His only play, *The Brave Irishman*, a rollicking farce written while he was still at Trinity, was produced at Smock Alley a few weeks after his début; its blustering hero, Captain O'Blunder (a near relation of his son's Sir Lucius O'Trigger), was an immediate favourite with Dublin audiences. He was invited to London the following year, where he played at Covent Garden and Drury Lane, and in 1745, after two seasons in England, he returned to Dublin as manager of Smock Alley, with the avowed intention of reforming it.

It was a bold undertaking. Dublin audiences were notoriously unruly. The upper galleries, where seats were cheapest, were the scene of constant brawling, especially after the third act when tickets were half price, bringing an influx of noisy spectators from the pubs.

Footmen, keeping places for their masters, fought with the audience in the pit or crowded the green-room with torches to light them home after the performance. Actors faced anything from hisses to a hail of stones and bottles if a performance failed to please; on the other hand, if they thought the house too thin to be worthwhile, they would refuse to play at all. Every stripling, as Thomas Sheridan expressed it, could bully his way behind scenes, while the stage was frequently so crowded with spectators that the actors could scarcely move between them. It was Thomas Sheridan's great achievement, begun in his first season, to clear the stage of spectators altogether – he was the first manager in the British Isles to do so.

Thomas Sheridan's first season at Smock Alley, made glorious by the presence of Garrick, whom he had invited from London on a profit-sharing basis, was so successful that he was able to purchase Quilca from his elder brother. His troubles began in the second, when the so-called Kelly riot set Dublin in an uproar, dividing the town, it was said, into parties 'as violent as Whig and Tory'. One evening in January 1745, when he was playing Aesop in Vanbrugh's comedy of that name, a drunken young man climbed over the spikes at the edge of the stage and proceeded to force his way behind scenes. Here he began abusing the actresses in 'the most nauseous bawdry and ill language . . . put his hand under their petticoats, and would have forced some of them (if his ability answer'd his inclination)' – the words are those of Edmund Burke, a Trinity student at the time. He was forcibly evicted by the theatre guards but reappeared soon after in the pit, where he started shouting insults and throwing oranges at Thomas Sheridan, who finally, goaded beyond endurance, took off the false nose he was wearing as Aesop to reply, 'I am as good a gentleman as you are.' Later, when the young man – a Mr E. Kelly from Galway – burst into his dressing-room with renewed abuse, he drove him off by beating him with Aesop's staff.

That an actor should dare mistreat a gentleman, still more that he should claim to be one, were offences enough to incite the rowdier members of the audience, already resentful of Thomas Sheridan's attempts to clear the stage. After two nights of disorder in the theatre, matters reached their climax on the third, when Thomas Sheridan was due to play again. He had been warned, however, that his life might be in danger and had reluctantly agreed to stay away.

The news was the signal for a full-scale riot. With a cry of 'Out with the ladies and down with the house!', a band of more than fifty 'Gentlemen', as Kelly's supporters were known, burst onto the stage and proceeded to rampage behind scenes, breaking down doors, smashing furniture, stabbing at the scenery and hangings with their swords, and destroying the entire theatrical wardrobe in a furious attempt to find the manager. They finally stormed off to his lodgings, but on learning he had gathered reinforcements they 'thought proper to retire'.

It was four weeks before the damage to the theatre, amounting to several thousand pounds, could be repaired. In the interval the quarrel continued in pamphlets and the press, the Gentlemen's party condemning the manager's presumption; Sheridan's supporters insisting on his right to self-defence. There were further disturbances when the theatre reopened, and it was not until the students of Trinity College, sympathetic to Sheridan as a former student, took the law into their own hands by marching on the lodgings of the leading rioters and forcing them to apologise that the violence finally died down.

Kelly, after unsuccessfully suing Thomas Sheridan for assault, was eventually tried for his part in the affair. In the course of the trial his defence counsel sneeringly remarked that he had seen a gentleman soldier and a gentleman tailor before, but never a gentleman actor. Bowing modestly, Thomas Sheridan replied, 'Sir, I hope you see one now.' He was much applauded for this dignified response; later when Kelly was sentenced to three months' imprisonment and a substantial fine Sheridan won further public sympathy by pleading successfully for the sentence to be set aside. Kelly, by now a broken man, was pathetically grateful for his intervention.

The Kelly riot, at first sight so disastrous, in fact brought Thomas Sheridan good luck. He gained authority from the episode, while his magnanimity towards Kelly made him the hero of the hour. It was at this time too, according to his granddaughter Alicia LeFanu, that he first made the acquaintance of his future wife. Amongst the spate of comments on the riot was an anonymous poem in the manager's defence whose opening line, 'Envy will merit still pursue', gave an indication of its general theme. On discovering the identity of the author, a Miss Frances Chamberlaine, he managed to obtain an introduction and, in his granddaughter's words, 'was so captivated by her conversation that a lively reciprocal attachment was the result of this first meeting'. They were married not long after.

Frances Chamberlaine, unlike her husband, was of English origin. Her father, the Archdeacon of Glendalough and Rector of St Nicholas Without in Dublin, belonged to a younger branch of the Chamberlaines of Kingsclere in Hampshire. (There was a baronetcy in the family, though he was not, as Alicia LeFanu asserted, the son of a baronet himself.) He held eccentric views on women's education, disapproving of teaching them to read or write for fear of encouraging 'the multiplication of love letters' when they grew up. But Frances Chamberlaine was taught in secret by her brothers and proved so apt a pupil that she wrote a two-volume novel, a lively romance called *Eugenia and Adelaide*, when she was only fifteen. Unpublished in her lifetime, it was later successfully adapted by her younger daughter for the stage.

Frances Sheridan was twenty-two when she married. She is described by her granddaughter as tall and dark-haired, 'not strictly handsome' but with fine dark eyes which her son Richard would inherit; her high complexion as she grew older was a less fortunate legacy to her son. A troubled life lay before her, but the first few years of her marriage were probably her happiest. Thomas Sheridan is often remembered as a cranky, misguided figure, obsessed with his theories of oratory, but to his wife, in the early days of their relationship, he appeared in a more romantic guise. She wrote of his acting,

> If every talent, every power to please,
> Sense joined with spirit, dignity with ease,
> If elocution of the noblest kind,
> Such as at once inflames and melts the mind,
> Looks strong and piercing as the bird of Jove,
> Address insinuating and soft as Love . . .
> If these can form a character complete,
> All these in Sheridan's performance meet.

Richard Brinsley was the Sheridans' second surviving son – their eldest child, Thomas, had died a year earlier at the age of three. The exact date of his birth – late September or October – has never been established but his christening, which must have followed shortly after, took place on 4 November 1751, in the parish church of St Mary's, Mary Street. His second name, Brinsley, was a family name of his godfather Lord Lanesborough, his first appearing mistakenly as Thomas, not Richard, in the church register. His elder brother, Charles Francis, had been born the previous year; two sisters, Alicia and Elizabeth, would follow in 1753 and 1757 respectively. A third brother, Sackville, died in infancy in 1754.

For the first few years of Richard's life his family divided their time between Dublin and Quilca, where Thomas Sheridan had taken on the role of country squire – he is described as 'immersed in Turf bogs' in one of his wife's letters. The once shabby house had been transformed by the scene painter John Lewis, with painted panels in almost every room, a landscape of clouds on the ceiling of the sitting-room, and classical medallions representing Shakespeare, Milton, Swift and Dr Sheridan on the walls below. Two portraits of Thomas Sheridan and his wife from about this time were probably the work of Lewis too, Thomas Sheridan sharp-featured and alert in a dressing-gown and velvet tam-o'-shanter, his wife in ermine and white satin, with the same long upper lip and humorous glance we see in portraits of her son.

With the Kelly riot behind him, Thomas Sheridan now dominated the Dublin theatre – a satirical poet of the day described him as 'King Tom'. Many of the reforms he had hoped for in the theatre had taken place. Actors were better paid and better rehearsed; audiences, at least for the time being, were better behaved. By abolishing half-price tickets after the third act, the drunken brawling in the galleries had been reduced. Footmen no longer waited in the green-room, or fought for places in the pit, and a one-way system had been devised to stop the crush of carriages after the theatre. The standard of entertainment had been raised. 'Good and chaste plays, decently represented,' as Thomas Sheridan put it, 'drew crowded Audiences, without the Assistance of *Dances*, *Pantomimes* or even *Farces*.' There were more plays by Shakespeare than ever before, often adapted by Sheridan himself to suit his audience's tastes. His version of *Coriolanus*, combining Shakespeare's tragedy with one by the eighteenth-century poet James Thomson, was still being used a generation later by the great Shakespearean actor John Philip Kemble.

Socially too his position had improved. Encouraged by his example and by the better conditions in the theatre, other 'gentleman' players had joined the company. He had founded a club, the Beef Steake, with the intention of mixing actors with distinguished members of the public. Presided over by the actress Peg Woffington, whose racy reputation prevented Mrs Sheridan from meeting her, it gathered together 'nearly all that the metropolis of Dublin could boast of talent, rank and fashion', and was especially popular with the viceregal court.

It was Thomas Sheridan's success in court circles, however, that indirectly brought about his downfall, for though he took no interest in politics he was generally associated with the Viceroy's policies. The first intimation of disaster came on 2 March 1754, with a performance of Voltaire's tragedy *Mahomet*. The play coincided with a bout of ill feeling towards the government, who were accused of using Irish revenues to pay English debts. Its fiery denunciations of tyranny were received with rapturous applause, while a speech at the end of the first act by the actor West Digges, condemning corruption in high places, was considered so apt that the audience demanded an encore.

If Thomas Sheridan had known what trouble lay ahead he would not have put on the play again. But he had developed the custom of asking the public to send in their requests for plays and had received so many for *Mahomet* that he rashly agreed to give it once more. Before doing so, he expressly asked his actors not to step out of character by repeating any passage; however, when Digges, who felt his remarks were aimed at him, asked him for specific instructions he replied with fatal ambiguity, 'I leave you to act in that matter as you think proper.'

When the performance took place on 2 March the whole house was waiting for Digges's speech at the end of the first act, and when it was given they demanded an encore. After some confusion Digges asked to be excused as 'compliance would be greatly injurious to him', whereupon the audience yelled for Sheridan, the man they thought responsible. But Sheridan, feeling that any confrontation would only enrage them more, ordered the curtains to be lowered and went home. Deprived of their prey, and unimpressed by Digges's belated assurances that Sheridan had not forbidden him to give an encore, the audience proceeded to wreck the theatre. By the time they had finished the inside was destroyed and the structure saved from fire only by some brave servants who had managed to extinguish a grate of burning coals which had been overturned. Sheridan was effectively ruined, eight years of hard work as manager gone for nothing. His wife had gone into premature labour on the news that her husband was in danger, and the baby – christened Sackville, after the Viceroy, the Duke of Dorset – died a few weeks later.

There was considerable sympathy for Sheridan in the disaster which had befallen him. The Duke of Dorset offered him a pension of £300, but Sheridan refused it on the grounds that the calumnies against him – of being in the pay of the government – would be confirmed if he accepted. Nor did he accept the help he was offered to repair the theatre. For the time being he was determined to sever his connections with Smock Alley. He was thirty-five and he had other plans.

It was only natural, considering his father's profession, that Thomas Sheridan should be interested in education. He spent the first few months of his retirement at Quilca preparing an 'academical project', later known as *British Education*, which he hoped would pave the way for an alternative career. In it, he set out the themes that would become the keynotes of his work – the importance of learning English as opposed to the classics, and the revival of the art of oratory.

By the time the book appeared Thomas Sheridan was in London, acting at Covent Garden. He was overshadowed, however, by the success of Garrick at Drury Lane and was perhaps not sorry when, in the spring of 1756, he was invited to return as manager to Smock Alley. He crossed the Irish Sea on the viceregal yacht, and was greeted on his first appearance at the theatre by an audience of over a thousand people. For a time all went well, but the honeymoon lasted only two years. Another actor, Spranger Barry, set up a rival theatre in Crow Street, enticing several of Sheridan's best players away. Dublin audiences were fickle. Deeply in debt, having borrowed to take up his share in the theatre, Thomas Sheridan decided to give up the struggle. He rented out the house and land at Quilca and sold the furniture and stock. In June 1758 he went to London to engage new actors for Smock Alley. He did not return, perhaps fearing his creditors, and resigned for good the following March.

Thomas Sheridan's eleven years as manager had ended in disaster for him personally, but they had been of supreme importance for the Dublin theatre. Like his father, he had never been much interested in money, ploughing back his profits for the benefit of the theatre, rather than lining his own pockets. He had insisted on high standards from his performers, luring the best London players with the salaries he offered and picking out new talent with an unerring eye. Above all, he had raised the expectations of his audiences, showing that the Dublin theatre could rival London's, and laid the foundations of a theatrical tradition that has lasted to this day. As his biographer Esther Sheldon remarks: 'Thomas Sheridan would have been pleased, but not surprised, at the Abbey Theatre.'

# II

Thomas Sheridan left Dublin with the most prosperous period of his life behind him. 'He wakes as from a dream,' he had written in a parting letter to the Dublin public, 'and finds that the best and most vigorous of his years have been employed to no purpose. Persecuted by implacable enemies, abandoned by many pretended friends . . . and daily experiencing the blackest instances of ingratitude from persons most obliged to him, he must look out for a new course of life, a new country and new friends.'

He did not give up acting altogether – his King John at Drury Lane in 1760 was said to outshine Garrick's – but from now on the main thrust of his interests lay with the subjects discussed in *British Education*, the promotion of oratory and educational reform. Many of Thomas Sheridan's ideas were far ahead of his time. In a period when the study of the classics took up a disproportionate amount of every schoolboy's time, he insisted on the importance of English language and literature in education. Whilst he was still in Dublin he had set up plans for a Hibernian Academy which he had hoped would discourage absenteeism from Ireland to the English public schools. Its prospectus was remarkably liberal: teaching was to be in small groups or seminars, no corporal punishment was permitted and special attention was to be paid to the pupils' individual talents. The plan had failed to materialise, largely due to prejudice against him as an actor, and he now hoped to propagate his views more widely by writing and lecturing in England.

The Sheridans set up house in Henrietta Street, near Covent Garden. Richard and his sister Alicia had been left behind in Ireland during the Sheridans' earlier stay in England, only Charles, the elder brother, accompanying his parents. The two children had attended the school run by their mother's cousin, Samuel Whyte, an enlightened teacher who shared many of Thomas Sheridan's views. Their mother had worried about them from a distance. 'How are my dear little ones,' she wrote to Whyte. 'Do they often talk of me? Keep me alive in their remembrances. I have all a mother's anxiety about them, and long to have them over with me.' She arranged for their nursemaid to go with them when they boarded, and made excuses when her husband failed to pay their fees. Poor woman, she often had to soothe her husband's creditors.

Richard was eight when he joined his parents in England. He would never return to Ireland again but the first few years of a child's life are said to be the most impressionable and his love for his country, reflected over the years in his championship of Catholic emancipation, went deep. In the character of Sir Lucius O'Trigger, touchy, proud, so poor he 'can't afford to do a dirty action', he drew a portrait of the impoverished Irish gentry to which his family belonged; whilst from his time at Quilca came a feeling for the Irish countryside and country people. In his poem 'Irish Biddy' he depicts the scenes he must have known in childhood:

> There rises up the cabin small,
> With roof of thatch, and low mud wall,
> The stagnant pool before the door,
> The grunting pig upon the floor,
> You know them, Biddy.
>
> But far beyond the mud and all,
> I see the mountains grand and tall,
> The beech and hawthorn in the bloom –
> The spot where lies my mother's tomb
> In Ireland, Biddy!

We do not know whether he attended the auction at Quilca, when the family's possessions were put up for sale, but perhaps some memory of it may have lingered in *The School for Scandal* when he wrote the picture auction scene. The particulars in *Faulkner's Dublin*

*Journal* give us a vivid picture of an eighteenth-century squireen's household, half farmhouse, half gentleman's residence:

## AUCTION AT QUILCA

To be sold by public cant [auction] at Quilca in the County of Cavan, on Friday the 5th day of May next 1758, all the Household Furniture belonging to Thomas Sheridan Esq., consisting of fine feather Beds and Bedding, Fourpost, Settee and Field Beds with Harateen and Linen Curtains, and Window Curtains of the same, Press and Settle Beds, Mahogany and Oak Card and Tea Tables, Chests of Drawers, Desks, Chairs, Sconces and other Glasses, some Coins, Flintware and Glasses, one fine Landscape in a handsome Frame, some Kitchen Furniture, utensils for the Dairy and Brewery, a large binn for Oats, and Chests, a good Bombcart, a Crane and Weights, Carrs and Carts, Ploughs, Harrows and Drafts, with other implements of Husbandry too tedious to mention. Also Milch Cows, Heifers in Calf, some three year old Bullocks, and some high-bred young Mares got by Mogul, Scar and Bashaw. The sale to begin at 11 o'clock and continue till all are sold. Dated 24th Day of April, 1758.

In London Thomas Sheridan and his wife were soon the centre of a lively circle which included such figures as Dr Johnson and the novelist Samuel Richardson. 'Mr Sheridan's well informed and bustling company never suffered the conversation to stagnate,' as Boswell wrote later, 'and Mrs Sheridan was a most agreable companion to an intellectual man.' On one of the evenings in Henrietta Street, Samuel Whyte, who was staying with them, looked out of the window to see the lumbering figure of Dr Johnson pausing, with the strange superstition his biographers record, to touch the top of each post beside the carriageway as he made his way to see his friends.

Thomas Sheridan's talks on oratory and elocution were a great success. His lectures at the Pewterers' Hall and Spring Gardens were attended by as many as sixteen hundred subscribers, paying a guinea apiece. He spoke at Oxford and Cambridge, receiving an honorary degree from each university. He travelled to Edinburgh, where he received yet another degree and where he gave lessons in pronunciation to notables concerned to lose their Scots accents, amongst them Alexander Wedderburn, later Lord Loughborough, and the young James Boswell. Boswell, with his natural tendency to hero worship, was an enthusiastic admirer of Thomas Sheridan. He called him 'my mentor, my Socrates', and so far benefited from his teaching that Dr Johnson, whom he met soon afterwards, told him kindly, 'Sir, your accent is not offensive.'

It was thanks to the influence of Lord Loughborough, and indirectly to Thomas Sheridan, that Dr Johnson received a pension of £300 in 1762. 'Sheridan rang the bell', as Loughborough put it. But when Thomas Sheridan, who had published a prospectus for a pronouncing dictionary of the English language, was awarded a pension of £200 shortly after, Johnson ungraciously exclaimed: 'What! Have they given *him* a pension? Then it is time for me to give up mine.'

His remark, repeated by 'some damn'd good-natured friend or other', caused a rift between the two men, and, though Johnson always claimed that he had added 'that he was glad Sheridan had got his pension for he was a very good man', they were never reconciled. Thomas Sheridan was generally supposed to have the wrong of this dispute by continuing to hold a grudge, but perhaps other remarks of Johnson's had also been repeated to him. It was hard for someone so devoted to the cause of oratory to hear that Johnson thought his efforts negligible: 'Sir, it is burning a farthing candle at Dover to show light at Calais'; still worse to be contemptuously summed up: 'Why Sir, Sherry is dull, naturally dull, but it must have taken him a great deal of pains to become what he is. Such an excess of stupidity is not in nature.'

Dismissive – and perhaps a little jealous – though he was of Thomas Sheridan, Johnson always had the highest admiration for his wife. In 1761, just before the two men quarrelled, Mrs Sheridan had published a three-volume novel, *The Memoirs of Miss Sydney Biddulph*, a book whose tone of tearful sensibility reflected the influence of Richardson and whose moral, according to Boswell, was 'impressed upon the mind by a series of as deep distress as can affect humanity'. She had written it with Richardson's encouragement and the author of *Clarissa* had been full of its praises. So too was Johnson, who told her after reading it, 'I know not, Madam, that you have a right, upon moral principles, to make your readers suffer so much.'

*Sydney Biddulph* was an immense success, and though it was

published anonymously the name of its author became well known. Two years later, at the invitation of Garrick, her play *The Discovery* was performed at Drury Lane. The comic spirit that had shown itself only in occasional flashes in *Sydney Biddulph* was given full rein in the play which Garrick declared to be one of the best comedies he had ever read. Garrick took the part of the procrastinating lover Sir Anthony Branville, Thomas Sheridan that of the insinuating Lord Medway, whose artful scheme to seduce Lady Flutter, while pretending to reconcile her with her husband, has a whiff of Richard's Joseph Surface about it. A second play, *The Dupe*, was less successful and was withdrawn after just one performance, supposedly because of an actress's cabal.

Some time before, while staying in Windsor, the Sheridans had made the acquaintance of an Eton schoolmaster, Robert Sumner. He was appointed headmaster of Harrow soon after, and in 1762, at the age of eleven, Richard was sent to school there. Charles, his elder brother, remained at home, a decision that has always seemed strange and which is only partly explained in a letter from his mother to Samuel Whyte: 'Dick has been at Harrow school since Christmas. As he may probably fall into a bustling life, we have a mind to accustom him to shift for himself. Charles's domestic and sedentary turn is best suited to a home education.'

Founded in 1570, with a charter from Queen Elizabeth, Harrow's prosperity had begun at the end of the seventeenth century when it began to take 'foreigners' or boys from other parishes. By the mid eighteenth century it had become a full-fledged public school, close to Eton in prestige, but less aristocratic in its intake, with the majority of the boys coming from professional backgrounds. Acting, however, was not considered an acceptable profession for a parent and Richard suffered misery in his early years at Harrow. Slighted by the masters and tormented by the boys as a poor player's son, he took such a dislike to the stage that he told Lord Holland years later that he had never seen any plays, except his own, right through from beginning to end – a statement that if not true at least had an imaginative truth about it.

His life at school became still harder when in 1764 his family moved to Blois. Still burdened by debts from Smock Alley, Thomas Sheridan had never shaken off his money troubles. In France he could not only escape his 'merciless creditors' but live far more cheaply than in England. Cut off from his family, Richard sometimes spent his holidays with Mr Aikenhead, a 'splendid West Indian' living at Richmond, but more often at Harrow where Mr Sumner's housekeeper, Mrs Purdon, took a motherly interest in him. The diarist Thomas Creevey, to whom he talked of his schooldays, records him as saying, 'that he was a very low spirited boy, much given to crying when he was alone; and he attributed this very much to being neglected by his father, to his being left without money, and to not being taken home at the regular holidays'.

Richard Chamberlaine, his mother's brother, a surgeon living in London, was his guardian as far as money was concerned and his nephew's first surviving letter is to him. It is easy to read his homesickness between the lines.

Dear Uncle – As it is not more than three weeks to the holy days, I should be greatly obliged to you, if you could get me some new clothes as soon as possible, for those which I have at present are very bad and as I have no others; I am almost ashamed to wear them on a sunday . . . Mr Somner asked me the other day if I had heard lately from my Brother and says he has not heard from them this long time; if you have had a letter recently I should be obliged to [you if] you would let me know how they are, and when they come to England for I long to see them.

I should be greatly obliged to you if you would let me have some cloaths as soon as possible, for when these want mending I have no others to wear. Mr and Mrs Somner are very well. I am Dear Uncle Your affectionate nephew R. B. Sheridan.

Meanwhile, in Blois, where Thomas Sheridan's lodgings had become a popular stopping place for young men and their tutors starting on the Grand Tour, Frances Sheridan had written two further volumes of her novel, culminating in the death of her heroine Sydney Biddulph after a lifetime of undeserved calamities: 'She stopped short, as if interrupted by some sudden and extraordinary emotion; a fine colour flushed at once into her face, and her eyes, which were before sunk and languishing, seemed in an instant to have recovered all their fire. I never saw so animated a figure; she sprang forward with energy, her arms extended, her eyes lifted up with rapture, and with an elevated voice she cried out "I come!"

Then, sinking down softly on her pillow, she closed her eyes and expired without a sigh.'

The deathbed scene she described was soon to be echoed in real life. In the autumn of 1766, hearing the news that an amnesty for insolvent debtors passed in England might extend to Ireland, Thomas Sheridan was preparing to go to Dublin when his wife fell ill. She died a fortnight later. Thomas Sheridan was inconsolable. 'I have lost, what the world cannot repair,' he wrote to Samuel Whyte, 'a bosom friend, another self. My children have lost – oh! their loss is neither to be expressed, nor repaired. But the will of God be done.'

For Richard the loss of a mother from whom he had so often been absent, first in Ireland and then at school, must have been a stunning blow. Writing to Richard in his last sad years of drink and debt, his sister Alicia blamed many of his troubles on the lack of his mother's care and guidance in his youth. He was too young to indulge in the luxury of his father's effusions. His letter to his uncle on the matter was brief and stoic:

> Dear Uncle – It is now almost a week since Mr Somner told me the melancholy news of my poor mother's death; and as Mr Somner has not heard what time my Father will be home, he desires me to write to you about mourning. I have wrote To Riley, who, with your orders, will make me a suit of Black. I should be obliged to you if you would let me know what time you expect my Father.
>
> You will excuse the shortness of this letter, as the subject is disagreeable, from your affectionate Nephew, R. B. Sheridan.
>
> P.S. I must have a new hat with a crape and black stokins and buckles. I should be glad of them on saturday.

Despite his sorrow at his mother's death, Richard's final years at Harrow were happier than his first. He had been a solitary boy, recalling years later how he used to study in the fields alone, with a piece of dry bread and sausage for refreshment, washed down with water from a brook or pond. But as he went up the school and gained in confidence he began to make friends. His natural geniality and charm revealed themselves, and though he was considered by his masters as a very idle, careless boy this did him no harm in his fellow pupils' eyes.

The learned Dr Parr, once described as a 'Whig Dr Johnson', was a young schoolmaster in Richard's last two years at Harrow, and a kindly influence in his life. In letters to his biographer Thomas Moore, he gives a sympathetic picture of his pupil, whom he remembered as inferior to many of his fellows in the ordinary business of the school, but with just sufficient industry to save him from disgrace.

'All the while,' he added, 'Sumner and myself saw in him the vestiges of a superior intellect. His eye, his countenance, his general manner were striking. His answers to any common question were prompt and acute. We knew the esteem, and even admiration, which, somehow or other, all his school fellows felt for him. He was mischievous enough, but his pranks were accompanied by a sort of vivacity and cheerfulness, which delighted Sumner and myself. I had much talk with him about his apple-loft, for the supply of which all the gardens in the neighbourhood were taxed, and some of the lower boys were employed to furnish it. I threatened, but without much asperity, to trace the depredations, through his associates, up to their leader. He, with perfect good humour set me at defiance, and I never could bring the charge home to him.'

Richard left Harrow in his seventeenth year, probably because there was no more money to cover his fees. He left behind his name, carved in the dark oak panelling of the Fourth Form Room, where it can still be seen, not far from that of Byron, who followed him thirty-eight years later. His early years at school had been unhappy, but he must have kept a pleasant memory of Harrow, for he would later take a house there, a fine Georgian mansion called The Grove, with marvellous views from the top of the hill. When Dr Sumner died Sheridan is said to have mourned him like a father, and on his own father's death his first wish was to bury him in the churchyard at Harrow, where Robert Sumner was already buried. Though the plan did not materialise, it showed his affection for the place where he had spent his school days, and Harrow in its turn came to think of him with pride. In a letter to Thomas Moore, Byron recalled how in his time 'we used to show his name – R. B. Sheridan, 1765 – as an honour to the walls'.

There was no question of Richard going to university. His father, who had returned to London with the worst of his debts behind him, had plans to educate his son himself, and Richard was able to rejoin his family at the house they had taken in Frith Street, Soho.

Years later his sister Alicia recalled the joy of her reunion with her brother:

'I saw him; and my childish attachment revived with double force. He was handsome, not merely in the eyes of a partial sister but generally allowed to be so. His cheeks had the glow of health, his eyes – the finest in the world – the brilliancy of genius, were as soft as a tender affectionate heart could render them. The same playful fancy, the same sterling and innocuous wit, that was shown afterwards in his writings, cheered and delighted the family circle. I admired him – I almost adored him. I would most willingly have sacrificed my life for him.'

Thomas Sheridan was a strict disciplinarian, managing his household, as one biographer remarked, as sternly as he did a theatre. There were morning prayers every day and on Sundays he would expound on a passage from the Bible or the sermon of the morning. Despite his differences with Dr Johnson he was a great admirer of Johnson's writing and his daughters would be made to read long passages from the *Rambler*, then wearied still further by his corrections of their faults. But he had a genial side to his nature as well: in the evening he liked to indulge in a mixture of brandy and hot water which he called his 'panacea', and his favourite toast as he looked down the table at his family was 'Healths, hearts and homes'.

Thomas Sheridan taught grammar and oratory to his sons, while an Irish tutor, Lewis Ker, gave them lessons in Latin and mathematics. They were instructed in riding and fencing by the great duelling master Domenick Angelo, an old friend of the family, whose manège and School of Arms were close by; Richard's lessons as a swordsman would later stand him in good stead. In return, Thomas Sheridan and Richard taught elocution to Angelo's son Henry, eleven years old, and Henry in his memoirs gives an amusing glimpse of their different methods:

'With the elder Sheridan all was pomposity and impatience. He had a trick of hemming, to clear his throat and, as I was not apt, he urged me on with – "Hem – hem – heiugh – em, boy, you mumble like a bee in a tar bottle; why do you not catch your tone from me? – Heiugh – heium – exalt your voice – up with it. *Caesar sends health to Cato*. Cannot you deliver your words – hem – hem – heiugh – m-m-m, with a perspicuous pronunciation, Sir."

'With his son Richard it was, "Bravo, Harry, now again; courage, my boy – Well said, my young Trojan!" '

Richard spent two years in London; he would describe them later as the time 'in which he acquired all the reading and learning he had upon any subject'. Amongst his papers from this period are sketches for stories and plays, including an adaptation of *The Vicar of Wakefield*; letters on politics in the style of Junius, then at the height of his fame; the opening number of a satirical newspaper, *Herman's Miscellany*, abandoned for lack of funds; and an unfinished essay on prosody in which, echoing his father, he dismissed the idea of modelling English poetry on Greek and Latin verse: 'We have lost all knowledge of the antient accent; – we have lost their Pronunciation; – all puzzling about [it] is ridiculous and trying to find the melody of our own verse by theirs is still worse. We should have had all our own metres, if we had never heard a word of their language.'

Richard had been a great reader of poetry at school, according to Dr Parr, and together with a friend, Nathaniel Brassey Halhed, had translated some of the poems of Theocritus into verse. Halhed was now at Oxford, and the two young men had embarked on another, longer verse translation from the Love Epistles of Aristaenetus, a series of mildly erotic fables, some humorous, some romantic, by an obscure Greek writer of the fifth or sixth century AD. Halhed, as the superior Greek scholar, provided the first draft, which Richard adapted and embellished as well as adding verses of his own. 'I have some time had full belief and confidence,' wrote the admiring Halhed, 'that every correction of yours would be an *emendation* and every *addition* a new perfection.'

Lewis Ker, the tutor, took it on himself to find a publisher and the translation finally appeared in 1771. Published anonymously, it ran into two small editions and was moderately well reviewed; one critic, Ker told Richard, had even ascribed it to Dr Johnson. Richard, however, took little pride in this work. Years later, when someone produced a copy of the book and taxed him with its authorship, he put it in his pocket and went off without a word.

A more frivolous co-production was a farce called *Jupiter*, set, as *The Critic* would be, during a rehearsal, and recounting the amours of gods and mortals, with Jupiter and Juno as usual in dispute. The playwright Simile, here seen supervising the action, is a dim foreshadowing of Mr Puff:

23

SIM. Now for a phoenix of a song.

*Song by* JUPITER
You dogs, I'm Jupiter imperial;
King, emperor and pope ethereal;
Master of th'ordnance of the sky.

SIM. Z—nds, where's the ordnance? Have you forgot the pistol? (*To the Orchestra.*)
ORCHESTRA (*to someone behind the scenes*). Tom, are not you prepared?
TOM (*from behind the scenes*). Yes, Sir, but I flash'd in the pan a little out of time, and had I stayed to prime, I should have shot a bar too late.

The two young men – whose joint ages, as Halhed remarked, did not amount to thirty-eight – had great hopes of making money with their play. 'The thoughts of £200 between us are enough to bring tears into one's eyes,' wrote Halhed. But though it was offered to Garrick at Drury Lane and Foote, the manager of the Haymarket theatre, it was never performed – perhaps a lucky thing in retrospect since it left the way clear for *The Critic*.

While Richard was trying his hand as a writer, his father had been busy with his usual round of acting, writing, lecturing, and working on his pronouncing dictionary – a project which annoyed Dr Johnson almost as much as his pension had done. When Boswell, in 1772, ventured to suggest that Sheridan's plan of marking the vowels to ascertain the right pronunciation was a good one, he was roundly contradicted: 'Why, Sir, consider how much easier it is to learn a language by the ear, than by any marks. Sheridan's Dictionary may do very well; but you cannot always carry it about with you; and when you want the word, you have not the Dictionary. It is like a man who has a sword that will not draw. It is an admirable sword to be sure: but while your enemy is cutting your throat, you are unable to use it. Besides Sir, what entitles Sheridan to fix the pronunciation of English?'

Side by side with his pronouncing dictionary – which would not appear till 1780 – Thomas Sheridan produced a further treatise on educational reform, *A Plan of Education for the Young Nobility and Gentry of Great Britain*. Published in 1769, it expanded on his earlier ideas and was dedicated to 'the Father of his People George III'. But its offer to devote his life to education – provided his pension was increased – not surprisingly went unanswered.

In the autumn of 1770, perhaps in search of cheaper lodgings, Thomas Sheridan decided to move his family to Bath. His ostensible reason was to set up a school in which his rejected theories could be put into practice and where his sons could assist him as 'rhetorical ushers'. An advertisement announcing 'An Academy for the regular instruction of Young Gentlemen in the art of reading and reciting and Grammatical Knowledge of the English tongue' was placed in the *Bath Chronicle* but seems to have attracted no replies. Richard told Creevey years later that the project was 'presently laughed off the stage'.

Fortunately, Thomas Sheridan had other strings to his bow. Some years before, he had devised a series of so-called Attic Entertainments, combining recitations from the English poets with vocal and instrumental music. It was a sweetening of the educational pill that suited his dramatic instincts; Mrs Siddons and John Philip Kemble would later follow the same formula. In Bath, with its public of fashionable idlers, he hoped to find a captive audience for his entertainments. Meanwhile his sons, reprieved from the drudgery of teaching, could plunge into the pleasures of the country's best-known watering place. For Richard, at the age of nineteen, Bath would be a social education.

# III

—⟨&⟩—

The Sheridans arrived in Bath at the end of September 1770. They found lodgings in Kingsmead Street, 'a very neat house, pleasantly situated and very cheap', as Richard described it in a letter to Mrs Angelo, giving her a mock ceremonial account of their proceedings:

> May it please your Majesty
> At a meeting of the Sheridanian society, in Parlour assembled, the following resolutions (amongst many others of great importance) were determined on, and I appointed to give your Majesty information of them.
> Thomas Sheridan esqr. in the chair – RBS Sec.
>
> 1. Resolved – that we are all alive. N.B. this pass'd nem. con.
> 2. Resolved – that her majesty be acquainted thereof.
> 3. That RBS be honoured with that commission . . .

He invited her to stay ('[which] will be much to the benefit of your Majesty's health and spirits') and added a further invitation from the presiding genius of the place:

> I have likewise another embassy to your Majesty; this is from King Bladud, who (as the Bath Guide inform[s] us) reigned in England about 900 years before Christ, and was the first discoverer of these springs. This King keeps his state on a fine rotten post in the middle of the water, decorated with a long account of his pedigree. His

Majesty whispered me the other day that having heard of your fame, he has long wished to see you; he says that, except his sister of Orange, he has not seen a royal female for a long time; and bid me at the same time assure your majesty, that tho' in his youth, about three thousand years ago, he was reckoned a man of Gallantry, yet he now never offers to take the least advantage of any lady bathing beneath his Throne, nor need the purest modesty be offended at his glances – So says his Majesty of Bladud: and in justice I must acknowledge that he seems to be as demure, grave and inoffensive a King as ever sat upon a – post.

Since the days of King Bladud, traditionally regarded as the founder of the city, Bath had been through many ups and downs. Celebrated as a spa in Roman times, and long known for the healing virtues of its waters, it had been a centre of the cloth trade in the Middle Ages and then fallen into comparative neglect. Two visits of Queen Anne and her husband in 1702 and 1703 helped to revive its reputation as a watering place, but it was not until the arrival of Beau Nash shortly after that Bath became really fashionable. Under his reign as Master of Ceremonies the Pump Room and the two lower Assembly Rooms were built, and a series of formal rules and regulations provided a social framework for visitors to the city, whether taking the waters or not. Stimulated by Nash, a wave of building began. Ralph Allen (who had made his fortune in the Post Office) developed the quarries which produced the honey-coloured local stone. The two Woods, father and son, led the way in rebuilding and expanding the city on classical lines. By 1770 most of the Palladian crescents, squares and terraces that made up eighteenth-century Bath had been laid out, though the New Assembly Rooms and Royal Crescent in the upper part of the town were not completed till the following year. From almost everywhere there were views of the surrounding hills, and the woods and fields that edged the town were never far away.

At a time when foreign travel was a major undertaking, and seaside holidays were only just becoming fashionable, Bath was a Mecca for those who sought distraction and a change of air as well as for those who came for their health. Jaded Londoners, country squires, quack doctors, scheming mothers, nabobs, noblemen, and young men on the make mixed freely in an atmosphere where acquaintances were quickly made and as quickly forgotten when the time came to leave. The formal etiquette first imposed by Nash replaced the usual distinctions of rank, and there were few places where those whose social credentials, like Richard's, were shaky could more easily enter society.

From the first peal of the Abbey bells that greeted distinguished new arrivals to the town, visitors to Bath fell into a holiday routine. "Tis a good lounge,' says Fag, the servant in the *The Rivals*; 'in the morning we go to the pump-room (though neither my Master nor I drink the waters); after breakfast we saunter on the parades or play a game at billiards; at night we dance: but d—n the place, I'm tired of it: their regular hours stupefy me – not a fiddle nor a card after eleven!'

With so much leisure to be filled there was a constant demand for entertainment. Coffee-houses, lending libraries, booksellers, milliners and print shops did a thriving trade. There were daily concerts in the Pump Room and the Assembly Rooms, subscription dances twice a week, and thrice-weekly performances at the theatre, where the latest plays from London could be seen. Portrait painters, music teachers – and lecturers on elocution – found a ready market for their wares, and Thomas Sheridan must have begun his Attic Entertainments with high hopes of success.

His first performance took place at Simpson's Assembly Rooms on 24 November 1770. He spoke on oratory and recited Dryden's 'Ode to St Cecilia', while Elizabeth Linley, a young singer with whom he had already worked in London, sang such songs as 'I have oft heard Mary say', 'Black-eyed Susan', and 'Rosey Bowers' by Purcell. Her performance on this occasion is said to have earned her the sobriquet of St Cecilia, and it is regrettably true that she, far more than Thomas Sheridan, was the draw.

Thomas Sheridan had known the Linley family since 1763 when his wife had accompanied him on a lecture tour to Bath and taken singing lessons from Elizabeth's father, Thomas Linley. To Mrs Sheridan, who had 'a fine voice and considerable taste in music', Thomas Linley's lessons 'opened a new world of harmony to her senses'. She carried her enthusiasm back to London where her daughter Alicia, who shared a room with her, remembered being kept awake by her mother repeating the last song she had learnt from Linley.

28

Thomas Linley, son of a carpenter, who had come to Bath in the building boom of the 1740s, had been apprenticed to the musician Thomas Chilcot, organist of Bath Abbey, and later studied under William Boyce. He had been appointed director of the public concerts in the Assembly Rooms in 1766 and was famous as a teacher of singing and the harpsichord. He was famous too as the father of a brilliantly gifted family of musicians, 'a nest of nightingales' as Dr Burney called them. In 1770, the year the Sheridans came to Bath, the Linleys' eldest son, also Thomas, was in Florence studying with the well-known violinist Nardini. It was here that he met the young Mozart, at the house of a 'learned poetess', Signora Corilla, and the two boys performed one after another throughout the evening, constantly embracing each other. They met again to play on the two following days, parting tearfully on the third, when the Mozarts left Florence. Leopold Mozart wrote of him: 'It would be impossible to hear a finer player, for beauty, purity and evenness of tone and singing quality.'

If Thomas was the pride of the Linleys as a violinist, and later as a composer, his elder sister Elizabeth was equally outstanding as a singer. She was sixteen when she first sang with Thomas Sheridan in Bath, and already a celebrity. Critics vied in praising her, as much for her beauty as for the 'indescribable sweetness' of her singing. Gainsborough's portraits of her capture the ethereal, other-worldly quality that led one admirer, the Bishop of Meath, to describe her as the connecting link between a woman and an angel. A newspaper story of that year showed how legends had begun to cluster round her:

At a Salisbury music meeting . . . while Miss Linley . . . was singing the air in the oratorio of *The Messiah*, 'I know that my Redeemer liveth', a little bullfinch that had found means . . . to secrete itself in the cathedral, was so struck by the inimitable sweetness, and harmonious simplicity of her manner of singing, that mistaking it for the voice of a feathered chorister of the woods, and far from being intimidated by the numerous assemblage of spectators, it perched immediately on the gallery over her head, and accompanied her with the musical warblings of its little throat through a great part of the song.

Her sister Mary, three and a half years her junior, was a prodigy second only to Elizabeth, and the younger Linleys, Maria, Ozias,

Samuel, Jane and William, would all show musical ability. 'We are all geniuses here,' Thomas the younger said gaily when a visitor questioned him on the family's talents. But in 1770 it was Elizabeth, the most beautiful and the most gifted of the sisters, who held the public eye. Her admirers were numerous, though firmly kept in check by her father, who knew the dangers to which female performers were exposed. The younger Sheridans may well have been amongst them, for the two families had soon become friends. But any dreams they may have had were cut short that December when Elizabeth became engaged to Walter Long, a wealthy landowner nearly forty years her senior.

Richard at least showed no signs of repining. According to his sister, he seemed entirely taken up with the amusements of his new surroundings. Years later he told Creevey that his happiness began in Bath, where 'he danced with all the women . . . wrote sonnets and verses in praise of some, satires and lampoons upon others, and in a very short time became the established wit and fashion of the place'.

It was here that he first tasted literary fame. His poem 'The Ridotto of Bath', a skit on the opening of the New or Upper Assembly Rooms on 30 September 1771, was published in the *Bath Chronicle* ten days later and proved so popular that it was twice reprinted as a separate pamphlet. Bath etiquette had slackened since the days of Beau Nash if the description of the rush for supper was to be believed:

> But – silence, ye hautboys! Ye fiddles be dumb!
> Ye dancers, stop instant – the *hour* is come;
> The great – the all-wonderful hour of eating!
> That hour, – for which ye all know ye've been waiting.
> Well, the doors were unbolted, and in they all rush'd;
> They crowded, they jostled, they jockey'd and push'd.
> Thus at a Mayor's feast, a disorderly mob
> Breaks in after dinner to plunder and rob.

A second poem, 'Clio's Protest', also published in the *Bath Chronicle* and reprinted as a pamphlet, was written in answer to 'The Bath Picture', an insipid poem on Bath's leading ladies by a certain Miles Peter Andrews, a fashionable dandy of the day. Today it is best remembered for its damning couplet,

> You write with ease to show your breeding;
> But *easy writing's* vile *hard reading*.

At the time it was celebrated for the lines – which were later set to music – on Lady Margaret Fordyce, one of the reigning beauties of the place,

> Mark'd you her cheek of rosy hue?
> Mark'd you her eyes of sparkling blue?
> That eye in liquid circles moving;
> That cheek, abashed at man's approving;
> The *one* – Love's arrows darting round,
> The other blushing for the wound:
> Did she not speak – did she not move –
> Now Pallas – now the Queen of Love.

In the spring of 1771 Elizabeth Linley's engagement to Walter Long was broken off amidst a flurry of scandal and speculation. The Sheridans were probably in the secret of what went wrong, for the younger members of the two families were in and out of one another's houses. (Thomas Sheridan, who thought himself a cut above the Linleys, preferred to keep his distance.) In Moore's version of the story Elizabeth told Long she could never be happy as his wife, and he chivalrously took the blame of breaking the engagement upon himself, paying off her father, who was threatening to sue him, by settling £3,000 upon her.

The playwright Samuel Foote, who had been in Bath at the time, gave a less romantic version of events. Bath news was always of interest in London and his quickly written play *The Maid of Bath* was an immediate success when it was first performed at the Haymarket Theatre at the end of June. It remained in the repertoire for many years. Richard himself would put it on when he came to be the manager of Drury Lane, though in 1771 he was indignant at Long's behaviour, attacking him anonymously in the *Bath Chronicle*:

> Spurr'd by a momentary letch of age
> You sought to gain a youthful virgin's heart;
> And trying first her friendship to engage
> You made that friendship but a mask for art . . .

31

Samuel Foote specialised in caricaturing people in the public eye. He had already made fun of Thomas Sheridan's rhetorical pretensions in an entertainment called *The Orators*. The only victim who had ever routed him was Dr Johnson, who, on hearing that Foote was threatening to lampoon him, simply asked where one could buy a stout cudgel; the hint was sufficient and the play was never written. Foote had lost a leg, due to a riding accident, and had used his disability to good effect in his play *The Devil on Two Sticks*. In *The Maid of Bath* he played Solomon Flint, the elderly suitor of the beautiful Miss Linnet, and brought in a younger would-be lover, Major Racket, as a counterweight. There was no attempt to portray Thomas Linley, a severe and serious man, who was said to strike awe into his pupils. But Mrs Linley, who was known to be vulgar and grasping, was not so far from Mrs Linnet, who is shown putting pressure on her daughter to marry her elderly admirer:

MRS LINNET. Ten thousand pounds a year! Gads, my life, there's not a lady in town would refuse him, let her rank be ever so.
MISS LINNET. Not his fortune, I firmly believe.
MRS LINNET. Well! Would you refuse an estate because it happens to be a little encumbered. You must consider the man in this case as a kind of mortgage.

Miss Linnet, who has accepted Flint to please her family, indignantly refuses him when he demands to spend a night with her before their marriage, and Flint, exasperated, decides to keep his money for himself. When the other admirer, Major Racket, proposes to Miss Linnet, she reminds him that he had seduced her friend Miss Prim the previous year and declares that she will remain independent and unmarried.

Elizabeth Linley comes out with credit from Foote's play; at a time when female performers were considered fair game it is a tribute to her character that her virtue was never in question. But the figure of the womanising Major Racket was not entirely fictional. For some time her name had been linked with that of another military figure, Thomas Mathews – variously known as Major or Captain Mathews, though he had left the army as an ensign three years before. His father had estates in Wales and Ireland, and he had made a prudent marriage to an heiress, Miss Jones of Fonmon Castle,

Glamorgan, some time earlier. This did not prevent him from pursuing Elizabeth, whom he had known and courted since her early teens. They were frequently seen together in public, presumably with her family's consent; it is possible that Long had released Elizabeth more willingly than he would otherwise have done because of her supposed involvement with Mathews.

With her engagement to Long behind her, Elizabeth was once more free to sing in public. For the rest of the year, while Mathews hovered in the background, she appeared at one concert after another, gathering new plaudits and admirers. In Oxford, where she inspired the undergraduates with a sort of 'contagious delirium', Richard's friend Halhed was one of those who heard her sing. 'I am petrified,' he wrote, 'my very faculties are annihilated with wonder; my conception could not form such a power of voice – such a melody – such a soft yet so audible a tone. Oh Dick . . . I wished myself hanged for not being able to commit my ideas to paper.'

Charles Sheridan was another of those who fell under her spell, though he did so most unwillingly. Now twenty-one, he was a pompous, serious-minded young man – very much the favourite of his father. Like his father, he took his background of gentility seriously; marriage to Elizabeth, a girl without family or fortune, would do nothing to help his future career. Interestingly, perhaps from his feeling that his sons, like him, were gentlemen, Thomas Sheridan had so far put no pressure on them to earn their living. A year later, thanks to the influence of a family friend, Charles would be appointed secretary to the British Legation in Sweden and Richard would eventually be set to studying law. But for the time being, despite his own precarious finances, their father left them to their own devices.

In November 1771, taking a copy of his play *The Brave Irishman* with him, Thomas Sheridan set off for Dublin. His Attic Entertainments had been well received in Bath and he had taught his favourite art of elocution to several distinguished pupils, amongst them the future Marquis of Buckingham, George Grenville. But Dublin offered greater possibilities. The stage there had fallen into disarray, with two rival theatres contending for a public that could support only one. Soon after arriving he called for legislation to give the monopoly to a single theatre, backing his arguments with a pamphlet based on his experiences of 1758; rumour went that if the legislation was successful the patent would be offered to him. In the meantime he was welcomed as an actor, his receipts were excellent, and 'no less than five persons of rank and fortune' were awaiting his leisure to become his pupils.

A good, if authoritarian, father, he kept in close touch with his family:

'My dear Richard,' he wrote on 7 December, 'How could you be so wrong headed as to commence cold bathing at such a season of the year and I suppose without any preparation too? You have been paid sufficiently for your folly but I hope the ill effects are now long over . . . Pray what is the reason of my hearing so seldom from Bath? Six weeks here, and but two letters! You were very tardy; what are your sisters about? I shall not easily forgive any further omissions.'

A letter from Richard on 2 February 1772 shows that his reproaches had been answered:

We have been for some time in hopes of receiving a letter that we might know that you had acquitted us of neglect in writing. At the same time we imagine that the time is not far when writing will be unnecessary . . . I am perpetually asked when Mr Sheridan is to have his Patent for the Theatre, which all the Irish here take for granted, and I often receive a great deal of information from them on the subject . . .

I could scarsely have concieved that the Winter was so near departing, were I not now writing after Dinner by day-light. Indeed the first Winter-season is not yet over at Bath: they have Balls, Concerts etc. at the Rooms, from the old subscription still, and the Spring ones are immediately to succeed them. They are like-wise going to perform Oratorios here: Mr Linley and his whole family, down to the seven years olds are to support one set at the new Rooms . . .

With this mention of the Linleys we return to the younger Sheridans' immediate concerns. Shortly after his father's departure for Ireland, Charles, determined to shake off his infatuation, left Bath to take rooms at a farmhouse some miles outside the town, sending a heartfelt letter of farewell to Elizabeth as he did so. Meanwhile, Elizabeth was being increasingly persecuted by Captain Mathews, who, 'taking advantage of a degree of countenance which, when almost a child, she had shown his attentions, now threatened

34

sometimes to destroy himself, at others to injure her character to the utmost of his power, if she persisted in refusing his addresses'.

The words are Alicia Sheridan's in an account she sent to Richard's second wife, a few months after his death in 1816, thus from a distance of over forty years. Devoted to Elizabeth's memory, she was bound to put the best complexion on the situation. From some previously deleted entries in Moore's journal, however, it seems that Elizabeth herself was deeply compromised. According to Samuel Rogers, Mathews used to boast that he had possessed her over and over again, though Mathews, wrote Moore, was 'not very worthy of credit'. He certainly seems an unattractive character. When Lord John Townshend, who called on him in Bath years later, remarked what a pretty woman she was, he replied, 'Yes – the prettiest creature stripped you ever saw.' The Reverend William Money, who knew him in old age, told Moore he had 'quite the impudent stare of the old debaucher ... the ruin of women's character has always been his chief pursuit'.

Whatever the exact degree of their involvement, Elizabeth seems to have been close to a nervous breakdown. A certain Miss White told Moore that she had actually tried to poison herself because of Mathews, mixing the poison, 'whatever it was', with 'pain powder' to disguise the taste. She dared not speak of her troubles to her parents, fearing the violence of her father's temper and the possibility of a duel. But she confided her misery to Alicia and Betsy Sheridan, and they in turn told Richard of her woes, 'thinking that one so handsome, clever and bold had been designed by Nature to act the part of a knight of olden time'.

Richard was delighted to play the knight errant. He agreed to talk to Captain Mathews, with whom he was on familiar terms, and apparently prevailed on him to give up his pursuit. But Mathews' word was not to be relied on and Elizabeth, 'now completely disgusted with a profession she had never liked' and sickened at the thought of further scandal, grew desperate to escape him altogether.

It was then, according to Alicia Sheridan, that she conceived the idea of retiring to a convent in France till she came of age, intending to compensate her father for her loss of earnings by giving up some of the money which Long had settled on her. She discussed her scheme with Richard, who talked it over with his sisters. Alicia offered to write letters of introduction to some ladies she had known in France and it was agreed that Richard should escort her to St Quentin, where they lived.

Their departure took place amidst all the trappings of an eighteenth-century opera or romance, though once again new entries from Moore's journal cast doubts on the accepted story. Elizabeth, to say the least, was still emotionally confused. According to Miss White she had agreed to go off with Mathews at the same time she was making plans with Richard; Richard himself told Mrs Crewe that she had been surprised to see *him*, not Mathews, when she arrived at their rendezvous. '*Can* this be true?' wrote Moore.

True or not, it was Richard's plan that won the day. On the evening of 18 March, when Thomas Linley, with two of his children, Thomas and Mary, were rehearsing, Elizabeth stayed behind on the plea of illness. Soon after their departure Richard sent a sedan chair to the Linleys' house in Royal Crescent, and Elizabeth was taken to a waiting carriage on the London road. Here Richard met her, with a maid he had hired to be her chaperone, and the three set off to London on the first stage of their journey.

# IV

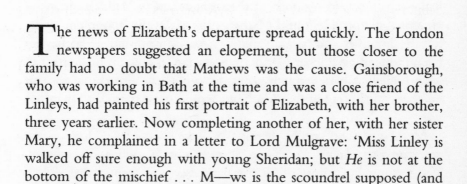

The news of Elizabeth's departure spread quickly. The London newspapers suggested an elopement, but those closer to the family had no doubt that Mathews was the cause. Gainsborough, who was working in Bath at the time and was a close friend of the Linleys, had painted his first portrait of Elizabeth, with her brother, three years earlier. Now completing another of her, with her sister Mary, he complained in a letter to Lord Mulgrave: 'Miss Linley is walked off sure enough with young Sheridan; but *He* is not at the bottom of the mischief . . . M—ws is the scoundrel supposed (and with much reason) to have undone the poor Girl − it vexes me much; I could fight about it, because I was just finishing her Picture for the Exhibition.' The painting was completed, nonetheless, and was shown under the title 'A Portrait of Two Ladies' at the Royal Academy that year.

Richard had left a letter for Elizabeth's father, describing Mathews' conduct, and it is possible that she may have written to him too. In any event, Thomas Linley's displeasure seems to have been directed towards Mathews rather than his daughter. A letter to Richard from William Brereton, a friend of both the Linleys and the Sheridans, throws light on Linley's attitude as well as that of Mathews.

> The morning after you left Mathews came to me and has repeated his visit several times. It is impossible to give an account of his conversation, it consisted of many dreadful oaths and curses upon

37

himself and his past life, but in my opinion they were little to the purpose. I am afraid his present situation and feelings are not to be envied. But, bad as his is the town has so little charity for him that they make [him] worse perhaps than he deserves. I carried two messages for him to Mr Linley, but he would not hearken to a word about him. He said he had been deceived once and would never trust him more, since that he has heard so many reports to his prejudice that their meeting may be of bad consequence, and I shall endeavour by all means to prevent it.

Meanwhile, the landlord at Kingsmead Street, alarmed at the thought that Alicia and Elizabeth Sheridan had no one to protect them, had gone to seek out Charles to tell him what had happened. Charles, who had known nothing of the couple's plans and felt he had been deceived by both of them, hastened to Bath in a state of violent agitation. He found Mathews already at the house, enquiring for the fugitives and 'outrageous,' as Alicia expressed it, 'at having been induced by Richard Brinsley Sheridan to give up his pursuit of Miss Linley'. Charles, much upset, let slip a few remarks against his brother, not knowing that Mathews would store them up for future use.

Mathews, who really seems to have become a little mad, continued to plague the young Sheridans with visits and enquiries. What stung him most of all, perhaps, was the feeling that public opinion was against him; it must have been because of this that on 8 April – just over two weeks after Elizabeth's departure – he inserted an announcement in the *Bath Chronicle*:

> Mr Richard S[heridan] having attempted, in a letter left behind him for that purpose, to account for his scandalous method of running away from this place, by insinuations derogating from my character, and that of a young lady, innocent as far as relates to me, or my knowledge, since which he has neither taken any notice of letters, or even informed his own family of the place where he had hid himself; I can no longer think he deserves the treatment of a gentleman, than in this public method, to post him as a L[iar] and a treacherous S[coundrel].

When Richard's sisters remonstrated with him, Mathews had 'the insolence and baseness' to claim that Charles had agreed to the announcement. Since Charles, however displeased with his brother, would never have considered such a thing he was angry enough to contemplate a duel. But Mathews left Bath at that moment and the matter came to nothing.

It was several weeks before Richard and Elizabeth heard what had been happening in Bath. They had arrived in London early on 19 March, and called first on some cousins of Richard's named Ewart – the younger Ewart, Simon, was Richard's particular friend. Richard introduced Elizabeth as 'an Heiress who had consented to be united with him in France' – thus openly expressing what must have been a secret wish. The Ewarts seem to have lent him money but it was another friend, the son of a brandy merchant named Field, who produced the most practical help – a free passage to Dunkirk in a ship of his father's that was just about to sail.

The crossing to France, coinciding with the equinoctial gales, was very stormy. Elizabeth became so ill that at one point Richard feared for her life. Such was his love for her, he wrote later, that had she then died he would 'assuredly have plunged with her body to the Grave'.

He had not yet revealed his feelings to Elizabeth though he had confided them earlier to his sisters. Whilst Charles had been struggling against what he would later call 'my very ridiculous attachment', Richard had been silently in love himself. It was not surprising that Charles had suspected nothing, for Elizabeth herself had known no better. As she wrote to Richard later: 'You are sensible that when I left Bath I had not an idea of you but as a friend. It was not your person that gained my affection. No, S—n, it was that delicacy, that tender compassion, that interest which you seemed to take in my welfare, that were the motives which induced me to love you.'

It was only when the fugitives left Dunkirk for Lille, where Field had given them letters of introduction, that Richard finally showed his hand.

'He told her,' wrote his sister, 'he could not be content to leave her in a Convent unless she consented to a previous marriage, which all along had been the object of his hopes, and she must be aware that after the step she had taken, she could not appear in England but as his wife. Miss Linley, who really preferred him greatly to any person, was not difficult to persuade, and at a village not far from

Calais the marriage ceremony was performed by a priest who was often known to be employed on such occasions.'

Sheridan's first biographer, Watkins, questions the story of the marriage, which in any case would have been invalid since both were Protestant and minors, with no possibility of their parents' consent. Neither seems to have looked on it as binding; at every place they stayed Richard made sure that Elizabeth was chaperoned by the landlady or some female companion. The following year, during a period of estrangement, Elizabeth was prepared to hear a proposal from another suitor, whilst in a letter to Richard after their return to England she writes of looking forward to a time when she can be his 'in every sense of the word'.

Richard, her twenty-year-old protector, was fiercely jealous of her honour. An amusing episode, which he described long afterwards to Samuel Rogers, took place one evening at the theatre, where two officers began ogling Elizabeth. Sheridan, who spoke not a word of French, could only put his arms akimbo and glare at them, while the officers, who spoke no English, were reduced to glaring in return.

On arrival at Lille, Richard found a place for Elizabeth in a convent while he himself remained in a hotel. From there he wrote a letter of explanation to his brother Charles. 'All is well I hope,' he told him. 'And I hope too that tho' you may have been ignorant for some time of our proceedings, *you* never could have been uneasy that anything could tempt me to depart even in a thought from the honour and consistency which engaged me at first.'

The letter was dated 15 April. Just over a week later Thomas Linley arrived in Lille to bring back his daughter. Elizabeth had fallen ill from fatigue and agitation and had been moved to the house of an English doctor. Linley's meeting with the runaways was surprisingly friendly, and though he insisted that Elizabeth should fulfil the engagements he had made for her he promised that she should cut down her appearances thereafter. The three of them set out for England together, apparently on the best of terms.

Till Linley's arrival, Richard had not heard of Mathews' advertisement in the *Bath Chronicle*. In his letter to his brother he had written airily: 'I wrote to M[athews] above a week ago, which I think [was ne]cessary and right. I hope he has acted the one proper

Part which was left him. And to speak from my *feelings* I cannot but say that I shall be very happy to find to[o] no further disagreeable consequence pursuing him. For what Brutus says of Caesar etc. – if I delay one moment I lose the Post.'

Now, at the news of Mathews' insults, Richard declared that he would never sleep in England till he had treated him as he deserved. On arriving in London with the Linleys on the evening of Wednesday 29 April, he left them at a hotel and went off accompanied by the younger Ewart to find Mathews. It was after twelve when they reached Mathews' lodgings, and for some time he refused to get up and let them in. When he eventually did so he seemed eager to be conciliatory, called Richard his 'dear friend' and forced him to sit down. On finding that Richard had not seen the offending announcement, he assured him that it had only been an advertisement enquiring for his whereabouts, and put the whole blame on his brother Charles and 'another gentleman from Bath'. His behaviour, wrote Charles later in a letter to his uncle, Richard Chamberlaine, 'was so very condescending that Dick let him off for a very small concession in the Bath paper'.

Richard left for Bath with the Linleys three days later, where his first step was to call on the offices of the *Bath Chronicle*. When he saw the actual text of Mathews' advertisement, he realised that he had been duped and returned home to demand an explanation from his brother. Charles easily cleared himself, though not without a few high words, and the two brothers set out for London that same evening. They travelled through the night, and called on the Ewarts the next morning, where Simon Ewart agreed to act as his second. Later that day Charles went round to Mathews' lodging to deliver Richard's challenge.

They met at the entrance to Hyde Park at six the following evening, Charles having tried vainly to extract an apology from Mathews. As the person challenged, Mathews had the right to choose weapons and chose swords. According to Henry Angelo he had 'learnt fencing in France and was considered very skilful in the science'. At first, however, he seemed reluctant to fight, at one moment objecting to the ground, at another that they might be seen by an officer, then suggesting that the duel should be postponed to the following day. After much shilly-shallying the meeting finally took place by candle-light that evening at a room in the Castle Tavern on the corner of Bedford and Henrietta Street. What followed is best told by Richard in an account he drew up on return to Bath: 'They engaged. Mr M. was disarm'd. Captain K[night, Mathews' second] ran in. Mr M. begg'd his life and afterwards denied the advantage. Mr S. was provoked by the (really well-me[a]nt) interposition of Captain K. and the elusion of Mr M. He insisted since Mr M. denied the advantage, that he should give up his sword. Mr M. denied but sooner than return to his ground he gave it up – it was broke. And Mr M. offer'd another. He was then call'd on to retract his abuse and beg Mr S.'s pardon. With much altercation and much ill grace He complied.'

The duel had taken place on Monday. Late on Tuesday evening the two brothers returned, exhausted, but bearing the text of Mathews' apology for insertion in the *Bath Chronicle*. It read:

> Being convinced that the Expressions I made use of to Mr Sheridan's Disadvantage were the Effects of Passion and Misrepresentation, I retract what I have said to that Gentleman's Disadvantage and particularly beg his pardon for my advertisment in the *Bath Chronicle*.

The affair seemed honourably over. Mathews left for Wales with his wife – there is no record, at this or any stage, of what she thought about it all. Alicia and Betsy Sheridan, who had been in a state of panic for their brothers, could breathe again; so too could Elizabeth, who had fainted when she heard the news of the expedition to London. Public opinion was on the couple's side – the papers were full of garbled versions of the duel, but Elizabeth's reputation stayed intact. As Charles expressed it, 'Most people are (notwithstanding the general tendency in mankind to judge unfavourably) inclined to think that he [Richard] behaved with the strictest honour in his late expedition with Miss Linley, when circumstances might allow of their being very dubious on this head.' Even Thomas Sheridan, who had come back from Ireland in great indignation at his son, was won round by the admiration he inspired.

This did not mean that either he or Thomas Linley were prepared to countenance a match between their children. Thomas Sheridan was still too proud of his ancestry and his status as a gentleman to wish his son to marry, as he thought, beneath him. Thomas Linley had no wish to lose his daughter to a young man without fortune or prospects. Both parents sought to separate their children and to keep them from meeting except in other people's houses or in public. But the two contrived to see each other secretly and one of these clandestine meetings, in the grotto of the Spring Gardens, was the scene of one of the best-known poems of their courtship:

> Uncouth is this moss covered grotto of Stone,
> And damp is the shade of this dew dropping tree;
> Yet I this rude grotto with rapture will own
> And willow, thy damps are refreshing to me.
>
> For this is the grotto where Laura reclined,
> As late I in secret her confidence sought,
> And this is the tree kept her safe from the wind,
> As blushing she heard the grave lesson I taught.
>
> Then tell me, thou grotto of moss covered stone,
> And tell me, thou willow with leaves dripping dew,
> Did Laura seem vexed when Horatio was gone?
> And did she confess her resentment to you? . . .

'I will call you Horatio –' wrote Elizabeth, 'that was the name you gave yourself in that sweet poem – write to me then, my dear Horatio, and tell that you are equally sincere and constant . . . My hand shakes so at this moment I can scarce hold the pen. My father came into my room this moment, and I had just time to stuff this letter behind the glass.'

And in another letter: 'My mother and me called on Miss Roscoe this evening, when we talked a great deal about you. Miss R. said she was sure you and I should make a match of it. Nay, she said the whole world was of the opinion that we should be married in a month. Only think of this, bright Hev'ns! God bless you, my dear, dear love. I am so weary I must go to bed. There is but one thing that would keep me awake and that is your company. Once more adieu.'

Elizabeth was still committed to singing engagements by her father and at the beginning of June she set off on tour. From Oxford she wrote to Richard again: 'How shall I account to my dear Horatio for my long silence? Will he permit me to excuse myself by pleading the continual hurry I have been in since I parted from him? Indeed nothing should have hindered my writing before but the shocking situation I was in, all day confined to my business, and at night my mother took away the candle for fear I should read. It was an absolute impossibility to elude her vigilance.' She went on to describe her adventures. In Chester she had attended a masquerade in fancy dress: 'The crowd was so great at the door, that, before I could get into the room, the fright overcame me and I fainted in the midst of them. On the return of my senses I found somebody was going to pull me by my legs, as you would a dead horse; this roused me, and I gave them a hearty kick.'

At Cambridge she fainted again during Handel's oratorio *Samson*: 'This raised no small bustle among the Cantabs, as they call them. I need not describe them to you, they are a strange set; although, upon the whole I really think they are more rational than the Oxonians. It seems that there is to be a very great riot here on one of the nights. They don't like the music and intend calling the Governors to an account. How it will end God knows.'

While Elizabeth was writing from Cambridge matters had taken a fresh turn in Bath. Charles's appointment as Secretary to the British Legation in Sweden had been confirmed and he had gone with his father to London to make the necessary preparations, while Richard remained with his sisters at Kingsmead Street. Meanwhile, Captain Mathews, having found himself cold-shouldered in Welsh society after the duel, had come back to Bath seeking revenge. Urged on by an officious friend named Barnett, he tried to force Richard to change his account of the duel – in particular the breaking of his sword – and then sent him a challenge and a letter 'filled with the most scurrilous abuse'. Richard had every right to refuse the challenge, having fought already, but Mathews' insults, as intended, roused his anger and he accepted it.

Early in the morning of 1 July they met at Kingsdown outside Bath. According to Mathews, Richard was drunk when he arrived; another version of the story, recorded in the painter Joseph Farington's diary, has Mathews also drunk and cursing at Richard for carrying off his mistress. Tempers in any case were high, and after some altercation as to whether to use sword or pistols, they set to with swords. The ground was uneven and after only a few paces both fell, Mathews uppermost, each breaking their swords: Richard's was snapped off within four inches of the hilt; Mathews' was shivered lower down leaving a jagged length of blade. Richard called out that he had nothing to defend himself with, whereupon Mathews, who had already wounded him in the stomach, seized the broken-off, pointed end of his sword and held it above him, telling him to beg for his life. The seconds too called on him to surrender, but Richard, replying, 'No, by God I won't,' caught hold of the blade with one hand so that the other could not disengage it. Mathews, 'uttering horrid curses', proceeded to stab him repeatedly with the hilt he was holding in his other hand. Richard fended off most of the blows with his free arm so that they breached only his coat, but was wounded five times before the seconds belatedly brought things to a halt.

Mathews, exclaiming, 'I have done for him,' drove off in a post chaise that was standing ready – he had arranged to go to France till the affair blew over. Richard, bleeding profusely, was carried to a nearby cottage, where he was given some water, then taken to the White Hart Inn in Bath, where surgeons were called in and his life, for a time, was thought to be in danger.

News of the second duel, with a report that Richard was seriously wounded, appeared in the *Bath Chronicle* the next day and was soon in all the papers. Elizabeth was due to sing in Oxford, and her father, who knew that she would never appear if she had heard about it, carefully kept the news from her. When she sang that day she was perhaps the only person present who knew nothing of the duel. Richard's friend Thomas Grenville told Alicia afterwards that her beauty and the thought of the calamity hanging over her sent a wave of chivalrous compassion through the hearts of her undergraduate audience.

Immediately after the performance the Linleys left Oxford for Bath. They were a few miles from home when they were met by a family friend, a clergyman named Panton, who proposed that Elizabeth should join him in his carriage for the rest of the journey. When she had done so he broke the news of Richard's duel as cautiously and tactfully as he could. 'But all these precautions,' wrote Alicia Sheridan, 'could not prevent her being dreadfully agitated by the stroke, and during her agitation she insisted on being permitted to see him, declaring she was his wife and as such entitled to see him.'

Richard had at first been pronounced too ill to be moved from the White Hart Inn. But his sisters, who had hurried there when they heard the news, found him so uncomfortable from the heat and noise that they persuaded the doctors to let him be taken home. Here they nursed him and here Thomas Sheridan arrived hotfoot from London, so incensed that at first he refused to even see his son. His daughters eventually pacified him but he strictly forbade them to have any communication with the Linleys. Richard, on his sickbed, seemed so distressed by this that Betsy, his youngest sister, contrived to carry messages to Elizabeth for him.

It was not until a week later that Richard was sufficiently recovered for his father to question him about the duel. On hearing the full story Thomas Sheridan came round completely. With a high, even touchy sense of honour himself, he found it impossible to blame his son for responding to Mathews' provocation. In fact he was proud of him. In a letter to Richard Chamberlaine he wrote:

'Never was more concern shown on any occasion than was to be seen in all classes of people on my son's account; for he bears an excellent character and is much beloved. And never were more execrations poured upon any head than that of the vile assassin. Never was man so universally hated, and I do verily believe that were he to appear in the streets of Bath by day he would be stoned to death.'

He wanted to have Mathews prosecuted for attempted murder, with affidavits from the various witnesses. Richard was unwilling to drag Elizabeth's name into the courts and the idea was dropped – but not before his father had made him promise not to see her, and to give 'an oath equivocal' not to marry her.

Elizabeth's parents felt equally strongly. Her father, she told Richard, 'declared he would sooner follow me to the grave than see me married to you as you would ruin me and yourself in a short time by your extravagance'.

She was packed off to Wells without seeing Richard, but was able to smuggle a letter to him through his second, Captain Paumier. 'Oh! my Horatio,' she wrote, 'I did not know till now how much I loved you. Believe me had you died I should certainly [have] dressed myself as a man and challenged M. He should have killed me or I should have revenged you and myself.'

Richard, slowly recovering, could bask in his status as a popular hero and amuse himself by reading the newspaper accounts, often wildly inaccurate, of his progress. 'Let me see what they report of me today,' his sister remembered him as saying; 'I wish to know whether I am dead or alive.'

But duels and elopements, however chivalrous their motives, do not come cheap. Richard had borrowed where he could, and the Ewarts, at least, were showing some impatience to be repaid. 'I am exceedingly unhappy at the situation I leave you in respect to money matters,' wrote Charles, 'the more so as it is totally out of my power to be of any use to you.' It was left to Thomas Sheridan to settle the most pressing debts, including those, as Richard put it, 'contracted later than they should have been, tho' to get rid of obligations of a former Date'.

Charles left for Sweden in early July. The rest of the family stayed on in Bath a few weeks more. George Grenville had come back to Thomas Sheridan for further lessons in elocution and would be cured of a chronic stammer as a result. He brought with him his tutor and his younger brother, Thomas Grenville, who would become one of Richard's lifelong friends. To him Richard must have confided his feelings for Elizabeth, for he was far from abiding by the 'oath equivocal' which he had given his father and had been seeing her secretly on her return from Wells.

Inevitably, their meetings were discovered. Thomas Sheridan had accepted another engagement for the autumn in Dublin, where his petition for a single theatre had failed, but a profitable season's acting lay ahead. He had planned to send Richard with his sisters to St Quentin – where Richard could learn French – while he was away. Now, declaring that his son was no fit guardian for Alicia and Betsy, he arranged that they should accompany him to Dublin, where Grenville and his party were to travel too. Richard was to be exiled to Waltham Abbey, in Essex, under the care of his father's 'particular friends', Mr and Mrs Parker, to repent of his follies and to study for the bar.

# V

Richard arrived at Waltham Abbey at the end of August 1772 in a mood of 'excessive melancholy', exacerbated by a toothache and a heavy cold. There must have been explanations with Elizabeth and a promise not to see or write to her before he left, for he was able to assure his father in a letter two days after his arrival that 'on this subject you shall never again have the smallest uneasiness'. But in a letter to Thomas Grenville that same day he poured out his misery at their parting:

'I am perfectly convinced that that unfortunate being called a Lover, if a true one, would better bear a separation from her he loves in a Desert than a Paradise . . . When I see a pair blest in peace and in each other Let me say, "Why am I shut out from this forever?" and 'tis torture. Let me sit in a beautiful scene, I exclaim – "What would her presence make this?" and 'tis worse than a wilderness. Let me hear musick and singing – "I cannot hear her sing and play", and the notes become the shrieks of the Damned.'

He had taken his resolution not to communicate with her more seriously than Elizabeth. 'I have received a letter from her, since I wrote to you (Counterband!),' he told Grenville three weeks later, 'fill'd with the violence of Affection & concluded with prayers, commands and entreaties that I should write to her.'

He was determined not to do so, less from the belief that he was doing right, than because he had given a solemn promise to his father: 'How strange is my situation; if I consult my Reason, or even one half of my Feelings I find conviction that I should end this unfortunate connexion – what draws the knot, rejects the influence of reason, and has its full moiety of Feelings (dearest! tenderest!) with the Passions for its hold.'

With such fluctuating emotions Richard passed the autumn. He was preparing for the bar with a tutor in the town. 'I have here at least one great inducement to study,' he told his father. 'Nothing else to do.' He worked hard, not only at the law, taking lessons in 'Mechanicks, Mensuration, Astronomy etc' from 'a very ingenious Man here', writing copious notes on history, geography and mathematics, and planning to learn Italian and French. But there were moments of distraction too. 'I wish you could on any pretence, come and spend a fortnight in Essex,' he wrote to Grenville in November. 'You shall hunt, & Shoot & Study in the prettiest rotation imaginable – at night you shall go on star-gazing Parties and with Ladies two: and conclude the Day with very good wine . . .'

Meanwhile Elizabeth had embarked on a round of engagements in Bath and nearby towns. Her father, who seemed to have forgotten his promise that she should appear less often in public, was determined to reap the benefit of her talents and his training. That he regarded her as a valuable source of income had been made clear by a letter the previous year when Colman, the manager of Covent Garden, had tried to engage her as actress. 'I think,' wrote Linley, 'as she has acquired a reputation, I ought to have the advantage of her first performing in London myself . . . I do not relish giving the prime of my daughter's performance to support the schemes of others.'

In the spring of 1773, suiting the action to the word, he brought Elizabeth and the rest of his family to London, to appear under his direction in a series of Lenten oratorios at Drury Lane. Tom Linley led the orchestra and played in concertos between the acts, and Mary joined her sister as a soprano soloist; but as ever it was Elizabeth who took the place by storm. 'The applause and admiration she has met with can only be compared to what is given Mr Garrick,' wrote Fanny Burney in her diary. 'The whole town seems distracted about her. Miss Linley alone engrosses all eyes, ears and hearts.'

Richard seemed the only person determined not to see her. 'Eliza is within an hour's ride of me and must have been for some time,' he told Grenville. 'Yet upon my honour, I have and do industriously avoid even knowing the particular Place that is blest with her inhabiting – I was obliged to go to London the other day – and I protest to you, no country Girl passing alone through a church-yard at midnight, ever dreaded more the appearance of a Ghost than I did to encounter this (for once I'll say) *terrest[r]ial* being.'

Richard would spend eight months at Waltham Abbey before entering the Middle Temple ('which I take to be the great Gate of Power') in April 1773. His own aspirations were high: 'It has been an everlasting Fashion to declaim against the Pursuits of Ambition, and the expectation of Happiness in the scenes of publick Life,' he wrote to Grenville in a revealing passage. 'Yet, may we not with some justice attempt to prove, that there is to be found there a surer Foundation to build on, than in any of the most captivating roads of private, and comparatively, solitary Enjoyments.'

In private life, he argued, men were at the mercy of the accidents of fate, the loss of friends or loved ones:

> – Ask the Fond Youth
> Why the cold Urn of Her whom long he lov'd
> So often fills his arms!

True ambition, on the contrary, could never be disappointed or circumscribed in its possibilities of doing good: 'It hopes most when most oppressed and the very scene which presents it with its misfortunes, denies it time to feel, or opportunity to indulge them. Then its object is as immortal as the source of it. Our Enjoyments here will never depend upon our selves, and our own abilities, in the other They can exist but on the verge of accident, and others' Caprice.'

Thomas Grenville was Sheridan's closest confidant during his stay in Essex. Four years younger than Sheridan, he admired him greatly and had suggested they should correspond. The point was important since Sheridan, conscious of Grenville's superior social status, was too proud to be the first to write. In Grenville he found a kindred spirit and could develop his thoughts on paper as though in conversation face to face. He had a serious idea of such exchanges: 'I would have every man *write* to his friend as he would *speak*. Yet not as he would speak to him at a dinner or assembly, but (if he pretends to be a man of sense) as he would speak to him in those uninterrupted, retired hours of mutual confidence and communication in which consist the spirit and enjoyment of friendship. And to such *this* will be to write with *ease.*'

His letters spoke of friendship and ambition; of Sidney's *Arcadia* and his liking for idealised romances; of love – with Elizabeth as the object – and a loathing of sordid encounters: 'A Lover (a true one) shall fly with rapture from the society of Courtezans, to contemplate but the Picture of his Mistress.'

Youthful philosophy changed to furious indignation on hearing from Bath that Mathews had persuaded Sheridan's second, Captain Paumier – on the threat of challenging him to a duel – to sign a false account of the near-fatal encounter between them. It was 'the basest, meanest, and most ungrateful Piece of Treachery that ever disgraced Human Nature', and he was determined to revenge it. Further reports absolved Paumier, but not Mathews' second, Barnett, who had drawn up the account. He protested to Barnett in a letter that he left unfinished, then grew sickened by the whole affair. 'Let them go –' he wrote to Grenville, 'I never now reflect on that Place, but it puts me out of sorts for writing on other matters.'

Grenville had done his best to calm his friend and to reassure him about a story, equally distracting, that Elizabeth had accepted an offer of marriage from a certain Sir Thomas Clarges. Clarges denied it to Grenville, but the offer had in fact been made before Elizabeth left Bath; she had refused it, as she had refused other offers, out of love for Richard.

Cut off from seeing or hearing from him for nearly six months her feelings had now changed dramatically. 'I have so been deceived by you and by every one that it has almost deprived me of my reason, but I have paid too, too dear for my experience ever to put [it] in your power, or anyone's to impose on me again', she wrote. She had heard gossip from Waltham Abbey, where Richard, as well as studying, seemed to have had some dalliance with a Miss C. and a Mrs L., apparently a doctor's wife in Waltham Abbey. In Miss C.'s case at least the matter was serious:

'Miss C., I own I pity,' wrote Elizabeth, when her first shock had died down. 'Why do you abuse her, what have you to alledge against her? If she was hurried on by the violence of her love for you to the commission of a crime, she has since repented. Surely the remorse, the anguish which she feels hourly joined to the opinion she is sensible you entertain for her is sufficient.'

It was evident that the correspondence between them had resumed, on Elizabeth's part with a demand that he should return her letters. Richard, his resolutions forgotten at the threat of losing her, seems to have answered that he would return them only when she declared that she loved someone else. 'Believe me,' she wrote, 'I am incapable of loving any man.' In her anguish at finding that he appeared to have abandoned her, she had sworn on her knees to her parents that she would never marry him. She had been prevailed on to agree that she would accept the first man, of suitable character, who proposed to her. Such a man had just appeared, and her father was urging her to accept him. She begged Richard again to return her letters. 'If not, I cannot compel you, but I hope your generosity will not permit you to make an improper use of them. For God's sake, write no more. I tremble at the consequences.'

Between this letter and their marriage two months later, in April 1773, lies an unexplained interval. Moore speaks of a 'serious misunderstanding' between the lovers, of Simon Ewart, Richard's friend and cousin, effecting a reconciliation, and of a 'series of stratagems and schemes which convinced Mr Linley that it was impossible much longer to keep them asunder'. But the four pages of Alicia Sheridan's narrative from which Moore drew his information were missing when he returned the papers he had borrowed for his biography, and no further details have been found.

Whatever his behaviour with Miss C. and Mrs L., Sheridan's thoughts had never been far from Elizabeth during their separation. Whilst keeping his promise to his father not to communicate with her, he had stolen up to London to see and hear her in public and once, according to Moore, disguised himself as a coachman so that he could drive her home from the theatre. He was still penniless, but he was now over twenty-one and entered at the Middle Temple, and Elizabeth had at least a portion of the £3,000 Long had settled on her. By the terms of her marriage settlement, £1,050 in 3 per cent consols was transferred to a trust run by Linley and his solicitor, with the dividends to be paid to her for life.

It was little enough to begin with, but the world might have thought that her singing would augment their income handsomely. Elizabeth was at the zenith of her fame. At a command performance at Drury Lane that spring George III had been enchanted by her. 'The King admires the last [Miss Linley],' wrote Horace Walpole to a friend, 'and ogles her as much as he dares to do in so holy a place as an oratorio, and at so devout a service as *Alexander's Feast*.' Only four days before Elizabeth's wedding the entire family were invited to perform before the king and queen and their children at Buckingham House. The king told Thomas Linley that he had never in his life heard so fine a voice as his daughter's, nor one so well instructed, and presented him with a bank note for £100.

But Sheridan's first action on their marriage was to refuse to allow his wife to sing in public any more. Dr Johnson applauded the decision: 'He resolved wisely and nobly to be sure. He is a brave man. Would not a gentleman be disgraced by having his wife singing publickly for hire? No, Sir, there can be no doubt here.'

Richard and Elizabeth were married on 13 April 1773, at Marylebone church, with her father and his solicitor as witnesses.

'After the ceremony,' reported the *Morning Chronicle* next day, 'they set out with her family and friends, and dined at the Star and Garter on Richmond Hill; in the evening they had a ball after which the family and friends returned to town, and left the young couple at a gentleman's house in Mitcham to consummate their nuptials.'

It was just over a year since the two had left for France together. If the intervening passage of time had been stormy they had reached a safe harbour at last. They spent the first months of their marriage in a cottage at East Burnham, a period they would both look back on with nostalgia. 'I have given orders concerning Betsy's harpsichord,' wrote Thomas Linley to his son-in-law, 'but she seems so delighted with her Nightingales, her great Elm tree and her Rooks, that all other amusement seems impertinent. Besides, she describes her *Maestro da Capella* as a Person of such consummate abilities, that in all I do, I shall approach him with fear and trembling . . .'

Richard was equally delighted with their choice.

'Had I hunted five years I don't believe I could have hit in a Place more suited to my mind, or more adapted to my present situation,' he told Grenville; '. . . I feel myself absolutely and perfectly happy. As for the little Clouds which the peering eye of Prudence would descry to be gathering against the Progress of the Lune, I have a consoling Cherub that whispers me, that before They threaten an adverse Shower, a slight gale or two of Fortune will disperse them.'

The only stumbling-block remained the attitude of Thomas Sheridan. His objections to Elizabeth as a public performer seem strange coming from one who was a performer himself. But Thomas Sheridan had always made a point of taking a share in the theatre's takings, rather than a salary, and considered the distinction important. In any case he would never have allowed his daughters to go on stage. He was in Ireland when he heard of his son's marriage and was so angry that he not only refused to have any contact with him, but also forbade his daughters to do so. Elizabeth, he declared, was 'a strumpet', and Richard 'without an atom of principle'. 'I consider myself now as having no other Son but *you*,' he wrote to Charles a few days later. 'Your sisters, too, know of no other brother, and would therefore naturally expect an increase of attention from you.'

To the outside world the affair seemed a storm in a teacup. As one wit put it, 'Who is to settle the precedence between the family consequence of the green-room and the orchestra?' Thomas Linley had soon come round to his son-in-law, whose 'captivating manners and superior address' he found hard to resist. It was true that Richard had no money, but his talents and ambitions promised much, and the only point of difference between them was Sheridan's refusal to allow his wife to go on singing. She had already been engaged to sing in Oxford and at the Three Choirs Festival in Worcester. Sheridan cancelled the engagements, explaining to his father-in-law that his wife could not be bound by undertakings made when she was unmarried: 'Nor . . . can you, who gave the promise, whatever it was, be in the least charged with the breach of it, as your daughter's marriage was an event which must always have been looked to by them as quite as natural a period to your rights over her as her death. And, in my opinion, it would have been just as reasonable to have applied to you to fulfil your engagement in the latter case as in the former.'

Under pressure Richard relented, on condition that she sang for nothing, and Elizabeth gave two farewell performances. The first was at the Sheldonian in Oxford, at the special request of Lord North, who was being installed as Chancellor of the university. A number of degrees were being conferred *honoris causa* and Lord North told Sheridan gracefully that he deserved one *uxoris causa* for allowing his wife to sing on this occasion. 'About 3,500 persons were present,' wrote the Scottish writer James Beattie who was receiving a degree. 'The band was led by Giardini, who is said to have declared it the finest he had ever seen . . . The first part of the concert consisted of Italian songs (sung by Mrs Sheridan and Miss Linley who are supposed to be the first singers now in England). Handel's Allegro and Penseroso formed the second part of the concert . . . Mrs Sheridan show'd amazing powers in the song "Sweet bird that shuns't" and Giardini excelled no less in its accompaniment . . . Never was there such a solemnity at Oxford.'

Elizabeth's second appearance, at the Three Choirs Festival, was a triumphant occasion for all the Linleys. It included the première of her brother's choral work 'Let God arise' and 'The Messiah', in which she sang with her sister and her father before an audience of over 1,400. She placed her fee, a banknote of £100, in the collection plate during a service at the cathedral, and took leave of her public, wrote the *Gloucester Journal,* 'in the full lustre of unrivalled talents, leaving the minds of her enraptured audience impressed with a remembrance not soon to be eradicated of her sweet and powerful tones, and charmed with her generosity and benevolence'.

It was her last public engagement and Linley, knowing the precarious state of the couple's finances, may well have sighed at the profits they had foregone – according to the *Morning Post* they turned down offers of more than 3,000 guineas in the months following their marriage. Perversely, Thomas Sheridan found this a new cause for offence. 'I found him very warm,' wrote a Bath friend, William Whateley. '. . . There is no moving him on one point, your refusing to let Mrs S. secure a Provision and Independence for herself and of consequence for you. That Part of your Conduct he says is contrary to the advice and wishes of every Friend you have.'

In the autumn of 1773 the Sheridans moved to London, at first as lodgers of Thomas Linley's friend the Italian musician Stephen Storace and then to a house of their own in Orchard Street. Here the Angelos joined them for a Christmas party. 'We kept it up to a late hour,' reported Henry Angelo; 'and music making part of the after-supper entertainment, Mamma Linley asked her daughter to sing a certain little favourite air; but a single glance from her juvenile lord and master kept her mute.'

Elizabeth seems to have acquiesced quite happily in her husband's refusal to let her sing in public. Fine musician though she was, she had always disliked the publicity to which she had been exposed. However, once settled in Orchard Street, where a music room had been set up, she sang in a number of private concerts to a selected audience. Alicia LeFanu, Sheridan's niece, insists that these were private entertainments, given in repayment for the hospitality they had received 'from many persons of fashion and consequence'. In fact the invitation was more general; according to a paragraph in the *Morning Post* of 4 February 1774: 'Sheridan has taken a house in Orchard St., Oxford St., where he purposes . . . to give concerts twice a week to the Nobility.' Not surprisingly they proved immensely popular. 'The highest circles of society were attracted to them by the talents, beauty and fashion of Mrs Sheridan,' wrote Fanny Burney in her diary. 'Entrance to them was sought not only by all the votaries of musical taste and excellence, but by the leaders of the *ton* and their followers and slaves.'

The concerts did much to ease the Sheridans' way into society; to a friend who taxed him with living beyond his means, he answered gaily, 'My dear friend, it is my means.' The transition did not always go smoothly. On one occasion Joshua Reynolds invited them to a large dinner party, expecting Elizabeth to entertain them afterwards. Having bought a new piano for the evening, he was much displeased when Sheridan declined to let her sing. 'What reason could they think I had for inviting them to dinner, unless it was to hear her sing? – for she cannot talk,' he remarked crossly next day. He soon changed his mind however, won over, as others would be, by Elizabeth's intelligence and charm. His portrait of her as St Cecilia, posed with two small angels at the keyboard, created a sensation when it was exhibited at the Royal Academy the following year and was, he considered, 'the best picture I ever painted'.

The Duchess of Devonshire was another who was at first dubious about the Sheridans. According to Lady Cork, who met them with some musical neighbours named Cootes (whose children were the models for the angels in Reynolds' portrait), she was anxious to have Mrs Sheridan sing at her house, but did not like to invite her husband – 'a player', as she called him. She was reminded of this by Lady Cork a few years later, on her keeping unoccupied for two months a house in Bath which she had rented at great expense, alleging for her reason that she and her party were detained from day to day at Chatsworth by the agreeableness of Sheridan's conversation.

Elizabeth was still the chief attraction at this time; Richard was known only as Mrs Sheridan's husband and as the hero of two duels for her sake. He had no intention of remaining in her shadow long. The law, once 'the great Gate of Power', now seemed too slow a route to fame and fortune. The world of letters, in one form or another, offered his best chance of distinguishing himself, and, with a confidence in his talents that disdained more prudent calculations, he soon gave up his studies at the Middle Temple for the riskier career of an author.

He did not find his way immediately. Amongst a number of unfinished projects dating from this period, the longest and most ambitious was an open letter to Queen Charlotte proposing a sanctuary and college for orphaned gentlewomen. In France the destitute daughters of the gentry could find refuge in a convent; in England there was no such resource. Perhaps the fate of his sisters should anything happen to his father was in his mind. In any case his suggestions for an educational establishment at Hampton Court along the lines of Madame de Maintenon's Saint Cyr were sensible and enlightened, if expressed in sometimes flowery language. The age of sensibility was dawning, and there were echoes of Rousseau in his description of the noble savage and his bride.

'The wild Huron shall become Gentle as his weary Rein-deer to the object of Love. He shall present to her the spoil of his Bow on his knee, he shall watch the scene where she sleeps with reward, he shall rob the Birds for Feather for her hair and dive for Pearl for her Neck, her Look shall be his Law and her Beauties his worship – This is Nature.'

Another, more fragmentary, project was a commentary on Lord Chesterfield's letters to his son, which had appeared posthumously in 1774. Moore quotes some characteristic extracts:

'Lord C's whole system in no one article calculated to make a great man – A noble youth should be ignorant of the things he wishes him to know; – such a one as he wants would be *too soon* a man . . .

'Emulation is a dangerous passion to encourage, in some points, in young men; it is so linked with envy. If you reproach your son for not surpassing his schoolfellows, he will hate those who are before him . . .

'His frequent directions for constant employment entirely ill founded: – a wise man is formed more by the action of his own thoughts than by continually feeding it. "Hurry," he says, "from play to study; never be doing nothing." I say "Frequently be unemployed; sit and Think . . ." '

Elizabeth's health had been an intermittent cause for worry since their marriage. She had had several miscarriages. In a letter to his son-in-law in June 1774, presumably after a recent alarm, Linley warned him that 'you must absolutely keep from her, for every time you touch her, you drive a Nail into her coffin'. She recovered, only to suffer a further set-back. Writing to Linley on 17 November, Sheridan told him: 'I must premise to you that Betsey is now very well, before I tell you abruptly that she has encountered another disappointment and consequent indisposition. However she is not getting entirely over it, and she shall never take any journey of the kind again. I inform you of this now, that you may not be alarmed by any accounts from some other quarter.'

Having broken this news he moved on to other matters: 'There will be a *Comedy* of mine in rehearsal at Covent-Garden within a few days . . . I have done it at Mr Harris's (the manager's) own request; it is now complete in his hands, and preparing for the stage. He, and some of his friends also who have heard it, assure me in the most flattering terms that there is not a doubt of its success. It will be very well played, and Harris tells me that the least shilling I shall get (if it succeeds) will be six hundred pounds. I shall make no secret of it towards the time of representation, that it may not lose any support my friends can give it.'

The play in question was *The Rivals*, and with its first performance on 19 January 1775 a new act in his life began.

# VI

Thomas Harris, the manager of Covent Garden theatre, had been a frequent visitor to Orchard Street, at first in the hope of luring Elizabeth on to the stage. Once it was obvious that she could not be persuaded to resume her professional career he had turned his attention to her husband. It cost him little to suggest that he should write a play. If the piece failed Sheridan would get nothing from it, while if it succeeded the theatre's profits would far exceed the £600 which its author hoped to make.

The first night of *The Rivals* was a failure. Sheridan had brought in his supporters from the fashionable world but the majority of the audience was so hostile that, as the *Town and Country Magazine* for January 1775 remarked, it was only 'after a pretty warm contest, towards the end of the last act, it was suffered to be given out for the ensuing night'.

Harris had helped Sheridan cut down the play, but it was still considered far too long and its language too extravagant and strained. Some of the characters gave offence. That of Sir Lucius O'Trigger in particular was regarded as an insult to the Irish section of the audience, while Lee, the actor playing him, was hopelessly unsuited to the part. His performance, wrote the *Morning Chronicle*, 'scarce equals the picture of a respectable Hottentot; gabbling in an uncouth dialect neither Welch, English nor Irish'. Lee played amidst violent heckling, and finally, on being struck by an apple from the pit, stepped forward to demand indignantly: 'By the powers, is it personal; is it me or the matter?' It was the only time, said Sheridan, that his Irish brogue was perfect.

Lee would be replaced for the second performance, which was postponed till ten days later, for Sheridan withdrew the play to revise it drastically and to soften the character of Sir Lucius from that of a bullying fortune hunter to one who, though quarrelsome, is so poor he 'can't afford to do a dirty action'. In his preface to the altered version he explained his changes, remarking, 'For my own part I see no reason why the Author of a Play should not regard a First Night's Audience as a candid and judicious Friend attending in behalf of the Public, at his last rehearsal.' At the same time he referred to his supposed offences over Ireland:

'It is not without pleasure that I catch at an opportunity of justifying myself from the charge of intending any national reflection in the character of *Sir Lucius O'Trigger*. If any Gentleman opposed the Piece from that idea, I thank them sincerely for their opposition; and if the condemnation of this Comedy (however misconceived the provocation) could have added one spark to the decaying flame of national attachment to the country supposed to be reflected on, I should have been happy in its fate.'

Elizabeth had been relieved by the initial failure of *The Rivals*. 'My dear Dick,' she told him, 'I am delighted. I always knew that it was impossible that you should make anything by writing plays; so now there is nothing for it but my beginning to sing publicly again, and we shall have as much money as we like.'

But the second night of *The Rivals*, so much altered that it was almost a new play, was an immediate success. It was received, wrote one newspaper, with 'the warmest bursts of approbation'; another quoted Garrick, the arbiter of the London stage, as saying at the beginning, 'I see this play will creep', and at the end, 'I see this play will run'.

*The Rivals* has kept its place in the hearts of audiences ever since. Less witty than *The School for Scandal*, it is more good-natured and more humorous. 'In the first,' as Hazlitt put it, 'you are always at the toilette or in the drawing room; in the last you pass into the open air, and take a turn in King's Mead.'

Bath is the setting for *The Rivals*. The Parades, King's Mead Fields, the Abbey – 'I am told there is very snug lying in the Abbey'

60

– are all included in the text. At the first performances, the realistic scenery, 'including a perspective view through the South Parade at Bath to the late Mr Allen's delightful villa', was much admired. But Sheridan's adventures there, contrary to the gossip of the time, had little to do with the plot. Perhaps there is something of the officious Barnett who urged on Mathews to his second duel in the scene where Sir Lucius O'Trigger dictates Bob Acres' challenge to the unknown Ensign Beverley, but the comparison cannot be taken very far:

SIR LUC. '*Sir*'—
ACRES. That's too civil by half.
SIR LUC. '*To prevent the confusion that might arise.*'
ACRES. Well—
SIR LUC. '*From our both addressing the same lady.*'
ACRES. Aye— there's the reason— '*same lady*'—Well—
SIR LUC. '*I shall expect the honour of your company*'—
ACRES. Z—ds! I'm not asking him to dinner.
SIR LUC. Pray be easy.
ACRES. Well then, 'honour of your company'—
SIR LUC. '*To settle our pretensions.*'
ACRES. Well.
SIR LUC. Let me see, aye, *King's Mead-Fields* will do.— '*In King's Mead-Fields.*'

Bob Acres becomes less belligerent as the duel grows nearer: 'My valour is certainly going! – it is sneaking off! – I feel it oozing out as it were at the palms of my hands!' But the blustering Sir Lucius is always ready for a fight. 'The quarrel is a very pretty quarrel as it stands – we should only spoil it by trying to explain it,' he tells Captain Absolute when he provokes him to a second duel.

As in *A Midsummer Night's Dream*, with whose fairy-tale atmosphere it has something in common, *The Rivals* has two pairs of lovers. In the hypersensitive Faulkland and the novel-reading Lydia Languish we see two aspects of romantic sensibility. Faulkland's feverish questioning of Julia's love, and the sentimental rhetoric he employs, are hard to put across today; in Sheridan's time they were admired as evidence of delicacy of feeling and may well have reflected some of his own doubts and fears during his courtship of Elizabeth. Lydia's extravagant romanticism, fed by the fiction she devours, is purely comical. She is not entirely taken in by it; she will marry Captain Absolute, even though he is not the penniless Ensign Beverley with whom she planned to run away, but she feels she has been cheated:

> There I had projected one of the most sentimental elopements! – So becoming a disguise! – so amiable a ladder of Ropes! – Conscious Moon – four horses – Scotch parson – with such surprise to Mrs Malaprop – such paragraphs in the News-papers! – O, I shall die with disappointment.

Mrs Malaprop, Lydia's aunt and unsuccessful chaperone, has given a new word to the language – in the *Oxford English Dictionary* a malapropism is defined as 'a ludicrous misuse of words'. She was said to have been based on Mrs Tryfort, one of the characters from Frances Sheridan's unfinished play *A Trip to Bath*. Mrs Tryfort uses the phrases 'a progeny of learning' and 'contagious countries' and declares that 'so much taciturnity does not become a young man', all of which are echoed in *The Rivals*. But Sheridan's father had given him the play to revise while he was in Bath and it is equally possible that these lines were his; and his father, normally quick to criticise, never suggested that he made use of his mother's comedy in *The Rivals*.

The character sketched in *A Trip to Bath* reaches new and joyous heights in Mrs Malaprop: 'A nice derangement of epitaphs'; 'as headstrong as an allegory on the banks of the Nile; 'you're not like Cerberus, three gentlemen at once'. The misapplications seem funny enough on paper, but they gain their fullest value when pronounced, as Hazlitt puts it, with 'all the vulgar self-sufficiency of pride and ignorance' on stage.

'Come, Mrs Malaprop, don't be cast down – you are in your bloom yet,' says Sir Anthony Absolute when she is spurned by Sir Lucius in the final scene. He himself has had his share of comic opportunities as the choleric father insisting that his son shall marry where he chooses: 'Odds life, Sir! if you have the estate, you must have it with the livestock as it stands.' When his son, who has meanwhile discovered his intended bride is Lydia Languish, asks coolly, 'And which is to be mine, sir, the Niece or the Aunt?', he is horrified:

SIR ANT. 'Why, you unfeeling, insensible Puppy, I despise you . . . The *Aunt*, indeed! Odd's life! when I ran away with your mother, I would not have touched anything old or ugly to gain an empire.'

ABSOLUTE. 'Not to please your father, Sir?'

SIR ANT. 'To please my father – Z—nds! not to please – O my father! – Oddso! – yes, yes! if my father indeed had desired – that's quite another matter . . .'

The overbearing father and his gallant son were familiar types in eighteenth-century comedy. So too were Sir Lucius, the stage Irishman, the clodhopping Bob Acres, the knowing servants, and the novel-reading Lydia Languish. (In Smollett's novel *Humphry Clinker*, published in 1770, the heroine, Lydia, 'has a languishing eye and reads romances'.) But if, like other writers of his time, Sheridan drew his characters from a common stock, he gave them all the life and vigour of originals.

'He was the furthest possible from a servile plagiarist,' wrote Hazlitt. '. . . . There is no excellence of former writers of which he has not availed himself, and which he has not converted to his own purposes, with equal spirit and success. He had great knowledge of the world; and if he did not create his own characters, he compared them with their prototypes in nature, and understood their bearings and qualities, before he undertook to make a different use of them. He had wit, fancy and sentiment at his command, enabling him to place the thoughts of others in a new light of his own, which reflected back an added lustre on the originals; whatever he touched he adorned with all the ease, grace and brilliancy of his style.'

At the age of twenty-four Sheridan had sprung up as a playwright fully armed. With the sure theatrical instinct inherited from his actor father and his playwright mother, he had made just one false start on stage. 'I have now got the last,' he is said to have remarked after rewriting *The Rivals*, 'and it shall not be my fault if I don't make the shoe to fit next time.'

He soon proved his skill once more with a two-act farce, *St Patrick's Day*. Written as a debt of gratitude for Clinch, the actor who had successfully replaced Lee as Sir Lucius O'Trigger, it was first performed for Clinch's benefit night on 2 May 1775, and had a great success on that and subsequent occasions. It is still occasionally revived today.

Though usually regarded as a trifle – Sheridan wrote it in forty-eight hours – *St Patrick's Day* is full of brilliant comic moments. Its hero, Lieutenant O'Connor, first played by Clinch, is a master of disguises; here, dressed up as a physician, he consults with Dr Rosy on the health of Justice Credulous:

LIEUT. Metto – dowsci pulseum.
DOCTOR. He desires to feel your pulse.
JUST. Can't he speak English?
DOCTOR. Not a word.
LIEUT. Palio-vivem-mortem-soonem.
DOCTOR. He says you have not six hours to live.

When the lieutenant undertakes to cure him for £3,000 Bridget (Mrs Credulous) thinks the price too high.

BRID. Three thousand halters – No, Lovee, you shall never submit
   to such an imposition – Die at once, my Life, and be a
   customer to none of them.
JUST. I will not die, Bridget – I do not like death.
BRID. Pshaw! there's nothing in it – a moment and it is over.
JUST. Aye, but it leaves a numbness behind, that lasts for a
   plaguey long time.

*St Patrick's Day* was a diversion and, in this *annus mirabilis* as a playwright, Sheridan was already considering a more ambitious project. But first his thoughts had turned to politics. By 1775 the American question had begun to loom large in British minds. Early that year Dr Johnson published his pamphlet *Taxation No Tyranny*, justifying British claims over the thirteen colonies. Sheridan's response shows him naturally taking the colonists' side. To Dr Johnson's point 'As all are born the subjects of some state or other, we may be said to have been all born consenting to some system of government,' he replied: 'This is the most slavish doctrine that ever was inculcated. If by our birth we gave a tacit bond for our acquiescence in that form of government under which we were born, there never would have been alteration of the first modes of government – no Revolution in England.'

Upon the argument deriving from Britain's right of conquest he observed with equal justice: 'This is the worst doctrine that can be with respect to America – if America is ours by conquest, it is the conquerors who settled there that are to claim these powers.'

Sheridan, perhaps, had no objection to taking issue with his father's old opponent. But his answer, fortunately, was neither published nor completed. If it had been, it might have prevented his being elected, as he was two years later, to the Literary Club – an honour that placed him among the foremost figures of the age.

The success of *The Rivals* had been marred for Sheridan by one poignant incident. Having heard that his father (who still refused to see him) meant to attend a performance with his daughters, Sheridan had taken a place by one of the side scenes directly opposite their box to watch them unobserved. On returning home he burst into tears, and, when asked what was the matter by his wife, told her how much it went to his heart 'to think that there sat his father and his sisters, and yet that he alone was not permitted to go near them or speak to them'.

All was not lost, however, for, perhaps influenced by his son's success, the Roman father was beginning to relent. On 21 October he made his first appearance at Covent Garden for sixteen years. 'My father was astonishingly well received on Saturday night as Cato,' wrote Sheridan to Thomas Linley. 'I think it will not be long before we will be reconciled.' According to Henry Angelo, it was his own parents who eventually brought about the peace between them, and by the end of the year father and son were again on speaking terms.

Neither *The Rivals* nor *St Patrick's Day* had wholly solved the younger Sheridan's financial difficulties. Elizabeth Linley was now pregnant and Thomas Linley felt justifiably concerned for their future. But Sheridan, on a rising tide of fortune, had perfect confidence in his powers to score another triumph if his father-in-law would only help. He was planning an opera, *The Duenna*, and looked to him to provide the music. Linley was at first unwilling: 'I would not have been concerned in this business at all,' he wrote to Garrick, 'but that I know there is an absolute necessity for him to endeavour to get some money by this means, as he will not be prevailed upon to let his wife sing, and indeed at present she is unable; and nature will not permit me to be indifferent to his success.'

Sheridan's letters to Linley on the subject show the easy

confidence that now existed between them, and cast a fascinating light on the composition of *The Duenna*. Without being musical himself, Sheridan had a clear idea of what he wanted and his wife could supply the musical knowledge that he lacked.

Many of the tunes for *The Duenna* were not original but, rather, familiar Scots or Irish airs reset to Sheridan's words by Linley. Some were still being written when the rehearsals had already started. Linley disapproved of this hand-to-mouth way of proceeding.

'I think he [Sheridan] ought first to have finished his opera with the songs he intended to introduce in it, and have got them entirely new set,' he told Garrick. 'No musician can set a song properly unless he understands the character, – and knows the performer who is to exhibit it.'

But Linley was too busy to leave Bath, where he was rehearsing for a concert at the New Assembly Rooms, and Sheridan had to do his best by correspondence.

'The inclosed are the words for "Wind, gentle evergreen"; a passionate song for Mattocks, and another for Miss Brown, which solicit to be clothed in melody by you and are all I want,' he wrote a few weeks before the first performance. 'Mattocks's I could wish to be a broken, passionate affair, and the first two lines may be recitative, or what you please, uncommon. Miss Brown sings hers in a joyful mood: we want her to show in it as much execution as she is capable of, which is pretty well; and, for variety, we want Mr Simpson's hautboy to cut a figure, with replying passages, etc., in the way of Fisher's *M'ami, il bel idol mio*, to abet which I have lugged in "Echo", who is always allowed to play her part.'

In the end the opera was a family affair, with the overture and five songs composed by the young Tom Linley, and others adapted or written by his father and a friend, the composer William Jackson. Thomas Linley arrived in London in time to supervise the final rehearsals, and to see his grandson, Thomas, who was born on 17 November, four days before the first performance.

*The Rivals* had made Sheridan's name as a playwright, but *The Duenna* was a still greater success. It ran for seventy-five days in its first season, ten days longer than *The Beggar's Opera* had done nearly half a century earlier. A popular broadsheet of the time compared the two:

> In days of Gay, They sing and say,
>   The Town was full of folly:
> For all day long, its sole sing-song,
>   Was Pretty, Pretty, Polly.
>
> So now-a-days, As 'twas in Gay's,
>   The world's run mad agen-a:
> From morn to night, Its whole delight
>   To cry up *The Duenna*.

The music to *The Duenna*, as its first published edition admitted, was a 'compilation'. It has subsequently been reset three times by other composers, the best known of whom is Prokofiev. Not only does the libretto sparkle, but its songs have a lyric quality which show Sheridan at his best as a poet. Many of them took their inspiration from his love affair with Elizabeth, and some perhaps were directly transcribed from letters he had written to her. How better could the pains of separation be expressed than by his heroine Louisa,

> What bard, O time discover,
>   With wings first made thee move;
> Ah! sure he was some lover,
>   Who ne'er had left his love.
>
> For who that once did prove,
> The pangs which absence brings,
>   Tho' but one day,
>   He were away,
> Could picture thee with wings.

And what could be more chivalrous than Carlos's promise to protect her, as Sheridan had done when he escorted Elizabeth to France,

> Had I a heart for falsehood framed,
>   I ne'er could injure you;
> For tho' your tongue no promise claimed,
>   Your charms wou'd make me true.
> To you no soul shall bear deceit,
>   Nor stranger offer wrong,
> But friends in all the aged you'll meet;
>   And lovers in the young . . .

As usual young love has to deal with intransigent old age in the opera and Don Jerome, Louisa's father, feels that he has much to bear,

> If a daughter you have, she's the plague of your life
> No peace shall you know, tho' you've buried your wife,
> At twenty she mocks at the duty you've taught her,
> O, what a plague is an obstinate daughter . . .'

The stratagems by which the rich Isaac Mendoza, the bridegroom intended for Louisa by her father, is tricked into marrying the Duenna instead, keep the plot turning over at a rollicking pace. When Isaac, who is marrying for money, first meets the disguised Duenna, he is surprised when Louisa's father, who thinks he has met his daughter, tells him she is only twenty:

ISSAC. Then, upon my soul, she is the oldest looking girl her age in Christendom.
JEROME. Do you think so? But I believe you will not see a prettier girl.
ISAAC. Here and there one.
JEROME. Louisa has the family face.
ISAAC. Yes, egad, I shou'd have taken it for the family face, and one that has been in the family some time too. [*Aside*]

For Garrick, the manager of Drury Lane, the brilliant success of *The Duenna* at the rival Covent Garden was a challenge. The greatest attraction he could offer was himself, and he threw himself into his most popular roles, amongst them Sir Anthony Branville in a revival of Frances Sheridan's *The Discovery*. So much activity was exhausting and, since he was then approaching sixty, a fellow actor quipped that 'the old woman [the Duenna] will be the death of the old man'. But Garrick bore no grudge against Sheridan, whom he admired and liked. He was planning to retire from Drury Lane and the idea that Sheridan might take a share in the management was already in his mind. The negotiations would begin in earnest early the following year.

For Sheridan, 1775, the year which had seen his theatrical fortunes soar, would end with a return to the subject of America. His poem 'The General Fast; A Lyric Ode', published as 'by the author of *The Duenna*' was a satire and an attack on the government for their conduct of the American campaign. Too long to quote here, its chief interest lies in the view expressed in his dedicatory introduction that 'the American War, founded in injustice and carried on by folly, must end in irretrievable disgrace, or in absolute destruction'. Ever since leaving Harrow Sheridan had been interested in politics, and it was an old Harrow friend, John Townshend, who would introduce him to Charles James Fox, the man who more than any other would shape his political ideas.

Sheridan's views on America coincided with those of Fox, but it was as the successful author of *The Rivals* that he was introduced to him. Townshend described the meeting:

'I made the first dinner party at which they met; having told Fox that all the notions he might have conceived of Sheridan's talents and genius from the comedy of *The Rivals*, etc. would fall infinitely short of the admiration of his astonishing powers, which I was sure he would entertain at his first interview. The first interview between them . . . I shall never forget. Fox told me, after breaking up from dinner, that he always thought Hare, after my uncle Charles Townshend, the wittiest man he ever met with, but that Sheridan surpassed them both infinitely; and Sheridan told me next day that he was quite lost in admiration of Fox, and that it was a puzzle to him to say what he admired most, his commanding superiority of talents, and universal knowledge, or his playful fancy, artless manners, and benevolence of heart which showed itself in every word.'

It was the start of a friendship that would last, though with lessening intensity, for more than thirty years, and an augury of the path which Sheridan was soon to follow. Meanwhile, the theatre claimed him, not only as an author but as the prospective proprietor of Drury Lane. The negotiations to raise money would be complex, but Sheridan had no doubts of succeeding. 'I'll answer for it,' he told his father-in-law, who was planning to join him in the enterprise, 'we shall see many golden campaigns'.

# VII

The patents for Drury Lane and Covent Garden, the theatrical charters which gave the two theatres the monopoly of spoken drama in London, went back to the reign of Charles II; they had been reconfirmed by the Licensing Act of 1737. A third playhouse, the Haymarket, had the right to perform plays in the summer when the other theatres were closed. Garrick, the manager of Drury Lane, also owned a half share of Drury Lane's patent, the other half being held on a mortgage of £31,500 from Garrick by a young man called Willougby Lacy. It was Garrick's half share, valued at £35,000, that he now planned to sell.

His first intention had been to sell to the playwright George Colman the elder, but Colman would only buy the whole, and Lacy would not sell his share. The way was now open for Sheridan, together with his father-in-law and Dr James Ford, a fashionable doctor who already held a mortgage on the theatre, to take up Garrick's share. They divided the purchase price into portions of £5,000, Sheridan and his father-in-law buying two shares each, and Ford three. Linley had property in Bath and elsewhere, on which he raised money by a mortgage from Garrick, but Sheridan could borrow only against the theatre itself. He did so with a mortgage on his share of the theatre of £7,700 from Ford, and a further £1,000 on two annuities from Garrick's solicitors; the last £1,300 he found himself, perhaps from his profits from *The Duenna*. The whole structure, as Sichel points out, was thus founded on 'the quicksands

70

of loans and mortgages'. But Sheridan had no doubts of making money. The theatre itself was worth £70,000, with annual interest payments of £3,500; 'while this is *cleared*,' he told his father-in-law, 'the proprietors are *safe*, – but I think it must be *infernal* management that does not double it.'

Drury Lane was crowded for Garrick's final performances, with parties coming from as far as France to see him act for the last time. Sheridan would always regret that he never saw Garrick act till the very end of his career. The story has it that this was owing to his father, who had told him that as he himself was the foremost actor of the age it was unnecessary to see inferior performers. This may have been unjust, for Thomas Sheridan, though jealous of Garrick, once admitted to Boswell that he regarded him as the greatest actor of his time.

Garrick was due to retire at the end of June 1776, the date when the transfer of the theatre was completed. As the time drew near his letters grew jubilant. 'I shall shake off my chains, and no culprit in a jail delivery will be happier. I really feel the joy I used to do when I was a boy, at breaking up.' His farewell performances alternated tragedy with comedy, King Lear and Richard III with Benedick and Abel Drugger from *The Alchemist*. He chose a comedy, *The Wonder*, for his final performance, his voice breaking when he came forward to give the epilogue. His last words were drowned by shouts of applause and cries of 'Farewell, farewell' as he slowly made his way off the stage. There was not a dry eye in the house.

Garrick had been in charge of Drury Lane for almost thirty years. Like Thomas Sheridan he had faced theatrical riots, but under his management Drury Lane had become the most important of the two main theatres. At a time when outside distractions and interests were few, it held a position in the life of the capital that is hard to imagine today. 'The theatre engrossed the minds of men to such a degree,' wrote Arthur Murphy in his life of Garrick, '. . . that there existed in England a *fourth estate*, King, Lords and Commons and *Drury Lane Playhouse*.'

Every section of London society, from the king and royal family downwards, was represented in the audience, their status roughly defined by their position in the theatre – in the boxes the aristocracy, above them merchants and tradesmen, in the galleries the lower orders, in the pit an indiscrimate collection ranging from footmen to critics and young bloods:

> Ye belles and ye beaux
>   Who adorn our low rows,
> Ye Gods who preside in the high ones;
>   Ye Critics who sit
>   All so snug in the pit –
> An assemblage of clever and sly ones . . .

The repertoire of Drury Lane, like that of Covent Garden, was as catholic as the composition of its audiences. On each evening there would be a main piece, lasting two or three hours, followed by an after-piece, usually of a light or humorous nature and often accompanied by music and dancing. It was perfectly normal to see, say, *King Lear* and a pantomime in a single evening's entertainment, though those who thought that five hours in the crowded and uncomfortable conditions of the pit were too much could come in after the second act of the main piece for half price.

A sense of intimacy between actors and audiences was fostered by the construction of the theatre, with a forestage jutting out into the auditorium and boxes above the side entrances, and by the fact that the theatre remained fully lit during performances. Though spectators were no longer allowed on the stage, the audience still regarded themselves very much as the arbiters of what went on there, rewarding their favourites with tumultuous applause and expressing their disapproval vociferously. Sometimes, as with the first Sir Lucius O'Trigger, the actors might be driven to answer back, but too much spirit on their part was not advisable. Even Garrick had once been forced to his knees by a rioting audience; in the end both management and actors had to abide by the basic tenet set out by Dr Johnson in his prologue for Garrick's opening night as manager:

> The drama's laws the drama's patrons give,
> For we who live to please must please to live.

In September 1776 the theatre opened for its first season under the new management. Thomas Linley was in charge of the music and director of the Lenten oratorios, while Sheridan combined the role of business and acting (or artistic) manager, responsible for casting and the choice of plays. The post of acting manager had first been offered to Thomas Sheridan but he had taken offence at the terms proposed and had set off for Ireland instead.

The new season began with a problem. Lacy, the co-owner of the theatre, now decided that he too wished to sell his half share, and, without consulting Sheridan, began negotiations with two friends to buy it. Sheridan was disgusted by what he considered Lacy's underhand behaviour and announced that he was giving up all part in the management and that Lacy must henceforth run the theatre. Poor Lacy, who had no experience, was confronted with rebellion from his actors, who one by one pleaded sickness and refused to play.

'Indeed,' wrote Sheridan to the sympathetic Garrick, 'there never was known such an uncommonly epidemick Disorder as has raged among our unfortunate Company – it differs from the Plague by attacking the better sort first – the manner too in which they are seiz'd I am told is very extraordinary – many who were in perfect Health at one moment, on receiving a Billet from the Prompter to summon them to their Business are seiz'd with sudden Qualms – and before they can get thro' the contents are totally unfit to leave their Rooms.'

Lacy, defeated, promised that he would never again try to part with his share without giving Sheridan and his partners first refusal, and the two potential buyers withdrew. Sheridan returned to the affairs of Drury Lane, where his first important contribution to the theatre's repertoire was an adaptation of Vanbrugh's comedy *The Relapse*, renamed – perhaps with his mother's *A Trip to Bath* in mind – *A Trip to Scarborough*.

Restoration comedy was considered too broad for later eight-eenth-century audiences. Garrick had toned down Wycherley's *The Country Wife* to the less offensive *The Country Girl*; Sheridan would do the same for *The Relapse*. He may have felt about adapting Vanbrugh as he did about Congreve, whose plays he also altered for the stage. 'His plays are, I own, somewhat licentious,' he told the singer Michael Kelly, 'but it is barbarous to mangle them; they are like horses, when you deprive them of their vice, they lose their vigour.'

But Sheridan's skilfully rewritten version was suited to his public.

'The comedy of *The Relapse* . . .' wrote the *Morning Chronicle*, 'was not only replete with gross allusions, but exhibited so glaring a picture of vice and immorality, that it has long been deemed unfit for representation. Mr Sheridan, impelled by a laudable desire to keep Sir John Vanbrugh, among the authors whose plays are in the stock list of the theatre, has given himself the task of altering *The Relapse*, and has (considering the heap of indecency he had to remove) achieved an Herculean task.'

Despite the author's good intentions, the first performance, on 14 February 1777, was met with a chorus of hisses from the audience, who had expected a new play, not a rehash of an old one. In her memoirs, the beautiful Mrs Robinson (later famous as Perdita to the Prince of Wales's Florizel) describes her terror when her fellow actress Mrs Yates, unable to bear the uproar any longer, fled from the stage, leaving her to face the hostile audience alone.

'I stood for some moments as if I had been petrified. Mr Sheridan, from the side-wing, desired me not to quit the boards: the late Duke of Cumberland from the stage-box bid me take courage – "It is not you, but the play they hiss," said his Royal Highness. I curtsied; and that curtsey seemed to electrify the whole house, for a thundering peal of encouraging applause followed. The comedy was suffered to go on, and is to this hour a stock-piece at Drury Lane theatre.'

Garrick had paid Sheridan the compliment of writing the prologue to *A Trip to Scarborough*. Sheridan did the same for Harris, the manager of Covent Garden, by writing a prologue to his production of a play by Richard Savage, *Sir Thomas Overbury*. Savage, who had died in poverty, had been the great friend of Dr Johnson's youth and the subject of his first biography. Sheridan's prologue, after describing the poet's wretched fate, paid a tribute to Savage's biographer:

> There shall his fame (if own'd tonight) survive,
> Fix'd by the hand that bids our language live.

This compliment to his dictionary, wrote Boswell, 'could not fail to be very pleasing to Johnson'. He had long wished to make up his differences with Sheridan's father, and was eager to show his appreciation of his son. He therefore proposed him as a member of the Literary Club, observing that 'He who has written the two best comedies of his age, is surely a considerable man.' (Johnson was referring to *The Rivals* and *The Duenna*, for *The School for Scandal* had not yet been written.)

Sheridan's election to the Literary Club was an honour that placed him on an equal footing with some of the most distinguished intellectual and artistic figures of the day, amongst them Gibbon, Reynolds, Burke and Charles James Fox. He was happy in his home and family life, devoted to his baby son, who, as he told his father-in-law, 'astonishes everybody by his vivacity his talents for musick and Poetry and the most perfect integrity of mind'. But he wished to shine in the fashionable world as well, and the great houses and great hostesses of the aristocracy had at least as much allure for him as the Turk's Head tavern. He had already been introduced to the Duchess of Devonshire and he would soon become friends, and more than friends, with her sister Lady Duncannon. But his first great friendship in the upper reaches of society was with the celebrated Mrs Crewe, then at the height of her worldly success.

Amoret, as she was known, was the daughter of the accomplished Mrs Greville, whose 'Ode to Indifference' was the best-known poem by a woman in the eighteenth century. She herself wrote poetry and prided herself on her intellectual friendships – in later life she would publish her reminiscences of Burke, with whom she maintained a correspondence over thirty years. Although exceptionally beautiful – 'she uglifies everything near her', wrote Fanny Burney – there was something essentially modest and retiring about her. As Sheridan expressed it,

> No state has *Amoret*! – No studied Mien!
> She apes no *Goddess*! – and she *moves* no *Queen*!
> The softer Charm that in her Manner lies
> Is framed to captivate, yet not surprise . . .

In the spring of 1775, fresh from the success of *The Rivals*, Sheridan had gone to a ball given by Mrs Crewe, attended by the most fashionable beauties of the day. Elizabeth, who was staying in Bath with her parents, was consoled by a poem from her husband, in the guise of Silvio, telling Laura that without her presence "tis not spring'. In a poem in reply she pictures him at the ball surrounded by an admiring throng, the ladies vying with each other to take the crown of beauty from his hands, and asks,

But where does Laura pass her lonely hours?
Does she still haunt the grot and willow-tree?
Shall Silvio from his wreath of various flow'rs
Neglect to cull one simple sweet for thee?

But she cannot doubt her Silvio, who reaffirms his love,

'Ah, Laura, no', the constant Silvio cries,
'For thee a never-fading wreath I'll twine,
Though bright the rose, its bloom too swiftly flies,
No emblem meet for love so true as mine.

For thee, my love, the myrtle, ever-green,
Shall every year its blossoms sweet disclose,
Which when our spring of youth no more is seen,
Shall still appear more lovely than the rose.'

Nearly two years had passed since then and Elizabeth, as well as her husband, had become close friends of Mrs Crewe, to whom Sheridan would dedicate the play he had been maturing since he came to Drury Lane, *The School for Scandal*. Some of the ideas behind it went back further, to his days in Bath, when his second duel had been a seven-day wonder in the press. A first sketch for the play was even set there, under the title 'The Slanderers, A Pump Room Scene'.

In his life of Sheridan, Moore traces the play's development, showing how it is an amalgam of two separate plots, one centred on Lady Sneerwell and her circle, the other on the Teazles, and quoting from successive drafts to show how the characters and situations evolve. The relationship between Sir Peter and Lady Teazle, for instance, develops into something far more interesting than the usual bickerings of an old man and his flighty young wife: both, it is clear, take pleasure in their verbal sparring and the attraction between them is implicit. In the same way the mischief-making of the scandalous college is tuned to such a pitch of fun and fantasy that Lady Teazle's enjoyment of their company becomes at least believable. Nor are their characters altogether black. Lady Sneerwell has been wounded by slander in her youth; Snake does a good deed by stealth, but is afraid to lose his evil reputation: 'If it were once known that I had been betray'd into an honest Action I should lose every Friend I have in the world.'

Sheridan took infinite pains with the play, polishing and cutting till every facet sparkled. Indeed, one of the criticisms against it was that the dialogue was too brilliant, that even such minor characters as the servant Trip were as witty as their masters. Sheridan might well have answered, with his own Mr Puff, that he 'was not for making slavish distinctions, and giving all the fine language to the upper sort of people'.

As always, Sheridan hid his hard work behind an appearance of insouciance. 'It was the fate of Mr Sheridan and, in a great degree, his policy –' wrote Moore, 'to gain credit for excessive indolence and carelessness, while few persons, with so much natural brilliancy of talents, ever displayed more art and circumspection in their display.' At the very last moment he was still correcting and rewriting, so that the play had already been announced before the whole of it was in the actors' hands. The manuscript of the last five scenes, Moore tells us, shows signs of being written in haste, and a note in Sheridan's handwriting at the bottom of the final page – 'Finished at last. Thank God. R. B. Sheridan' – had a heartfelt postscript by the prompter – 'Amen! W. Hopkins'.

The first night of *The School for Scandal*, on 8 May 1777, was one of the great dates in theatrical history. Eagerly anticipated, it was attended by all the luminaries of the fashionable world, Mrs Crewe and the Duchess of Devonshire conspicious amongst them. Garrick, who had superintended the rehearsals and written the prologue, was observed applauding in the highest spirits at his successor's triumph. The curtain went up at six o'clock; some time later the playwright Frederick Reynolds, who was passing outside the theatre, heard such a roar from within that, thinking the building was collapsing, he took to his heels and ran. It was the shout of applause that greeted the falling of the screen in the fourth act. So great was Sheridan's elation at his success, he told Byron years later, that 'he was knocked down and put in the watch-house for making a row in the streets and for being found intoxicated by the watchman'.

'Amidst the mortifying circumstances attendant upon growing old, it is something to have seen the *School for Scandal* in its glory', wrote Charles Lamb in 1822. No piece, he considered, had ever been so well cast when it first appeared. Sheridan knew his company well, and their parts displayed them to their best advantage.

In the opening scene at Lady Sneerwell's, Crabtree and Sir Benjamin Backbite, 'the wasp and the butterfly' as Lamb described them, were played by Parsons, the first Sir Fretful Plagiary, and Dodd, 'the prince of pink heels and empty eminence'. Miss Pope, 'the perfect gentlewoman', was said to be type-cast as Mrs Candour; off stage as well as on, her sweetness had a hidden sting. When Maria, disgusted by their criticism of Charles, leaves the room on pretence of feeling ill, she is all solicitude.

> MRS CANDOUR. O dear, she chang'd colour very much –!
> LADY SNEERWELL. Do Mrs Candour follow her – she may want assistance.
> MRS CANDOUR. That I will with all my soul. Ma'am – poor dear Girl – who knows – what her situation may be!

Mrs Abington, the finest comic actress of the day, was Lady Teazle. Behind scenes she was formidable – she was one of the three actresses whose quarrels and tantrums were said to have driven Garrick from the stage – but on stage she was charm personified. She had begun life as a tavern girl, but excelled in playing fashionable ladies; no one, it was said, could handle a fan more delightfully, or point a witty phrase more gracefully. It was easy to believe that Sir Peter found her irresistible, even when they most disagreed: 'With what a charming air she contradicts everything I say – and how pleasingly she shows her contempt of my authority – well tho' I can't make her love me there is a great Satisfaction in quarrelling with her and I think she never appears to such advantage as when she's doing everything in her Power to plague me.'

Tom King, one of the most reliable members of the company, was Sir Peter. His acting, wrote Hazlitt, 'left a taste on the palate, sweet and sharp like a quince; with an old, hard, rough withered face, like a John apple, puckered up into a thousand wrinkles; with shrewd hints and sharp replies'. Maria, his ward, was originally intended for Mrs Robinson, but she was pregnant and too 'unshaped' to play the part which was taken by the prompter's daughter Priscilla Hopkins. Perhaps it was because of this that Sheridan once told Samuel Rogers that he had not written a love scene between her and Charles Surface, as his actors were not suitable.

The two Surfaces, Charles and Joseph, were perfectly matched.

The gay and jovial Charles, first seen with his companions 'at a Table with Wine etc.' was played by William, or 'Gentleman' Smith, late of Eton and Cambridge and noted for his easy, aristocratic manner. Thomas Linley had composed the music for their famous drinking song:

Here's to the maiden of Bashful fifteen,
Here's to the Widow of Fifty . . .

John Palmer, otherwise known as 'Plausible Jack', was Joseph, the lightest and most elegant of scheming hypocrites. 'With what an air he trod the stage! —' wrote Hazlitt. 'With what pomp he handed Lady Teazle to a chair! With what elaborate duplicity he knelt to Maria!'

For Charles Surface the deciding moment of the play is the picture auction scene when his refusal to sell his uncle's portrait, despite his friend's disparaging description — 'as Stern a looking Rogue as ever I saw — an Unforgiving Eye and a damn'd disinheriting Countenance' — transforms him in his uncle's eyes. For the disguised Sir Oliver he is now 'A Dear, extravagant rogue!', while Joseph, the man of sentiment, is soon to be found out.

Joseph's come-uppance is the climax of the famous screen scene. As the screen falls to reveal Lady Teazle to Charles Surface and her astonished husband — 'Lady Teazle! by all that's wonderful!'; 'Lady Teazle! by all that's Horrible!' — the full extent of his hypocrisy is exposed. It is unfortunate that his uncle, posing as his poor relation Stanley, comes to see him just when his pretensions to virtue have been overthrown: 'Sure Fortune never play'd a man of my Policy — such a Trick — before — my character with Sir Peter! my hopes with Maria! — I'm in a rare humour to listen to other People's Distresses! — I shan't be able to bestow even a benevolent sentiment on Stanley.'

It is hard not to feel a sneaking sympathy for him in his embarrassments, though the 'scandalous college' stays poisonous to the last. Lady Sneerwell's parting shot to Lady Teazle — 'May your Husband live these fifty years!' — loses its sting in the reconciliation between husband and wife. For all the malice of the scandal mongers, there is a warmth and optimism in the play which bring it naturally to its happy ending.

Sheridan had joined Garrick in overseeing the rehearsals and ensuring that each line was given its right value. There is a story handed down to Ellen Terry, and recorded in her autobiography, of his correcting the formidable Mrs Abington when she spoke the line 'How dare you abuse my relations?' 'That will not do,' he said, 'it must not be pettish. That's shallow, shallow! You must go up the stage with, "You are just like my cousin Sophy said you would be", and then turn and sweep down on Sir Peter like a volcano: "You are a great bear to abuse my relations! How dare you abuse my relations!" '

Garrick, like the man of theatre that he was, kept a careful eye on the actors, even after the first night. 'Mr Garrick's best wishes and compliments to Mr Sheridan,' he wrote a few days later. 'How is the Saint [Elizabeth] today? A gentleman who is as mad as myself about ye School remark'd, that the characters upon the stage at ye falling of the screen stand too long before they speak; – I thought so too ye first night: – he said it was the same on ye 2nd, and was remark'd by others; – tho' they should be astonish'd, and a little petrify'd, yet it may be carry'd to too great a length – All praise at Lord Lucan's last night.'

From the days of Garrick onwards actors have delighted in *The School for Scandal*. Productions vary with the generations but, as with the music in an operatic aria, the language to a large extent imposes its own rhythm and Sheridan, the actor's son, must have written with the sound of it in mind: 'Sheridan wrote for the actor as Handel wrote for the singer,' remarked Bernard Shaw, reviewing a production of the play in 1896, 'setting him a combination of strokes which, however difficult some of them may be to execute finely, are familiar to all practised actors as strokes which experience has shown to be proper to the nature and capacity of the stage player as a dramatic instrument. With Sheridan you are never in the plight of the gentleman who stamped on a sheet of Beethoven's music in a rage, declaring that what cannot be played should not be written.'

Fifty years later, in an essay on his production of 1947, in which he played Sir Peter Teazle, Laurence Olivier wrote of a producer's duty to regard his author as the 'all-important lantern', whose beams of light must be followed in interpreting him to a contemporary audience. Sheridan was not for those who sought to update him by supposedly satirical treatment; he himself was the only satirist needed. The play worked best when approached with a devoted understanding of its eighteenth-century setting and by actors grounded in a feeling for the period. For Olivier its appeal was evergreen. Writing in his dressing-room, fresh from playing the second quarrel scene with Lady Teazle, he described 'the inexpressible feeling of fulfilment that possesses at least one humble actor as he feels the play's life and spirit pulsating through his body and soul' and paraphrased Charles Lamb: 'I am prepared to swear that whatever mortifying circumstances attend the life of the Theatre throughout the world, this play will never grow old.'

*The School for Scandal* made £15,000 in its first two seasons – £5,000 more than Sheridan's original stake in the theatre. For some time thereafter, in the words of the prompter, it 'dampened' all other new productions, and till the end of the century it was performed more often than any other play in London. It was translated into German and French. In Russia, Catherine the Great commissioned a translation and performance for the coming of age of her grandson, the future Alexander I; in the United States, where it quickly acquired the status of a classic, it was said to be George Washington's favourite play.

As with the translations, the American performances of the play were based on a pirated or unofficial version, taken from a copy Richard had given his sister to be used in Dublin. Sheridan never authorised its publication in his lifetime – nineteen years later he told its would-be publisher Mr Ridgway that he was still endeavouring to satisfy himself with its style, but had not yet succeeded. Perhaps he was also unwilling to let the other London theatres have the use of it; unpublished, the play was Drury Lane's single most valuable property.

Sheridan presented a manuscript of his play to Amoret, '*Thee* my Inspirer – and my *Model* – Crewe!', singing her praises in a four-page dedication which may have caused Elizabeth a pang. Silvio was still, in theory, faithful to his Laura, but the morals of the set which he was joining were far freer than those she was accustomed to. A few years later Elizabeth would write rather ruefully to a friend, 'S. is in Town – and so is Mrs Crewe – *I* am in the country and so is Mr *Crewe* – a very convenient arrangement is it not?' For the moment, however, she was happy to bask in her husband's glory; she had had enough adulation on her own account to take it in her stride.

# VIII

---

A midst the chorus of praise which greeted *The School for Scandal* it was Thomas Sheridan who sounded a dissenting note. 'Talk of the merit of Dick's play, there's nothing in it,' he said sourly, 'he had but to dip the pen in his own heart and he'd find there the characters of both Joseph and Charles Surface.'

It was true that Sheridan's character had its devious side. He had shown it in his reaction to Lacy's behaviour and in the way he had kept the secret of his love for Elizabeth; in later life he delighted in political and amorous intrigue. But there was far more of the open-hearted Charles than Joseph Surface in him; his generosity, like Charles's, might be at his tradesmen's expense, but there was no doubting its reality. To his sisters it was their more calculating elder brother who was the real Joseph, and they often spoke of him as such amongst themselves.

Charles Sheridan had spent three years in Sweden, where he had arrived at the time of the royal *coup d'état* which established Gustavus III in power. His eyewitness account of events there, published in 1778, attracted considerable attention and was later translated into French. Boswell, in his life of Johnson, gives an amusing picture of the great man reading it: 'Before dinner Dr Johnson seized upon Mr Charles Sheridan's *Account of the late Revolution in Sweden*, and seemed to read it ravenously, as if he devoured it, which was to all appearance his method of studying ... He kept it wrapt up in the table-cloth in his lap during the time of dinner, from an avidity to have one entertainment in readiness when he should have finished another; resembling (if I may use so coarse a simile) a dog who holds a bone in his paws in reserve, while he eats something else which has been thrown to him.'

Charles, now living in Dublin and a member of the Irish Parliament, remained his father's favourite child. Thomas Sheridan, in Elizabeth's opinion, had a tincture of the 'damnatus obstinatus mulio' about him. It must have been a consolation to her to see how well her husband got on with her own family, not only with her father but with her younger brothers and sisters with whom he was always happy to romp and play games. 'Oh, how I long for Sheridan to roll with me on the carpet again,' wrote Mary to her sister.

The Linleys had left Bath for London, where they took a house in Norfolk Street off the Strand, conveniently close to Drury Lane. For Elizabeth, separated from her family since her marriage, it was a pleasure to be close to them once more, in particular to see Mary, her closest confidant and 'the sister of my heart', on an everyday basis.

Since Elizabeth's retirement, Mary had taken her place as a singer at oratorios, festivals and concerts, but she had always suffered from comparisons between them. Fanny Burney described her as 'very handsome but nothing like her sister' and her soprano voice lacked the particular sweetness of Elizabeth's. She was still one of the leading singers of the day and, together with her brother Tom, the bright hope of her father, who stood to make a considerable amount of money from them both.

Tom Linley's creative powers had developed amazingly since his days as a child prodigy in Italy. A virtuoso violinist, he had composed over twenty concertos for the violin, many of them performed between the acts in the oratorio season at Drury Lane, where they were received 'with the most unbounded applause'. As well as his contributions to *The Duenna*, he had written other works for the theatre: a choral *Ode on the Spirits of Shakespeare*, music for *The Tempest*, and an oratorio, *The Song of Moses*, described by a critic of the time as 'one of the finest specimens of the Simple, Affecting, Grand and Sublime styles that was ever produced by the pen of a musician'. Mozart told the singer Michael Kelly when he met him in Vienna some years later that Linley was a 'true genius' who, had he lived, 'would have been one of the greatest ornaments of the musical world'.

In August 1778 Tom and his sisters went to stay at Grimthorpe Castle in Lincolnshire, the home of the Duke and Duchess of Ancaster. The introduction had come through Sheridan, and, though they were probably expected to help with music-making, they were treated as guests rather than performers. On 7 August Tom Linley, with two companions, was sailing on the lake beside the house when a wind got up and overturned the boat. After clinging to the rigging for some time he decided to strike out for shore to fetch help; hampered by his boots and heavy topcoat he drowned within a hundred yards of the boat. He was twenty-two years old.

Elizabeth mourned her brother's loss in a poem, 'On my brother's Violin':

> Sweet instrument of him for whom I mourn,
>     Tuneful companion of my Lycid's hours,
> How liest thou now neglected and folorn!
>     What skilful hand shall now call forth thy powers?
>
> Ah! none like his can reach those liquid notes,
>     So soft, so sweet, so eloquently clear,
> To live beyond the touch, and gently float
>     In dying modulations on the ear . . .

Thomas Linley's grief was deep-felt and long-lasting. The singer Mrs Crouch, one of his students at the time, remembered him sitting at the harpsichord at a rehearsal of a play, *Henry and Emma*, in which the actor playing Henry's tutor describes a young man of outstanding promise. 'The feelings of Mr Linley could not be repressed,' she wrote, 'the tears of mental agony rolled down his cheeks; nor did he weep alone, the cause of his distress was too well known not to obtain the tears of sympathy from the many who beheld *his* flow so fast.'

In December of that same year tragedy struck again when his second son, Samuel, now a midshipman aboard the HMS *Thunderer*, died of a fever caught at sea. The nest of nightingales was emptying fast.

1778, a year of bereavement for the Linleys, was an unhappy one

84

for Drury Lane. Garrick had begun it with high hopes, boasting, according to his biographer Arthur Murphy, 'of the genius to whom he had consigned the conduct of the theatre'. There were those who murmured that *The School for Scandal* alone would not support the theatre long, and who mourned his departure from the management. 'To you, Mr Garrick,' said one, 'I must say, "the Atlas that propped the stage has left his station".' 'Has he?' said Garrick cheerfully. 'If that be the case he has found another Hercules to succeed in the office.'

Sheridan's mood was equally sanguine, and when Lacy announced that he was prepared to sell his half share in the theatre for £10,000 more than Garrick's half he agreed to buy it. He paid for it in part by selling his previous share to Ford and Linley at a price somewhere between Garrick's and Lacy's, and by taking out two annuities of £500 each. Lacy's share had been mortgaged to Garrick for £31,500 and Sheridan took over the responsibility for the interest payments. Since Linley and Ford had also taken out mortgages with Garrick, the former manager was still closely involved with the fortunes of the theatre.

On paper there was nothing inherently risky in Sheridan's investment. Garrick had borrowed to take up his original share in the theatre and had seen it flourish under his management. But Garrick had devoted all his energies to the theatre and to the complex business of running it. Sheridan's ability and flair were not in question, but he was already distracted by the claims of social life and his growing interest in politics. To complicate matters further he had recently purchased a half share in the opera house at the King's Theatre, Haymarket, with Harris, the proprietor of Covent Garden – a short-lived arrangement that he would abandon after two seasons. Meanwhile, Drury Lane suffered. Playwrights complained that he had failed to answer their letters, actors that their salaries were unpaid. They retaliated by withdrawing their labour, feigning sickness or simply refusing to turn up. William Hopkins, the prompter, was often in despair.

Complaints came back to Garrick. 'Every one is raving against Mr Sheridan,' wrote the veteran actress Kitty Clive; 'there never was in nature such a contrast as Garrick and Sheridan.' The playwright Richard Cumberland, whose tragedy *The Battle of Hastings* had been accepted on Garrick's recommendation, was indignant at Sheridan's careless attitude. 'I read the tragedy in the ears of the performers on Friday morning . . .' he told Garrick, 'but your successor in management is not a representative of your polite attention to authors on such occasions, *for he came in yawning at the fifth act*, with no other apology than having sat up two nights running.'

Garrick himself was not immune. In May 1778 he was given notice that in future he could not be paid the interest he was owed till the other expenses on the theatre had been met. He wrote back sternly to the proprietors that he imagined his mortgage was as fair a charge as any other on the theatre and that he expected it to be paid off at the date agreed in the deeds. By their original agreement they stood in penalty of £44,000 – 'a thumper!' as Garrick endorsed it – if they failed to discharge the mortgage on demand.

In September 1778, in an attempt to improve matters, Sheridan and his partners again offered his father the post of acting manager and this time Thomas Sheridan accepted. But he was affronted at the condition imposed by Sheridan, and seconded by Charles (who also wished to keep his father from the stage), that he should not act at the same time. Age and disappointment had soured him. Mrs Linley, who had taken on the role of wardrobe mistress, christened him 'Old Surly Boots'. He started the job in an ill humour; five years later in a letter to Charles he poured out his grievances against his younger son.

At length a scene opened which promised better days. Garrick's retiring, whose jealousy had long shut the London theatres against me, such an open[ing] was made for me both as manager and actor as might soon have retrieved my affairs . . . But here a son of mine steps into possession, whose first step was to exclude me wholly from having any share in it. Afterwards when by extreme ill conduct they were threatened with ruin, he agreed to put the management into my hands upon condition that I should not appear as a performer and in this he got his brother to join him with such earnestness, that merely to gratify him I acquiesced . . . I desire to know whether if the theatre of Drury Lane had fallen into the hands of the worst enemy I had in the world, determined upon ruining me and my family, he could have taken more effective means of doing it, than those which have been pursued by my own son.

Thomas Sheridan was far less successful at Drury Lane than in his great days at Smock Alley. He was no longer regarded with the respect he had commanded as Dublin's most brilliant young actor, and he had grown inflexible with age. Not only did the actors find him so overbearing that his powers were eventually curtailed by the management, he even contrived to insult Garrick when he good-naturedly offered advice at a rehearsal. It was true that the play was *Mahomet*, the ill-fated work which had led to the destruction of Smock Alley, and that Thomas Sheridan knew the part in question well; he had played it at the time of the riot which had ruined him. Garrick wrote to Richard in dignified protest: 'Pray assure your father I meant not to interfere in his department: I imagined (foolishly indeed) my attending Bannister's rehearsal of the part I once played, and which your father never saw, might have assisted the cause, without giving the least offence. I love my ease too well to be thought an interloper, and I should not have been impertinent enough to have attended any rehearsal, had not you, sir, in a very particular manner desired me. However, upon no consideration will I ever interfere again in this business, nor be liable to receive such another message as was brought me by young Bannister.'

It was a graceless end to Thomas Sheridan's relationship with Garrick, who had overshadowed him at almost every turn of his career. But despite provocations from the father, Garrick continued to take a kindly interest in the son. Matters were obviously patched up and, according to the playwright John O'Keeffe, it was at a rehearsal of a topical after-piece, *The Camp*, in October 1778, that Garrick caught the cold that led to his death.

*The Camp* was said to be the work of Sheridan in conjunction with General Burgoyne, whose recent defeat at Saratoga had not affected his career as a successful playwright. It was written as a skit on the preparations for resisting invasion from France, which had declared war on Britain earlier that year in support of the American colonies. Militia regiments had been formed, and camps set up along the coast – the largest, at Coxheath in Kent, where the Duke of Devonshire was in command of the Derbyshire militia, was the setting for the play. The great scenic artist de Loutherberg, first introduced to Drury Lane by Garrick, surpassed himself in his realistic portrayal of Coxheath; Garrick had attended the rehearsal to have a preview of the sets. The cold he caught on this occasion led to complications, and by the end of the year it was clear that he would not recover. He died on 20 January 1779. Drury Lane remained closed that evening, as a mark of respect to the man who had guided its fortunes for so many years.

Garrick's death, in Johnson's memorable phrase, 'eclipsed the gaiety of nations'; the magnificence of his funeral at Westminster Abbey was a tribute to the achievement of one who, in the equally well known words of Burke, 'had raised the character of his profession to a liberal art'. Sheridan was chief mourner, theatrically dressed in black velvet with a train carried by six pages. When the funeral was over, he spent the rest of the day in silence.

Sheridan's monody 'Verses on the Memory of Garrick' was given from the stage of Drury Lane a few weeks later. Accompanied by 'solemn airs' and spoken by the actress Mrs Yates, it dwelt above all on the fleeting nature of the actor's fame,

> Th' expressive glance – whose subtle comment draws
> Entranced attention and a mute applause;
> Gesture that marks, with force and feeling fraught,
> A sense in silence, and a will in thought . . .
> Passion's wild break – and frown that awes the sense,
> And every charm of gentle eloquence,
> All perishable! like the electric fire
> But strike the frame and as it strikes expire . . .

The verses were published some months later, prefixed by a fulsome dedication to 'the Right Honourable Countess Spencer, whose approbation and esteem were justly considered by Mr Garrick as the highest panegyric his talents or conduct could acquire'. Lady Spencer was also the mother of the Duchess of Devonshire and Lady Duncannon and it was partly thanks to her influence that Sheridan would first acquire a seat in Parliament. Byron thought his monody the finest of its kind, but he also relates that Sheridan, on rereading the dedication in his company some thirty years later, flew into a rage and went on for half an hour abusing the object of it, declaring that he had never in his life dedicated anything to such a 'damned canting bitch'. Perhaps he disliked to be reminded of his erstwhile deference.

'Talents in literature,' remarked Moore, '. . . may lead to

association with the great, but rarely to equality.' At a time when politics were still the natural preserve of the aristocracy, it was only as a Member of Parliament that Sheridan could hope to be accepted fully into the 'little great world' of eighteenth-century society. Through his membership of the Literary Club he had come to know Burke; and in the years since their first meeting he had become intimate with Fox. He and Fox had become members of the so-called Westminster Committee, a group dedicated to electoral reform, and had begun a joint newspaper, *The Englishman*, chiefly devoted to attacks on the government. Sheridan wrote the first two numbers, Fox the third, but its appearances became increasingly irregular and it petered out a few months later. 'I knew what would come of it,' said Fox. 'Our d—d punctuality would be the ruin of it.'

These were opening moves in Sheridan's campaign to become a Member of Parliament. Before he did so he had one last masterpiece to give the theatre, his skit on heroic tragedy, *The Critic*. Few people were better placed than Sheridan to write it. Since taking over three years earlier he had always kept the task of reading new plays for himself and was thus the natural target of playwrights seeking to have their plays put on at Drury Lane. The authors of tragedy were the most persistent, and Richard Cumberland, in particular, had pursued him without mercy. In *The Critic* Sheridan would have his revenge.

Richard Cumberland was a well-known figure in his time. He was the author of fifty plays, one of which, *The West Indian*, had almost the status of a classic. But despite his achievements he was ludicrously envious of other writers. He was said to have been so jealous of *The School for Scandal* that when he saw it during its first run he had pinched his children to stop them laughing. 'It was very ungrateful of Cumberland to have been displeased with his poor children for laughing at my comedy,' said Sheridan when he heard of it, 'for I went the other night to see his tragedy, and laughed at it from beginning to end.'

Whether or not Cumberland was the original of Sir Fretful Plagiary in *The Critic*, he was generally considered to be so. '*No one* could mistake the Character who knows Mr Cumberland,' a friend told Fanny Burney's sister Susan soon after the first night. 'His *son* found it out immediately – He is in the Guards – I dined with him a few days ago and he cursed at Mr S. pretty heartily.'

It was not like Sheridan to be malicious. 'A Talent for ridicule even to bitterness and severity has not been wanting among such as I possess,' he told his second wife years later, 'but a certain Portion of good sense and more of good nature very early decided me to forego the use of it.' The portrait of the hypersensitive Sir Fretful was an exception, though it is the officious Mr Puff, not Sir Fretful, whose tragedy is burlesqued in *The Critic*.

The idea of a play within a play, or rather a tragedy within a farce, was not a new one. It had already been used with brilliant success in the Duke of Buckingham's *The Rehearsal* in 1671, still popular in Sheridan's time, and Sheridan's youthful comedy of *Ixion* had followed the same formula. In *The Critic* he would have the last word on the subject.

As with *The School for Scandal*, Sheridan procrastinated till the last moment with *The Critic*. In the end, Tom King, the actor playing Mr Puff, was driven to desperate measures. Two days before the performance, with the last scene still unwritten, he called Sheridan into the green-room on some slight excuse. Here a table with writing materials, two bottles of claret and a plate of anchovy sandwiches had been set out before the fire. No sooner were they in the room than King stepped out, locking the door behind him. Linley and Ford, the other two proprietors, announced that they would not let him out until the scene was written and Sheridan, under compulsion, finished the play, the claret and the sandwiches together.

Sheridan's dilatory habits were becoming a legend. The *Morning Chronicle* told the story of two men gazing at the bill outside the theatre on the opening night and wondering why the spelling was 'critic' rather than 'critick', the more normal eighteenth-century usage. 'Lord, Sir,' exclaimed a passing prompter's boy, 'that was owing to a joke of my Master's, who meant to intimate by his short spelling that the piece was not finished when the play was printed.'

First performed on 30 October 1779, *The Critic* followed *Hamlet* as an after-piece – a contrast perhaps no greater than when in 1945 it was played as a double bill with Yeats's version of *Oedipus Rex*, with Laurence Olivier both as Oedipus and Mr Puff. At the time of its first performance the play had a topical content whose context is now long forgotten. In June 1779 Spain had followed France in recognising American independence and declaring war on Britain, and in August the French and Spanish fleets were sighted in the Channel. The invasion scare had since died down, but not before it had been reflected in the theatre with a patriotic opera at Sadler's Wells entitled *The Prophecy, or Queen Elizabeth at Tilbury*. The piece may well have been the target of the so-called tragedy by Mr Puff.

The tragedy forms the last two acts of *The Critic*. The first act takes place at the house of Mr Dangle, an amateur of the theatre, who is discovered at breakfast reading the newspapers with his wife: 'BRUTUS to LORD NORTH − "Letter the second on the STATE OF THE ARMY" − Pshaw! "To the first L dash D of the A dash Y" . . . Pshaw! − Nothing but about the fleet and the nation! − and I hate all politics but theatrical politics.'

With the arrival of Sir Fretful Plagiary the destruction of Cumberland − if such was Sheridan's intention − begins. He was played on the first night by the veteran actor William Parsons, who made it one of his most celebrated parts.

'I have repeatedly enjoyed this rich treat,' wrote the theatrical historian James Boaden, 'and become sensible how painful laughter might be, when such a man as Parsons chose to throw his whole force into the character. When he stood under the castigation of Sneer affecting to enjoy criticisms, which made him writhe in agony; when the tears were in his eyes, and he suddenly checked his unnatural laugh, to enable him to stare aghast at his tormentors; a picture was exhibited of mental anguish and frantic rage, or mortified vanity and affected contempt which would almost deter an author from his pen, unless he could be sure of his firmness under provocation.'

But Sheridan could never be entirely cruel, and Sir Fretful has his own *bon mot*. 'You are quite right, Sir Fretful,' says Dangle, 'never to read such nonsense.' 'To be sure,' he replies, '− for if there is anything to one's praise, it is a foolish vanity to be gratified at it, and if it is abuse − why one is always sure to hear about it from some dam'd good natured friend or another!'

If Cumberland was the model for the character of Sir Fretful Plagiary, Mr Puff's mock tragedy in the next two acts was a skit on the whole genre. The theme is ostensibly patriotic, as England awaits the arrival of the Armada. However, as the governor of Tilbury Fort tells Tilburnia,

91

The Spanish fleet thou *canst* not see – because –
  It is not yet in sight!'

Tilburnia's love for the Spanish Don Whiskerandos ends in tears
and he falls to the Beefeater's sword:

WHISKERANDOS. . . . Captain, thou hast fenced well!
  And Whiskerandos quits this bustling scene
  For all eter—
BEEFEATER. —nity – He would have added, but stern death
  Cut short his being, and the noun at once!

Tilburnia enters to the famous stage direction 'Enter Tilburnia
stark mad in white satin, and her confidante in white linen'. 'O
Lord, Sir – when a heroine goes mad, she always goes into white
satin – don't she, Dangle?' says Puff.
  Meanwhile a sub-plot is unfolding with the recognition of the
'prisoner youth', Tom Jenkins. As Puff remarks: 'relationship, like
murder, will out'.

JUSTICE. No orphan, nor without a friend art thou—
  *I* am thy father, *here's* thy mother, *there*
  Thy uncle – this thy first cousin, and those
  Are all your near relations!
MOTHER. O ecstasy of bliss!
SON. O most unlooked for happiness!
JUSTICE. O wonderful event!
    *They faint alternately in each other's arms.*

But it is Puff who is the real hero of the play, dealing with
recalcitrant actors: 'I can't stay here dying all night', Whiskerandos
complains; chivying the Thames in the final procession: 'but hey!
what the plague! you have got both your banks on one side – Here
Sir, come round'; refuting the charge of plagiarism: 'all that can be
said is, that two people happened to hit on the same thought – And
Shakespeare made use of it first, that's all'; explaining Lord Burleigh's
silent shake of his head:
  'Why, by that shake of the head, he gave you to understand that
even tho' they had more justice in their cause and wisdom in their
measures – yet if there was not a greater spirit shown on the part of
the people – the country would at last fall a sacrifice to the hostile

ambition of the Spanish monarchy.' 'The devil!' says Sneer, '– did he mean all that by shaking his head?' 'Every word of it,' Puff answers, '– if he shook his head as I taught him.'

*The Critic* ended with a grand spectacle – 'Now for my magnificence! – my battle! – my noise! – and my procession!' says Puff – in which de Loutherberg again surpassed himself. The stage directions began, '*Flourish of drums – trumpets – cannon, &c. &c. Scene changes to the sea – the fleets engage – the musick plays "Britons strike home" – Spanish fleet destroyed by fire-ships, &c. English fleet advances – music plays "Rule Britannia" . . .*'

After the farce of Puff's tragedy the final pageant united the audience in a genuinely patriotic mood. The Spanish fleet, though not in sight, had not been forgotten by either the audience or the author.

Still more than *The School for Scandal*, *The Critic* was written with the company at Drury Lane in mind. It was full of shared jokes with the audience. Miss Pope, who played Tilburnia, took off the celebrated tragic actress Mrs Crawford; the grave Lord Burleigh was a caricature of the Prime Minister Lord North. Even Sheridan had a mention. '*Writes himself*! – I know he does', says Sneer to a whispered aside from Sir Fretful, who is afraid of plagiarism if he sends his play to Drury Lane: 'Why, Sir, for ought I know, he might take out some of the best things in my tragedy, and put them into his own comedy.'

The first night of *The Critic* was another triumph for its author. Fox and the Duchess of Devonshire sat in Mrs Sheridan's box and joined in the applause. 'It is vastly good,' wrote the duchess to her mother that same evening, 'it occasioned peals of laughter ev'ry minute.' In five years Sheridan had produced six great theatrical successes, three of them, *The Rivals*, *The School for Scandal* and *The Critic*, destined to become immortal. He was the most successful playwright of the age. Young, charming, with a wife whose fame matched his own, he was lionised in the drawing-rooms of London. Fanny Burney, who met the Sheridans for the first time that year with the fashionable hostess Mrs Cholmondeley, gave an enchanted description of them in a letter to her sister Susan:

'The elegance of Mrs Sheridan's beauty is unequalled by any that I ever saw, except Mrs Crewe . . . She is much more lively and agreeable than I had any idea of finding her; she was very gay and unaffected and totally free of airs of any kind . . . Mr Sheridan has a fine figure and a good, though I don't think a handsome face. He is tall and very upright, and his appearance and address are at once manly and fashionable, without the smallest tincture of foppery or modish graces. In short, I like him vastly, and think him in every way worthy of his beautiful companion.'

At twenty-six, Fanny Burney was in the first flush of her popularity as the author of *Evelina* and in her own quiet way was much enjoying her success. She was certainly not immune to Sheridan's flattery, or his compliments about her novel, which she recorded proudly in a letter to her sister:

'And now I must tell you a little conversation which I did not hear myself till I came home; it was between Mr Sheridan and my father.

"Dr Burney", cried the former, "have you no older daughters? Can this possibly be the authoress of 'Evelina'?"

And then he said an abundance of fine things and begged my father to introduce him to me.

"Why, it will be a very formidable thing to her", answered he, "to be introduced by you."

"Well then, by-and-by" returned he.

Some time after this, my eyes happening to meet his, he waived the ceremony of introduction and in a low voice said:

"I have been telling Dr Burney that I have long expected to see in Miss Burney a lady of the gravest appearance, with the quickest parts."

Of course I could make no verbal answer, and he proceeded then to speak of "Evelina" in terms of the highest praise; but I was in such a ferment from surprise (not to say pleasure), that I have no recollection of his expressions. I only remember telling him that I was much amazed he had spared time to read it and that he repeatedly called it a most surprising book; and after some time he added: "But I hope, Miss Burney, you don't intend to throw away your pen?" '

The evening ended with a request that she should write a comedy for Drury Lane. Fanny Burney wrote the play, but after showing it to a friend who condemned it decided not to put it forward. Sheridan protested to her father that he would not accept her refusal and asked his permission to call on her to try and persuade her to change her mind. Not surprisingly perhaps, to those who knew him, he never came. Caught up in a multiplicity of occupations, he all too often promised what he could not perform. In any case he was now engaged on the next great adventure of his life. Drury Lane and its affairs took second place as he turned towards the wider stage of politics.

# IX

─────────────⌇─────────────

Sheridan's first appearance in the political arena took place at a mass meeting in Westminster Hall on 2 February 1780, in which Fox, as the chairman of the Westminster Committee, presented his resolutions in favour of electoral reform. Sheridan shared the platform and signed the sub-committee's report. In the long run, however, he regarded its more radical demands – for annual parliaments and universal suffrage – as too sweeping to be practical politically. 'Whenever any one proposes to you a specific plan of Reform,' he would say jokingly, 'always answer that you are for nothing short of Annual Parliaments and Universal Suffrage – there you are safe.'

Sheridan's participation in the Westminster Committee established him firmly in the ranks of the Whig opposition. Many were figures already familiar to him: John Townshend, Edmund Burke, Thomas Grenville and his brother William, William Windham, whom he had first met in Bath, and Charles Fitzpatrick, whose sister had married Fox's brother and who had written the prologue to *The Critic*. Their political loyalties would not always be constant – Parliament at that time was a place of shifting groups attached to one or other interest, rather than of clearly defined parties – but for the moment they were united in their opposition to the war with America and what they regarded as the excessive influence of the Crown.

Fox was their chief spokesman in the House of Commons. A year older than Sheridan, he was already a parliamentary veteran, having become a member in 1768 at the age of nineteen. His success there had been immediate and he quickly established himself as one of the best debaters in the House, with an impromptu brilliance that amazed his hearers. Heavily built and swarthy, with thick black eyebrows over his brilliant dark eyes, his looks harked back to Charles II, his maternal great-great-grandfather – his mother was the daughter of the Duke of Richmond, a title given to the son of Charles II's mistress Louise de Keroualle. He had all the Stuart recklessness and lack of judgement – he had gambled away a fortune of over a million pounds in today's values by the time he was twenty-five – and all his share of Stuart charm as well. His warmth of heart and sweetness of disposition disarmed even his political opponents. At the height of his attacks in Parliament on the Prime Minister, Lord North, the two remained on friendly terms in private. 'I am glad you did not fall on me today,' said North, after Fox had made a particularly violent speech against his Minister of War, 'for you was in full feather.'

By 1780, after five years of conflict, the prospect of winning the American War seemed remoter than ever. The defeat of General Burgoyne at Saratoga at the end of 1777 had had a decisive effect on European opinion. Since then, both France and Spain had declared war on Britain; Russia, Denmark and Sweden were about to form a league of Armed Neutrality, whose main object was to deny the British navy the right of search of neutral vessels; by the end of 1780 Holland, France and Spain had joined the league, and Holland was at war with Britain too.

With almost all of Europe arrayed against Britain, and no end to the war in America in sight, the opposition's demands for opening peace negotiations gained new force. The general public disliked the war because of its cost; those involved in it, on the other hand, grew rich from the loans and contracts it created. At the Westminster meeting of 2 February the committee had called for 'economical reform' to curb corrupt expenditure of public funds. In the House of Commons on 6 April, John Dunning, the MP for Calne, moved his resolution 'that the influence of the Crown has increased, is increasing, and ought to be diminished', a direct attack on the spread of royal patronage arising from the war. It was passed by a small majority, but further propositions were defeated. The Gordon 'No Popery' riots, which broke out in June, and which for five days held London at the mercy of the mob, alarmed the independent members of the House, while the king's good sense and firmness on this occasion did much to restore his prestige.

This was the state of affairs when Parliament dissolved on 1 September; Sheridan was to stand as a member for Stafford in the election that followed. It had not been easy to find a seat. He might take pride in the Irish kings and chieftains who had been his forebears, but Irish distinctions cut little ice in England. He was the son of an actor, with no fortune beyond his share in Drury Lane, and above all with no relations among the network of powerful families who dominated British politics. Lady Holland would dismiss his origins as 'mean', but Fox's father, the first Lord Holland, had risen from obscurity to great wealth by blatant profiteering as Paymaster General during the Seven Years War; Pitt's great-grandfather, Thomas Pitt, had founded the family fortunes by acquiring, when Governor of Madras, the famous stone known as the Pitt Diamond, in a manner which, in the words of one historian, 'would hardly survive serious scrutiny'. As so often, respectability was largely a matter of dates.

Unlike those whose interests or connections made their election a matter of course – Pitt would enter Parliament for the first time that year for one of the nine seats at the disposal of Sir James Lowther – Sheridan began his search for a seat without a patron. He tried first for Honiton, a pocket borough in the hands of a family called Younge, but was passed over for another candidate, Alexander Macleod, who already had connections there. 'They are damn'd Fellows if they think to mend themselves by choosing a Scotsman and a *Mac* too!' wrote Sheridan, the Irishman, to a friend.

Another attempt, at Wootton Basset, was also unsuccessful. In the end it was thanks to the influence of the Duchess of Devonshire, the leading hostess of the Whig party, that Sheridan was able to stand for Stafford – an independent borough, not in the gift of any patron but in which her family, the Spencers, had an interest. Sheridan's fellow candidate was Edward Monckton, son of Lord Galway, whose sister, later Lady Cork, was an *habitué* of Devonshire House. The two men became close friends; Lady Cork recalled how Sheridan would sometimes leave his carriage waiting all day at Monckton's house while he played cricket with Monckton's children.

As an independent borough, with about 320 voters, almost all of them local tradesmen, Stafford was at the time one of the most democratic seats in the country. (Westminster, with 9,000 voters, had the widest franchise.) This must have pleased Sheridan's own independent spirit – his pride was always at the ready – but it did not mean that the votes could be had for nothing. There were tickets for ale and dinners to be handed out, subscriptions to charities, five guineas each for local burgesses, house rent, taxes and servants' wages – all in all, the election cost Sheridan well over £1,000, some coming from subscription, some presumably borrowed against his share in Drury Lane.

On 12 September, he and Monckton were duly elected as members for Stafford, and expressed their thanks to their electors in a joint letter:

'We have found you men of your words – we will deserve the continuance of your friendship by serving you faithfully, *as you have served us* – if we deceive you, you will have no difficulty in turning us out again, as we shall deserve; independent candidates will no more be afraid to offer themselves, for you have now made it appear that you are the *masters of your own rights*, and that you are determined to hold them in your own hands, and to keep your Borough free.'

Sheridan would remain a member for Stafford for twenty-six years. Long afterwards he was asked by Creevey if he could fix upon a moment in his life that was happier than any other. He replied that it was after dinner on the day of his first election for Stafford, 'when he stole away by himself to speculate upon those prospects of distinguishing himself which had been opened to him'.

Lady Cork would later claim the credit of having introduced Sheridan to her brother and opening the way to his election. But it was to the Duchess of Devonshire that Sheridan felt most indebted. His letter of thanks, a few days later, showed the distance which still existed between them at the time:

'I am entirely at a loss how to thank Your Grace for the Honor and service which your Grace's condescending to interest yourself in my election at Stafford has been of to me . . . It is no Flattery to say that the Duchess of Devonshire's name commands an implicit admiration whenever it is mentioned, and I found some that had had opportunities of often seeing and hearing more of your Grace who were so proud of the Distinction as to require no other motive to support any one who appear'd honor'd with your Graces recommendation.'

On 6 October 1780, Sheridan took his seat in the House of Commons. He made his first speech three weeks later. His fame as a dramatist had gone before him and he was heard, according to the Parliamentary History, 'with particular attention, the House being uncommonly still while he spoke'.

The subject itself was uninspiring – an answer to a petition brought against him and Monckton for bribery during the election for Stafford. Money had certainly passed hands – election expenses would be a heavy charge throughout his political career – but this was common practice in the context of the time and the petition, by the defeated member for Stafford, was later dismissed. For Sheridan it was an obvious opening. Had he begun with a more ambitious topic he might have seemed too eager for attention, a fault not to be forgiven in an actor's son.

He dealt with the petition soberly, deploring the ease with which such vexatious cases could be brought and the reflection it cast on the independence of his voters. They were disingenuous arguments perhaps, but when Rigby, the Paymaster of the Forces, tried to ridicule them Fox sprang warmly to his defence. Rigby, he observed, might be one of those ministerial members who, having robbed and plundered his constituents, affected to despise them; but those, like Sheridan, 'who felt properly the nature of the trust allotted to him, would always treat them with respect'. The speaker brought an end to the exchanges, and Sheridan, no doubt, kept Rigby in mind to be dealt with at a later date.

Moore reports that Woodfall, the parliamentary reporter, met Sheridan in the gallery after his speech and answered his anxious enquiry how it had gone by telling him frankly that politics were not his line – that he had far better stick to Drury Lane. Sheridan, apparently, put his head in his hands for a few minutes, then vehemently exclaimed: 'It is in me, however, and by God, it shall come out!' Other biographers question the timing of this story, suggesting that the exchange must have taken place some months later, after Sheridan's first big speech in the House, on the subject of the Gordon riots, in March 1781.

Whatever the truth of the matter, Sheridan trod delicately during his first months in Parliament, determined to avoid the slightest suspicion of theatrical excess. Outside, however, new worlds were opening to him. He was elected to Brooks's Club, the heartland of Fox's brand of Whiggery, aristocratic, hard drinking and careless of public opinion. Here Fox ran a Faro bank, in an attempt to stave off his horde of creditors, arriving there late from his lodgings in St James's Place, after holding a levée for his followers. 'His bristly black person and shaggy breast,' wrote Horace Walpole, 'quite open and rarely purified by any ablutions, was wrapped in a foul nightgown, and his bushy black hair dishevelled. In these Cynic weeds, and with Epicurean good humour did he dictate his politics.'

If Brooks's was the political headquarters of the Whigs, Devonshire House was its social rallying point. The Duchess of Devonshire had come there on her marriage three years before and had quickly attracted a brilliant circle round her. Fox was at its centre, as attractive to her husband, a reserved, rather frigid figure, as to herself.

'I have always thought that the great merit of C. Fox is his amazing quickness in seazing any subject,' she wrote from Chatsworth to her mother; 'he seems to have the particular talent of knowing more about what he is saying and with less pains than anyone else. His conversation is like a brilliant player at billiards, the strokes follow one another, piff paff . . .'

Georgiana, Duchess of Devonshire, was now twenty-two, tall and full-figured, with reddish-gold hair and very bright blue eyes. Impulsive, warm-hearted and ingenuous, her vivid personality was such that, in the words of Horace Walpole, she 'effaces all without being a beauty', and her charm and fascination cast a glow on the gatherings at which she presided. Sheridan's wit and his wife's beauty were passports to her inner circle. Sponsored by Fox, he was soon a familiar figure at Devonshire House and at Chatsworth, where, in another of Georgiana's letters to her mother, we catch a pleasing glimpse of him a few years later: 'Sheridan goes tomorrow; we kept him today by main force absolutely. He is amazingly entertaining. He is going to Weirstay to shoot for silver arrow, he is such a boy.'

1780, the year of Sheridan's election, was the year when the

Prince of Wales reached the age of eighteen and was given his first taste of independence. Whilst still residing at Buckingham House, he was allowed to give private dinner parties to 'Lords, Grooms and Equerries' twice weekly; to own sixteen horses; to visit the theatre or the opera provided he gave previous notice; and was expected to attend all court levées and accompany his father on his morning ride. The king considered his provisions to be liberal and enlightened but it was not a programme to attract a spirited young man. One by one, George III would see his sons react against their strait-laced upbringing and stuffy family life. The Prince of Wales did so spectacularly, running up debts, pursuing actresses and drinking 'like a Leviathan'. The previous year he had fallen in love with Mrs Robinson, the beautiful Perdita, who later had to be bought off for £20,000 when she threatened to publish his letters to her. He had now gravitated to Devonshire House to the fury of his father, who regarded its inhabitants, and Fox in particular, as anathema. Here the prince and the duchess referred to each other as brother and sister, and Sheridan and Fox became his drinking companions and friends.

It was not surprising that the prince should be drawn by Fox's magical charm, or by the genius of Sheridan, who had written *The Rivals* when little older than himself. But the prince on his side had much to offer beside his royal birth. He was far more intelligent and accomplished than most of Europe's other princelings, a brilliant mimic, an easy and agreeable talker. Over the decades Sheridan would be one of his most disinterested friends, never presuming on their friendship till his last sad years, while the prince, far more than Sheridan's political colleagues, understood and appreciated his qualities. It would be hard to find a more perceptive epitaph for Sheridan than that which the prince pronounced to Peter Moore, the member for Coventry, when he received him after his funeral:

'Sheridan was a great man, but in the simplicity of his nature he never knew his own greatness. His heart was too much enlarged to be governed by his head. He had an abounding confidence in every man; and although his pen indicated a knowledge of human nature, yet that knowledge was confined to his pen alone, for in all his acts he rendered himself the dupe of the fool and the designing knave . . . He was a proud man, sir, a very proud man, with certain conscientious scruples always operating against his own interests. He was a firm and sound adviser; but he was so systematically jealous of his own honour, that he was always willing to grant what he was not willing to accept in return – favours, which might be interpreted as affecting his own independence.'

It is worthwhile, at the start of Sheridan's political career, to be reminded of the principles that would underlie it. In a period when political jobbery was the norm and sinecures and peerages the natural reward for services rendered, he hung on to his integrity. He would put himself out for others, for his brother, for whom he found the place of Under-Secretary of Military Affairs in Dublin, for his sisters and his wife's relations, but he refused to do so for himself. His quixotry resembled his grandfather's. On reading Dr Sheridan's correspondence in a life of Swift soon after 'poor Sheridan's' death, George IV told Croker that he was amazed at the likeness between them.

In February 1781, the twenty-one-year-old William Pitt, like Sheridan a newcomer that session, made his maiden speech in favour of a bill for the revision of the Civil List. Much had been expected of him as the son of the great Prime Minister Lord Chatham, and he rose triumphantly to the occasion. His icy brilliance and self command, the clarity of his arguments and the readiness of his answers, showed that a new political star had been born. Lord North described it as the best first speech he had ever heard. 'It is not a chip off the old block,' said the enthusiastic Burke, 'it is the old block itself.'

Sheridan, inevitably, made his way more slowly. He spoke seldom, and always concisely and unassumingly, having carefully written out his words beforehand. Fox, his greatest supporter at the time, regarded his self-effacing conduct as the surest way to win the confidence of the House, suspicious as they might have been of any premature display of eloquence. He was rewarded for his discretion when, on 5 March, he was chosen by Fox to introduce the motion 'For the better regulation of the Police of Westminster', in which he criticised the use of the army in quelling the Gordon Riots of the previous year, and added his mite to the Whig opposition's undermining of the Crown:

'What! was his Majesty's power at that moment to have trampled on the liberties of the country and to have introduced military government in the place of the present constitution. If this doctrine was to be laid down and the Crown could give orders to the military to interfere when, where and for what length of time it pleases, then we might bid farewell to freedom.'

The motion was defeated but the speech had been well received by his friends, who welcomed him as a valuable new ally. Over the next year he gradually began to build up his political experience and to spread his wings as a debater. 'By constant practice in small matters and before private committees,' wrote Lord Brougham, 'by diligent attendance on all debates, by habitual intercourse with all dealers in political wares, from the chiefs of parties and their more refined coteries to the providers of daily discussion for the public and the chroniclers of parliamentary speeches, he trained himself to a facility of speaking, absolutely essential to all but first class genius, and all but necessary even to that.'

On 25 November 1781, two days before Parliament was due to reassemble after the autumn recess, came the news of the British defeat and surrender at Yorktown. It was now obvious to everyone, except George III, that victory on land in America was impossible. The harassed Lord North, who had stayed on in power only from a sense of obligation to the king, fought a last losing battle against the attacks of the opposition. Sheridan joined in, and in the course of a speech supporting a resolution censuring the government was able to take his revenge on Rigby, whose professed disapproval of the war was at odds with his determination to retain the fruits of his office as Paymaster for as long as possible:

'The Right Hon. Gentleman . . . had acted in this day's debate with perfect consistency. He had assured the House that he thought the Noble Lord [North] ought to resign his office; and yet he would give his vote for his remaining in it. In the same manner he had long declared, that he thought the American war ought to be abandoned; yet had uniformly given his vote for its continuance. He did not mean however to insinuate any motives for such conduct; – he believed the Right Hon. Gentleman to have been sincere; he believed that, as a member of Parliament, as a Privy Counsellor, as a private gentleman, he had always detested the American War as much as any man; but that he had never been able to persuade the Paymaster that it was a bad war; and unfortunately, in whatever character he spoke, it was the Paymaster who always voted in that House.'

In March 1782, Lord North resigned. A new government was formed under the prime ministership of the Marquis of Rockingham, in which Fox and Lord Shelburne were joint Secretaries of State, Burke was Paymaster of the Forces and Sheridan Under-Secretary of State for the Northern Office. After less than two years in Parliament he was a member of the government. Wags of the day maintained that a notice on his door while he was Under-Secretary announced, 'No application to be received here on Sundays, nor any business done during the remainder of the week', but Sheridan was determined to disprove his reputation.

'Dear Charles,' he wrote to his brother, who had written to congratulate him on the opposition's victory, 'Tho' I have time only to send you a very few lines to Night I will not omit to convince you how very much a man of Business I have become, by acknowledging the receipt of a Letter from you this Day – I take it for granted that you know from our Newspapers that it is *The Under secretary of State* who is become thus punctual.'

Negotiations for peace with America were the first concern of the Rockingham administration. Almost at once a rift opened up between the two Secretaries of State, Fox with responsibility for Foreign Affairs, Shelburne in charge of the colonies. Fox had always detested Shelburne, an old political antagonist of his father's; able, intellectual, but arrogant and devious in his dealings, he was commonly known as 'the Jesuit of Berkeley Square'. Shelburne considered negotiations with the American colonies as his affair and wished to use the recognition of their independence as a bargaining counter in establishing a general peace. Fox, as Foreign Secretary, insisted that American independence, already existing in fact, should be granted immediately and that the peace with France and Spain should be worked out thereafter. Both men sent emissaries to Paris, Shelburne's to treat with the American commissioner Benjamin Franklin, and Fox's, Thomas Grenville, as envoy to the French government. It was a situation bound to cause confusion. 'If the business of an American treaty seemed likely to prosper in your hands,' wrote Sheridan to Grenville, on 21 May 1782, 'I should not think it improbable that Lord Shelburne would try to thwart it.'

Five days later, writing to Grenville at Fox's request, he spelt out the reasoning behind Fox's attitude:

> Surely, whatever the preliminaries of a treaty for peace with France may be, it would be our interest, if we could, to drop even mentioning the Americans in them; at least the seeming to grant anything to them as at the requisition of France. France now denies our ceding Independence to America to be anything given to them, and declines to allow anything for it. In my opinion it would be wiser in them to insist ostentatiously (and even to make a point of allowing something for it) on the Independence of America being as the first article of their treating; and this would forever furnish them with a claim on the friendship and confidence of the Americans after the peace. But since they do not do this, surely it would not be bad policy, even if we gave up more to France in other respects, to prevent her appearing in the treaty as in any respect the champion of America, or as having made any claims for her ... Were I the Minister, I would give France an island or two to choose, if it would expose her selfishness, sooner than let her gain the *esteem of the Americans* by claiming anything essential for them in apparent preference to her own interest and ambition.

Fox's policy of granting independence to the American colonies as a preliminary to the general peace was defeated when he raised the question in the Cabinet on 3 July. He was already considering resigning in protest when the sudden death from influenza of Lord Rockingham the following day brought matters to a head. Rockingham had been the link between the rival factions in the government. When the king called on Shelburne to succeed him Fox resigned, taking his loyal lieutenant Sheridan with him. Most other members of the government, including Fox's uncle, the Duke of Richmond, stayed on. Fox's resignation was based more on his personal dislike of Shelburne than any major political differences between them. It was true that they disagreed about the methods of negotiating the peace, but Shelburne had long been opposed to the war and was sympathetic to the idea of electoral and economical reform. The rift would be fatal in the long term, and in the short term left the government greatly weakened.

It soon became clear that Shelburne could not command a majority in the House of Commons. Fox, his obvious ally, would not join him; his followers had attacked Lord North too often to make a combination with him likely. The twenty-three-year-old William Pitt, who had refused to serve under Rockingham in a subordinate position, had now been appointed Chancellor of the Exchequer. In February 1783, despairing of carrying on the government without support, Shelburne sent Pitt to sound out Fox about a possible coalition. Fox asked if it was proposed that Shelburne should remain Prime Minister. Pitt answered that it was. 'It is impossible for me,' said Fox, 'to belong to any administration of which Lord Shelburne is the head.' 'Then we need discuss the matter no further,' said Pitt. 'I did not come here to betray Lord Shelburne.'

The two men parted coldly. Shortly afterwards, to the amazement of those who had listened night after night to Fox's diatribes against his conduct of the war, Fox made an alliance with Lord North. 'It is not my nature to bear malice or live in ill will,' he explained blandly to an astounded House. 'My friendships are perpetual, my enmities are not so.' Sheridan had done his best to persuade his friend against the ill-assorted union, which one indignant member described as a union between Herod and Pontius Pilate, but Fox was adamant. His resolution, he declared, was 'as fixed as the Hanover succession'. Sheridan was forced to comply. Over forty years later, in conversation with Fox's nephew Lord Holland, Lord John Townshend poured scorn on the idea that Sheridan had been against the alliance: 'Sheridan . . . instead of being averse to the coalition, as I dare say you have often heard the vapouring rogue declare, was on the contrary, I assure you, one of the most eager and clamorous for it.' But the Holland House set, in their loyalty to Fox's memory, had always been unjust to Sheridan. In February 1784, when the Coalition had already fallen, Sheridan spoke on the matter in a debate. When Fox had first suggested the idea of a coalition to him, he said, he had advised him by no means to accede to it, as it 'would infallibly produce the loss of his popularity, character and general estimation', adding loyally that he now 'rejoiced at it even in contradiction to his own advice'. No one questioned his statement either then or in his lifetime, so it seems that, as with other ageing statesmen, Lord John's memory could not always be relied on.

The alliance of Fox and North made the defeat of the government inevitable. On 24 February 1783, Shelburne resigned. For five weeks the country was without an administration as the king struggled in vain to find an alternative to the Coalition. He begged Pitt to form a government, but Pitt, after consenting for a few hours, decided his moment had not yet come. In the end, the new ministers, with the Duke of Portland as their nominal leader, came into office. Lord North was in charge of Home Affairs, Fox was Foreign Secretary. Sheridan was appointed Secretary to the Treasury, a post he shared with Burke's son Richard. However, as one acute observer remarked, it was obvious that the new administration would not last long for the king, on Fox's kissing hands on his appointment, 'turned back his ears and eyes just like the horse at Astley's when the tailor he had determined to throw was getting on him.'

# X

'For God's sake,' Sheridan's brother had written to him, when he was first appointed to the government, 'improve the opportunity to the utmost, and don't let dreams of empty fame (of which you have had enough in all conscience) carry you away from your solid interests.' Richard had helped his brother to a sinecure in Ireland but he was far more eager to shine in public than to win any similar advantage for himself. Vanity and the desire for admiration, he admitted, were his overriding faults. 'They talk of avarice, lust, ambition, as great passions,' he once said to Lord Holland. 'It is a mistake; they are little passions. Vanity is the great commanding passion of all.' It seemed as though the neglected schoolboy, despised for his poverty and parentage, could never have enough of praise thereafter.

After a deliberately slow beginning he was becoming known as one of the best speakers in the House. His face and features, 'indicative at once of intellect, humour and gaiety', were extraordinarily attractive, his Irish geniality was infectious. Even in the most heated debates he never lost his self-possession or his power to hold his audience's attention. Fox could tire the House by repetition, Burke, for all his intellect and power of reasoning, was often coughed down, but a speech by Sheridan was always eagerly awaited. Even Pitt, whose tip-tilted nose, as Romney remarked, seemed to be turned up at mankind, could not get the better of him. In a debate when the Coalition had first been revealed, he had taunted Sheridan with his theatrical associations. 'No man,' said Pitt, 'admired more than he did the abilities of the Right Honourable Gentleman, the elegant sallies of his thought, the gay effusions of his fancy, his dramatic turns and his epigramatic point; and if they were reserved for the proper stage, they would no doubt, receive what the Honourable Gentleman's abilities always did receive, the plaudits of the audience . . . But this was not the proper place for the exhibition of those elegancies.'

Sheridan rose to answer. He noted the personality, he said, and made no comment on it; its propriety, taste, and gentlemanly point must have been obvious to the House. 'But,' he added, 'let me assure the Right Honourable Gentleman, that I do now, and will at any time he chooses to repeat this sort of allusion, meet it with the most sincere good-humour. Nay, I will say more – flattered and encouraged by the Right Honourable Gentleman's panegyric on my talents, if ever I again engage in the compositions he alludes to, I may be tempted to an act of presumption – to attempt an improvement on one of Ben Jonson's best characters, the character of the Angry Boy in the Alchemist.'

If Sheridan's weak point was the stage, Pitt's was his youth. The retort, which Pitt's brother-in-law Lord Stanhope regarded as the severest he ever received, not only silenced him effectively but put an end to further sneers at Sheridan's theatrical connections. At a time when duelling between political opponents was not uncommon it was also remembered that Sheridan had two duels behind him.

Sheridan treasured the memory of his riposte; amongst the numerous papers found on his death was a scribbled *jeu d'esprit* in which he took the idea further, casting *The Alchemist* with the various political characters of the day. Pitt was the Angry Boy (a name which stuck to him for life), Shelburne was Subtle and the king, 'His —', was Surly.

However much Sheridan disliked allusions to the theatre in the House of Commons, Drury Lane remained the basis of his fortunes and his only certain source of income. There was a kind of magic surrounding the borrowings with which he had built up his share in the theatre. When questioned about the details he would mutter 'the philosopher's stone' and change the subject. But he was not as careless about his investment as first appeared. The financial ingenuity he had shown in making it was matched by a sure sense of theatre and an instinct for what the public liked. Though he officially resigned his role as business manager to his father-in-law in 1783, in order to devote more time to politics, as chief proprietor he still had the final word on its affairs and insisted on reading all new plays.

His own father's reign as acting manager had ended badly, and during his last season there, from September 1779 to June 1780, receipts had been lower than at any time since Sheridan took over. This was partly due to inattention: Thomas Sheridan had been distracted by preparing his long-awaited pronouncing dictionary for publication. A landmark of its kind, it was an immediate success when it appeared in 1780, and went into eleven editions before the end of the century. At a time when regional differences in pronunciation were far greater than today, his attempts to set a common standard were especially welcome. 'A correct pronunciation,' wrote one reviewer, 'is the foundation of all correct reading and speaking . . . The author of the book before us has very properly attempted to point out the true pronunciation of every common word in the English language, and opened the way for the acquisition of a just and graceful delivery.'

It seems sad that Thomas Sheridan, who had devoted so much of his life to promoting better elocution, should get so little pleasure from his son's triumphs as an orator. But relations between them had not improved during his period as acting manager. Sheridan, the harassed man in the middle between his father and the rest of the company, had been in an impossible position. In June 1780 Thomas Sheridan resigned his post by mutual consent, to the secret relief of all concerned. He would subsequently blame his son for his departure, though at the time of leaving they were still on relatively good terms; in fact he was expecting to return to Drury Lane two seasons later. It was only afterwards, when it became clear that no new invitation would be forthcoming and Tom King, the first Sir Peter Teazle, became acting manager, that he turned against 'that wretch', his younger son. Thrown back on lecturing and a revival of his Attic Entertainments, he again refused to speak to him for several years.

Before the final breach, however, he had done the theatre one great service. It was thanks to his efforts and initiative that Drury

Lane acquired its brightest star in Mrs Siddons. Her tear-compelling first performance as Isabella in the tragedy of that name on 6 October 1782 immediately established her as the greatest tragic actress of the age. Thomas Sheridan, she wrote later, had been the father of her fortune and her fame.

Sarah Siddons had already appeared at Drury Lane during Garrick's final season seven years earlier. At that time she was twenty-one, timid and inexperienced, and her engagement had not been renewed when the new proprietors took over. (Sheridan later blamed this oversight on Garrick.) The shock of her dismissal had almost destroyed her, but over the next few years she had become famous as a tragic actress, playing alternately in Bath and Bristol. Thomas Sheridan, on a visit to Bath in 1777, had immediately recognised her potential. He offered to coach her and it is tempting to see a reflection of his ideas on oratory in the grand, declamatory manner which she made her own. Later, as manager of Drury Lane, he undertook the first approaches to her and in the summer of 1782, after many hesitations on her part, she was engaged for the forthcoming season at Drury Lane.

She chose the part of Isabella in Garrick's adaptation of Southerne's tragedy *The Fatal Marriage* for her opening performance. She had been guided in her choice by Thomas Sheridan, who rehearsed her in the part, accompanying her to the theatre, 'where *alone*,' she told her biographer James Boaden, 'she could shew him exactly what she could do at night'. It was a role which drew on all her powers of pathos and had never failed to reduce her audience in Bath to tears. But with memories of her former failure still vivid, she approached her first night at Drury Lane in a state of agitation and terror.

'At length,' she wrote, 'I was called to my fierey trial . . . The awful consciousness that one is the sole object of attention to that immense space, lined as it were with human intellect from top to bottom, and on all sides round, may perhaps be imagined but cannot be described, and never never to be forgotten.'

The evening was a triumph. The sobs and hysterics of the audience and the acclamations of the press next day confirmed the occasion as the greatest first performance since Garrick's début as Richard III forty-one years earlier. Over the rest of the season, as

Siddonian idolatry reached fever pitch, she played eighty times in seven different parts, though the strain of such continued exertions was so great that she frequently fainted at the end of a performance. The cream of London society, fashionable and intellectual, flocked to see her. Sir Joshua Reynolds, trumpet to his ear, could be seen in the orchestra; there too – 'O glorious constellation!' wrote Mrs Siddons – sat Gibbon, Burke, Sheridan and Fox, the latter frequently in tears. The Prince of Wales called on her in her dressing-room. George III, forgetting his disapproval of Sheridan's politics, came with the royal family to see her in all the characters she played. He hid his tears behind his eyeglass, while the queen, as she told Mrs Siddons, was at times so overcome that she was forced to turn her back on the stage protesting 'it was indeed too disagreable'.

Receipts reflected Mrs Siddons' triumph; the takings on Siddons evenings were £200 more than on other days. After the doldrums of the previous few years the prospects for Drury Lane looked golden. Once again it seemed that everything Sheridan touched succeeded. Already, however, there were warning signs. There were still large debts to be serviced, and the principal eventually to be repaid. Garrick had been so careful that he was said to have turned back in the road 'because he saw the ghost of a shilling'. Sheridan, like his grandfather, was recklessly extravagant, relying on the morrow and his own talents to provide. Moving amongst those far richer than himself, his spending inevitably outran his income, and though, as a Member of Parliament, he was immune from being arrested for debt, his house was already haunted by duns.

He had a restless passion for changing houses and had already moved several times since the Orchard Street days, ending up in elegant new premises in Bruton Street, not far from Devonshire House. He had also taken a country house at Heston, then changed it for 'a very pretty place', The Grove, on the top of Harrow Hill, with stabling for sixteen horses. In vain Elizabeth warned that they were living beyond their means and suggested moving to a cottage and giving up their London home for something cheaper.

'When you were oblig'd to be in Town, a ready furnished house would do as well as another for us, and would be a trifling expense in comparison with Bruton Street. I wish to God you would reconcile yourself to this. Suppose people say you could not live in so large a house, where would be the Disgrace? And what *can* they say more than they do at present, you never will persuade People you are very rich if you were to spend three times as much as you do.'

Sheridan's drinking, though not yet excessive, was another cloud on the horizon. It was an age of heavy drinkers. Even Pitt, so cool and dignified, frequently arrived drunk at the House of Commons and had once been sick behind the Speaker's Chair. At Brooks's Club the Earl of Surrey, later the Duke of Norfolk, was regularly carried home insensible. Fox drank deeply and Sheridan likewise, but whereas Fox's splendid constitution stood up to any amount of punishment, Sheridan's high-strung nervous system was easily overset by wine. It was some time before he acquired the red face and bottle nose that would be a gift to caricaturists but he was beginning to lose his youthful good looks. In 1784 his sister Betsy, after a three-year absence in Dublin, found him much heavier than before, with a 'good deal of scurvy' in his face. Once again, it was Elizabeth who sounded a note of warning:

'I see you are ever so affronted with me, but upon my life without the least cause . . . I must say whatever is in my mind to say on all subjects, you know, and when you tell me how vexed and grieved you was at not being able to speak that Monday on account of your making yourself so ill on Sunday, would you have me say drinking to that excess is *not an abominable habit?*'

The clouds were still small ones. For every occasional word of reproach in Elizabeth's letters there were twenty more of warm affection. He was her Sherry or Cheri, her Dear Soul, her dearest Dick. During periods apart – Sheridan attending the House of Commons, Elizabeth in the country – their letters formed a loving dialogue, and Sheridan, notoriously careless in answering letters, seldom missed a note to her. Sadly his letters have been lost, but we catch their echoes in hers, full of the little family phrases ('e' for you, 'fiff' for note, and so on) that she shared with all the Linleys.

'Thank'e Dearest Love for not disappointing me,' she wrote from Delapré Abbey, the home of the great Whig hostess Mrs Bouverie, 'never – no not once have 'e missed writing – 'e dear good boy. When I see 'e I will kiss 'e up as never 'e was kissed before.'

And in another letter, this time from Crewe Hall, the Crewe's country house in Cheshire:

'I forgot to tell you how delighted every body here was with the parts of your Letter that I read to them and how I was envied by them all for having such a kind, Good-Natur'd attentive little Bodye of a husband, but I told 'em 'ee didn't love me a bit better than I deserved, for I car'd for nothing in the world but 'ee.'

In 1780, Elizabeth's sister Mary had married one of Sheridan's greatest friends, Richard Tickell. Tickell, whom Sheridan had first met in Bath, was a journalist and dramatist, best known for his satirical pamphlet 'Anticipation', a skit on the House of Commons in 1778, which had earned him the name of 'Anticipation Tickell'. Like Sheridan, he had studied law, but preferred to live by his wits and a place in the Stamp Office, bestowed by Lord North, which brought him a small pension. A faithful ally in Sheridan's theatrical and parliamentary enterprises, he supported the one by writing plays and prologues and the other by his political journalism, which was always on the Foxite side. He was generally regarded as a minor version of his brother-in-law or, as he was described, Sheridan *in petto*.

The two men vied with one another as a wit, Tickell coarser in his humour and more eager to draw attention to himself: 'Tickel[l] had more of vanity, Sheridan more of pride,' wrote a friend, the publisher John Taylor. 'Tickel[l] was perpetually gay and ambitious to shine in society; he was therefore always on the watch for some opportunity of making a brilliant sally and often succeeded. Sheridan was contented to be easy and observing, and quietly waited till the stream of conversation should bear something worthy of his notice.'

Both shared a taste for elaborate practical jokes. On one occasion they dressed up as highwaymen and ambushed Thomas Linley's coach. On another, doubtless with Tickell's connivance, Sheridan arranged a spoof attack on Pitt, who had been dining with a friend at Brooks's and was proceeding across St James's Street to his party's natural habitat at White's. 'In the midst of the scuffle,' writes Moore in a previously deleted passage from his journal, 'Sheridan himself ran out, apparently shocked at the outrage, and giving his arm to Pitt who was very drunk, begged to be allowed to see him in safety to White's which he did & got great credit thereby.'

Elizabeth's and Mary's letters give vivid glimpses of their wayward husbands, sometimes drinking till the early hours – 'I heard every cruel Pop of that odious five shilling claret which entirely hindered my closing my eyes,' wrote Mary; or splashing one another as they emerged, puffing and dripping 'like two Tritons in a Sea piece', from different boats on the river at Broadlands, where they were staying with the Lord Palmerston of the day. Sometimes the joke was on the wives; once when staying at Crewe Hall, Elizabeth went driving with Mrs Crewe, whilst Sheridan and Tickell rode ahead; suddenly they came on Sheridan stretched out on the ground apparently in the agonies of death, and Tickell standing over him in a theatrical attitude of despair.

On a more serious level the interests of the two were closely linked. Drury Lane was very much a family affair, Tickell sometimes acting as viceregent when the 'great head', as Mary called her brother-in-law, was away. Meanwhile, Mrs Linley, well known for her cheeseparing at home, used her talents for economy on the wardrobe and productions. She is recorded as snipping the ends off the actresses' trains to use for covering pincushions; Mrs Tickell, in a letter to her sister, gives an amusing description of her fury at the extra expenses for a musical adaptation of Dryden's *King Arthur.*

'He [Tickell] found my mother in the most violent agitation in the World. "Oh, Tickell, I am fretted to Death. Those Devils, but it is all Mr King's fault." "Why, what's the matter, Ma'am?" "Matter! Why, do you know they have hired a whole regiment of Guards amost for Arthur and for what? as I said, for you know there's plenty of common men in our house [meaning the theatre] that always come on as Sailors and why should they not make good *soldiers*. What, because forsooth they can't march in time, Ma'am, but my husband is such a fool." '

Thomas Linley, already overstretched as musical director, found the additional role of business manager almost too much for him. He worried about receipts and was cast into despair when the king – 'I wish his great wooden head was stuck on Temple Bar', wrote Mrs Tickell – visited Covent Garden on two nights running. His daughters did their best to help him, though Mary, who had three children in quick succession, had less time than her sister. Elizabeth was in her element in the theatre. She kept accounts, auditioned singers, arranged and adapted music, and provided English words for foreign songs; when the singer Michael Kelly first joined the company at Drury Lane, he won great applause in 'Love, thou maddening power', a song she had written to an aria of Gluck's.

Tickell too could turn out lyrics on demand, and used his contacts with the press to publicise new plays, an art in which Sheridan was also adept. His biographer Fraser Rae quotes a paragraph in his handwriting, evidently intended for insertion into the *Public Advertiser*, and not unworthy of his Mr Puff:

The manager has got it up in his usual style of liberality; the performers highly merit the thanks of the author, the manager and the public. The performers were all at home in their respective parts . . . and received from a most crowded and brilliant audience, repeated bursts of applause.

In the autumn of 1783 Mrs Siddons' brother, John Philip Kemble, made his début as Hamlet at Drury Lane. Tall, dark-eyed and Roman-nosed, with a full share of his sister's dramatic good looks, he would eventually become the great tragic actor of his age, though his progress was less immediate than hers. Other actors blocked his way to many of the best parts and, except on first nights and benefit performances, could not be asked to give them up. But his studied, courtly Hamlet, suffused with melancholy sensibility, was much admired. For some critics it was over-studied. Great play was made of his 'new readings' of certain lines. Shakespearean commentary, revived by Garrick's worship of the bard, was a prestigious occupation in scholarly circles. A wealth of controversy was engendered, for instance, by Kemble's change of emphasis when questioning Horatio about the ghost from the commonly accepted 'Did you not *speak* to it?' to 'Did *you* not speak to it?' Such debate, however, served only to underline the fact that Kemble was an actor to be taken seriously and his début, though less sensational than his sister's, established him at the forefront of his profession.

Mrs Siddons had faced less opposition and in any case swept all before her. Her lofty style of acting was reflected in Reynolds' painting of her as the Tragic Muse that year; the pose, suggestive of one of Michelangelo's Sybils, was of her own choosing. She was as awe-inspiring off the stage as on, making herself respected by the aristocracy as no actress had ever been before. Northcote, the painter, speaks of seeing 'young ladies of the quality, Lady Marys and Lady Dorothys, peeping into a room where Mrs Siddons was sitting, with all the same timidity and curiosity as if it were a praeternatural being'. Even Sheridan found her daunting. 'Your admiration for Mrs

Siddons is so high', Samuel Rogers once remarked, 'that I wonder you do not make open love to her.' 'To her!' said Sheridan. 'To that magnificent and appalling creature! I should as soon have thought of making love to the Archbishop of Canterbury!'

In 1785 Mrs Siddons made her first appearance as Lady Macbeth, the most legendary of all her roles. In her memoirs she describes how Sheridan, his theatrical judgement for once at fault, made a last-minute intervention on the opening night:

'Just as I had finished my toilette and was pondering with fearfulness my first appearance in the grand fiendish part, comes Mr Sheridan knocking at my door ... What was my distress and astonishment when I found that he wanted me even at this moment of anxiety and terror to adopt another mode of acting the sleeping scene! He told me he had heard with the greatest surprise and concern that I meant to act it without holding the candle in my hand; and when I argued the impracticality of washing out that "*damned spot*" that was certainly implied by both her own words and those of her gentlewoman, he insisted, that if I did put the candle out of my hand it would be thought a presumptuous innovation as Mrs Pritchard had always retained it in hers. My mind, however, was made up, and it was then too late to make me alter it, for I was too agitated to adopt another method.'

Sheridan's fear of the audience's reaction was not altogether unreasonable. Familiar with the play through the classic perform-ances of Garrick and Mrs Pritchard (immortalised in Zoffany's painting of the dagger scene), they were fully capable of rioting at a departure from tradition. His father's fate in Dublin was an ever-present warning.

In the event the sleep-walking scene was the most applauded in the play. It is true that Mrs Siddons' dress, a sweeping white garment, half-way between a night-gown and a robe, was criticised. 'Lady Macbeth is supposed to be *asleep* and not *mad*,' wrote the *Morning Post* next day, 'so that custom itself cannot be alleged as a justification for her appearance in white sattin.' But her actions on entering the stage – setting down the light and washing her hands, pouring water from an imaginary ewer as she did so – established a tradition for generations of Lady Macbeths, and the audience, enthralled, accepted them at once.

As soon as the performance was over Sheridan hastened round to Mrs Siddons' dressing-room to congratulate her – 'most ingenuously' she wrote – on her obstinacy. When he had gone, she began to undress. Standing in front of her mirror, her mind still full of the emotions of the evening, she repeated aloud in the tones she had used on stage, 'Here's the smell of blood still', to the amazement of her dresser who innocently exclaimed, 'Dear me, ma'am, how very hysterical you are tonight; I protest and vow, ma'am, it was not blood but rose pink and water, for I saw the property man mix it with my very eyes.'

# XI

⁂

The ill-matched coalition of Fox and North lasted from April to December 1783. It was Sheridan's fellow Irishman Burke who played the leading role in putting forward its most controversial policy, the reform of the affairs of the East India Company. Twenty-two years older than Sheridan, Burke had long been the prophet and propagandist of the Foxite Whigs, raising their claims to be the heirs of the Glorious Revolution and defenders of Parliament's rights against the Crown to the level of a political philosophy. Lacking the essential eighteenth-century credentials of wealth and grand connections, he had never reached the highest offices in government, though the violence with which he expressed his opinions may have also played a part in keeping him back. More than once, when roused to anger in a debate, Burke had to be physically restrained: on one occasion he flung a book of estimates at the Speaker; on another, Sheridan, who was sitting next to him, held him down by his coat tails to keep him from leaping up in fury.

Burke's ideas of liberty stopped short of constitutional change; he had been unwilling to join his fellow Whigs in the movement to widen the franchise and abolish anomalies in the electoral system. But he had been one of the moving spirits in pressing for 'economical reform' and lessening the extent of royal patronage. In the affairs of the East India Company he believed he was fighting abuses on a far larger scale. What had begun two centuries before as a sparse collection of trading stations was beginning to acquire the status of an empire. Still largely independent of the British government, it administered a yearly revenue of £7 million, commanded an army of 60,000 men, and governed a population of some 30 million. Under Shelburne, Dundas, later to be Pitt's right-hand man, had already put forward a bill for bringing the Company under greater government control; but the Shelburne ministry had fallen before it could be carried through. Burke, who had studied the problem far more deeply and knew India, it was said, 'better than any other man who had never been there', laid the ground for the Coalition's version of the India Bill, though it was Fox who introduced it and did the most to argue it through the Commons.

Sheridan's attitude differed from both Burke's and Fox's. Burke's passionate feeling for the suffering millions under the East India Company's control, combined with a growing hatred for the man who seemed to epitomise its misdeeds, the governor Warren Hastings, found its echo in Fox's warmly emotional nature. Sheridan was more moderate. He saw no point in taking retrospective measures against Hastings. 'There is good reason to believe,' wrote a parliamentary colleague, Sir Nathaniel Wraxall, 'that Sheridan deprecated from the beginning the too great energy, or rather the confiscation and ambition, which characterised the East India Bill'; and Moore, in the course of writing his biography, noted in his journal: 'It is said that Sheridan was against the India Bill.'

The debates about the bill in Parliament began in November 1783. In the meantime treaties of peace with France and America had been signed on terms very little different from those negotiated by Shelburne. The king chafed impotently under the yoke of his new ministers, his discontents increased by their support for his eldest son, who having now reached twenty-one required a financial establishment of his own. Fox suggested an income of £100,000 a year; the king dug his heels in at £50,000, though eventually agreeing to a special grant from Parliament of a further £60,000 to cover his immediate debts and the costs of completing Carlton House. He held the government responsible for encouraging his son's demands, referring bitterly to Fox as the chief of 'my son's ministers'.

The introduction of the India Bill confirmed the king's worst suspicions of the Coalition. In many ways it was a continuation of the idea of 'economical reform'. The powers of the East India Company were to be curbed, but not, to begin with, by increasing those of the Crown. Instead, a commission of seven men, appointed in the first instance by Parliament and then, after four years, by the king, was to take over control of its affairs. Since the nominees to the commission were all supporters of the Ministry, the bill, in practice, gave the whole vast patronage of the East India Company to Fox's friends. Fox was caricatured as Carlo Khan, the would-be dictator of India; he was shown triumphantly entering Leadenhall Street – where the Company's headquarters were – dressed in Indian costume and riding on an elephant with the face of Lord North, with Burke alongside as a trumpeter.

Sheridan spoke for the bill at its third reading. Only fragments of his speech, which was said to have been exceptionally well argued, have been recorded, but one pleasantry remains. In an impassioned attack on the bill, John Scott, a Tory member, drew a parallel with a passage from the Book of Revelations – Babylon being the East India Company, Fox and his seven commissioners the Beast with the seven heads, and the marks on the hand and forehead, imprinted by the Beast on those around him, meaning evidently, he said, the peerages, pensions and places distributed by the minister. 'In answering this strange sally of forensic wit,' writes Moore, 'Mr Sheridan quoted other passages from the same Sacred Book, which (as the Reporter gravely assures us) "told strongly for the Bill" and which proved that Lord Fitzwilliam and his fellow Commissioners, instead of being the seven heads of the Beast, were seven Angels "clothed in pure and white linen"!'

On 8 December 1783, in the teeth of violent opposition, the bill was passed by a majority of 208 to 102. But though it had been carried in the Commons it was widely resented by the public at large, as well as by the Company itself. The bill was considered unjust and excessive, an act of confiscation that set a dangerous precedent. The fact that it attempted to address genuine abuses was ignored in the general outcry against it. For once the king and people were united in opposing the Ministry.

The king kept his reservations to himself. He was hoping that the bill would be defeated in the House of Lords and the Ministry dismissed in consequence, but this could not happen until a replacement could be found. After a series of secret negotiations through intermediaries, William Pitt at last agreed to take the post of Prime Minister. The king was free to act. He let it be known, in a note to Pitt's kinsman Lord Temple, that 'whoever voted for the India Bill was not only not his friend, but would be considered by him as an enemy; and if these words were not strong enough, Earl Temple might use whatever words he might deem stronger and more to the purpose'. On 17 December the bill was defeated by a majority of nineteen on its second reading in the Lords. Fox, who had been behind the throne throughout the proceedings, was in a state of the greatest agitation. 'I am told,' reported the Shelburnite member Thomas Orde, 'that his countenance, gesture, and expressions were in the highest degree ludicrous from the extremity of distortion and rage, going off with an exclamation of despair, lugging G. [Lord] North along with him and calling out for Sheridan.'

The next day the king sent messages to North and Fox, requesting them to send him the seals of their departments; he refused to receive them personally 'as Audiences on such occasions must be unpleasant'. On the day after, the twenty-four-year-old Pitt kissed hands as First Lord of the Treasury and Chancellor of the Exchequer,

A sight to make surrounding nations stare,
A kingdom trusted to a schoolboy's care.

Fox's gamble had failed. Sheridan had warned against the Coalition, he had been doubtful of the wisdom of the East India Bill, but he followed him loyally into political exile. At first it seemed that Pitt's term of office would be short. There was still a large majority against him in the Commons. Mrs Crewe said that it would be a 'mince pie administration', which would be over by Christmas or soon after. But Pitt knew he had the support of opinion outside the House. For three months he struggled on against lessening odds, steadfastly refusing to resign as the Coalition's majority gradually diminished. While Fox and Sheridan attacked the new Prime Minister for acting unconstitutionally, Pitt, supported by the influence of the Crown, was diligently gathering allies. He was helped above all by John Robinson, the Secretary of the Treasury, and a master of political intrigue. It was not to be wondered, said Sheridan, that the Coalition's majority was decreasing 'when a member is employed to corrupt everybody in order to get votes'. There were indignant cries of of 'Name him! Name him!' from the Pittite side.

'I shall not name the person,' said Sheridan to the Speaker. 'It is an unpleasant and invidious thing to do, and therefore I shall not name him. But don't suppose, Sir, that, I abstain through any difficulty in naming. I could do that, Sir, as soon as you could say Jack Robinson.'

On 24 March 1784, after a coalition motion which was carried by only one vote – a virtual defeat for Fox – Parliament was dissolved. In the election that followed, 160 coalition candidates, 'Fox's Martyrs' as they were known, were routed. Pitt was returned with a majority of over two hundred; he would remain in power for nineteen out of the next twenty-two years.

Sheridan had not been one of Fox's martyrs. He and Monckton were returned for Stafford, Sheridan heading the poll. Fox's own campaign at Westminster, where he was standing against the Pittite candidates Lord Hood and Sir Cecil Wray, had all the elements of a saturnalia. The polling took place over forty days; supporters of the rival factions crowded into the area round Covent Garden as the electoral battle raged. Wearing the buff and blue of Washington's army, a dress he first adopted during the American War of Independence, Fox was supported by a bevy of beauties, the Duchess of Devonshire and her sister Lady Duncannon among them. The Duchess of Devonshire was said, though she denied it, to have exchanged kisses for votes; the Prince of Wales himself, sporting the cockade of a fox's brush, joined in the canvassing for his friend. Sheridan, abandoning his Stafford constituents, was in the thick of the fray, writing speeches and skits and attending dinners at the various Whig taverns, where he proposed his favourite toast, 'the Liberty of the Press'. When Fox was finally elected, after a furious contest in the course of which at least one person had been killed, Sheridan was behind him on the platform as the results were being declared and followed him in triumph as he was chaired to Devonshire House.

Their victory was celebrated with a day-long *fête champêtre* in the garden of Carlton House; the king, on his way down the Mall to open Parliament, had the irritation of glimpsing a crowd of his son's friends, apparently dressed in Washington's uniform, through the colonnades. In the evening Mrs Crewe gave a ball in Fox's honour at her house in Lower Grosvenor Street, in the course of which the Prince of Wales proposed the toast, 'Buff and blue and Mrs Crewe', to which she answered, 'Buff and blue and all of *you*!' More parties and euphoria followed, but the underlying facts were less inviting. Fox and his friends were now in opposition. Pitt, with an overwhelming mandate, was in command.

If personalities had been excluded, there was much in Pitt's programme to appeal to his opponents. Still calling himself a Whig (though forced to rely on the support of royalist and Tory members), he shared the Whig desire for parliamentary reform. In 1785 he put forward a bill to abolish some of the worst rotten boroughs; it was rejected, however, by a large majority and he was forced to abandon the attempt. His India Bill, putting control of its affairs into the hands of a commission, or Board of Control, nominated by the Crown, but leaving its patronage to the East India Company, set the pattern of Indian government for the next three-quarters of a century and temporarily calmed its critics at home. He determined to tackle the country's finances, at a low ebb after the drain of the American war. He increased some taxes, whilst lowering others which were strangling trade, and during 1786 and 1787 introduced the famous Sinking Fund, designed to bring down the National Debt. The fund, originally intended to be financed by a million pounds from the surplus of government income each year, eventually had to be maintained by borrowing after war with France broke out in 1793. Sheridan, who could be surprisingly effective as a debater on financial matters, dealt with this essential flaw. 'It was clear,' he said, 'there was no surplus; and the only means which suggested themselves to him were, a loan of a million for the especial purpose – for the Right Hon. Gentleman might say, with the person in the comedy, "If you won't lend me the money, how can I pay you?" '

There was one subject, more than any other, with which Sheridan was passionately concerned and which Pitt now set himself to address, the question of Ireland. No one could be less self-consciously Irish than Sheridan. He was as proud of his mother's English blood as of his father's Irish ancestry and he had been given a thoroughly English education at Harrow. Despite his miseries as a child, his friendships and formation there had given him an insight into English life that his elder brother had been denied. In a way, it was this measure of distance which made it easier for him to take up the cudgels on behalf of his fellow countrymen. Burke, whose father had been a convert from Catholicism in order to practise as a lawyer, was always in danger of being dubbed a Papist and sometimes trod warily where Irish questions were concerned. Sheridan, from a family which had been Protestant for at least five generations, could speak for the Irish Catholics, who still made up three quarters of the population, without such reservations.

The American War of Independence had brought the problems of Ireland sharply into focus. Embattled elsewhere, the British government had been forced to make concessions to Ireland, where the largely Protestant Irish Volunteer army, ostensibly raised to defend the country against invasion, was in fact a potential threat to British authority. In 1778 a number of the trade restrictions barring Ireland from the British market had been lifted, while at the same time laws preventing Catholics from inheriting land and taking leases on the same basis as Protestants were repealed. More importantly, by the repeal of the (Irish) Declaratory Act of 1719 under Rockingham in 1782, the Irish parliament was made independent. The Crown and the chain of patronage depending from it were, in theory at least, its only link with Westminster.

The transfer of power to Dublin had done nothing for the population of Ireland at large, merely exchanging a corrupt and Protestant-dominated elite for that of Westminster. Meanwhile, with English tariffs still cramping Irish trade and widespread distress in consequence, there were commercial questions to be raised. Pitt's propositions for establishing free trade between the two countries, at first accepted by the Irish parliament, were greeted by cries of outrage from the British manufacturers, who felt that their vested interests were at risk. The modifications and safeguards they obtained so distorted the purpose of the original bill that the Irish parliament withdrew its consent. Sheridan spoke strongly in opposition to the altered bill, above all to its new proposition that free trade for Ireland should be dependent on its being bound by British navigation laws – an abdication of the Irish parliament's hard-won independence from external legislation:

'All had been delusion, trick and fallacy; a new scheme of commercial arrangement is proposed to Ireland as a boon; and the surrender of their Constitution is tacked to it as a mercantile regulation. Ireland, newly escaped from harsh trammels and severe discipline, is treated like a high mettled horse, hard to catch; and the Irish Secretary is to return to the field, soothing and coaxing him, with a sieve of provender in one hand, but with a bridle in the other, ready to slip over his head while he is snuffling at the food. But this political jockeying, he was convinced, would not succeed.'

The bill, which at its outset would have met almost all of Ireland's wishes (and whose modifications had been largely forced through by the opposition), was eventually withdrawn. Sheridan, as its chief opponent in the House of Commons, was the hero of the hour in Ireland. His speech on the subject was published in Dublin as a pamphlet; the Irish parliament sang his praises. 'We hear astonishing accounts of your greatness,' wrote Sheridan's friend Stratford Canning from Ireland; 'Paddy will I suppose, some *beau jour* be voting you another £50,000 [a sum that had been recently voted to the Irish statesman Henry Grattan], if you go on as you have done.' Mrs Sheridan meanwhile was writing to Stratford Canning's wife, Mehitabel, her greatest friend, from Crewe Hall: 'They tell me Sheridan has made the best speech on the Irish business . . . that ever was heard – I hear nothing but his praises, which (between you and I) I have great pleasure in "tho' he is my Husband".'

With Sheridan, Burke and Fox against him, Pitt faced a formidable opposition. But he had one strength they had always lacked, the whole-hearted support of the king. There was no more question of the Crown undermining government policies. Standing as he did between the king and the return of the hated coalition, Pitt could virtually dictate his own terms. He did not abuse his position, while the follies and extravagances of the Prince of Wales, who had thrown in his lot with Fox and his friends, served to underline the dangers of the alternative.

The prince's love affairs, from Perdita onwards, had always been a source of scandal. More serious was his passion for Mrs Fitzherbert. Twice widowed and a Catholic, Mrs Fitzherbert had first met the prince in 1784. She was then twenty-eight, the prince twenty-two. The prince fell madly in love with her, but Mrs Fitzherbert, unlike his earlier conquests, was not prepared to be his mistress. Marriage presented grave, if not insuperable, obstacles. In the first place, by the terms of the Royal Marriage Act of 1772, no member of the royal family under twenty-five could marry without the king's consent; in the second, under the Act of Settlement of 1701, any prince who married a Papist automatically forfeited his right to succeed to the throne. But the prince was infatuated. He attempted to stab himself. Mrs Fitzherbert, summoned in alarm to Carlton House, took the Duchess of Devonshire with her as a chaperone, to find him rolling about in agony, besprinkled with blood and in paroxysms of despair. She calmed him by agreeing to accept a ring as a sign of their betrothal, but the next day left the country. She was determined not to jeopardise her co-religionists by a scandal which could be turned against them, nor to embroil the succession to the Crown in controversy.

The prince was beside himself. He poured out his woes at Devonshire House, calling there so frequently that even the phlegmatic duke showed signs of taking umbrage; he sent interminable letters to Mrs Fitzherbert; and finally, in November 1785, after writing her a passionate missive of forty-two pages, succeeded in persuading her to return to England.

Fox was extremely anxious when he heard the news. The Prince of Wales was the hope of the Whigs; should he disqualify himself from the succession by marrying, their best chance of returning to office was gone. He sought assurances from the prince that he was not going to take the 'very desperate step (pardon the expression) of marrying at this moment', and was reassured by a flat denial from the prince: 'Make yourself easy, my dear friend. Believe me, the world will soon be convinced that there not only is, but never was any ground for these reports which, of late, have been so malevolently circulated.'

Four days later, on 15 December 1785, the prince married Mrs Fitzherbert secretly according to the rites of the Church of England – the curate who conducted the service having been bribed by the promise of a bishopric when the prince came to the throne. Over the next year and a half, although they lived in separate houses, they were seen continually together and rumours of their marriage were widely circulated. Meanwhile, the problems of the Prince of Wales's finances had raised their head again. By the spring of 1787 his debts, including £54,000 for setting up Mrs Fitzherbert, had grown to such astronomical proportions that some immediate measure of relief was necessary. Wisely forestalling a full-scale debate – which might have opened up the question of the marriage – Pitt agreed to recommend that Parliament should settle his outstanding liabilities, as well as voting him a further sum for Carlton House. However, during discussions in the Commons a Tory member, John Rolle (whose attempts to silence Burke by orchestrating a barrage of coughing and spitting during his speeches had given his name to a series of anti-government satires known as the *Rolliad*), asked members to take note of 'a question which went immediately to affect our constitution in Church and State'. It was generally assumed that Rolle was alluding to the reported marriage.

Sheridan, who was in little doubt as to the true state of affairs, did his best to turn aside the question. But Fox, with the prince's letter as his justification, seized the opportunity to deny that the marriage had taken place: 'It not only never could have happened legally, but it never did happen in any way whatsoever, and had from the beginning been a base and malicious falsehood.' Rolle was silenced, but Mrs Fitzherbert, who had been content to leave the matter in discreet ambiguity, was outraged at this reflection on her honour. She was furious with Fox – he had rolled her, she said, 'in the kennel like a street walker' – while Fox in his turn felt that the prince had deliberately deceived him.

It was left to Sheridan to put matters right. According to Lord Holland's memoirs, the Prince of Wales, in a state of great agitation, first called on the young Charles Grey, who had made his début in the Commons that year, to deny Fox's statement. Grey refused to take on the impossible task, whereupon the prince, abruptly terminating the interview, threw himself on a sofa and muttered: 'Well, if nobody else will, Sheridan must.'

George IV, in conversation with Croker years later, maintained that Sheridan's intervention was purely accidental, stemming chiefly from his sympathy for Mrs Fitzherbert and his desire to keep the peace between her and Fox. In a speech the next day Sheridan deliberately avoided mentioning Fox's statement. Instead, after complimenting the House on the 'dignity and decorum' they had shown in taking the question no further, he gracefully restored the lady's reputation:

'But whilst his Royal Highness's feelings had no doubt been considered on this occasion, he must take the liberty of saying, however some might think it a subordinate consideration, that there was another person entitled, in every delicate and honourable mind, to the same attention; one whom he would not otherwise venture to describe or allude to, but by saying it was a name, which malice or ignorance alone could attempt to injure, and whose character and conduct claimed and were entitled to the truest respect.'

No one could weave words like Sheridan, or throw a veil of meaningless phrases over awkward truth more skilfully. Lord Holland, who did not hear the speech, dismissed it later as 'unintelligible sentimental trash'. But it served its purpose at the time. Memories of the 'No Popery' riots cast a long shadow; few people wished to provoke a constitutional crisis by bringing the question of the marriage's validity out into the open. Sheridan's speech had saved the situation not only for the prince but for the country as a whole.

# XII

Sheridan's prowess as a speaker had won him the respect of the House of Commons; outside the House it was less easy to defend himself. The press was a many-headed monster, its attacks too numerous to be dealt with by a smart riposte. His theatrical origins and shaky finances provided all the fuel that was needed. Watkins, his first biographer, quotes a characteristic entry from *The Royal Register* of 1784, a satirical publication purporting to be written by the king.

## THE POLITICAL ADVENTURER

It could not happen in any country but England:

That a young man, the son of a player, who had . . . married the daughter of a musician, should refuse though in very distressed circumstances, to let his wife sing at a royal concert, and at an enormous salary, because it would degrade his character as a *gentleman*:

That this *gentleman*, after having written a successful piece or two at one theatre, should find the means of raising sufficient sums of money to become the purchaser of a considerable share in another . . .

That this *author* and *manager*, having by the success and merit of his productions, established the character of a man of wit, and by his wife's concerts made an acquaintance with the fashionable world, should live in a style of elegance and expense that would soon beggar a large fortune:

That this *man of fashion*, being so embarrassed as not to find the most common credit . . . should desert the common muse for politics; contrive, with the last guinea of a borrowed purse, to get elected into parliament, and set up, at once, for an active politician . . . and living in defiance of economy himself, become an economist for the nation.

Sheridan's moments in office had been brief; they would not return again for another eighteen years. In the 1780s, however, the picture still looked promising. The king was nearing fifty, a considerable age for that time, and the opposition's hopes were fixed on the accession of his son. Sheridan had earned the Prince of Wales's gratitude and had made himself essential to the opposition. He had no occasion to feel discouraged and showed little sign of being so. 'God bless thee my Dear Soul,' wrote Elizabeth in one of her charming 'fiffs'. 'Thank ye for the good News of Politics. I hope all is really good, but 'e are such a sanguine Pig, there's no knowing.'

With Mrs Siddons as a risen and Kemble as a rising star the affairs of Drury Lane were also going well. In October 1785 a new figure made her appearance there, the comic actress Mrs Jordan. If Mrs Siddons, according to the writers of the day was Melpomene, Mrs Jordan was Thalia, or the comic muse. She was at her best in romping roles such as Peggy, the artless heroine of *The Country Girl*, or the bouncing Miss Hoyden in Sheridan's *A Trip to Scarborough*. To see her in this part, wrote Leigh Hunt later, 'shed blubbering tears for some disappointment, and eat all the while a great thick slice of bread and butter, weeping and moaning and munching, and eyeing at every bite the part she meant to bite next was a lesson . . . worth a hundred sermons.'

After the stormy passions of Mrs Siddons, Mrs Jordan burst like sunshine on to the London stage. Her trim figure, best displayed in 'breeches parts', was pronounced perfection by so grave a critic as Sir Joshua Reynolds, her gaiety and high spirits were irresistible. Before long she was drawing crowds as great as those on Siddons nights.

Theatre-going in those days could be a perilous business. Sheridan's sister Betsy described the fight to reach her box to see Mrs Jordan in *The Country Girl*.

'When we got to the House,' she wrote in a letter to her sister, 'we found ourselves in such a Croud as I never before encounter'd . . . After we had nearly reach'd the Box Office a cry of Pick-pocket raised a general confusion and those at the top of the Stairs were forcibly push'd down by the pursuers of the said Gentleman. At this instant I saw a door open into a sort of lobby, into which I made Mrs M— enter but found it impossible to accompany her and was by the Croud brought Back to the Street. What made the Croud so intollerable was that I firmly believe three parts of it were pick-pockets, for the Constables Bawl'd themselves Hoarse in telling them the house was full without making the least difference in the number. Again the Torrent push'd me up to the spot where I had left Mrs Morris where we had the pleasure of cooling our heels for half an hour, during which time we heard various lamentations about purses etc. that had been convey'd away. At length we got admittance but the fright and additional cold I had got made me pay dear for the evening's amusement.'

Betsy Sheridan had arrived in London to stay with her father the previous autumn. Her letters to her sister Alicia, who had married a member of a Huguenot banking family, Joseph LeFanu, in Dublin three years earlier, give intimate glimpses of the Sheridans' life at this period. For her other brother, Charles, Betsy Sheridan had nothing but dislike. After her sister's marriage she had been obliged to live with him and his wife and had known the bitterness of being a poor relation; her letters are full of her brother's hypocrisy and meanness. Sheridan and his wife, by contrast, immediately made her welcome, though her father, still nursing his grudges, refused to join her when she called on them.

Richard was evidently saddened by the renewed estrangement. At his first meeting with his sister he immediately turned the conversation to their father, and hoped that now she had come to London she might make peace between them. He asked her many questions about Ireland – 'which made me smile,' she wrote, 'as one would have supposed I came from the furthest part of America' – and complained of Charles's neglect in keeping him in touch with matters there. 'Dick is a very warm friend to the Irish,' she noted. 'Mrs S. cannot conceive the violent attachment he has to that country.'

Charles had not thought it necessary to resign his post as military under-secretary when the Whigs lost office. 'The system, the circumstances and the manners of the two countries are so totally different,' he told his brother in a somewhat laboured letter of self-justification, 'that I can assure you nothing could be so absurd as any attempt to extend the party-distinctions which prevail on your side of the water to this.'

Dining with the Linleys in Norfolk Street, where Mrs Linley 'gave us a bad dinner not to make a stranger of me', Betsy found her hostess grown much older. Another tragedy had struck the family. Maria, the last of the the Linley daughters to sing in public, had died of brain fever on 5 September 1784, aged twenty-one. Her death-bed scene became part of the Linley legend: shortly before her death she had raised herself up in bed and, with 'an unexpected and momentary animation', had sung a part of the anthem 'I know that my Redeemer liveth'.

This new bereavement cast Thomas Linley into deeper gloom. He complained of rheumatism and excruciating headaches and ran the gauntlet of the appalling cures that were then thought suitable. We read of blistering and leeches being applied; on one occasion a friendly apothecary, Mr Pratton, suggested shaving his head so that a blister might be raised on the crown. Mrs Linley had a wig prepared, but, wrote Elizabeth, 'when he saw the formidable Grizzle display'd upon my hand his heart fail'd him and he was as unprevailable as ever'.

Elizabeth had written verses on her sister's death which according to Mary were 'some of the sweetest lines you ever wrote'. But her life was too hectic for prolonged mourning. The responsibilities of the theatre, late nights and fashionable entertainments took a heavy toll. Calling at two o'clock one afternoon, Betsy found her brother and sister-in-law sitting down to breakfast. Such hours were not unusual. 'Indeed,' wrote Betsy of Mrs Sheridan, 'the life she leads would kill a horse, but she said one must do as other people do.'

In the summer of 1786 the Tickells and the Sheridans took a seaside holiday at Weymouth. The brothers-in-law enjoyed their usual jaunts and jokes, but Sheridan, walking on the beach alone, had moments of melancholy reflection. There had always been a dark side to the brilliant surface that he presented the world, something within 'that gives a check to my most pleasurable ideas ... that contradicts my best Passions, repines at the enjoyment of them, and cries out "Non est Tanti" to every Pursuit of my Life'. The remains of a shipwreck washed up on the rocks inspired a fragment of gloomily romantic reverie:

I saw many carry off the . . . prizes, some humanely looking to the living wretches, exhausted yet clinging to the wreck . . . I alone remained. I looked on the Sea and the Sky and thought of the feeling of those who had thus lost Friends. My soul was awed by the scene, and I resolved to bury the officer left and as far as my memory recollected, to perform the rites of Sepulture. I dug a grave. I, on my knees began to say, Hast thou no mother – who is the dearest Friend that will regret thy loss? – if it be Parents, speak in this glory, this shade – if thy Brother—. At that name I thought a whisper in the glade. – Is it thy Lover? – a Cupid appeared . . . a pale, a meagre form, no laughing roses on his cheek. He said '. . . I am Love, a ghastly figure . . . the lying cheat in me behold. Ask me no more, I bear her tears that would embalm his grave' . . . The pale Cherub stooping o'er the space dropped two tears and vanished . . . and I turned the sand upon his tomb.

Perhaps, like 'La belle dame sans merci', the passage held a premonition. The shadow of consumption lay over the two sisters. Elizabeth had always been the more delicate, and both Mary and Sheridan were constantly haunted by the fear of her falling ill. But it was Mary who would succumb first. During their holiday she complained of a painful stitch in her side which prevented her from bathing. She was suffering from what she thought was rheumatism and was taking constant opiates to dull the pain. 'I wonder I don't sprout at my finger-ends Daphne-like with the loads of Bark I have Swallowed', she wrote to Mrs Canning.

Her symptoms, taken lightly to begin with, were the first signs of the pulmonary tuberculosis, or consumption, from which she would die the following year. In a paper dated 24 August 1791, attached to a collection of her sister's letters, Elizabeth recorded the agonising progress of her illness:

In February 1787 my Dear Sister came to Town in a bad state of Health. On the 15th of May she return'd to Hampton Court [where the Tickells had an apartment] without having receiv'd any benefit from the various Remedies prescrib'd for her. The three last letters were written between the 15th and 25th when she was once more brought to Town dangerously ill of a Fever which turn'd to a Hectic that never afterwards left her. On the 13th of June she was carried back to Hampton Court where I remained with her, and on the 19th we went by slow stages to Clifton Hill near the Hot-Wells with a faint hope that the air and waters would restore her, but after struggling with this most dreadful of all diseases and bearing with gentlest Patience and Resignation the various pains and Horrors which mark its fatal Progress. On the 27th of July she ceased to suffer, and I for ever lost the Friend and Companion of my youth, the beloved Sister of my Heart, whose loss can never be repaired.

Elizabeth took her sister's three children to live with them, devoting herself to their upbringing as a distraction from her grief. Sheridan, always warm-hearted, had done all he could to comfort the family during Mary's illness – 'he is sadly taken up with managing us all here in our Distress', wrote Elizabeth. Mary had always loved and understood him – 'I in particular', she said, 'am one who think you cannot be half kind enough to Sheridan' – and Sheridan had reciprocated her affection. As for Tickell, he was so overcome by grief that he vowed he would never marry again and had to be prevented from inscribing his promise on the plate on his wife's coffin. Less than two years later, as Elizabeth noted indignantly, he was married again, to 'a beautiful young woman of eighteen!!!'

In the midst of this family tragedy Sheridan's theatrical and political life had never been busier. As well as the normal problems of running a theatre, he had faced a threat to Drury Lane's most precious asset, the theatre's patent – the royal charter by which the monopoly of spoken drama was confined to London's two main theatres.

The challenge had come from the Drury Lane actor John Palmer, the first Joseph Surface, who attempted to set up a new theatre in Wellclose Square, near the Tower of London, to meet the demands of east London's growing population. The foundation stone was laid in 1785, and in a prospectus which did justice to Palmer's nickname of 'Plausible Jack' investors were assured that the enterprise had a legal basis, the details of which would be revealed in due course. It was not until 1787, when the theatre had been completed, that the proprietors of the patent theatres, united in defence of their monopoly, rose up to challenge him. Palmer's so-called authority proved to be no more than a permission granted by the local magistrates and a licence from the governor of the Tower of London. Weighed in the balance against an Act of Parliament which had forbidden all theatrical performances in London not previously allowed by royal patent or licensed by the Lord Chamberlain, it turned out to be worthless. After only one night, at the end of which Palmer was forced to admit he had no legal case, the theatre was closed down. It was subsequently permitted to reopen for specifically non-spoken entertainments, but went bankrupt less than two years later.

When Palmer, defeated but unrepentant, rejoined the company at Drury Lane, there was considerable interest amongst his colleagues as to how his first meeting with Sheridan would go. Palmer, it appears, made quite a scene of it.

'After a profound bow', wrote Boaden, 'he approached the author of *The School for Scandal* with an air of penitent humility; his head declined, the whites of his eyes turned upwards, his hands clasped together and his whole air exactly that of Joseph Surface before Sir Peter Teazle.

'He began thus:

' "My dear Mr Sheridan, if you could but know what I feel at this moment *here*" (laying one hand upon his heart).

'Sheridan, with inimitable readiness stopped him. "Why Jack! You forget I wrote it!" '

Meanwhile, on the political front, the vexed affairs of India were coming to a head. Sheridan's speech in the House of Commons demanding the impeachment of Warren Hastings was the great event of 1787. Hastings' trial, the longest and most famous in British legal history, would begin before the Lords the following year.

In 1785 Hastings had resigned his post as governor-general and returned to England, where at first he was well received. The king made much of him at court and the directors of the East India Company, taking their cue from the monarch, passed a unanimous vote of thanks for his services. Behind the scenes, however, his enemies were gaining strength. Burke had never wavered in his conviction that Hastings had been guilty of oppression and corruption on a gigantic scale. Urged on by Philip Francis, Hastings' bitter enemy and former colleague on the governing Council, he had gathered up a dossier of Hastings' so-called crimes. The fact that Hastings had saved India for Britain at a time when the American War of Independence was at its height and almost all of Europe was against her, that he had established some kind of peace and order out of anarchy, and laid the foundations of a lasting system of administration over its vast territories, was conveniently forgotten. By comparison with other servants of the Company Hastings had made very little personally during his thirty years in India. He had taken a closer interest in Indian culture and civilisation than any previous governor; he had financed from his own pocket the founding of the Madrasah, a college of Arabic studies in Calcutta; he had encouraged and written the introduction to the first translation of the Bhagavid Gita, and become the first patron of the Asiatic Society of Bengal. Wherever possible he had left administration in Indian hands and, although devout himself, had always discouraged missionary activity. It was wrong, he felt, to force a foreign faith on India's millions; the Almighty would doubtless reform them in his own good time.

Burke's crusade against Hastings, undertaken out of passionate conviction, had much that was irrational and intemperate about it. But it reflected a growing feeling that Britain should take responsibility for the welfare of those under its rule and that the policy of self-enrichment and plunder practised by the East India Company – which Hastings had done his best to mitigate – should be checked. Politics entered into the equation. Pitt and his government, harassed on the economic front, saw a chance of diverting the Foxite opposition's energies elsewhere. Hastings, after thirty years' absence from England, was bad at presenting his case or assessing the strength of his opponents.

When Burke, in April 1786, brought forward twenty-two charges of 'high Crimes and Misdemeanors' against him in the House of Commons, Hastings, instead of defending himself in general terms, chose to answer each charge at such interminable length that the house was half empty by the time he had finished. Inevitably there were mistakes over details on which Burke, returning to the attack, could build when the charges were debated. Nonetheless, the first charge, that of provoking war against the Rohillas, Afghan tribesmen who were threatening the state of Oudh, was defeated. On the second charge, however, that of driving Chait Singh, the ruler of Benares, to revolt, Pitt voted against Hastings, bringing enough of his supporters with him to carry the motion. It was the turning point in the case. The third charge, the alleged spoliation of the Begums of Oudh, was presented by Sheridan when the House reassembled the following year.

The state of Oudh, nominally independent, was important to the East India Company as a buffer zone between their territories in Bengal and the warlike Mahratta tribes of the north-west. Beginning as an ally, it had become little more than a protectorate by the late 1770s. Company troops were stationed there in exchange for a fixed subsidy, and a resident appointed to represent Hastings with the Nawab, Asaph-al-Dowlah. Following the outbreak of war between Britain and France in 1778, the East India Company found itself threatened by France's allies on two fronts, the Mahrattas in the west and Haidar Ali of Mysore in the south. With its very existence in India at stake, the Company was desperately in need of extra funds. Hastings' peremptory demands on Chait Singh, the ruler of Benares, for increased contributions to the war had driven him to rebellion in 1781. Chait Singh had been overthrown; Asaph-al-Dowlah, owing the Company arrears of more than a million pounds, was eager not to suffer the same fate. Since he had no immediate means of finding such a sum, it was agreed that he should be released from maintaining British troops in Oudh, and that in order to repay what he already owed he should be allowed to take back the jaghirs (land revenues) belonging to his mother and grandmother, the Begums of Oudh.

The Begums naturally objected. They had inherited vast lands and revenues from the previous Nawab, together with a treasury estimated at over two million pounds. Their right to so large a share of the inheritance was dubious but, since they refused to give it up and since Asaph-al-Dowlah was in urgent need of ready money on his accession, he had agreed to guarantee it in exchange for cash gifts of some three-quarters of a million pounds. That money had long since been expended. In December 1781, under strong pressure from Hastings, who claimed that the Begums had forfeited their rights by supporting the rebellion of Chait Singh, the Nawab took back the Begums' jaghirs with a promise of compensation in return.

His real goal, however, was the Begums' store of treasures. Hastings maintained that as part of the former Nawab's treasury it should have been inherited by his son; his opponents, probably incorrectly, insisted that it was the Begums' personal property. In any case the need for cash was pressing and, since the Begums – who detested the Nawab – refused to hand over any part of it, he marched on their palace at Fyzabad to enforce his demands.

After a preliminary resistance the palace was captured, but neither the Begums nor the two eunuchs who effectively ran the place would agree to reveal the treasure's whereabouts. Urged on by Hastings and Middleton, his agent on the spot, the Nawab confined the Begums to their quarters and ordered the eunuchs to be put in irons. By using 'some few severities', the extent of which was much debated later, the eunuchs were persuaded to disclose the secret of the treasure in early February, though they continued to be kept in irons till the end of the year. The Nawab was able to seize the best part of a million pounds; but, since the Begums kept a residue of at least £120,000, they could not be said to have been left in penury. As for the eunuchs, though they may have been roughly treated, they did not appear to have suffered any long-term ill effects. Twenty years later Lord Valentia met one of the two in Lucknow; he remarked that he was 'upwards of eighty, full six feet high and stout in proportion . . . supposed to be worth half a million of money'.

Sheridan, as his stance in 1783 had shown, had originally hoped to spare Hastings. Since then the climate of opinion and his own attitude had changed. Swept along by Burke, his imagination took fire at the Begums' wrongs. The appeal to his chivalry, the exoticism of the setting, his hatred of oppression gave a natural opening for his powers of oratory. The charge concerning the Begums was amongst the most dramatic in Burke's list of crimes and misdemeanours and Burke had at first coveted it for himself. In the end he was pleased to relinquish it to Sheridan, from whom he expected great things. In a letter to Philip Francis at the beginning of January 1787 Burke reported with satisfaction: 'The D. of Portland tells me that Sheridan has warmed with a sort of love passion to our Begums. Genl. Smith [a Foxite nabob] says he will make such a figure on that Subject as has not hitherto been seen.'

# XIII

———✦———

S heridan's speech on the Begums of Oudh, delivered before the committee of the whole House of Commons on 7 February 1787, was hailed as the greatest feat of parliamentary oratory of his own or any previous age. His speech, declared Burke, was 'the most astonishing effort of eloquence, argument and wit united, of which there was any record or tradition'. Fox agreed: 'All that he had ever heard – all that he had ever read – when compared with it dwindled into nothing and vanished like vapour before the sun.' Pitt, not normally given to enthusiasm, acknowledged 'that it surpassed all the eloquence of ancient and modern times, and possessed everything that genius or art could furnish, to agitate and controul the human mind'.

These comments are recorded at the head of the summary of his oration in the collection of Sheridan's speeches published in 1816, the year of his death. Owing to the inadequacies of parliamentary reporting at the time, neither this nor the version in *The Parliamentary History*, covering only nineteen pages, give more than a fragmentary picture of the speech, which lasted for five hours and forty minutes. Sheridan never agreed to its publication. Perhaps he remembered Fox's dictum that speeches which read well on paper are seldom successful when delivered – an observation that applied especially to Burke whose power of emptying the house when speaking had earned him the nickname of the 'dinner bell'. The extracts with which we are left do little to convey the effect which it created at the time – 'the flash of Wit – the bright Intelligence' that illuminated his features, the extraordinary fascination of his speaking voice. But we can follow the course of his arguments even if, as one historian suggests, they were too over-simplified to carry much conviction when the effect of his oratory had worn off.

He began by making the general point that Britain had been disgraced by the crimes carried out in its name in India. He 'professed to God that he felt in his own bosom the strongest personal conviction' that in his treatment of those 'illustrious women', the Begums, Hastings was guilty of rapacity, treachery, cruelty and oppression. Basing his narrative on Hastings' own letters and reports, and the reports of the Supreme Council in Calcutta, he proceeded to detail the events leading up to the attack on their palace at Fyzabad.

Sir Elijah Impey, the Chief Justice in Bengal, had reported Hastings as saying that Benares and Oudh were his only resources in paying for the war.

'What was he to derive from those two resources?' demanded Sheridan. 'Not the collection of a just revenue, not the voluntary contributions of a people attached to the Company from sincere motives of gratitude and esteem, but the exaction and extortion of pretended debts and the plunder of the innocent. It was exactly like the malversation of a highwayman, who, in justification of his crimes, should say he had only two resources – Bagshot or Hounslow!'

Hastings' defenders had claimed that his faults were excused by his greatness of mind. Sheridan saw no evidence of such greatness. 'We see nothing solid or penetrating, nothing noble or magnanimous, nothing open, direct, liberal, manly or superior, in his measures or his mind. All is dark, insidious, sordid and insincere.'

Dundas, the head of the Board of Control of the East India Company, had said that 'the greatest defect in the politics of India was that they were uniformly founded on mercantile maxims'. Hastings had carried this system to its utmost extent.

'It was in this manner that nations have been extirpated for a sum of money, whole tracts of country laid waste by fire and sword, to furnish investments; revolutions occasioned by an affidavit, an army employed in executing an arrest, a prince expelled for the balance of an account . . . a truncheon contrasted with the implements of a counting house; and the British Government exhibited in every part of Hindostan holding a bloody sceptre in one hand and picking pockets with the other.'

No document had shown conclusively that the Begums had abetted the rebellion of Chait Singh. Sir Elijah Impey had been sent to Lucknow to obtain affidavits proving their complicity but these had been obtained retrospectively. The Begums' only treason was their possession of the treasure, and Sheridan's rhetoric took wing as he described the invasion of their palace.

'I am utterly at a loss in what terms to describe the attack on the zenana . . . The confusion, the uproar, the screaming of females, the barbarity of the troops, and the trepidation of the neighbourhood are unrecountable . . . Let the Committee picture to themselves any of the British Royal Family thus surrounded, assailed, and forced to surrender their property and their servants, their bosom friends at the point of a bayonet. To us at least who live in a land where every man's house is his sanctuary, where the arm of power dares not intrude, where the Constitution has erected an insuperable barrier to every encroachment or outrage, such an instance of violence cannot but appear monstrous and atrocious beyond all example or idea.'

In concluding Sheridan called for all considerations of party to be thrown aside. 'When the majesty of justice is to be supported, it is our duty, our glory, our interest to be unanimous . . . We are challenged by the laws of God and man to relieve millions of our fellow creatures from a state of misery and oppression . . . Would not the omnipotence of Britain be demonstrated to the wonder of nations by stretching its mighty arm across the deep and saving by its *fiat* distant millions from destruction? And would the blessings of the people thus saved dissipate in empty air? No! If I may dare to use the figure, – we shall constitute Heaven itself our proxy, to receive for us the blessings of their pious gratitude, and the prayers of their thanksgiving. It is with confidence, therefore, Sir, that I move you on this charge, "that Warren Hastings be impeached".'

The following year a partial translation of Sheridan's speech was read to the Princesses of Oudh. They appeared quite unmoved by his recital of their wrongs, reported Hastings' agent Major Scott, 'though they expressed great remarks of astonishment on the occasion'.

Far otherwise was the reaction in the House of Commons. 'I have not slept *one wink*', wrote Sir Gilbert Elliot, a future governor-general of India, to his wife next day. 'Nothing whatever was the matter with me, except the impressions of what had been passing still vibrating on my brain . . . The *bone* rose repeatedly in my throat, and tears in my eyes – not of grief, but merely of strongly excited sensibility . . . The conclusion, in which the whole force of the case was collected, and where his whole powers were employed to their utmost stretch . . . worked the House into such a paroxysm of passionate enthusiasm on the subject, and of admiration for him, that the moment he sat down there was a universal shout, nay even clapping, for half a second; every man was on the floor, and all his friends throwing themselves on his neck in raptures of joy and exultation.'

Another of those present, a Mr Logan, had come into the House convinced of Hastings' innocence. At the end of the first hour he said to a friend, 'All this is declamatory assertion without proof'; when the second was finished, 'This is a most wonderful oration'; at the end of the third, 'Mr Hastings has acted very unjustifiably'; of the fourth, 'Mr Hastings is a most atrocious criminal'; and at last, 'Of all the monsters of inquity the most enormous is Warren Hastings!'

So great was the emotion created by the speech that it was decided to adjourn proceedings till the following day when the first excitement had subsided. Sheridan, it seemed, had bewitched the House.

'How should such a fellow as Sheridan, who has no diamonds to bestow, fascinate all the world?' wrote Horace Walpole to his friend Lady Ossory. 'Yet witchcraft, no doubt there has been, for when did simple eloquence ever convince a majority? . . . Well at least there is a new crime, sorcery, to charge on the opposition!'

Sheridan's family greeted his triumph with delight. His brother, writing from Dublin, described the sense of national pride – 'good honest *Irish* pride' – that Sheridan, an Irishman, had brought such honour to his country. He had read accounts of his speech with tears of exultation and seen them bring tears to the eyes of many who had never met him. His sister Alicia wrote of her own joy and affection for him. She gloried in his achievement; even her father, she noted, had been gratified, 'in a degree that I did not expect', by the attention his son had excited. 'He seems truly pleased that men should say, "There goes the father of Gaul".'

With Sheridan's speech on the Begums the proceedings against Hastings became inevitable. Sheridan spoke again on the seventh charge against the governor-general, that of corruptly awarding contracts and receiving bribes, but did not repeat his previous *tour de force*. More than ever it was clear that Hastings was the scapegoat for the system under which he had to operate, but the tide of opinion against him had gone too far. On 21 May he was arrested by the sergeant-at-arms and taken to the bar of the House of Lords. Here he had to endure the single thing he felt most in all his long ordeal, the ceremonial of kneeling before the Lords – a punishment, he wrote, not only before conviction, but before the accusation.

He was released on a bail of £50,000. His trial would take place at the beginning of the following year. A committee of eighteen members of the House of Commons was appointed to manage the proceedings. Headed by Burke and including Fox and Sheridan, it was drawn entirely from the ranks of the Whig opposition. Pitt, though willing to support the impeachment, would take no active part in managing it. Philip Francis, while eager to participate, was deliberately excluded. He was too obviously biased against Hastings, though Burke continued to take his advice behind the scenes.

Although the threat of impeachment had been often made in Parliament – Fox, for instance, had repeatedly called for North's impeachment during the American War of Independence – it was more than forty years since it had last been carried out. On that occasion it had been used against the Jacobite losers after the rebellion of 1745 – a political proceeding without much relevance to the Hastings' case. For Burke it was important that the case should be judged on the grounds of natural justice as well as those of common law, thus giving his charges a wider scope and enabling him to appeal to morality when facts were missing or deficient. The conflict would run through the whole trial, and the final decision in favour of the common law would play a major part in securing Hastings' acquittal.

On 6 February 1788, Hastings went to see the preparations at Westminster Hall, where he would appear 'as a criminal' the following week. Workmen were putting the finishing touches to a vast improvised theatre. On the right were rows of red-covered seats for the peers; on the left, covered in green, the seats for the Commons; above them the galleries for ticket holders and peeresses. At the far end, under the great window, were the throne and royal boxes, with seats for the Chancellor, judges and heralds below them. For Hastings himself there was a little box near the door, facing the throne and separated only by the witness box from the seats of his accusers; today a plaque on the wall marks his place.

The trial began on 13 February. A hundred and seventy peers, in their coronation robes of red and ermine, escorted by heralds dressed in gold, processed to take their places on the right side of the hall; the Commons were already seated opposite. In the galleries, the ambassadors of the great European kingdoms, having decided to treat this as a state occasion, sat dressed in their full orders, their plumes and diamonds vying with those of the fashionable ladies round them. The queen and the princesses were in the Duke of Newcastle's box; Fanny Burney, her quick eyes missing nothing, was amongst the ladies-in-waiting in attendance. Mrs Fitzherbert was in the royal box. The Prince of Wales, after taking part in the opening procession, sat talking too loudly with Sheridan in the managers' enclosure.

Hastings was summoned to the hall at noon. A small emaciated figure in poppy-coloured silk, he was escorted to his box, and, advancing to the bar, once more knelt before the court.

'What an awful moment was this for such a man!' wrote Fanny Burney. 'A man fallen from such height of power to a situation so humiliating – from the almost unlimited command of so large a part of the Eastern world to be cast at the feet of his enemies, of the great tribunal of his country, and of the nation at large, assembled thus in a body to try and to judge him!'

Fanny Burney was a passionate supporter of Hastings. Her sister Charlotte had recently married the son of Hastings' doctor, Clement Francis – no relation to the malevolent Philip Francis – and the whole family were ardent admirers of the governor-general. To see him now, so harassed, pale and altered, brought her close to tears. That Burke, who had flattered and charmed her when she first emerged into the world, should be his prosecutor was especially hard to bear.

Burke's opening speech, remarkable as a work of art and

imagination, bore little relation to the facts of Indian history. Painting a picture of a prosperous Bengal blighted by Hastings' crimes, he launched into a torrent of invective against Hastings, describing him variously as 'a ravenous vulture who feeds on the dead and enfeebled', 'a swindling Maecenas', 'the Captain-General of Iniquity', 'a heart dyed deep in blackness – gangrened to the very core'.

It was an impressive performance. Hastings himself declared that 'for half an hour I looked up at the orator in a reverie of wonder, and actually felt myself the most culpable man. But,' he added, 'I recurred to my own bosom, and there found a consciousness which consoled me under all I heard and suffered.'

Sheridan's speech did not take place till the beginning of June. Fox had suggested that he repeat the oration he had given in the House of Commons, but Sheridan was determined to produce one that was entirely new. For weeks beforehand his entire household was involved in its preparation, some busy with pen and scissors, making extracts, others pasting and stitching together his scattered memorandums. A pamphlet of more than two hundred pages survives amongst his papers, copied out in Elizabeth's neat hand. Throughout the proceedings his wife was Sheridan's greatest help, though her health was still affected by her sister's death, and at one point he had to excuse himself from attending Burke's committee meetings in order to be with her in the country.

After the excitement of Burke's opening speech public interest in the Hastings trial largely died down. The prospect of Sheridan's speech revived it and the demand for places was so great that tickets changed hands for as much as fifty guineas.

The speech was scheduled to begin at midday on 3 June. By eight on the morning of that day, so the Parliamentary Report informs us, the avenues leading to the court through the New and Old Palace Yards were crowded with peeresses and 'persons of the first distinction'; when the gates were opened one hour later, the crush to get places was so frantic that it 'nearly proved fatal to many'.

Sheridan began his speech at noon before an audience of all that was most brilliant in the world of fashion, art and politics. Unaccustomed to the greater size of Westminster Hall it was difficult at first to make himself heard. But he soon found the right level, getting into his stride as he described the profanation of the Begums' inner sanctum, the zenana. The Begums' claim to the treasure, he maintained, rested on the fact that it had been lodged there by the previous Nawab.

'To dispute with the Counsel about the original right to those treasures – to talk of a title to them by the Mahometan law! – their title to them is the title of a Saint to the relics upon an altar, placed there by Piety, guarded by holy Superstition, and to be snatched from thence only by Sacrilege.'

This passage was rather roughly handled by one of Hastings' defending counsels, William Law, a few years later, when he asked how a Begum could be considered as a saint, or how the camels which formed part of the treasure were to be placed upon an altar. Sheridan could only reply lamely that it was the first time he had ever heard of special pleading against a metaphor.

Many of Sheridan's arguments had been heard in his previous oration in the House of Commons, though greatly elaborated and recast. Fox considered his style was more florid and overworked than it had been on that occasion. He objected to its passages of 'poetic prose, or worse still, prosaic poetry', and would later deplore its influence on Burke's writing. But there was no mistaking its effect at the time or its power to sway the feelings of its audience. Sheridan's own emotions were wrought to their highest pitch. On the night after his second appearance on 6 June he was taken so ill and vomited so severely that it was doubtful whether he would be able to continue. He recovered enough to reappear on 10 June, but had to stop short before concluding. His final appearance, on 13 June, set the seal on a performance worthy in its way of Mrs Siddons – who is said to have fainted at the climax of his speech.

He dwelt once more on the enormity of Hastings' crimes, against which, he claimed, those recorded in 'the deep searching annals of Tacitus – the luminous philosophy of Gibbon' dwindled into insignificance. Gibbon noted the reference in his memoirs: 'It is not my province,' he wrote gravely, 'to absolve or condemn the Governor of India; but Mr Sheridan's eloquence commanded my applause; nor could I hear without emotion the personal compliment he paid me in the presence of the British nation.' Moore, however, tells us that when asked by some brother Whig, at the conclusion of the speech, how he came to compliment Gibbon with the epithet 'luminous', Sheridan answered in a half whisper, 'I said voluminous.'

Hastings' disregard of natural ties in inciting the Nawab to attack his own mother was the theme of one of Sheridan's most purple passages:

'Filial Piety! It is the primal bond of society! . . . It is the sacrament of our nature! − not only the duty, but the indulgence of man − it is his first great privilege − it is amongst his most enduring delights! − it causes the bosom to glow with reverberated love! − it requites the visitations of nature, and returns the blessings that have been received! . . . hangs over each vicissitude of all that must pass away − aids the melancholy virtues in their last sad tasks of life, to cheer the languors of decreptitude and age . . . and breathes sweet consolation even in the awful moment of dissolution!'

In the cold light of the printed page and the garbled rendering of the reporter, it is hard to imagine the effect created by this homily. But Sheridan had caught up his hearers and himself into a world of make-believe, or what Coleridge describes as a willing suspension of disbelief. Most of the audience were in tears; Sir Gilbert Elliot, who was on the committee of managers, told his wife that he could not recollect ever crying 'so heartily and copiously on any public occasion'.

Sheridan's final peroration was a call for justice − 'justice august and pure; the abstract idea of all that would be perfect in the spirits and aspirings of men!'

'On that justice,' he concluded, 'I rely; deliberate and sure, abstracted from all party purpose and political speculations! not on words but on facts . . . This is the call on all, to administer to truth and equity, as they would satisfy the laws and satisfy themselves, with the most exalted bliss possible, or conceivable for our nature − the self-approving consciousness of virtue, when the condemnation we look for will be one of the most ample mercies accomplished for mankind since the creation of the world.

'My Lords, I have done!'

He fell back half fainting into the arms of Burke, who was waiting to support him. 'A good actor,' noted Gibbon next day. 'I saw him this morning; he is perfectly well.'

The speech on the Begums, had Sheridan known it, marked the

zenith of his political career. Never again would he soar to such heights or be greeted with such universal praise.

'It is impossible, my dear woman,' wrote Elizabeth to Alicia four days later, 'to convey to you the delight, the astonishment, the adoration, he has excited in the breasts of every class of people! Every party prejudice has been overcome by a display of genius, eloquence and goodness, which no one, with anything like a heart about them, could have listened to without being the wiser or the better for the rest of their lives. What must *my* feelings be! – you can only imagine. To tell you the truth it is with some difficulty that I can "let down my mind" as Mr Burke said afterwards, to talk or think on any other subject. But pleasure, too exquisite, becomes pain, and I am this moment suffering for the delightful anxieties of this week.'

The trial of Warren Hastings dragged on for seven years. Parliament sat for only four or five months a year, and during this period the sittings of the Court were limited to a few weeks and sometimes only a few days. Hastings remained at liberty in the intervals, though Burke, increasingly obsessional, had bitterly opposed his bail. In 1795 Hastings was finally acquitted on all charges by the Lords, the whole House rising to salute him when the verdict was announced. Long before this Sheridan had grown heartily sick of the trial. 'He wishes Hastings would run away and Burke after him,' the Duchess of Devonshire recorded in her diary for 20 November 1788.

Ten years after the trial had ended Sheridan was introduced to Hastings by the Prince of Wales in Brighton. Hastings, now seventy-three, had long been recognised for the great man he was and, though he never received the peerage he had hoped for, was enjoying an honoured retirement. Sheridan, wrote Creevey, 'lost no time in attempting to cajole old Hastings, begging him to believe that any part he had ever taken against him was purely political, and that no one had a greater respect for him than himself &c., &c., upon which old Hastings said with great gravity that "it would be a great consolation to him in his declining days if Mr Sheridan would make that sentence more publick"; but Sheridan was obliged to mutter and get out of such an engagement as well as he could.'

Had Sheridan been sincere at the time of his two famous speeches?

It is hardly possible to believe that he could have spoken with such emotion if he had not been convinced of the justice of his cause. There had been much that had been indefensible in the policies of the East India Company. However mistaken in its persecution of Hastings, the trial had been motivated by a moral impulse. As one of the managers bringing forward the case for the prosecution, Sheridan was not obliged to look too closely at the arguments for the defence. Or so, at least, he seems to have reasoned. 'The counsel,' he wrote in a fragment found amongst his papers, 'is not only not bound to ask his conscience but he is bound *not* to do it. He has a duty and a trust which ought to receive no aid from conviction.'

The point is debatable. Hastings' trial, according to the legal historian Sir James Stephen, was a blot on our judicial history. But by dramatising the question of Britain's responsibility for the peoples under its rule it brought about lasting changes in our attitude to India. Not all were desirable. Hastings had ruled alongside the Indians, entering far more fully into their laws and customs than any governors after him. His successors had a more colonialist approach. The plundering of the East India Company had been checked, but relations between Indians and British were never so natural again. Nonetheless a new era was beginning, based, in theory at least, on more humanitarian ideals. Sheridan had voiced them in unforgett-able terms. Byron, who described the speech on the Begums in the House of Commons as 'the very best Oration . . . ever conceived or heard in this country', was expressing something more than a poetic truth when he wrote in his 'Monody on the Death of Sheridan',

> When the loud cry of trampled Hindostan
> Arose to Heaven in her appeal from man,
> His was the thunder – his the avenging rod
> The wrath – the delegated voice of God!
> Which shook the nations through his lips – and blazed
> Till vanquish'd senates trembled as they praised.

# XIV

In July 1788 Thomas Sheridan arrived in London from Dublin, accompanied by his daughter Betsy. They were greeted on their first evening by his old manservant, William Thompson, who called at their lodgings to have supper with them. He was full of Sheridan's praises, repeatedly saying, 'Sir, your Son is the first Man in England – You will find every one of that opinion.'

'I thought my father seem'd rather pleased,' wrote Betsy. Later, when he had gone to bed Thompson stayed on to talk of his 'dear Master Richard', getting up to act out his concluding words. 'Bad as the attempt must have been,' she told her sister, 'yet it convey'd some idea of the manner in which he spoke those words "My Lords I have done" which so haunted you.'

Betsy called on her brother and his wife the following day. 'Mrs Sheridan received me very kindly,' she wrote, 'but my Brother seem'd very much affected. His eyes fill'd with tears and his voice choak'd. After embracing me very affectionately he hurried out of the room. Mrs S. said he was *nervous* but would return to us soon, which he did and . . . spoke very kindly of my Father.'

The next day the Sheridans called at Thomas Sheridan's lodgings. 'My father a little stately at first,' wrote Betsy, 'but soon thoroughly cordial with his Son.'

Thomas Sheridan had returned from Dublin a sick and disappointed man. He had gone there two years earlier with a new plan for improving Irish education and for founding a 'Lyceum' in which his principles could be applied. For a time the prospects had looked good. Thomas Orde, Secretary to the Viceroy, had drawn up a bill to introduce a National Educational System along the lines of his proposals, and it had been intended that Thomas Sheridan should have the overall direction of the scheme. But the sudden death of the Viceroy and the illness of Thomas Orde had led to the plan being dropped; it seemed unlikely that the next administration would renew it.

Thomas Sheridan could look back on substantial achievements in the last few years – the publication of his dictionary, and in 1784 a massive edition of the works of his first mentor, Swift. But now he had lost heart. Betsy's letters to her sister talk of visits to the doctor and a plan to go to Lisbon to recover his health. The journey was thought to be too daunting and it was decided instead that they should go to Margate to try what sea air could do.

Thomas Sheridan's illness, later described as 'a dropsy', seems to have been the culmination of some kind of digestive disorder from which he had suffered much of his life. The doctor prescribed a diet of slops, but even on the lightest food he had frequent attacks of vomiting; he felt the cold intensely and complained of headaches. He had been in Margate only a few days when a hot-water salt bath, which he had taken against the doctor's orders, brought on a high fever. Sheridan hastened to his bedside.

'It is to no purpose to use many words in communicating to you the melancholy situation in which I have found my father at this place,' he wrote to his brother on 12 August. 'He is I fear past all hope . . . No view of sickness or decay while death is at a distance gives an idea of the frightful scene of being present at the last moments of such a person and so circumstanced. You will prepare and inform my sister [Alicia] in the properest manner. Poor Betsy is almost laid up.'

At the very last, father and son were reconciled. Dr Jarvis, the doctor attending Thomas Sheridan, records how his son watched by his bedside day and night, snatching a few hours' sleep when the doctor was there to relieve him. Thomas Sheridan appeared much moved by his son's attentions, saying, 'with considerable emotion', 'Oh! Dick, I give you a great deal of trouble.' He died on 14 August, four days after his son's arrival.

Thomas Sheridan's old adversary Dr Johnson had died four years before. Their quarrel had never been made up, though shortly before his death Johnson had asked Boswell to tell him that he would be glad to see him and shake hands. Thomas Sheridan had not responded. 'It is to me,' said Boswell, 'very wonderful that resentment should be kept up so long.' 'Why, Sir,' Johnson answered, 'it is not altogether resentment that he does not visit me; it is partly falling out of habit, partly disgust, as one has of a drug that has made him sick. Besides, he knows that I laugh at his oratory.'

Thomas Sheridan's achievements had never been fully recognised in his lifetime. Only in his heyday as manager of Smock Alley and his first years as a lecturer had he known any real success. But many of the seeds that he had sown would bear fruit later. His ideas on education, on pronunciation and the importance of the art of public speaking are as relevant as ever. If he had never reached the first rank as an actor he had inspired the greatest actress of the age and laid the foundations of Dublin's theatrical pre-eminence. Best remembered now as the father of his greater son, Thomas Sheridan has his own claims on posterity.

Sheridan's first wish was that his father should be buried at Harrow, next to his old friend Dr Sumner. But a special provision in his will, drawn up three years before, directed that his body should be buried in the parish where he happened to die and 'in as private and cheap a manner as may be'. The funeral therefore took place in Margate, with Sheridan and his brother-in-law Tickell as the only family mourners.

He took his sister Betsy home with him to Deepdene in Surrey, where the Duke of Norfolk, an ardent Whig supporter, had lent them a house. Mrs Sheridan greeted Betsy affectionately. Privately she had had misgivings about this new addition to her household. But Sheridan, she told Mrs Canning, had been so good to all her family that she could not refuse him.

Betsy Sheridan never guessed that she was less than welcome. Elizabeth, she wrote later, received her like a sister and showed her constant kindness and consideration at a time when she was at her most dependent. She stayed with the Sheridans for just under a year, leaving them in July 1789 to marry Henry LeFanu, the younger brother of her sister Alicia's husband. It was Sheridan who arranged to give her the allowance that made it possible for her to marry; Charles, true to his character as Joseph Surface, had only fine phrases to contribute.

With the first stage in the Hastings trial behind him, Sheridan's most immediate concern was the affairs of Drury Lane. Writing at the beginning of October, Betsy describes him as being 'entirely engross'd by the Theatre'. He had recently purchased Ford's share of Drury Lane for £18,000, though how he had conjured up the money, wrote Betsy, was a secret even to his wife. 'She declares She is often astonish'd at the points apparently almost impossible which he accomplishes. He now says his great object is to make as much money as he can and she is certain he will succeed.'

A month before, on the eve of the new season, Tom King, the acting manager, had resigned in despair.

'Should any one . . . ask me,' he wrote in a letter to the public, '"What was my post at Drury Lane? and if I was not manager, who was?" I should be forced to answer . . . to the first, *I don't know* – and to the last, *I can't tell*. I can only once more positively assert, that I was *not manager*, for I had not the power, by any agreement, nor indeed had I the wish, to approve or reject, any new dramatic work; the liberty of engaging, encouraging or discharging any one performer – nor sufficient authority to command the cleaning of a coat, or adding, by way of decoration, a yard of copper lace; both of which, it must be allowed, were often much wanted.'

Sheridan and Linley, caught unawares by King's defection, were compelled to replace him at short notice. Their natural choice was Mrs Siddons' brother, John Philip Kemble, now coming into his own as the older actors who had blocked his way retired. Sheridan's political commitments and the urgency of finding a manager before the season began gave Kemble the leverage to demand and obtain a far greater degree of authority than King had been allowed. Over the next few years he would establish his ascendancy at Drury Lane, and though there were some who complained of his 'uncommon asperity' behind scenes there were few who doubted his integrity or his devotion to the theatre as a whole.

Kemble's appointment had been made in the nick of time. By early November 1788 it became clear that George III was ill. Suffering in fact from the hereditary disease of porphyria, he showed all the symptoms of insanity. In the medical parlance of the day, the gout from which he suffered had flown to his head. For the next four months Sheridan would be the Prince of Wales's closest adviser in the regency discussions which followed and a central figure in the councils of the Whig opposition. In demand on all sides, he had less time than ever for the theatre. Betsy Sheridan's letters to her sister describe them all as being 'in the midst of news and politics', with the king's illness as the only topic of conversation.

George III's health had been causing concern since May that year. Worn out with hard work and worry, he had complained of sleeplessness and a bilious disorder. A visit to Cheltenham to take the waters had done little to improve his condition. His speech became hurried and his behaviour increasingly eccentric. Anecdotes of his oddities abounded: he had mistaken an oak tree in Windsor Park for the King of Prussia, he had run a race with a horse, he had snatched a courtier's wig and made him go down on his knees to look at the stars. Over dinner on 3 November he broke down in delirium and the facts of his condition could not longer be concealed. For a time it was feared he would die, and the Prince of Wales, in full court dress, sat up at Windsor two nights running awaiting the event.

By the end of the month the king's life was no longer in danger, but his mental condition showed no signs of improvement. Locked in his room and often tied down on his bed, he was purged, bled and blistered by a succession of doctors each more ignorant than the last. In a despairing moment of lucidity he was heard to pray 'that either God be pleased to restore him to his senses, or permit that he might die immediately'. It seemed unlikely that he would ever be fit to rule again.

At Brooks's Club gamblers said 'I play the lunatic' when they meant the king. For Sheridan and his friends, after five years in the wilderness, an intoxicating vista of power and patronage seemed to be opening out. Already they were planning to share the spoils. The Duke of Portland, as leader of the party, would be the First Lord of the Treasury, Fox the Foreign Secretary. Sheridan, according to the Duchess of Devonshire, could have become the Chancellor of the Exchequer if he chose but preferred to progress by degrees and wait till he had proved himself to the public. In the meantime he would have the post of Treasurer of the Navy.

Fox, who had been touring in Italy with his mistress Mrs Armistead, hurried back to London when he heard the news. Arriving on 24 November, exhausted and ill after travelling post haste across Europe, he was soon plunged into political discussions. Betsy writes of her brother as being 'taken up entirely with Charles Fox and the Prince of Wales'. 'I should tell you,' she adds proudly, 'the latter Gentleman has more esteem and friendship for him than for any Man in England.'

Good-natured though he was, Fox was not best pleased to find Sheridan, his former lieutenant, taking the lead in negotiations with Pitt's Lord Chancellor Lord Thurlow. It was taken for granted that the majority of the new government would be chosen from the Foxite Whigs, but it was important to have some legal stiffening from the other side. Thurlow, whose brusqueness and bad manners had earned him an undeserved reputation for straightforwardness, was regarded as the ablest lawyer of the day. Devoted to the king, he got on badly with Pitt and had let it be known that he might be prepared to join the new administration. Fox was far from happy at the prospect. He would have preferred to see Lord Loughborough as Lord Chancellor and agreed to Thurlow only under sufferance. 'I have swallowed the pill,' he wrote to Sheridan on 13 December, '– and a most bitter one it was . . . I do not remember ever feeling so uneasy about any political thing I ever did.'

In the event, Thurlow gave no immediate answer to the opposition's offer, preferring to hope that the king might yet recover. 'When I forget my King,' he said in a famous outburst in the Lords, 'may God forget me.' 'God forget you,' muttered Wilkes, who happened to be sitting at the foot of the throne, 'he'll see you damned first.' 'The sooner the better,' added Burke.

Thurlow's double-dealing was discovered when his hat was found in the Prince of Wales's closet while Pitt was visiting the king at Windsor. By this time, however, he had decided to gamble on the king's recovery, and despite the revelation of his treachery was too powerful for Pitt to dispense with. Fox's candidate, Lord Loughborough, agreed to take the Woolsack in his place; Lord Thurlow, said Sheridan, was a great rogue and a shilly-shallying fellow.

From the opposition's point of view the episode was significant as the first sign of a rift between Fox and Sheridan. It was an impression fostered by Fox's supporters, who accused him of courting the Prince of Wales at Fox's expense. But Sheridan never wished to rival Fox as leader; he was far more interested in being a power behind the scenes. The Duchess of Devonshire, whose journal for the period gives a fascinating background to the regency negotiations, acquitted him of all suspicion of disloyalty. 'I do not mean to accuse him of any duplicity,' she wrote in a preface to the journal some years later; 'in fact He has stood the test of even poverty and I feel convinc'd of the honor of his political sentiments – but he cannot resist playing a sly game; he cannot resist the pleasure of acting alone, and this, added to his natural want of judgment and dislike of consultation frequently has made him commit his friends and himself.'

Sheridan's strongest point was his influence with the Prince of Wales. Mrs Fitzherbert was still furious with Fox and did not fail to make her feelings felt. The Duke of Portland had been one of those who had opposed the payment of the prince's debts in the recent discussions in Parliament; it needed Fox's best persuasions to reconcile them. Burke, so long the mentor of the Foxite Whigs, felt himself excluded from the prince's councils. 'I know no more,' he said sourly, 'of Carlton House than I do of Buckingham House.'

These rifts between allies were exacerbated by the weaknesses in the prince's own character, 'the facility,' as the Duchess of Devonshire put it, 'with which [he] yields to the pleasure of making himself agreable to those with whom he happens to associate – his aptitude to yield over his better opinions to foolish, and even ridiculous counsellors if they happen to convince him'.

There were basic differences too between Sheridan's and Fox's tactics. Pitt's proposals for a regency hedged about with limitations were unacceptable to Fox. Sheridan, on the other hand, thought it better that the prince should take the regency on any terms; there would always be time to change them later.

Matters came to a head when Fox put forward in the House of Commons the doctrine that the Prince of Wales possessed 'as clear a right to assume the reins of Government, and to exercise the sovereign power during his Majesty's incapacity, as he would have in the case of his natural demise' – a remark which caused Pitt to exclaim with satisfaction that he would unwhig the gentleman for ever.

That Fox, the avowed opponent of the Crown, should assert the prince's rights against those of Parliament was a change of position so blatant that all later attempts to gloss it over failed. Privately, Sheridan took Fox to task for raising the subject at all. Fox insisted that it was always better to take the bull by the horns, to which, reports the duchess, Sheridan replied: 'Yes but you need not have drove him into the room that you might take him by ye horns.'

Fox's tactlessness turned the uncommitted members of the House of Commons – the 'armed neutrality', as the supporters of North and Shelburne were known – against him. On 16 December Pitt's resolutions for a bill of regency, severely limiting the prince's powers, were carried by a majority of sixty-four. Two weeks later he wrote to the prince announcing the bill's provisions: with certain exceptions the prince was prevented from making peers (and hence from controlling the House of Lords), while the king's person and household, together with most of his patronage, was placed in the hands of the queen.

The opposition was indignant. The letter, announced the duchess, was 'insolently couch'd'; the fact that Pitt had sent it by a footman was a further insult. But they had no alternative but to accept. Burke, Loughborough and Sheridan were set to work to draft an answer combining dignified consent with a hint of wounded feelings and deliberately addressed not to Pitt but to the Cabinet. Burke's answer was so weightily argued that it took an hour and a half to read; Loughborough's was unsuitably dry and legalistic. The final version, described by George IV's biographer Shane Leslie as 'one of the ablest State-papers ever written', was long thought to be Burke's. The Duchess of Devonshire's diary makes clear that it was Sheridan's:

'Saw Sheridan at Night', she wrote on 1 January, '– he came here tho' he ought to have been writing the Prince's answer – Burke had wrote one he sd, all fire and tow, Ld Loughboro' one, all ice and snow - and he was to make one out of Both – its to go tomorrow.'

He stayed so late at Devonshire House that the promised letter was not ready till two the following afternoon, and there was no time to clear it with Fox before taking it round to the prince. 'I have had a great hand in it, for I copied it twice,' wrote Elizabeth to Mrs Canning, 'and the Copy actually sent to the Cabinet was written by

Me & sign'd by the Prince. I intend when he is Regent to claim something good for myself for *Secret Service*.'

Fox was displeased by Sheridan's failure to consult him.

'When he [Sheridan] came to Charles with the Prince,' wrote the duchess, 'he found [Thomas] Grenville and Fitzpatrick there, and the note he wrote here last night saying he should be ready by 9, pin[n'd] up on the chimney – Charles spoke crossly to him – and s$^d$ something (he won't tell what), to which Sheridan answer'd – I am as God made me and hate personalitys and they have been boudéing each other all day.'

So much activity was exhausting – 'poor S. has not been in his Bed one Night since I have been in town till five or six o'clock; he is quite worn out with fagging so much,' wrote Mrs Sheridan. But till then the opposition's spirits had been buoyed up by the prospects ahead of them. By early January, however, there were rumours that the king was beginning to recover. A new doctor, Dr Willis, 'a clergyman used to the care of madmen', had been appointed. He believed in treating his patients by a mixture of kindness and coercion, even keeping a pack of hounds for them and allowing them to hunt and shoot. His methods, surprisingly, proved successful and on 19 February the Lord Chancellor was able to announce in the House of Lords that the king was in 'a state of convalescence'.

The news was a body blow for Sheridan. Far more than his aristocratic colleagues, he had needed the salary and status that a ministerial post would bring. But he took it with characteristic aplomb:

'He entered his own house at dinner-time with the news,' wrote Moore. 'There were present – besides Mrs Sheridan and his sister – Tickell who, on the change of administration, was to have been immediately brought into Parliament – Joseph Richardson, who was to have had Tickell's place of Commissioner of the Stamp-office – Mr Reid and some others. Not one of the company but had cherished expectations from the approaching change – not one of them, however, had lost so much as Mr Sheridan. With his wonted equanimity he announced the sudden turn affairs had taken, and looking around him cheerfully, as he filled a large glass, said – "Let us all join in drinking to his Majesty's speedy recovery." '

On 24 February 1789, the king was declared to be completely

cured. The following day, by an ironic stroke, a deputation from the Irish Parliament arrived in London to offer the prince the Irish regency with no restrictions at all. They were ridiculed for arriving 'one day after the fair' and, though they were fêted by the Prince of Wales and his supporters, were seen to have suffered a major defeat. Those who, like Sheridan's brother Charles, had been most fervent for a regency would subsequently lose their posts; Charles, a natural survivor, contrived to obtain a pension instead.

In England the king's recovery was celebrated on all sides. The Prince of Wales was deeply unpopular – his extravagance, his dissipation, the rumours of his irregular marriage contrasted painfully with his father's obvious sense of duty, his frugality, his boring but exemplary family life. The opposition had lost the respect they once had as guardians of the rights of Parliament against the Crown – Fox's rash assertion of the prince's inherent right to rule had shown that party politics overrode the principles he claimed to stand for. Sheridan would suffer sorely for his friend's mistakes.

Meanwhile, he flung himself wholeheartedly into the festivities for the king's recovery. The queen and the royal princesses made their first public appearance at Covent Garden, ostentatiously shunning Drury Lane out of disapproval for its owner. But Sheridan, not to be outdone in showing loyalty, was the moving spirit behind a splendid gala evening, with a concert and ball, given by Brooks's Club at the Opera House in the Haymarket. Mrs Siddons, dressed as Britannia, declaimed a patriotic ode he had composed for the occasion and at the end of it sat down to great applause in the exact position of the figure on a penny piece.

# XV

Throughout the thrilling months of the regency negotiations
Betsy Sheridan had been a quiet observer behind the scenes.
Her letters to her sister give intriguing vignettes of the characters
involved. Sheridan 'wrapped in a fine Pellisse the Prince had given
him' setting off to Carlton House to deliver the answer to Pitt's
conditions; Mrs Sheridan sitting up without a fire with Mrs Bouverie
till six in the morning to hear the result of a parliamentary debate and
falling ill in consequence; the Duke of York and the Prince of Wales
arriving at Bruton Street when Sheridan had planned to spend the
day in studying legal precedents, 'both boring him and preventing
him reading the said papers'; Fox surprising Betsy by his plain and
unaffected manners, 'If one did not know that he was a great man,
the idea that one would take up would be merely that he was good
natured and good humoured to the greatest degree.'

Never had politics and friendship been more closely linked. Party
differences spilled over into social life. The Duke of York fought a
duel with a fellow officer for toasting Pitt in the Prince of Wales's
presence. At a reception at Lady Buckinghamshire's the Irish
delegates were groaned and hooted at by the ladies on the
government side – 'what say you to Female Delicacy?' asked Betsy.
Even the servants were involved. When the Sheridans' butler was
hired for the evening for a gala given by White's Club to celebrate
the king's recovery he was treated as a rat by the other members of
the household because he might be asked to wait on Pitt.

Naturally reserved and with none of her sister-in-law's beauty or her brother's social gifts, Betsy Sheridan usually preferred to remain in the background, staying at home when they went out and retiring early to her room when there was company. Occasionally, however, she was persuaded to join in and thanks to this we get a vivid picture of the Sheridans at the last great gala of the season, a grand masquerade – or fancy-dress party – given in honour of the Prince of Wales and his two brothers by a fashionable hostess, Mrs Sturt.

'Sunday, 14th June', she writes, '. . . We went to Hammersmith about ten o'clock – Mrs and Miss Bouverie, a Mrs Stanhope (a very beautiful Woman), Mrs S & I, all as Gypsies . . . Mrs Sturt's House formerly belong'd to the famous Lord Melcombe – The Hall & Staircase very lofty and ornamented with colour'd Lamps – the Duke of York's band playing – We enter'd first a very fine Gallery paved with different sorts of Marble & ornamented with some uncommonly fine pillars, lighted with colour'd Lamps . . . From thence we went through two or three pretty Rooms to a very Spacious Ball Room and then through small rooms again round to the Gallery, so that though there was a great deal of company there was no unpleasant croud. I stuck close to Mrs S— and we unmask'd very soon. She was of course accosted by a great many with an abundance of fine things and I came in for a share of civility.

'About One the Princes arrived all dressed alike 'as Highland Cheifs; nothing could be more Elegant or becoming than their dress. The Prince came up to Mrs S: to enquire for Dick and gave such an enquiring Stare at me that She thought it best to introduce me, for he has his Father's Passion for knowing who and what every one is.

'At two the Supper Rooms were open'd. The Etiquette is always to have a Room for the Prince who chuzes his company, So that neither Rank nor the Lady of the House decides that point. He as usual ask'd Mrs S— and She kept fast hold of me 'till we got into the Room. The Duke of Clarence took the head of the table and the Prince placed himself on one side, Mrs S— at his right hand, the Duchess of Ancaster (as *Hecate*) on his left. I sat next and *le Cher Frère* next to me (who by the bye is always particularly civil to me in Public, unlike a certain sneaking Puppy [Charles] of our acquaintance). Opposite to us Lady Duncannon as a *Soeur Grise*, casting many tender looks across the table which to my great joy did not seem much attended to . . .

163

'When Supper was near over Some excellent Catch Singers belonging to the *Je ne sais quoi* Club sung some very good catches. After a little while the Prince call'd them round and proposed to Mrs S— to join him in a Trio, which She did at once tho' She has not practised anything of the kind for many months and was quite taken by Surprise. The Company as you may suppose were all delighted with this unexpected pleasure . . .

'We sat about an hour at table and then return'd to the Gallery. We intended going home at first, but Dick who came in a black domino put on a disguise after supper and made a great deal of diversion, as he was unknown to every one but us; having plagued several people sufficiently he resumed his Domino and return'd to the company, pretending he had just left a party at Supper . . . After we all unmask'd Dick walk'd about a good deal with us and several of the masks remark'd that having such a Partner it was no wonder he kept by her: I think I never saw Mrs S— look handsomer.'

They returned home at a 'shamefully late or rather early hour', Betsy reflecting that though she had seen the 'Raree Show of the great world' she would be happy enough with her broiled bone and her husband. She married Harry LeFanu a few weeks later, on 4 July 1789. In the evening Mrs Sheridan sang for them – 'the best celebration of a day I consider'd as happy', wrote Betsy – and they parted with tears of affection on both sides.

Betsy would always be grateful for her brother's kindness. 'His tenderness to me I can never forget', she had written when her father died. But she was not blind to the flaws in his character, his tendency to promise more than he could possibly perform, his hopeless unreliability and unpunctuality. It was one of his charms that he recognised them too, as a characteristic letter to his sister shows:

'Ma Chère Soeur, Je suis much disappointed at not having the Pleasure of seeing your fair eyes this morning. I am sure it must be something more than a Hairdressing that has made you break an appointment, tho' possibly my own habit of punctuality, which indeed I carry to a degree of almost ridiculous precision, makes me think more of things than they deserve . . .'

As a member of the household Betsy had also not failed to notice that as far as morals were concerned her brother and sister-in-law had very different ideas from hers. Discussing the subject, Mrs

Sheridan told her that she had managed to convert her friend Mrs Canning, who was 'uncommonly rigid' in her notions, to her point of view. She hoped to do the same for Betsy.

'I assured her,' wrote Betsy, 'that her chance was much worse with me than Mrs C. – for that so far from being *rigid* I was convinced I was *indulgent* to the utmost verge of propriety and that therefore I must *err* to extend my latitude in the smallest degree.' She added that she would no more argue with a woman on such matters than she would with a Mahometan about religion, and the two agreed to differ amicably.

It was true that the circles in which the Sheridans moved took sexual matters lightly. The Duchess of Devonshire, noted Betsy, 'is by no means supposed to be sparing of her *smiles* at least', and was now in love with the brilliant young Whig orator Charles Grey, by whom she would later have a child. The duke was the lover of her best friend, Lady Elizabeth Foster, and the father of two of her children. As for Sheridan, his womanising had become notorious. Unlike Fox, who had inherited Mrs Robinson from the Prince of Wales and whose current mistress Mrs Armistead had started life as a courtesan, he tended to confine his love affairs to the fashionable world. Few people were more mercilessly attacked in cartoons and caricatures – his red face, his drunkenness, his lack of money would be persistent themes. The only sin of which he was never accused was association with loose women, or even the actresses of Drury Lane. In love, as in so much else, his vanity played an overwhelming part.

'Sheridan is a great gallant and intriguer among fine ladies . . .' wrote Sir Gilbert Elliot to his wife in 1789. 'He employs a great deal of art with a great deal of pains to gratify, not the proper passion in these affairs, but vanity; and he deals in the most intricate plotting and under-plotting, like a Spanish play.'

Time and the prudery of the period have effaced the names in most of Sheridan's love affairs. A new passage from Moore's journal, however, gives us a story of Sheridan and Lady Holland, then eighteen years old and just married to her first husband, Sir Geoffrey Webster.

'Shall I tell you,' she told Moore, 'how he made love to me? – he took it into his head that there was something between me & a person, for whom I certainly did not care the least – and he used to say "I can get possession of your letters to —, and I can ruin you by means of these letters, if you will not listen to me favourably" – when I defied this threat he took another most extraordinary method – I was told one day that a servant had brought a message which he would deliver to no one but myself, & before I could order him to be admitted, in entered Sheridan, wrapped up in a great watch-coat & after my servant had quitted the room, rushed up to me & with a ferociousness quite frightful bit my cheek so violently that the blood ran on down my neck – I had just enough sense to ring the bell & he withdrew.'

She added that at the time he was attempting to make love to her, Elizabeth was flirting with Lord Lorne, elder son of the Duke of Argyll, but that 'both of them would willingly have given us up for each other, if they could have come to some explanation between them'. Between love and infidelity and jealousy, wrote Moore, their life was one continual scene.

The links between Elizabeth and her husband were still strong. Together they had conquered society; in the theatre as in politics she had thrown herself into his interests. They had shared and supported one another through family sorrows, and Tom, their son, now twelve years old and studying with Sheridan's old tutor Dr Parr, was equally adored by both. But both were artists, emotional and highly strung. Mrs Canning, Elizabeth's greatest friend, describes how Sheridan would tease his wife into a nervous frenzy, till she was ready to dash her head against the wall – she had seen her burst into tears and leave the room, and then 'the scene changed and the wall seemed fully as likely to receive his head as hers'. And Mrs Crewe, not without malice, described how in their jealousy of one another each would rush to be first at the letterbox at Crewe Hall to read the other's letters.

Sheridan's affair with Amoret had long since ended. 'You know', wrote Betsy to her sister, '. . . that Mrs Crewe among her other Lovers (favor'd ones I mean) has had our Brother in her train. As his fame and consequence in Life have increased, her charms have diminished, and passion no longer the tie between them, his affection, attention and esteem return'd to their proper channel. And he has never seem'd or I believe never was in truth so attached to his wife as of late and this her *dear friend* cannot bear. Mrs S. tells me that while they were at Crewe Hall she took little pains to conceal her jealousy. A strange system you will say altogether and for such people to associate and disgrace the name of friendship is truly disgusting. Yet such I am told is the way of the great world.'

By far the most serious of Sheridan's new romances was his affair with the Duchess of Devonshire's younger sister, Lady Duncannon. Less ebullient but more intellectual than her sister, she appears in her youthful portraits as a slender, elegant figure, with dark eyes and a clever, fine-featured face beneath a froth of powdered hair. (It is hard to imagine her grown middle-aged and overblown as Byron's Lady Blarney, the mother of the tempestuous Lady Caroline Lamb.) Betsy Sheridan described her as casting tender glances at her brother at the masquerade in June; a letter to her from Sheridan that summer, in the playfully flirtatious baby language affected by the duchess and her circle, gives the flavour of the relationship between them.

> I must bid *'oo* good Night, for by the Light passing to and fro near your room I hope you are going to bed, and to sleep happily, with a hundred little cherubs fanning their white wings over you in approbation of your goodness . . .
>
> Grace shines around you with serenest beams and whispering Angels prompt your golden dreams and yet and yet – Beware!! Milton will tell you that even in Paradise Serpents found their way to the ear of slumbering innocence.—
>
> Then to be sure poor Eve had no watchful guardian to pace up and down beneath her windows or clear sighted friend to warn her of the sly approaches of T's and F's and W's and a long list of wicked letters. And Adam I suppose was – at Brook[s]'s! – 'fye Mr S' – I answer 'fye fye Lord D.'

Till then, despite her provocations, Elizabeth had remained untouched by scandal. She had never lacked admirers, the Prince of Wales and Fox among them. She took their gallantries light-heartedly, turning away advances without causing offence. Recently, however, a more persistent contender had become a daily visitor to Bruton Street. The Duke of Clarence, George III's third son, had been serving in the navy in the West Indies when he heard the news of his father's illness and had immediately set off for England without waiting for permission. By the time he reached home in April 1789 the regency crisis was over and with it his hopes that his brother would appoint him to some high post in the Admiralty. His father, though displeased at his unauthorised departure, had allowed him to remain in London, with his own set of rooms in St James's Palace, and had created him a duke. Bluff, boisterous and ten years younger than Mrs Sheridan – he was twenty-six – he had fallen as madly and indiscreetly in love with her as his elder brother had with Mrs Fitzherbert.

'The D. of C. persists in his Passion – and writes me Letters here enough to melt a heart of stone,' wrote Elizabeth to Mrs Canning on 27 January 1790. 'He is very ill poor Man and confin'd to his Bed – and a Person in his confidence wrote me word that his illness was entirely occasion'd by my refusing to answer his Letters . . . God knows how it will end.'

Meanwhile, matters between Sheridan and Lady Duncannon had reached such a point that Lord Duncannon had begun proceedings against them in the Doctors Commons (the ecclesiastical court dealing with divorce). They had been saved from public scandal and humiliation by the Duke of Devonshire, who came home from abroad to persuade his brother-in-law to drop the case. Largely out of consideration for his father, old Lord Bessborough, Lord Duncannon allowed himself to be talked round, and it was arranged that he and his wife should stay with the Devonshires in Brussels till things had quietened down. 'I should not be sorry to hear she had drown'd on the way,' wrote the loyal Betsy.

The drama had blown up while both the Sheridans were staying at Crewe Hall. Elizabeth was naturally much distressed, Sheridan full of repentance and promises to reform.

'But can you believe it possible,' wrote Elizabeth to Mrs Canning, 'that at the very time when S— was pleading [for] forgiveness to me, on this Account, before it was certain that it w[ou]ld be hush'd up, at the Moment almost in wh[ich] he was swearing and imprecating all sorts of Curses on himself, on Me, his Child, if ever he was led away by any Motive to be false to me again he threw the whole family at Crewe into Confusion, and Distress, by playing the fool with Miss Jd (little Emmas Governess) and contriving so awkwardly too, as to be discover'd by the whole House lock'd up with her in a Bed-Chamber in an unfrequented part of the House.

'I confess to you my dear Hitty that this last instance of his duplicity, the apparent total want of all feeling for me, all sense of Honor, Delicacy, propriety, considering the *Person*, the *Place*, and the *time* when he endulged so unwarrantable an inclination – provoked me so much beyond all bounds that I am confident that had the D[uke] of C[larence] been Six & thirty instead of six & twenty I shd have run away with him directly though most probably I shd have hang'd myself a week afterwards.'

She left Crewe Hall, determined on a separation from her husband, arriving back in London to find the Duke of Clarence 'like one out of Bedlam' in the violence of his passion for her. With cooler judgement, she was appalled by how close she had been to bringing 'eternal disgrace and misery' on herself and reproached herself for having danced on the edge of a precipice for so long. But it was easier, she found, to raise a spirit than to lay it. It was only with the help of Fox and Mrs Bouverie (herself, it was rumoured, a former flame of Sheridan's), together with the Prince of Wales, who 'moved heaven and earth to bring him to himself', that the duke was finally persuaded to let her go. She had become quite ill in the process, while the duke, in a state of hysterical despair, retired to the country in a shattered state of health. He would find consolation the following year in the arms of the enchanting Mrs Jordan.

The same friends who had pleaded with the duke on Elizabeth's behalf now set about talking her into a reconciliation with her husband. Sheridan, wrote Elizabeth, had been so terribly frightened and affected by her behaviour, and seemed so full of sorrow for the temptations he had exposed her to – 'wh[ich] God knows how I have hitherto escaped' – that in the end she softened and agreed to take him back. But she had lost all confidence in his promises to be faithful, at least for the time being. 'We are now both descending the Hill pretty fast,' she told Mrs Canning, 'and tho' we take Different Paths, perhaps We shall meet at the Bottom at last and then our Wanderings and Deviations, may serve for Moralising in our Chimney Corner some twenty years hence.'

Meanwhile, with a feverishness that owed something to desperation, she flung herself into a round of pleasures, or 'raking' as she called it. 'Mrs S. is giving great parties and making up for last year's moderation,' wrote Betsy. 'I am sorry to see the Pharaoh table always makes part of the entertainments.'

Gambling was the fashionable passion of the day. Fox, it was said, had been born for the salvation of the Jews (or money lenders). The Duchess of Devonshire cost her husband nearly £1,000,000 at today's values; her sister, though gambling on a lesser scale, was once actually arrested for her debts. Sheridan was often their confidant in these disasters and may well have helped financially too. According to Farington, 'he gave away vast sums of money to women of quality who applied to Him when they were distressed'. He himself was never a heavy gambler, though Elizabeth played deeper than their beleaguered finances could afford. 'Lost my money again, Sir' was a rueful refrain in her letters. The prudent Elizabeth was becoming reckless.

In the spring of 1790 a romantic new figure made his appearance in the Devonshire House circle. He was Fox's first cousin Lord Edward Fitzgerald, a slight young man of twenty-six, who had just returned from Canada, where he had been serving in the army. Filled with Rousseau-like enthusiasm for the wild country in which he found himself, he had completed his time there with an adventurous journey by compass through the forest from Frederickstown to Quebec, where he had been adopted by the Bear Tribe, and made one of their chiefs. He spent only a few months in London before he was called back to Ireland, where his brother, the Duke of Leinster, had nominated him as Member of Parliament for Kildare. But it was during this period that he first met Mrs Sheridan and fell madly in love with her.

For Elizabeth, the adoration of Lord Edward, also ten years younger than she was, but sensitive and high-minded rather than crude and boisterous like the Duke of Clarence, was something quite new. Though Sheridan and she had remained on affectionate terms since their reconciliation, she was ready to be consoled. Early the following year when he returned to London, she and Lord Edward became lovers.

Elizabeth's health had always been fragile. Betsy writes of her frequent coughs and sometimes of her spitting blood, while she was staying with her in 1788 and 1789. She suffered a number of miscarriages and never succeeded in bearing her husband another child, perhaps fortunately as far as her health was concerned. (The fatal illness of her sister Mary had almost certainly been triggered by her successive pregnancies.) In the summer of 1791, however, she became pregnant by Lord Edward.

Mrs Canning – 'Sister Christian', as Elizabeth called her – was so disapproving that she broke off all communication with her. Sheridan, on the other hand, always at his tenderest when his wife was ill, was as solicitous as though the baby she expected was his own. He accompanied her to Southampton, where he hoped the air would do her good, taking time off from a political scene which was becoming increasingly tempestuous. For the last two years the French Revolution had drawn all eyes across the Channel, dividing opinions in England and polarising the Whigs in opposition. While Burke thundered his disapproval, Sheridan had followed Fox's lead in greeting the fall of the Bastille as 'the greatest Event . . . that ever happened in the World!' For the rest of his career his political attitudes would be largely defined by what was happening in France.

# XVI

The king's recovery in the spring of 1789 had left the Foxite Whigs in disarray. Pitt, his authority greatly strengthened by their mistakes, was able to concentrate on the subjects nearest to his heart, the establishment of a sound economy at home and peaceful relationships abroad. The French Revolution at first seemed no great threat to Britain; the overthrow of the old absolutist government was welcomed if anything as a compliment to its superior constitution.

The Hastings trial continued, already something of an embarrassment to Fox and Sheridan, who mistrusted Burke's fanaticism. Burke on the other hand was spoiling for a fight. He had resented Sheridan's pre-eminence in the regency negotiations. As a fellow Irishman, unsanctified by wealth or hereditary privilege, he had been tolerable only in the role of disciple.

The simmering ill will between them broke out in February 1790. The violence that had accompanied the fall of the Bastille and the horrifying spectacle of the mob's march on Versailles had begun to cause misgivings in the average British heart. Pitt had no intention of becoming involved with disputes across the Channel; as a precautionary measure, however, he called for a small increase in the Army estimates. Fox opposed him, using the occasion to praise the Revolution. He was opposed in turn by Burke, who launched into a furious tirade against the excesses of a ferocious, bloody and tyrannical democracy and the wickedness of those who sought an imitation of the French reforms in England. Fox was placatory in reply but Sheridan, who felt Burke's criticisms were aimed at him, was not prepared to let the matter pass. The French Revolution, he declared, was as just as the Glorious Revolution of 1688, and stemmed from far worse provocations. Its excesses, though deplorable, arose from the cruel and despotic system of government preceding them. In describing the National Assembly as ferocious, bloody and tyrannical, Burke traduced the whole French nation.

For Burke the moment of rupture had arrived. The honourable gentleman, he said, had cruelly misrepresented his arguments and 'had thought proper to charge him with being the advocate of despotism'. He had not referred to the National Assembly, which he regarded as irrelevant, but to the 'outrageous democracy' of the republics of Paris and the provinces which held the real power in France. He might have expected greater kindness, if not fairness, from one he had hitherto regarded as a friend. From henceforth he and Sheridan were 'separated in politics'.

A schism gaped in the opposition's ranks. Had personalities alone been involved it might have been possible to patch things up. But their differences were too real for that. Burke, who was beginning to write his *Reflections on the Revolution in France*, was already moving from his earlier position as a reformer and defender of Parliament's rights against the Crown. His view of government had always been paternalistic and aristocratic; appalled at the prospect, as he saw it, of anarchy spreading to Britain, he fell back on the bulwarks of tradition and the status quo. Perhaps his opinions were coloured by the fact that he saw no chance of the opposition's return to power. Pitt, who had begun life as a Whig and a supporter of parliamentary reform, had been pragmatic in bowing to conservative opinion in both houses. Between him and Burke there was no inherent difference of principle. In the new situation created by the Revolution Burke might well find a welcome in the government ranks.

No such considerations weighed with Sheridan. The break with Burke, though it left him visibly shaken, was bound to have happened sooner or later. His sympathy for the Revolution was instinctive. The ideal of liberty, if sometimes too generalised to have much practical application, was central to all his political thinking. Like Burke, he revered the British constitution, but not as something static, rather as open to continual improvement. 'It is the best part of our constitution,' he once wrote, 'that it contains a principle of reform in its very nature . . . Indeed it is a bad compliment to the constitution to say it is a building we cannot touch without danger of its overthrow.' How far Burke had moved from this attitude was revealed the following month when he refused to vote for the repeal of the Test and Corporation Acts (discriminating against Catholics and Dissenters) on the grounds that it was not the moment to weaken the safeguards of the established church. This speech, from a former champion of religious tolerance, said Fox, filled him with grief and shame.

In June 1790 Parliament was dissolved and Sheridan was faced with a new election at Stafford. The contest was hard fought and expensive and though he and Monckton were returned in triumph the government came back with an increased majority.

'I am more than ever convinced,' wrote Elizabeth, 'that we must look to other resources for wealth and independence, and consider politics merely as an amusement – and in that light 'tis best to be in opposition, which I am afraid we are likely to be for some years again.'

As usual Elizabeth's was the voice of common sense. It was in the theatre, not the House of Commons, that Sheridan's best interests lay. But the lure of politics beckoned him on. No sooner had he won at Stafford than he hurried to the aid of Fox in Westminster, where a violent battle was again under way. This time Fox and his former opponent Lord Hood, who had agreed to share the seat between them, faced unexpected opposition from an independent candidate, Horne Tooke. A former clergyman and radical, who had used the example of the Revolution to revive demands for electoral reform, Tooke was one of the few men who could rival Sheridan in repartee. In Parliament, when he later took a seat, it was a different matter and he never held the attention of the House. On the hustings, however, he exchanged insult for insult with a virulence and coarseness that Sheridan could not match. On one occasion when Fox retired from the platform leaving Sheridan to address the crowd Tooke remarked that it was the custom of quack doctors to leave their Merry Andrews (or buffoons) behind them when they left the stage. It was always possible to get a laugh from Sheridan's association with the theatre.

Horne Tooke was defeated. By the time that Parliament reassembled, events in Paris had moved on. Though France was still theoretically a constitutional monarchy, the king and queen were virtually prisoners in the Tuileries. In November 1790 Burke published his *Reflections on the Revolution in France*, warning of its disastrous consequences and deploring the indignities suffered by the royal family. His famous passage on Marie Antoinette was written, he said later, with tears falling onto his page. 'Little did I dream that I should have lived to see disasters fallen upon her in a nation of gallant men, in a nation of men of honour, and of cavaliers. I thought ten thousand swords must have leaped from their scabbards to avenge even a look that threatened her with insult. But the age of chivalry is gone.'

'He pities the plumage, but forgets the dying bird,' wrote Tom Paine in his answering *Rights of Man*.

Burke's *Reflections*, which was reprinted eleven times in its first year, had a profound effect on public opinion not only in Britain but across Europe. His own convictions were still more entrenched, his attitude towards the Revolution had become a crusade. He had refused all suggestions of renewing his friendship, if not his political association, with Sheridan. 'Burke continues quite implacable . . .' wrote a Whig MP, James Hare. 'I despair of a cure. He says it is only the "Dissolution of a Friendship, not the Creation of an Enmity", which You know, is just what he would say if he were determined to poison Sheridan.'

On 6 May 1791 Burke's celebrated split with Fox took place when, during a debate on a constitution for Quebec, each took the opportunity to reiterate their views on the Revolution. Fox, though privately hostile to the *Reflections*, had always taken care to express his admiration for Burke in public. This time Burke went too far, launching into a violent attack on the 'mischievous' doctrine of the rights of man, and by implication Fox's support for it. Fox, in answering, accused Burke of inconsistency in his political opinions and repeated his admiration for the Revolution as 'one of the most glorious events in the history of mankind'.

Burke had reached breaking-point. Fox's speech, he said, had 'ripped up the whole course and tenour of his public life'; he had frequently differed with him in the past, but their friendship had never been affected. This time, whatever the personal cost, he would risk all and, as public duty and private prudence instructed him, exclaim with his last words, 'Fly from the French Constitution.'

Leaning across to him, Fox whispered that there was no loss of friends. Burke answered out loud, 'Yes, there was a loss of friends – he knew the price of his conduct – he had done his duty at the price of his friend – their friendship was at an end.'

For once Fox was unable to speak. In the words of the *Parliamentary History*, which recorded the exchange: 'Mr Fox rose to reply; but his mind was so much agitated, and his heart so much affected by what had fallen from Mr Burke, that it was some minutes before he could proceed. Tears trickled down his cheeks, and he strove in vain to give utterance to feelings that dignified and exalted his nature. The sensibility of every member of the House appeared uncommonly excited on the occasion.'

An anonymous caricature of the time, appropriately titled 'The Wrangling Friends', depicts the scene. Burke, tall and bespectacled, swings away from a black-jowled Fox who has tears pouring from his eyes. Pitt, pleasantly relaxed by the opposition's troubles, leans back in his chair on Burke's left; Sheridan is on his feet on Fox's right calling for 'Order, order'. In the political iconography of the day Sheridan, his nose growing redder with the years, is always shown at Fox's side.

The strains within the party were growing, though loyalty to Fox still held his followers together. Burke remained an isolated figure, cut off from his former friends but not yet acceptable to the Right. Meanwhile, the opposition had been encouraged by a major victory over the government in the debates on Russia's occupation of the Turkish port of Ochakov on the Black Sea. Pitt, who regarded the Turkish Empire as a buffer against Russian penetration to the Mediterranean, had issued an ultimatum to Russia to withdraw and had mobilised the navy. The opposition, however, thought his fears of Russian expansion overdone and in any case outside the sphere of British interests. Fox, Grey and Sheridan denounced the ultimatum in a series of brilliant debates that revived the great days of Whig oratory and came closer to destroying Pitt's ministry than any issue since he came to power. The government was forced to retreat, a decision which Pitt declared was the 'greatest mortification he had

Sheridan's grandfather, Dr Thomas Sheridan, 'doubtless the best instructor of youth in these kingdoms and perhaps in Europe,' according to his friend Dean Swift.

Thomas Linley, Sheridan's father-in-law and co-owner of Drury Lane, by Gainsborough.

Sheridan's father, Thomas Sheridan, probably by John Lewis, the scene painter at Smock Alley.

Sheridan's mother, Mrs Frances Sheridan, also probably by Lewis.

*A Portrait of Two Ladies*
Gainsborough's portrait of
the Linley sisters,
Elizabeth (standing) and
Mary (seated), was painted
in the spring of 1771. The
sittings were interrupted
by Elizabeth's flight to
France with Sheridan.
'It vexes me much; I
could fight about it,'
wrote Gainsborough when
he heard the news.

*Mrs Sheridan as St Cecilia*
by Reynolds. Exhibited at
the Royal Academy in
1775 it was, considered
Reynolds, the finest
picture he had ever
painted.

*Left* 'Amoret', or Mrs Crewe, to whom Sheridan dedicated *The School for Scandal*, from a drawing by Downman in 1777, the year of the play's first performance. *Right* George IV as Prince of Wales. He regarded Sheridan as 'a man that any prince might be proud of as a friend'.

*A Gaming Table at Devonshire House* by Rowlandson. The Duchess of Devonshire and her sister Lady Duncannon (*later* Bessborough) are shown playing faro, the Duchess throwing the dice, her sister taking money from her purse.

'Ye falling of the screen' in the fourth act of *The School for Scandal*.

*A Peep Behind the Curtain at Drury Lane.* The occasion is the regency crisis; Sheridan is shown objecting when the orchestra plays 'God save the King'.

*Mrs Siddons as the Tragic Muse* by Reynolds.

Kemble as Rolla in *Pizarro*, after the painting by Thomas Lawrence.

Sheridan caricatured by Gillray as Pizarro contemplating the riches of his 'new Peruvian Mine'.

Drury Lane Theatre on fire, 24 February 1809.

Charles James Fox.

William Pitt the Younger.

*Uncorking Old Sherry*: In Gillray's cartoon of 1805 Pitt
draws the cork from a bottle-shaped Sheridan to release
a volley of lies, abuse and stolen jests. Fox, in one of the
unopened bottles, is labelled 'True French Wine'.

Sheridan's second wife, Esther, with
their son, Charles Francis.

Tom Sheridan, Sheridan's son by his
first wife, Elizabeth.

The Sheridan portrait at
Clandeboye, home of his
great grandson, the first
Marquess of Dufferin and
Ava. 'It is a cautious
picture,' wrote Harold
Nicolson in his memoir
of Lord Dufferin, *Helen's
Tower.* 'There is no hint
of the candle-laden
atmosphere of Brooks's
. . . nor yet of those
unending brandies and
sodas with which, at late
Parliamentary sittings, he
would wash down
Mr Bellamy's veal pies
. . . Nor would the
observer deduce from this
portrait that it represents
one of the kindest and
most amusing men that
ever lived.'

Sheridan, painted by Reynolds in 1789, the year of
his great speech on Warren Hastings in Westminster
Hall. The portrait was considered an exceptionally
good likeness. 'It is not a canvas and a colour,'
wrote Horace Walpole when it was exhibited at the
Royal Academy that year, 'it is animated nature;
all the unaffected manner and character of the
admired original.'

ever experienced', and Catherine the Great sent for a bust of Fox to display with those of Cicero and Demosthenes in the Cameron gallery at Tsarkoe Selo.

Sheridan had supported Fox, though he was only half convinced of Russia's good intentions. 'For Ma'am,' as he wrote in a playful letter to Lady Duncannon, now back in England and staying at Bessborough House, the family villa in Roehampton, 'if the Empress can gain an ascendancy in Poland and by commanding the navigation of the Dnieper and the Dniester get complete possession of the Black Sea then Ma'am with the future connivance or assistance of the Emperor [of Austria] She may certainly get actual Possession of Constantinople and the European Provinces of Turkey which is all that's necessary and then Ma'am turning the Black Sea into a Wet Dock and floating down her Stores from the North fit out such a fleet when no one can peep at her that out they will come to the Mediterranean, swallow up all the States of Italy like larks, and at last a Russian Brigadier may be quarter'd at Roehampton for aught I know within these hundred years.'

On 4 June 1791, at the end of the summer season, the old theatre at Drury Lane was closed down. For some time the structure of the building had been in a dangerous condition. Built by Wren, it had reached a state when it could no longer be repaired. Undisturbed by regrets for departed glories, Sheridan had embarked on a grandiose new scheme, that of erecting an entirely new theatre, capable of accommodating twice the numbers of the previous one. The proposition had much to commend it in commercial terms; the value of the monopoly was growing steadily as London's population and the demand for entertainment expanded and it made sense to exploit it to the utmost. The same idea had occurred to the proprietors of Covent Garden, who were commissioning the architect Henry Holland to remodel the interior and to increase its seating capacity. Sheridan, going further, had commissioned Holland to design a vast new playhouse; new land to provide the extra space was acquired and £150,000 worth of debentures was issued and taken up by the public.

Pending the rebuilding of the theatre, the company found temporary homes, first at the King's Theatre in the Haymarket, where the vast stage, intended for displays of ballet and opera, dwarfed the scenery transferred from Drury Lane, and then at the smaller Haymarket Theatre, till then permitted only to play straight drama in the summer months. Three seasons were to pass till the new theatre was ready. Building was delayed by negotiations over a third or dormant patent which had been overlooked, and was now largely owned by Harris, the manager of Covent Garden. Its possession, removing the threat of a third theatre, was essential to Drury Lane's new shareholders, but neither Harris nor his co-owners were prepared to part with their share cheaply. While the bargaining dragged on, the cost of ground rents on the empty site and the expense of hiring space elsewhere added greatly to the theatre's burdens, casting a shadow on its future profits.

Kemble, as acting manager, found the delays particularly frustrating. Though given a freer hand than King, he chafed at the difficulties of dealing with Sheridan, who insisted on being consulted on all but the smallest financial decisions and could seldom be pinned down for long enough to give them. Nor would he abandon the task of reading all new plays, though he had neither the time nor the inclination to attend to it. Authors might as soon abandon hope as send their work to Drury Lane.

'Melancholy proofs of this,' wrote Boaden, 'appeared in the piles of long forgotten tragedies and comedies which he had promised to consider and never opened. Mr Kemble, whom I one day found sitting in the great man's library, pointed to this funeral pile and added to his action the declaration of his belief that in these morning attendances he had read more of these productions than ever had or would the proprietor.'

'Sheridan's habit,' he continued, 'was to keep his visitors distributed variously, according to their rank and intimacy with him. Some, like ourselves, penetrated into the library; others tired the chairs in parlours; and tradesmen lost their time in the hall, the butler's room and other scenical divisions of the premises. A door opening above stairs moved all hopes below; but when he came down his hair was drest for the day, and his countenance for the occasion; and so cordial were his manners, his glance so masterly and his address so captivating, that the people, for the most part, seemed to forget what they actually wanted, and went away as if they had only come to look at him.'

Perhaps it was Sheridan's charm, and their admiration for his genius as a playwright, that held his company together against all odds. It was certainly not his business methods. The one stable feature in his procrastinating rule was his reluctance to part with any money unless absolutely forced to do so. Nonetheless the first few years of Kemble's management were a golden age in theatre history. Kemble, one of the greatest classical actors of all time, was coming into his prime, at his best in tragic or heroic roles, above all by his favourite author, Shakespeare. His Shakespearean productions, often featuring spectacular processions, with banners, solemn music and skilfully handled crowds of extras, brought a new element of pageantry to the stage. Mrs Siddons and Mrs Jordan personified the Muses of tragedy and comedy, whilst the elegant Miss Farren ran Mrs Jordan a close second on the comic side. Mrs Jordan shone in bouncing, *ingénue* roles; Miss Farren, who later became the Countess of Derby, had a near monopoly in 'fine lady' parts; no one could equal her in 'the flutter of a fan or the agony of a drawing room curtsy'.

Musically, too, Drury Lane was enjoying a revival. Though the death of Tom Linley had deprived them of one of their most promising composers, new talent had appeared in the person of the young Stephen Storace, with whose family the Sheridans had lodged when they were first married. He had been a friend of Mozart's in Vienna, where in 1786 his sister Nancy had sung the role of Susanna in the first performance of *The Marriage of Figaro*. At Drury Lane his Mozartian opera *The Haunted Tower* had been the great attraction of 1790. Nancy Storace and a young Irish tenor, Michael Kelly, who also sang in the first *Figaro*, took the leading roles. Trained in the opera houses of Italy and Vienna, Kelly and Nancy Storace would raise the vocal standards of Drury Lane to new heights, Kelly in particular making musical history as the first playhouse tenor *not* to sing his high notes *falsetto*. With his mistress, the beautiful singer Mrs Crouch, another rising star at Drury Lane, Kelly kept open house after the theatre; Sheridan, arriving from the House of Commons, and Kemble from Drury Lane would settle more points at such gatherings than in hours of seeking a decision in the day.

Kemble, solemn and conscientious, would unbend at Kelly's cheerful board. 'Come, Kemble,' Kelly would call down the table, 'open thy ponderous and marble jaws and give us your opinion.' For Sheridan as a writer he had an admiration just short of idolatry; only Shakespeare came higher in his pantheon of literary gods. Sharing with Sheridan a vast capacity for claret, which according to Walter Scott he used to take in 'pailfuls', he would drink late into the night; Sheridan, who seldom got up before lunch time, was at his most convivial in the small hours. Occasionally, remembering his many grievances as manager, Kemble would wax indignant in his cups, even going so far as to throw a decanter at his unreliable proprietor. But these were temporary outbursts, soon to be forgotten under Sheridan's blandishments, though once, when he had been more than usually tried, he announced his fixed intention to resign.

The scene took place in Kelly's house, where Kemble, expecting Sheridan's arrival after the House of Commons had risen, had set about fortifying his resolution with claret. 'At length,' wrote Boaden, 'Sheridan arrived, took his seat next to Mrs Crouch at table, looked at Kemble with kindness, but the kindness was neither returned nor acknowledged. The great actor now looked unutterable things, and occasionally emitted a *humming* sound like that of a bee, and groaned in spirit inwardly. A considerable time elapsed and frequent repetitions of the sound before mentioned occurred; when at last, "like a pillar of state", slowly uprose Kemble, and in these words addressed the astonished proprietor; "I am an EAGLE, whose wings have been bound down by frosts and snows; but I now shake my pinions and cleave into the general air, into which I am born." He then deliberately resumed his seat and looked as if he had relieved himself from insupportable thralldom.'

But Sheridan, continued Boaden, 'knew the complacency of the man under the notion of a fine figure; he rose, took a chair next to the great actor; in two minutes resumed his old ascendancy. The tragedian soon softened into his usual forgiving temper; and I am ashamed to say how late it was when, cordial as brothers, I took one arm of Kemble and Sheridan the other, and resolutions were formed "that melted as breath into the passing wind".'

# XVII

On 30 March 1792, Mrs Sheridan gave birth to a daughter whom she christened Mary in memory of her beloved sister. She had been very ill during her pregnancy and at first it was hoped that she would rally after the baby was born. It soon became clear that she was not improving. Sheridan, remembering Mary's illness five years earlier, had few illusions about the seriousness of her condition. He wrote to Mrs Canning, who had always been her dearest friend, to beg her to end the estrangement between them – an estrangement, he insisted, that had been his fault, not hers.

My dear Mrs C. You do not know the state she has been in, and how perilous and critical her situation now is, or indeed you would upbraid yourself for harbouring one alter'd thought or even for abating in the least degree the warmest zeal of Friendship! of such Friendship as nothing in Nature could ever have prevented *her* heart shewing *you*. Pray forgive my writing to you thus, but convinced as I am that there is *no chance of saving her Life*, but by tranquillizing her mind, and knowing as I do and as I did hope you knew that God never form'd a better heart, and that she has no errors but what are the Faults of those [himself and FitzGerald] whose conduct has created them in her against her nature, I feel it impossible for me not to own that the idea of unkindness or coldness towards her *from you* smote me most sensibly, as I see it does her to the soul.

I have said more than I meant, when I have the satisfaction of seeing you tomorrow I am sure you will enable me to heal her mind on this subject, or real Love charity and candour exist nowhere . . .

How could Mrs Canning resist this appeal? How deeply Sheridan felt his own responsibility was revealed not long after when Mrs Canning, as she told the tutor William Smyth, made some slight allusion to Elizabeth's affair. Sheridan, it appears, was thrown into a 'perfect paroxysm of grief and remorse'. 'Oh! not a word of that kind,' he said, 'she is an angel if ever there was one. It is all my fault; – it is I, I, that was the guilty fiend.' He sank into a chair, covering his face with his hands, convulsed with the agony of his feelings.

Lord Edward had followed Elizabeth's pregnancy anxiously, visiting her at Southampton and hurrying to be beside her when the baby was born. The devotion he had shown her, she told him, almost made up for her being so ill. But for the sake of her reputation he was forced to be discreet, and it was Sheridan who was with her in her final months and who would suffer most at the prospect of her death. From Southampton, shortly before Elizabeth's confinement, he had written to Lady Duncannon in a mood of deepest melancholy.

I am just returned from a long solitary walk on the beach. Night Silence Solitude and the Sea combined will unhinge the cheerfulness of anyone, when there has been length of Life long enough to bring regret in reflecting on many past scenes, and to offer slender hope in anticipating the future . . .

How many years have pass'd since on these unceasing restless waters which this Night I have been gazing at and listening to, I bore poor *E.*, who is now so near me fading in sickness from all her natural attachments and affections, and then loved her so that had she died as I once thought she would in the Passage I should assuredly have plunged with her body to the Grave. What times and what changes have passed! . . . what has the interval of my Life been, and what is left me – but misery from Memory and a horror of Ref[l]exion?

At the beginning of May, Elizabeth set off for Hotwells, Bristol, well known for its medicinal waters. Sheridan had persuaded Mrs Canning to go with her. 'There never was in the World a more friendly act than her doing so,' he told Lady Duncannon. 'She has left her daughter and all her children whom she dotes on for this office.'

Sheridan went with them, leaving theatrical negotiations and political commitments in a state of ruinous confusion, but, as he wrote to Dr Parr, 'I can put nothing in competition with my feelings for her.'

Elizabeth bore the journey 'amazingly well', and the local physician, Dr Bain, a specialist in consumptive cases, called on her next day. Sheridan dared not ask him directly what he thought, but took some cheer from Mrs Canning's manner that she might not be so ill as he had feared. Deep down, however, he had little hope, and his letters to Lady Duncannon and her sister, his closest confidants during this period, are some of the saddest and most revealing that he ever wrote.

'I do not feel as if I should pursue my plan of writing to you and sharing the melancholy moments I pass here, for the only time I am away from her at Night I get into such gloomy fits that I can do nothing,' he wrote to the duchess the evening after their arrival. 'I stopt yesterday evening as we came over King's Down, while poor E.'s chaise was going down the Hill – and went to the spot where my life was strangely saved once [after his second duel] . . . What an interval has passed since, and scarce one promise that I then made to my own soul have I attempted to fulfill. I looked at the carriage that bore her down the same road, and it wrung my heart to think over the interval, the present and the too probable conclusion. My nerves are shook to pieces. The irregularity of all my Life and pursuits, the restless contriving Temper with which I have persevered in wrong Pursuits and Passions makes [*word erased*] reflexion worse to me than even to those who have acted worse.'

Any optimism that Mrs Canning may have felt about her friend was soon dispelled by Dr Bain. Writing to her daughter on 13 May she told her that he now considered her a hopeless case; her lungs were completely ulcerated and she would not last six months. She and Sheridan did their best to keep up their spirits before her, but Elizabeth had no doubts as to the seriousness of her condition.

'Ever since she has been brought to bed,' Sheridan told Lady Duncannon, 'she has turned her mind wholly to think and talk and read on religious subjects and her Fortitude and calmness have astonished me. She has put by any other contemplation . . . Last Night she desired to be placed at the Piano-Forte. – Looking like a Shadow of her own Picture she played some Notes with the tears dropping on her thin arms. Her mind is become heavenly, but her mortal form is fading from my sight – and I look in vain into my own mind for assent to her apparent conviction that all will not perish. I mean to send for my son and she wishes for him.'

The fate of her other child, the baby Mary, was very much in Elizabeth's mind. Tom was now fourteen, well cared for in Dr Parr's small school, and Sheridan for all his distractions was a devoted father. But Mary was Lord Edward's daughter. They had talked long of what to do, kissing and weeping over the baby together, and had decided that it would be best if she was brought up as Sheridan's child. The world was tolerant enough of the misdoings of the aristocracy, but Lord Edward was a younger son, with his own way to make, and Mary's position would always be ambivalent. Sheridan was happy to call the child his own, but Elizabeth knew him too well to think that he would be a suitable guardian for her. A few days before she died she wrote her last testament, confiding the baby to Mrs Canning's care and asking Sheridan to sign a promise that he would not interfere with her upbringing.

The final scenes were harrowing. On 26 June Elizabeth took to her bed. Sheridan had fetched Tom from school; her parents and family were called for. On the morning of her death they came to her bedside one by one to say goodbye.

'The women bore it very well,' wrote Mrs Canning to Sheridan's sister Alicia, 'but all our feelings were awakened for her poor father. The interview between him and the dear angel was afflicting and heart-breaking to the greatest degree. I was afraid she would have sunk under the cruel agitation: – she said it was indeed too much for her. She gave some kind injunction to each of them, and said everything she could to comfort them under this severe trial. They then parted, in the hopes of seeing her again in the evening, but they never saw her more!'

Sheridan and Mrs Canning sat up all that night with her, as Sheridan had done for several nights before. At about four in the morning they saw an alarming change in her and sent for Dr Bain. Elizabeth asked him if there was any hope, or, if not, whether he could give her some laudanum to help her through the final parting with her husband, Tom and little Betty Tickell.

'Your brother behaved most wonderfully, though his heart was breaking,' wrote Mrs Canning to Alicia, 'and at times his feelings were so violent, that I feared he would have been quite ungovernable at the last. Yet he summoned up the courage to kneel by her bedside, till he felt the last pulse of expiring excellence, and then withdrew. She died at five o'clock in the morning, 28th of June.'

Elizabeth's funeral took place at Wells Cathedral, where her sister Mary had been buried five years earlier. Though it was many years since she had sung in public she was still a cult figure, the most beautiful and best known of the Linleys. There were crowds all along the way to the cathedral, which was filled to overflowing, with curious spectators pushing and crowding round the vault. Fourteen years later, after attending the country burial of Elizabeth's sister Jane, Sheridan contrasted its simplicity to 'the gaudy parade and show' of Elizabeth's. 'The recollection of the scene and of the journey has always pained me, independently of the occasion itself,' he wrote to his second wife Hecca, 'and has decided me, who am a friend without superstition to attention and attendance on these occasions, to prefer the mode I witnessed this morning – and so shall be my own passage to the grave.'

For Mrs Canning, the crowd that pressed round them in some ways helped to make the ceremony more bearable, distracting a little from its solemnity and helping them to keep their emotions in check. Sheridan, she wrote, remained composed throughout, though there was a wildness in his looks towards the end. That evening he descended to the vault alone, where he spent several hours in prayer and silence beside Elizabeth's coffin before leaving her for ever. A fragment found by Moore amongst his papers gives some impression of his feelings at the time: 'The loss of the breath from a beloved object, long suffering in pain and certainty to die, is not so great a privation as the loss of her beautiful remains, if they remain so. The Victory of the Grave is sharper than the sting of Death.'

Sheridan was forty when Elizabeth died. In more ways than one her death marked a turning point in his fortunes. Essentially a simple person, she had held her own amongst the raffish and sophisticated society in which they both moved. But she had always insisted that she would have been just as happy in a cottage, and she was never taken in by wealth and power. Sheridan's talents and integrity, she once wrote to his sister Alicia, would always place him above those with 'richer purses and more contracted minds'. She had not been able to keep him faithful: how could she match the worldly glamour of Lady Duncannon or Mrs Crewe? Even if she had lived, she could have done little to influence him, for Sheridan was a law unto himself, and there is no evidence that he listened to her good advice. But she had understood him probably better than anyone else, and whether copying out his notes for speeches, arranging music, writing songs, or grappling with the Drury Lane accounts, had given him unstinting practical support. Without her he was rudderless indeed.

After his wife's death Sheridan clung eagerly to her survivors. For Thomas Linley he seemed more like a son than any of his own, and he kept the two children close to him, taking a house near Mrs Canning's in Wanstead, so that she could supervise the baby's upbringing, and withdrawing Tom from school with Dr Parr. Tom, reported Mrs Canning, behaved with 'constant and tender affection' to his father. He had been deeply affected when his mother died; 'but at his age, the impressions of grief are not lasting; and his mind is naturally too lively and cheerful to dwell long on melancholy subjects'.

Lord Edward, in a series of letters to his mother, lamented the loss of the angel, as he called her, and mourned at the necessity of parting with his daughter. But Sheridan, he was sure, would behave generously towards her. 'Poor man, he has gone through a good deal. I feel for him thoroughly; he loved her and feels his loss. I love him for it. I hear he has the child constantly with him. What a comfort it must be!'

The memory of Elizabeth, inextricably mingled with the hopes and triumphs of his youth, would always have a poetry for Sheridan. Kelly, who recalled how Sheridan would cry like a child at a song of his own composition, 'They bore her to her grassy grave', also set some lines of Sheridan's to music, as lyrical and tender as any he had written in their courtship:

> No more shall the spring my lost pleasure restore;
>     Uncheered, I still wander alone,
> And sunk in dejection, for ever deplore
>     The sweets of the days that are gone.
> When the sun as it rises, to others shines bright,
>     I think how it formerly shone;

186

While others cull blossoms, I find but a blight,
  And sigh for the days that are gone.

I stray, where the dew falls through moon-lighted groves
  And list to the nightingale's song:
Her plaints still remind me of long banished joys,
  And the sweets of the days that are gone,
Each dew-drop that steals from the dark eye of night
  Is a tear for the bliss that is flown;
While others cull blossoms, I find but a blight,
  And sigh for the days that are gone.

Sheridan's grief might have been profound – Moore writes that a 'noble friend' who happened to sleep in the room next to him at about this time heard him sobbing through the greater part of the night – but the demands of the theatre and politics were too pressing to be denied and he was soon in the thick of them once more. Socially, too, he sought distraction where he could, drinking at Brooks's, gossiping at Devonshire House and even pretending to fall in love. An encounter that autumn with Madame de Genlis and her beautiful adopted daughter Pamela forms a curious pendant to the story of Lord Edward and his wife.

Madame de Genlis was the former mistress of the Duc d'Orléans, or Philippe Egalité as he now described himself, and had been the governess to his children. In October of the previous year, fleeing the gathering storm in France, she had arrived in England accompanied by his daughter Adèle d'Orléans, and the eighteen-year-old Pamela, who was rumoured to be her daughter by the Duc. Sheridan had met them with a friend the following February. He was immediately smitten – or claimed to be smitten – by Pamela's charms and had spent most of the evening writing verses to her in his very imperfect French. Later, describing her to Elizabeth and Lord Edward, who happened to be present, Sheridan said how much she reminded him of his wife in her first bloom of youth and beauty. When he had left the room Elizabeth, turning to Lord Edward, said with a melancholy smile: 'When I am dead, I should like you to marry that girl.'

In October 1792, four months after Elizabeth's death, we hear of Sheridan's renewing his acquaintance with Madame de Genlis and her charges. He invited them to Isleworth, where he had taken an expensive villa on the Thames. Perhaps Pamela's resemblance to his wife struck a chord in his still-grieving heart, for a letter from Lady Malmesbury to her sister Lady Elliot on 24 October speaks of Sheridan being 'so much in love with Madame de Genlis's Pamela, that he means to marry her if she will have him'.

It is not clear how seriously we should take this story. Philippe Egalité had sent for his daughter Adèle and Madame de Genlis had agreed to escort her back to Paris, intending to return to England with Pamela a fortnight later. On the eve of their departure, she tells us in her memoirs, Sheridan proposed to Pamela, who, 'touched by his reputation and his amiability', had accepted the offer of his hand. According to Madame de Genlis, who favoured the idea, it was agreed that they should marry on her return from France. However, Sir Gilbert Elliot, writing to his wife, says that Pamela rejected Sheridan. More than twenty years her senior, red-faced and sometimes the worse for drink, he may not have struck her as the ideal partner. Even Madame de Genlis, whilst praising his talents as a dramatist and statesman, admitted that he had his faults: 'He had a steady, wide and far seeing mind, but his character was light, inconsistent and lazy. His heart was excellent, his society charming, but his conduct was very disordered.'

Whatever the truth, the matter was never put to the test. In early November, accompanied by his son Tom, Sheridan escorted Madame de Genlis' party to Dover. They parted with feelings of 'inexpressible sadness', wrote Madame de Genlis, though it does not seem that Sheridan suffered any lasting ill effects. As for Pamela, she had scarcely been in Paris for two weeks when a chance meeting with Lord Edward, who was drowning his sorrows in revolutionary politics, put all thoughts of Sheridan out of her mind. Struck by her extraordinary resemblance to Elizabeth, Lord Edward fell instantly and violently in love. They were married shortly afterwards – a marriage which lasted only six years. The final twist in the story came with Lord Edward's death in the Irish rebellion of 1798. Wounded whilst resisting arrest for his part in the uprising, he died in prison, a martyr in the cause of Irish independence.

Long before that, the daughter that had linked his life to Sheridan's had died. Elizabeth's baby had never thrived despite the devoted care of Mrs Canning. She died at seventeen months. Sheridan had been extravagantly fond of her, seeing in her the reflection of his wife. He would linger for hours over her cot trying to amuse her and always brought some toy or ribbon for her when he arrived from London. According to Mrs Canning he was perfectly frantic at her death and for several days would scarcely leave the room where her body was laid out. After the funeral he left for London, returning home a few days later apparently in good health and spirits. 'But however he may assume the appearance of ease or cheerfulness,' wrote Mrs Canning, 'his heart is not of a nature to be quickly reconciled to the loss of anything he loves. He suffers deeply and secretly; and I dare say he will long and bitterly lament both the mother and the child.'

Now only Tom remained, a charming boy, light-hearted and lively, but, according to Dr Parr, incapable of application. Since Elizabeth's death Sheridan had engaged a tutor, William Smyth, a young man just down from Cambridge, to look after him. Smyth's memoirs, a fascinating record of Sheridan's home life, bear witness to his anxious solicitude for his son. It could sometimes be taken to excessive lengths.

'For instance,' noted Smyth, 'it was a severe frost, I remember, and had been long, when down he came one evening to dine after his usual manner . . . and he had scarcely drunk his claret and got the room filled with wax lights, without which he could not exist, when he sent for me and lo, and behold, the business was, that he was miserable on account of Tom's being on the ice, that he would certainly be drowned etc. etc. and that he begged it of me, as the greatest favour I could do him, in some way or other to prevent it.'

Smyth expostulated that all was safe, that there was a servant with a rope and ladder on the bank, and Sheridan, seeing him growing almost angry, eventually yielded to his arguments. He then called for his carriage, saying he must be at Drury Lane that night, though it was already eleven o'clock and the theatre was nine miles off. Half an hour later, when Smyth was just getting ready for bed, there was a violent ringing at the gate.

'I was wanted,' he wrote, 'and sure enough, what could I see, glaring through the bars, and outshining the lamps on the carriage, but the fine eyes of Sheridan. "Now do not laugh at me Smyth," he said, "but I cannot rest or think about anything but this d—d ice and this skating, and you must promise me that there shall be no more of it." I said what may be supposed and in short was at last obliged to thrust my hand through the bars, which he shook violently, in token that his wishes should be obeyed.'

'Never was such a nonsensical person as this father of yours,' said Smyth to Tom when he had left, and both were half laughing, half crying at their fate, for Smyth liked skating as much as his pupil. 'Have a glass case constructed for your son at once', Grey once remarked to Sheridan – a joke, wrote Smyth, which Tom used to quote with 'particular approbation and delight'.

# XVIII

The movement for parliamentary reform, which had lost its impetus since Pitt's rejected bill in 1785, had been revived by the example of the French Revolution. Clubs had sprung up all over Britain, with a view to promoting constitutional discussion. In March 1792 the Society for Constitutional Information, or Constitutional Society, of which Sheridan had been a founder member in 1780, was reactivated by Horne Tooke and rapidly became a focus of middle-class radical opinion. The London Corresponding Society, founded two months earlier by the shoemaker Thomas Hardy, with a subscription of a penny a week, took the debate to working-class level and set up links with similar societies across the country. The liberal members of the Foxite opposition saw the leadership of the reform movement slipping from their hands. In April 1792, in an attempt to take back the initiative, Sheridan, with Grey and other leading Foxite Whigs, formed their own association, the Society of the Friends of the People. Devoted to 'temperate reform' and disclaiming any wish to borrow remedies from France, its objects, set out in its opening address, were deliberately moderate.

*First.* To restore the freedom of election, and a more equal representation of the people in Parliament;
*Secondly.* To secure to the People a more frequent exercise of their Right of electing their Representatives.

These were aims to which Pitt would cheerfully have subscribed a few years earlier. However, times had changed. When Grey announced his intention of introducing a motion for electoral reform in the next session of Parliament, it was denounced by Pitt on suspicion of its being 'the preliminary to the overthrow of the whole system of government'.

In later years the Society of the Friends of the People would be dismissed as something of an aristocratic folly, conceived in a spirit of euphoria by a group of would-be Mirabeaus and never of much practical significance. Symbolically, though, it was of great import-ance. There were twenty-five MPs amongst its founder members. (Fox, still hoping to keep his party together, did not join them.) By giving a respectable voice to the movement for reform it sought to channel popular protest away from more extremist courses, provid-ing a moderate alternative to the outright republicanism of Tom Paine and keeping the subject open in the House of Commons. In the short term it was unsuccessful, discredited by the excesses of the Revolution; in the long run it pointed the way to the Reform Bill of 1832, and Grey, who lived to pilot it through Parliament, would refer to his membership with pride.

In the summer and autumn of 1792 there seemed every reason for the government to be alarmed by suggestions of reform. Events in France were moving with terrifying speed. In April the National Assembly had declared war on Austria, the start of a struggle which would tear Europe apart for almost a quarter of a century. On 24 July, Prussia threw in her lot with Austria and the Prussian Commander-in-Chief, the Duke of Brunswick, issued his manifesto threatening Paris with destruction if the royal family were harmed. On 10 August, with the storming of the Tuileries and the massacre of the Swiss Guard, the monarchy in France was overthrown. On 2 September, as enemy troops streamed across the frontiers, the horrifying massacres in the prisons began; over five days, on the pretext that they were spies and counter-revolutionaries, more than a thousand prisoners were murdered by the Paris mob. Less than three weeks later, on 30 September, the tide of battle turned for France with the resounding victory of Valmy; by 9 October the last foreign troops had been driven off French soil.

No one had been more reluctant than Pitt to interfere in French internal politics, still less to become involved with her wars. Burke's warnings had found no echo in his heart; the strengthening of the British economy and the expansion of her trade abroad remained his main objectives. But from September onwards it became harder and harder to keep aloof. The September massacres had horrified British opinion. Men of property everywhere, from the landed aristocracy to the merest shopkeeper, shuddered at the thought of the French contagion spreading. The National Convention's decree of 19 November, offering fraternal support to all peoples seeking to 'break their chains', did nothing to allay their fears. Meanwhile, the French invasion of Belgium, their opening of the river the Scheldt to commerce in defiance of treaties, the threat to Britain's vital interests in Holland, which the French army was poised to invade, had thrown Pitt's policy of studied neutrality into confusion. However much he might have wished to hold back, the pressure for war from his own side of the House was becoming overwhelming.

On 13 December, in his speech at the opening of Parliament, the king announced that in view of France's policy of 'conquest and aggrandisment' the army and naval estimates were to be increased, and that the militia was to be brought in to deal with the threat of insurrection at home. Fox reacted with indignation. Sheridan supported him.

He hoped, said Sheridan, 'it was not understood that those who rejoiced at the revolution likewise approved of all the subsequent excesses'. The 'formidable band of republicans' mentioned existed chiefly in the imaginations of the ministers who had raised the alarm; if there were any such persons in the country their numbers were as small as their designs were detestable.

As to the question of a war, he should vote 'that English ministers be impeached, who should enter into a war, for the purpose of re-establishing the former despotism in France, who should dare in such a cause, to spend one guinea, or spill one drop of English blood'. He did not regard the opening of the Scheldt as a sufficient ground for war, nor did he believe that the Dutch would apply to the British to interfere on their behalf, unless they had been previously instructed to do so.

Sheridan and Fox were swimming against the tide. Fox's amendment to the king's speech, questioning all its premises, was supported by only fifty votes. Meanwhile the trial of Louis XVI in

Paris had just begun, striking even the most advanced admirers of the Revolution with consternation and dismay. 'God keep us all safe and quiet!' exclaimed the staunchly Tory Fanny Burney. 'If the Jacobins hear that Fox has called him "an unfortunate monarch", that Sheridan has said that "his execution would be an act of injustice", and Grey that "we ought to have spared that *one blast to their glories* by earlier negotiation", surely the worst of these wretches will not risk losing their only abettors and palliators in this kingdom.'

On 28 December, in a further measure of internal security, Pitt brought in a bill requiring all French citizens to register as aliens and authorising their expulsion should it be thought necessary. (A year later Talleyrand would be expelled under the terms of this Alien Bill.) Burke, who had crossed to the government benches two weeks earlier, supported the bill vehemently. He was convinced that there were spies and foreign agents fomenting revolution in their midst, and at the climax of his speech dramatically flung down a Birmingham dagger, which had been concealed in his coat, on the floor of the House. Sheridan spoilt his effect by enquiring *sotto voce* where was the fork, but Burke, disdaining such levity, continued with his peroration. The British Constitution was in danger: 'It is my object to keep the French infection from this country: their principles from our minds: their daggers from out hearts ... When they smile, I see blood trickling down their faces: I see their insidious purposes: I see that the object of all their cajoling is – blood!'

Against such hysteria the protests of the opposition were to no avail. Sheridan, who could not resist a further dig at Burke, suggested that ladies should be exempted from the bill, which would not defeat its object, but show 'that the age of chivalry was not gone in this country, whatever might have become of it anywhere else'.

On 21 January 1793, Louis XVI was executed. The news, which reached Britain late on 23 January, sent a shock of horror through the country. The Court and Parliament went into mourning; the London theatres were closed. (Kemble, who had cancelled the next night's performance on his own initiative, was later berated by Sheridan for allowing foreign politics to interfere with his receipts.) Chauvelin, the French ambassador, was expelled from London the following day. Four days later, pre-empting the British government, France declared war on Britain and Holland.

The onset of war drove the final wedge between Fox and many of his followers. It would be some time before they would desert him altogether – the fascination of his company and the charm of his friendship were still so strong that the Duke of Portland, the official leader of the party, wept at the very thought of leaving him. But they could not agree with his opposition to the war, nor to his protests at the increasingly draconian measures the government was taking to suppress dissent at home. The number of his supporters dwindled in the House of Commons. Sheridan and Grey, the most influential of his remaining followers, made up in eloquence and passion what they lacked in votes.

Sheridan's belief in individual liberty was fundamental to his politics. Opposition came naturally to him, and perhaps his most important role during the long years ahead was to keep alive the ideas of tolerance and freedom without which, as one historian put it, 'what Pitt saved might have been much less worth saving'. Since Elizabeth's death the outlines of his character had hardened. His speeches during this period reflect a growing authority and maturity. His great feats of oratory in the Hastings trial had drawn on a general hatred of oppression and a feeling, rightly or wrongly, that he was on the side of India's suffering masses. India had been far away, its zenanas and wronged princesses had been coloured by his imagination. He was now dealing with reality: war with France and its repercussions at home.

Unlike Fox, who consistently opposed the war, Sheridan was not for peace on any terms. In December 1792, when Holland was first threatened, he had warned the French ambassador Chauvelin that the opposition wanted peace, but not if Holland were attacked. He was certainly against war for ideological reasons, but so too was Pitt. He accepted its present necessity, whilst criticising the incompetence with which it was conducted in its early stages. But his energies were chiefly directed to defending civil liberties at home. During the first years of the war fear of Jacobinism led to an exaggerated reaction. Tom Paine, who had fled to France in September 1792, had been officially outlawed three months later. In August and September 1793, the trial took place in Scotland of two leading advocates of reform, the lawyer Thomas Muir and the Reverend Thomas Palmer, whose chief offences had been to recommend Paine's writings. Their savage sentences of fourteen and five years' transportation respectively shocked even conservative opinion and were strongly condemned by Fox and Sheridan. In May 1794, the Habeas Corpus Act was suspended, amidst furious protests from the Foxite opposition.

It was, said Sheridan, 'the most daring, the most abominable, and most unprecedented' of measures; he should not be sorry to find that 'any minister who should advise his Majesty to pass a bill of this magnitude, should lose his head upon the scaffold'. Pitt assured him coldly that he hoped that no member's head was in danger, since French tribunals had not yet been introduced in Britain.

That summer, after much agonised negotiation, the Duke of Portland, with the bulk of the Whig opposition, made the final break with Fox. The duke became Home Secretary; others who followed him across the floor included the Duchess of Devonshire's brother, Lord Spencer, Lord Fitzwilliam, William Windham and Sheridan's old friend Thomas Grenville. The opposition was reduced to a mere fifty. 'I wish,' said Sheridan, 'that he [Pitt] would take some of our Whig principles from us; instead of Whig members.'

Sheridan had nothing to gain from his loyalty to Fox. The defecting Whigs found themselves amply rewarded, either with government posts – William Windham, for instance, became Secretary for War – or with sinecures and titles. In a powerful speech in answer to Lord Mornington at the beginning of the year, Sheridan had attacked the proliferation of government patronage at a time when the country was at war and taxation pressed heavily on the poor:

'What! in such an hour as this, at a moment pregnant with national fate . . . can it be that people of high rank . . . should seek to thrive on the spoils of misery and fatten on the meals wrested from industrious poverty?' What a contrast was the spirit of self-sacrifice and furious resistance displayed by France, a fury to which they had been driven by the hostility of other nations. Wild and unsettled as the sudden grasp of power had made the French government, 'the surrounding States had goaded them into a still more savage state of madness, fury and desperation . . . We had unsettled their reason, we had reviled their humanity. We had baited them like wild beasts till at length we made them so.'

The French were fighting for their lives; the British, so they said, in order to support the throne.

'The Throne is in danger! – "we will support the throne; but let us share the smiles of Royalty;" – the order of Nobility is in danger! – "I will fight for Nobility," says the Viscount, "but my zeal would be much greater if I were made an Earl." "Rouse all the Marquis within me," exclaims the Earl, "and the peerage never turned forth a more undaunted champion in its cause than I shall prove." "Stain my green riband blue," cries out the illustrious Knight, "and the fountain of honour will have a fast and faithful servant." What are people to think of our sincerity? – What credit are they to give to our professions? – Is this a system to be persevered in? Is there nothing that whispers to that right honourable gentleman [Lord Mornington] that the crisis is too big, that the times are too gigantic, to be ruled by the little hackneyed and every-day means of ordinary corruption?'

Sheridan could not foresee that the war would last for more than twenty years, that France, at present beleaguered, would come to dominate the whole of Europe. It was far easier to criticise than to conduct the war, and Pitt, as a practical politician, used the means of patronage at hand to control his followers. Again it is easy now to say that Pitt over-reacted to the dangers of sedition, but France's slide from good order into anarchy had taken place in a terrifyingly short space of time, and Pitt had the duty, as he saw it, of ensuring that the pattern was not repeated in Britain. But Sheridan's voice was an essential one. His sympathies were always with the underdog, whether revolutionary France or the victims of repression at home; his own incorruptibility, though at times too much insisted on, was beyond question. Amongst the little band of faithful still attached to Fox, Sheridan was perhaps the most persuasive speaker, his eloquence and invective accompanied by a humour that enlivened the often interminable wastes of parliamentary debate. (At a time when speeches sometimes lasted for five hours a joke was something to be prized.) Pitt, according to Moore's diaries, feared Sheridan even more than Fox, while to Sheridan, since the break with Shelburne, Pitt had been the one great foe. Pitt's lofty scorn and hauteur, which crushed even the boldest spirits, could never quell or silence Sheridan. Both respected, whilst cordially disliking, each other, and their verbal exchanges were among the great set pieces of the period.

In the midst of his parliamentary battles, Sheridan had been struggling with the problems of rebuilding Drury Lane, beset by financial difficulties on all sides. On 12 March 1794, after long delays, the new theatre was opened to the public for the first time, with a concert of sacred music to mark the beginning of Lent. Its dramatic inauguration took place six weeks later with a new production of *Macbeth*. Kemble and Mrs Siddons played the leading roles, Mrs Siddons undeterred by being six months pregnant. 'I suppose,' said one wit, 'she means to carry all before her.'

The epilogue for the evening was given by Miss Farren, who, in the guise of housekeeper to a noble lord, showed off the new building to the audience. In obedience to her wand, an iron safety curtain interposed itself between stage and audience, and, on being raised again, revealed an artificial lake and a cascade of water from a tank above. But though these elaborate precautions were reassuring, Miss Farren's boastful challenge to the powers of fire might be seen as tempting fate.

> The very ravages of fire we scout,
> For we have wherewithal to put it out:
> In ample reservoirs our firm reliance
> Whose streams set conflagrations at defiance.

Meanwhile, though the outside remained unfinished for lack of funds, the splendour of the interior delighted the audience. Surprisingly light and airy for its vast size, it was likened to a giant bird cage from the way the lines dividing the boxes converged in the centre of the ceiling. The decorations were in the neoclassical manner; a multiplicity of cut-glass candelabra lit the interior as brightly, said one bedazzled spectator, as the sun at noon. A wider proscenium arch, with far greater depth behind the stage, made possible scenic effects well beyond the scope of the former theatre. The auditorium itself held 3,611 spectators, 2,000 more than previously, and the actors' voices had to project a hundred feet rather than sixty as before. The difference was all-important. With so much distance to command it was inevitable that much of the intimacy between actor and audience would be lost. Henceforth, wrote

Richard Cumberland, there were 'theatres for spectators rather than playhouses for hearers . . . On the stage of Old Drury in the days of Garrick the moving brow and penetrating eye of that marvellous actor came home to the spectator. As the passions shifted and were reflected in the mirror of his expressive countenance, nothing was lost; upon the scale of modern Drury many of the finest touches of his art were necessarily lost.'

Mrs Siddons herself soon sensed how much had been lost by the change of scale which forced on her a bolder, larger style. 'I am glad you are come to Drury Lane,' she wrote to the actor William Dowton when he made his début in 1796, 'but you are come to a wilderness of a place, and God knows, if I had not made my reputation in a small theatre I should never have made it.'

The effect on the actors was not the only consequence of the theatre's greatly increased size. The rush for seats and the frequent overcrowding in the old Drury Lane had the effect of stimulating the public's appetite; the ease of access and the cheerless look of the vast new theatre when half empty were correspondingly discouraging. To gather together some three and a half thousand people, new and spectacular attractions must constantly be sought. It was to Kemble's credit that, thanks to his own and his sister's acting and the splendour of the productions, the popularity of Shakespeare continued unabated. But increasingly as time went by Drury Lane and the newly enlarged Covent Garden edged towards the repertoire of the non-patent theatres (whose right to perform legitimate theatre they continued to deny) in their efforts to attract a wider public. Pantomimes, processions and dashing melodramas played an increasing role; performing animals – horses, dogs, even elephants – were brought on to the stage. 'Why do they take my horses?' asked the proprietor of Astley's Amphitheatre plaintively. 'I never tried to engage Mrs Siddons.'

For Sheridan personally the construction of the new Drury Lane, on which he had embarked with such high hopes, was an eventual disaster. The purchase of the third or dormant patent had cost him an unexpected £20,000; the cost of rebuilding the theatre had overrun the original estimate by £70,000. Whatever the difficulties caused by his carelessness in running the old Drury Lane, the theatre had always been potentially viable. Now, with greatly increased costs and encumbrances far heavier than he had foreseen, he was entangled in such a confusion of mortgages and liabilities that it seemed impossible he could ever extricate himself.

For the moment, however, all was optimism, and Kemble, descending from his Shakespearean heights, applied himself with enthusiasm to providing lighter entertainments. Amongst the most successful was a musical romance, *Lodoiska*, which Kemble had translated and adapted from the French. Set in Poland, with a cast of wicked baron, captured princess and gallant rescuer, its climax was the storming of a blazing castle by a band of Tartars – a sensational scene that nearly ended in disaster on the opening night when the wind blew the flames the wrong way and Mrs Crouch, the heroine in the tower, was in imminent danger of being burnt. Michael Kelly, who played the hero, was rushing up the bridge which led to her tower to save her when a carpenter inadvertently removed a support and he fell to the ground. A minute later, the blazing tower, with Mrs Crouch still inside it, collapsed with a violent crash. Mrs Crouch screamed with terror, but Kelly, luckily unhurt, was just in time to catch her in his arms and carry her, amid 'loud and continued applause', to the forefront of the stage.

After the accident, recalled Kelly in his memoirs, 'Mr Sheridan came to sup with me and I told him I was lucky in not having broken my neck. He left us earlier than usual to go to the Duchess of Devonshire's. The Duchess, who had been at the theatre, asked if I had been much hurt; to which (with his usual good nature in making blunders for me) he replied: "Not in the least; I have just left him very well and in good spirits; but he has been putting a very puzzling question to me which was – Suppose, Mr Sheridan, I had been killed by my fall, who would have *maintained* me for the rest of my life?" '

# XIX

---

L*odoiska*, with Kelly's fortuitous rescue repeated in each sub-sequent performance, was the money-spinner of the new Drury Lane's first season. It was closely followed in popularity by a rapidly concocted piece, *The Glorious First of June*, in celebration of Lord Howe's naval victory against the French. Written, rehearsed and produced in only three days, its climax was a splendid stage battle between the two fleets, whose pasteboard manoeuvres had been supervised by the Duke of Clarence; the future sailor king, now the lover of Mrs Jordan, took a friendly interest in the theatre's affairs.

Sheridan had produced much of the dialogue, handing it over on scraps of paper during the rehearsals. He still continued to oversee new plays for Drury Lane. A collection of manuscripts of plays of this period, now in the British Museum and many of them annotated in his handwriting, show how skilfully he could cut and edit when he wished. But since *The Critic* he had written nothing substantial of his own, though he would often talk of writing a new comedy.

'Not you,' said Michael Kelly to him once, 'you will never write again; you are afraid to write.'

'He fixed his penetrating eye on me,' wrote Kelly, 'and said "Of whom am I afraid?"

' "You are afraid," said I, "of the author of *The School for Scandal*." '

It was no coincidence that Sheridan's playwriting career had come to an end at the time of his first entry into Parliament. It is part of the

Sheridan legend that he lived in a state of continual disorder, that drink, carelessness and indolence were his besetting faults. It was certainly true that his private affairs were chaotic. William Smyth, when he first became Tom's tutor, found him possessed of a large, forlorn and dirty house in Grosvenor Street (he had been evicted from Bruton Street some time before) but living in a hotel as he could not bear to stay there alone; he had two more houses, one at Wanstead, one at Isleworth, but it was doubtful if the rent was paid on any of them. 'It is not to be expressed,' wrote Smyth, 'the rage and paroxysms of fury people to do with Sheridan were thrown into. Letters were unanswered, promises, engagements, the most natural expectations totally disregarded.' So thoughtless was he about money that his faithful valet Edwards once found the windows of his bedroom stuffed with banknotes to keep them from rattling; he had come in drunk the previous evening, and fumbling in his pockets in the dark had used the first papers that came to hand. He owed money on all sides, but was just as often cheated; Moore worked out that for every £100 he owed he paid £150.

Against this background of confusion Sheridan's parliamentary speeches, running to five closely printed volumes, are models of vigour, intelligence and clarity. They might be prepared in bed, where he would retire with box loads of papers and pamphlets and from which he seldom rose till noon, but they represented hours of hard and detailed study. Touching on a wide variety of subjects they were almost always on the side of the individual against the State. As well as his running battle with the government on the conduct of the war and civil rights at home, he spoke against the harshness of the game laws, took on the almost hopeless cause of reforming the royal Scottish boroughs, where the electoral system, even by the standards of the day, was exceptionally corrupt, denounced the cruelty of bull-baiting and the appalling condition of the London prisons, supported Wilberforce in his campaign for the abolition of the slave trade, and continued to press for fairer treatment for Ireland and the end of discrimination against Catholics. He was assiduous in his parliamentary attendances and constantly besieged outside the House by hard-luck stories and petitions. Judging from the fraction that have survived, the number and importunity of the requests with which he was assailed are amazing. Begging letters arrived in an unending

202

stream, asking him to use his interest, now to save a Stafford woman from transportation for horse stealing, now to rescue a poulterer whose stock had been ruined by hot weather, now to fund a plan for reducing the national debt, now to help a destitute family or an army veteran in distress, now to obtain a clerical living or government post for some deserving candidate. When added to these were innumerable requests to do with the theatre, his correspondence alone was enough to swamp a lesser, or more conscientious, man. To keep his head above water in politics, and to run, however negligently, London's leading theatre at the same time, was enough for even his ambitions.

The great event of the autumn of 1794 was the trial of Horne Tooke, Thomas Hardy and other members of the Society for Constitutional Information and the London Corresponding Society on charges of high treason. With the threat of execution hanging over them the trial provoked enormous public interest and sent a chill through even the most moderate supporters of reform. 'If Hardy is hanged,' wrote Grey to his wife, 'I do not know how soon my turn will come.' Their acquittal, thanks to the persuasive powers of the great Whig advocate Thomas Erskine, had removed the threat of further prosecutions, but the danger they had run cast a blight on all reforming movements. The Society of the Friends of the People, outpaced by more extremist groups, was already dwindling into extinction; the Society for Constitutional Information seems never to have met after the trials. The London Corresponding Society and its affiliates lasted longer but was eventually crushed, as much by the weight of public opinion as by government measures.

Sheridan had given evidence for Horne Tooke though he had never liked him personally. He returned to the attack in January 1795 with a motion to restore the Habeas Corpus Act. In the course of his speech he spoke of the 'late trials', remarking on the extraordinary pains that had been taken to obtain convictions and ridiculing the evidence which had been put forward:

'On the first trial one pike was produced, and afterwards withdrawn from mere shame. A formidable instrument was talked of to be employed against the cavalry; it appeared upon evidence to be a teetotum in a window in Sheffield. There was a camp in a back shop, an arsenal provided with nine muskets and an exchequer containing £10 and one bad shilling – all to be directed against the whole armed force and established Government of Great Britain.'

The 'bad shilling' was a typical Sheridan touch, but the underlying tone was serious. He knew that there was little hope of the motion being carried, but he was wholly in earnest about the principle involved. The question, he said, was not whether the Habeas Corpus Act should be suspended for a certain period, but that it should be suspended at all. Once this was admitted, there was no situation in which the government would not be provided with some argument for 'suspending this chief bulwark of the rights and liberties of Englishmen'.

The motion was defeated but the speech had carried weight, and Pitt, quick to sense the current of opinion in the House, agreed that the act should not be suspended between Parliamentary sessions. It was a partial victory for the Foxite opposition, but there were soon new measures to oppose. On 29 October 1795, when the king was on his way to Westminster for the opening of Parliament, his carriage was mobbed by a huge crowd in the Mall and the window broken by a shot. Pitt's enemies declared that he had deliberately engineered the incident in order to tighten up security at home, but though this was unlikely the government was quick to exploit it.

In the House of Lords Lord Grenville (Thomas Grenville's elder brother) introduced the Treasonable Practices Bill, by which even those who spoke or wrote against the constitution came under penalties for treason and might be transported for seven years. As Fox exclaimed indignantly, if he criticised a system which allotted two members to Old Sarum and none to Manchester, he might be sent to Botany Bay. In the Commons Pitt moved the Seditious Meetings Bill, proposing that before any meeting of more than fifty citizens which was not convened by the local authorities notice must be given to a magistrate, who would also have the power to stop any meeting and order the arrest of the speaker. 'To have recourse to such laws,' cried Sheridan, 'was characteristic of a feeble and cruel policy, equally impotent as detestable . . . We tell the country that if these bills pass the Constitution is lost! Good God! What a situation they were reduced to! A system of terror was begun, they were going to be trampled under the feet of a new Robespierre.'

The bills were passed but in the event there was little need to enforce them. Economic distress, rather than Jacobinism, had lain behind the last disturbance. The ideological ferment initiated by the French Revolution was subsiding. The overthrow of Robespierre in July 1794 had brought the reign of terror to an end. The ideals, however distorted, on which the Revolution had been based had ceased to be an inspiration. Power in France had passed to lesser men, cynics rather than fanatics, committed to continue the war, since without it they could not control the army or prevent a royalist reaction. France could now be seen, once more, as the traditional enemy of Britain; even those who, like the Corresponding Societies, continued to press for reform made it clear that they would fight to the death against invasion. In this atmosphere the opposition's criticisms of the government and supposed sympathy with France were regarded as almost traitorous. Gillray's caricatures of the period abound in hostile images of Fox and Sheridan, now bartering their country for bags of gold, now shooting at a target shaped like George III. Fox, black-browed and corpulent, is generally the central figure; Sheridan, red-faced and carrying a bottle, supports him drunkenly.

Sheridan's drinking was nothing new, but its effects were now clearly visible in his ruined looks. His fine dark eyes were as brilliant as ever, but his cheeks were pimpled and the lower part of his face had grown coarse and heavy; he looked, it was said, like the old lion Hector in the zoo. Elizabeth's beloved Sheri, the romantic young man who had fought two duels for her sake and won her in the teeth of opposition from their parents, was becoming the Old Sherry of Gillray's cartoons; in the most famous of them, 'Uncorking Old Sherry', Pitt draws the cork from a bottle-shaped Sheridan to release a volley of slanders, lies and stolen jests. Sheridan was used to verbal criticism and usually gave as good as he got; such visual abuse could only be endured. Vain as he was, he was not prepared to give up drinking for the sake of his looks. In any case, he had lost none of his charm – 'there has been nothing like it since the days of Orpheus', wrote Byron – and was as interested as ever in amorous pursuits.

He was seldom coarse in conversation, and his poems, if not political or satirical, generally gave a romantic, idealised view of love. One poem, however, 'The Geranium', has found its way into various collections of erotic verse.

In the close covert of a grove
By nature formed for scenes of love,
Said Susan in a lucky hour:
'Observe yon sweet geranium flower.
How straight upon its stalk it stands,
And tempts our violating hands,
Whilst the soft bud, as yet unspread,
Hangs down its pale declining head.
Yet soon as it is ripe to blow
The stem shall rise, the head shall glow.'
'Nature,' said I, 'my lovely Sue,
To all her followers lends a clue . . .

The poem was not printed in his lifetime, and it is not clear at what point it was written. But it certainly shows a lively interest in the other sex; in later life his womanising was as much a part of his reputation as his drinking. In 1807 the painter Joseph Farington, in his diary, says that Thomas Lawrence had been at a dinner party with Samuel Rogers and others, at which Sheridan's profligacy with women was much talked of and many examples of it were mentioned; it was even said that a woman with any character to lose scarcely dared be left alone in a room with him.

But this was in the future. In 1795, three years after Elizabeth's death, Sheridan married again. His bride was a Miss Esther Ogle, daughter of the Dean of Winchester. She was nineteen, he was forty-three. They met at a party at Devonshire House; Miss Ogle, who prided herself on saying the first thing that came into her head, called out, 'Keep away, you fright, you terrible creature!' when Sheridan, whom she had never met, came close to where she was sitting.

Sheridan was piqued. 'He resolved that she should feel his power,' wrote Smyth, 'so after some little contrivance he obtained a more civil word from her; at the next party a little conversation. Then she proclaimed that though quite a monster he was very clever; then that though to be sure ugly enough, he was very agreable. It then occurred to her more forcibly than at first that he was one of the most celebrated men in the kingdom; and that to make a conquest of such a man . . . was not at all unpleasant.'

In the end it was a love match on both sides, with Esther declaring that Sheridan was 'the handsomest and honestest man in England'. As for Sheridan, he doted on Esther, or 'Hecca' as he named her.

Tall, with green eyes and dark hair, she was his 'soul's beloved', his 'only delight in life', 'prettiest of all my eyes ever thought pretty, dearest of all that was ever dear to my heart'. His friends were less enthusiastic. Fox, who had loved Elizabeth, had little in common with the pert new wife, and one more link between Sheridan's two men weakened. George Canning, Mehitabel Canning's nephew, who had recently entered Parliament under Pitt's protection but remained devoted to Sheridan as a family friend, found her eccentric to the point of oddity.

'She is not very pretty, I think,' he wrote when Sheridan first introduced him to her, 'but wilder and more strange in her air, dress, and manners than anything human, or at least anything female than I ever saw.' He was forced to admit, however, that there was something interesting and animated in her countenance: 'Her friskiness and vivacity if they were not carried to such an excess as to look like impudence, would have an air of innocence not unpleasing.'

For Sheridan this vivacity was part of Hecca's attraction. She was neither beautiful nor talented as Elizabeth had been, but she was good-hearted and high-spirited and above all had the charm of youth. He was renewed by his love for her. She might be eccentric, she was extravagant and frivolous, with none of Elizabeth's common sense or understanding of her husband's interests. But she made no claims to be better than she was, and there is something touching in her self-assessment, written shortly after Sheridan's death, in a letter to his sister Alicia LeFanu: 'I am not handsome, I am full of faults and very ignorant. I have a tolerable heart, and not a little mind, and I adore merit in others and that is all that I can say for myself.'

Sheridan and Hecca might be deeply in love, but this time he was marrying into the gentry, not a music master's daughter. Her father, the Dean, had no intention of letting his daughter be married without a suitable financial settlement. She had a dowry of £8,000; Sheridan agreed to settle a further £12,000 on her, to be held in trust with Charles Grey and the brewer Samuel Whitbread, both cousins of hers, as trustees. Somehow he contrived to find the money; Moore, in his journal, suggests that he raised it on the Linleys' shares in Drury Lane in return for annuities which were never paid. The Dean was sufficiently cautious to insist that the funds should be safely lodged with the bankers before the marriage could take place. Some £12,000 of the settlement was later used to buy the estate of Polesden Lacey, near Leatherhead in Surrey, where Sheridan flung himself with enthusiasm into the role of country squire. To his credit he bound himself not to touch the interest on the capital till it had doubled; whatever his own financial problems, Hecca's trust would stay intact.

Tom, now aged nineteen, received the news of his father's impending marriage in characteristic fashion. He was staying with his tutor at Bognor when a letter came from Sheridan instructing him to meet him for dinner in Guildford at six o'clock the following Wednesday; he particularly wanted to speak to him. Tom set out in high delight, having decided with his tutor that his father was planning to find him a seat in Parliament or an heiress. ('Take a wife', his father used to tell him, to which Tom answered: 'Whose, sir?') After nearly a week, Smyth got a letter from his pupil:

'Here I am and have been and am likely to be. My father I have never seen, and all I can learn of him is, that instead of dining with me at six on Wednesday last, he passed through Guildford on his way to London, with four horses and lamps, about twelve. I have written to him letter after letter, to beg he will send me his orders, for I have only a few shillings left, having paid the turnpike faithfully; and I am so bored and wearied out with being here, and seeing neither father nor money, nor anything but the stable and the street, that I almost begin to wish myself with you and the books again.'

Several weeks went by, and Smyth, marooned in Bognor, with no money to pay the bills and his salary a year overdue, was beginning to despair of any news, when a second letter came from Tom.

'It is not I that is to be married, nor you. Set your mind at rest, it is my father himself; the lady a Miss Ogle, who lives at Winchester . . . About my own age; better me to marry her, you will say. I am not of that opinion. My father talked to me two hours last night, and made out to me that it was the most sensible thing he could do. Was not this very clever of him? Well, my dear Mr Smyth, you should have been tutor to him, you see. I am incomparably the most rational of the two.'

Hecca got on very well with Tom. She called herself his 'aged parent' but treated him more like a brother. She always insisted that his interests should be looked after; her own son, Charles, born the year after her marriage, would have her marriage settlement to rely on. 'I trust you will be able to do something positive for Tom about money,' she wrote to Sheridan a few years later, when Tom's future was being discussed. 'I am willing to make any sacrifice in the world for that purpose and to live in any way whatever.'

Sheridan was married at Southampton on 27 April 1795. The ceremony had been deferred to take place after the marriage of the Prince of Wales to Caroline of Brunswick, an ill-omened occasion which ended with the prince falling drunk into the grate on their wedding night. Sheridan's own marriage would have disastrous ups and downs, and poor Hecca had as much or more to suffer than Elizabeth. But nothing could be happier than its opening stages, a honeymoon at Wanstead and a summer spent boating with her family on the river at Southampton. Sailing with Hecca by his side, in a little cutter called the Phaedria (after the magic boat in *The Faerie Queene*), Sheridan could forget his debts, the theatre and the House of Commons for a while. A friend who happened to be staying, the poet William Bowles, captured the pleasure of the moment in verses Sheridan particularly admired:

> Smooth went our boat upon the summer seas,
> Leaving (for so it seem'd) the world behind,
> Its cares, its sounds, its shadows: we reclin'd
> Upon the sunny deck, heard but the breeze . . .

Returning to London after his honeymoon, Sheridan found the House of Commons plunged into a discussion of the Prince of Wales's debts, which amounted to a staggering £600,000. Having married a Protestant princess and broken with Mrs Fitzherbert because his father would not pay his debts on any other terms, he now expected his reward. Opinions were divided as to whether the debts should be settled gradually from the increased income of his new establishment as a married man, or whether Parliament should bear the brunt of them at once. The government favoured the first solution. Sheridan hedged his bets. On the one hand, he said, the debts 'ought to be paid immediately, for the dignity of the country and the Prince'; on the other, the public should not be burdened by a hair's weight with their payment. He would not vote upon the question either way, as he had not yet made up his mind.

Pitt, affecting to ignore the reason for his recent absence, rebuked him coldly for his indecision. He 'must take the liberty to say, that if the honourable gentleman had given his attendance to the former discussions on the subject, as he ought to have done . . . he would have heard enough to make up his mind upon.'

'It was unnecessary,' said Sheridan, 'for him to state to the house the reasons which prevented his attendance, and were he to state them, they most probably would be unintelligible to that right honourable gentleman' – a thrust which was received with boisterous guffaws from the opposition side. Pitt's bachelor status was a favourite stick to beat him with. Whig satirists, reflecting on his seeming indifference to women, attributed it uncharitably to impotence. Fresh from his honeymoon and in high good humour, Sheridan was happy to repeat the taunt.

# XX

On 19 November 1795, Thomas Linley died at the age of sixty-two. He had never really recovered from the death of Elizabeth, the fifth of his adult children to die before him and perhaps the dearest of them all. Forced by ill health to give up the musical directorship of Drury Lane, he was thrown back on the company of his wife, with whom he was on increasingly acrimonious terms. Mrs Linley had grown no less garrulous or vulgar with age and the two of them would sit at opposite sides of the fireplace '*groaning* against each other'.

The family had suffered yet another tragedy when in October 1793 Richard Tickell had fallen to his death from the window of his apartment at Hampton Court. Subject to fits of depression, despite his genial exterior, and unhappily married to a second wife, he had probably flung himself over deliberately. Sheridan, however, used his influence to prevent an official inquiry and the matter was treated as an accident. Thereafter he took a continuing interest in Tickell's wife and children. The two boys were found places in the Navy and the East India Company, while Betty, the youngest, was sent to a boarding school in Bath run by a family friend.

Linley named Sheridan his executor, a touching if misguided proof of his faith in his son-in-law's financial abilities. On paper it was a logical decision. Most of his estate was directly or indirectly tied up in Drury Lane, his shares in the theatre itself and the properties in Bath which he had mortgaged to buy them in the first place. Neither source of income was certain, above all in Sheridan's hands, and Mrs Linley and her three surviving children were sometimes as hard put as any of his leading actors to get the money that was due to them.

Already the optimism with which Drury Lane had opened was giving way to something approaching desperation. Despite its opening successes the burden of debt incurred in building the new theatre was proving increasingly difficult to carry; Sheridan's borrowings for his own expenses drained the treasury still further. For Kemble, strictly honest and straightforward, 'a child even in the forms of business', the strains of his position as manager were proving intolerable. Tradesmen, doubting their chances of repayment from the treasurer, took to demanding pledges from him before they would supply goods; actors and workmen, with equal trust in his good faith, would do the same. Kemble's good nature and his devotion to the theatre led him to sign a number of such guarantees, which for a time were honoured by the treasury. But when one day he found himself arrested for debt his indignation was extreme. It was the last in a series of exasperations and at the end of April 1796, only two years after the reopening, he resigned his post as manager. Before this, however, he had been involved in one of Drury Lane's most sensational fiascos, the so-called Shakespearean tragedy of *Vortigern*.

Since the beginning of 1795 the learned world had been humming with news of a remarkable discovery: a cache of previously unknown works by Shakespeare. Their discoverer had been a seventeen-year-old attorney's clerk, William Henry Ireland, who claimed to have found them in the attic of an unnamed friend. The documents, like the attic, were fictitious, but tantalising scraps of writing were produced to whet the appetites of Shakespearean scholars. Written on parchment cut off from the foot of ancient legal deeds, they owed their inspiration to the forgeries of Thomas Chatterton, whose suicide in a garret at the age of seventeen had helped to establish his legend as a neglected genius. William Henry, who also felt himself neglected, though he was certainly not a genius, was amazed by the success of his deception. When Boswell, who came to inspect them, fell down on his knees before the samples he had produced for him, exclaiming, 'I now kiss the invaluable relics of our bard; and thanks to God that I have lived to see them', William Henry was scarcely able to believe his ears.

The crowning discovery of all was said to be the unknown tragedy of *Vortigern*, which Sheridan, topping rival bids from Covent Garden, had accepted sight unseen for Drury Lane. The task of forging five acts, as well as composing them, was too much for even William Henry's powers. He contented himself with producing a 'transcript' of the supposed original, counting every line of one of Shakespeare's plays (his *Confessions* do not say which) in order to keep to the same length. Alas, he had chosen one of Shakespeare's longest plays and when Sheridan was presented with the final copy he remarked that the purchase of the play was at any rate a good one, as there were two and a half instead of one.

*Vortigern* was finished in two months, but in the interval the actors showed signs of getting cold feet. The unbelievers were gathering their forces, early supporters were having second thoughts and skits were appearing almost daily in the press. As for Sheridan, the more he read of the play the more dubious he became. Putting down the manuscript he observed thoughtfully: 'There are certainly some bold ideas but very crude and ill digested. It is very odd; one would be led to think that Shakespeare must have been very young when he wrote the play.'

Rehearsals got under way slowly. Public scepticism was growing and a pamphlet by the great Shakespearean scholar Edmund Malone condemning the papers as forgeries was at the printer's waiting to be published. Mrs Siddons, who was to have played the heroine Rowena, developed a convenient illness, while Kemble, who had unwillingly agreed to take the title role, announced his intention of putting on the first performance on April Fool's Day.

This dastardly plan was foiled and the first night was in fact on 2 April 1796. Two days before, Malone's pamphlet, totally damning, was published to the confusion of William Henry and the pro-Shakespearean party. *Vortigern* therefore took on the status of a test case, and every seat in the theatre was sold out, as the cynical Sheridan had foreseen. Public curiosity would certainly fill the house for the night, even at inflated prices, for, 'you know,' said Sheridan to Kemble, 'every Englishman considers himself as good a judge of Shakespeare as of his pint of porter'.

On the first night the Duke of Clarence, with Mrs Jordan, was in the royal box. William Henry, whose state of nerves can be imagined, watched anxiously from behind the scenes. The prologue stated the case:

No common cause your verdict now demands;
Before the court immortal Shakespeare stands.

The first two acts went fairly well, with polite attention from the audience. The trouble started in the third when the piping voice of a minor actor, Mr Dignum, who called for trumpeters to 'bellow on' had the house in fits of laughter. Worse was to follow in the fourth with the death of the Saxon general Horsus. Stricken by the fatal blow, he 'so placed his unfortunate carcass that on the falling of the drop-curtain he was literally divided between the audience and his brethren of the sock and buskin'. Groaning beneath the weight, he struggled to extricate himself, 'which for a dead man,' wrote William Henry, 'was something in the style of Mr Bannister jun. in The Critic, who tells Mr Puff that he "cannot stay there dying all night".'

From then on *Vortigern* was doomed. Kemble, abandoning all attempts to play it seriously, dealt it the *coup de grâce* when in the final act, in 'the most sepulchral tone of voice possible', he uttered the words 'And when this solemn mockery is o'er . . .', laying such peculiar stress on the line as to make it the cue for a howl of execration from the pit. The clamour continued for ten minutes, till Kemble, calling for silence, stepped forward and with 'even more solemn grimace' repeated the offending lines.

Kemble's deliberate guying of his part effectively brought the great Shakespearean controversy to an end. Sheridan, who had hoped that continuing uncertainty about its authorship would ensure the play a lengthy run, was much displeased. Taken off after only one performance, it had involved the theatre in a considerable loss. As a manager Kemble might have deplored this; as a lover of Shakespeare, forced to undertake the play against his will, he was unrepentant. In any case his patience with Sheridan was coming to an end. He had already been threatening to resign for several months. His arrest for debt was the final indignity and this time he carried out his threat in earnest.

Kemble's resignation as manager at least had the good effect of releasing his energies as an actor. After much hard bargaining he agreed to go on playing leading roles, leaving a lesser actor, Richard Wroughton, to take on the thankless task of management in his place. 'The distracted state of the concern was obvious from the very playbills,' wrote Boaden, 'and Wroughton was, perhaps, as little the object of envy as manager ever was.' Sheridan, however, had lost none of his capacity to pull rabbits out of a hat, and the following season, to the amazement of everyone except himself, saw three sensational successes at Drury Lane.

The first of them, *The Castle Spectre*, was written by Matthew or 'Monk' Lewis, whose gothic bestseller *The Monk* had appeared two years before. Complete with ghosts and gloomy dungeons, it ran a record forty-seven nights in its first season. 'It is a vile thing,' noted Kemble, who had played the hero, 'but the audience applauded very much.' Sheridan shared his low opinion of the play; when, in the course of an argument with Lewis, the author offered to bet him all it had made for Drury Lane, he answered that he could not afford it. 'But I'll tell you what,' he added, 'I'll bet you all it is worth.'

*Blue Beard*, the second success of the season, was a musical version of Perrault's fairy tale. Elaborately got up, the stage directions called for a procession, with elephants, through a mountain pass and a thrilling glimpse of Blue Beard's chamber, a sepulchral apartment, filled with tombs and 'streaked with vivid streams of Blood . . . in the midst of which ghastly and supernatural forms are seen'; in the centre was a skeleton seated on a tomb, with the words 'THE PUNISHMENT OF CURIOSITY' in characters of blood above his head.

The gothic thrills of *The Castle Spectre* and *Blue Beard* reflected one aspect of the transition to romanticism which was beginning to take place in the theatre as in every other branch of the arts. Another very different aspect of the same movement was reflected in the third great success of the season, Kotzebue's play *The Stranger*.

'The eager fancy for German sentiment, which was then steadily increasing,' writes Kemble's Victorian biographer Percy Fitzgerald, 'might seem to us almost incomprehensible. The sickly perversion of all moral relations which pervaded it ought to have been foreign to British tastes.' Incomprehensible or not, there was a growing passion for German drama and the works of Kotzebue, translated by various hands, became immensely popular; between 1796 and 1801 twenty of his plays were published in England. Mrs Inchbald wrote a translation of his *Lover's Vows*, for ever celebrated as the play whose proposed performance so shocked Sir Thomas Bertram in *Mansfield Park*. By the standards of the time the plot of *The Stranger*, in which a wife who has deserted her husband and children for a lover is finally reunited with her husband, was equally immoral. Adultery was being condoned. It would not be long, complained one critic, before 'not a child in England will have its head patted by its legitimate father'. Nevertheless the play, with Mrs Siddons as Mrs Haller, the repentant wife, and Kemble, the Stranger, as her husband, stirred emotions untouched by English writers of the day. Romantic sensibility ran riot in the final scene:

> MRS HALLER. Forget a wretch who will never forget you – and
> when my penance shall have broken my heart – when we
> again meet in a better world –
> STRANGER. There, Adelaide, you shall be mine again.
> *They part weeping, but as they are going, she encounters the Boy and
> the Girl*
> CHILDREN. Dear father! Dear mother!
> *They press the children in their arms with speechless affection; then tear
> themselves away – gaze at each other – spread their arms and rush
> into an embrace. The children run and cling round their parents, the
> curtain falls.*

Kemble, released from the cares of management, was able to give his all to the part of the Stranger. Friends who visited him while he was studying it found him deep in 'gloomy abstraction' and displaying an unusual carelessness in his dress. 'He brooded over the recollection of disappointed hope till it became part of himself . . .' wrote Hazlitt. 'The weight of sentiment which oppressed him was never suspended: the spring at his heart was never lightened – it seemed as if his whole life had been a suppressed sigh!'

Sheridan, who had taken a close interest in the play – he claimed to have rewritten most of it – also wrote a song for it, which the Duchess of Devonshire set to music:

> I have a silent sorrow here,
> A grief I'll ne'er impart.
> It breathes no sigh, it sheds no tear,

But it consumes my heart.
This cherished woe, this loved despair,
My lot for ever be,
So my soul's lord, the pangs I bear
Be never known by thee.

Green-room gossips had it that during rehearsals he pointed to his pocket and was heard to mutter: 'I have a silent bottle here.'

Sheridan was well pleased with his theatrical successes, which brought a welcome boost to Drury Lane's finances. But they had taken place against the background of a national situation more alarming than any since the beginning of the war. One by one Britain's allies had made a separate peace with the French Republic. By April 1797, with a financial crisis and naval mutinies at home, with Ireland teetering on the brink of rebellion, and invasion threatening from the Low Countries, Britain confronted France alone.

Pitt had begun the war by subsidising Britain's European allies, preferring to concentrate his own forces on attacking French possessions in the West Indies. He had hoped by doing so to contribute towards the expenses of the war, but the price in lives, with 40,000 dead, had been enormous. In December 1795 when the government, encouraged by the replacement of the French Convention by the Directory, put out feelers for peace, Sheridan was quick to remind them of the 'calamitous waste of treasure and of blood' caused by their delay in doing what Fox had suggested three years before. The government's pretext that the system in France was now milder and more moderate did not hold water; four of the five Directors had voted for the death of Louis XVI. It had always been wrong to make peace dependent on the internal situation in France.

Whatever the internal situation, France's external ambitions had not changed. She insisted on keeping all her conquests up to the Rhine, regardless of the threat to British security. By October 1796, the peace negotiations had been abandoned. Meanwhile, Prussia, Holland and Spain had signed treaties with France, and the Austrian Netherlands had been incorporated into the French republic. Austria, Britain's last important ally, had been driven out of Italy by Bonaparte's invading army. In 1797, by the treaty of Campo Formio, she bought peace and the conquered Venetian territories for herself at the price of consenting to the Rhine frontier for France.

To the last, Pitt had sought to keep Austria on the British side by massive subsidies. In the summer of 1796, when Parliament was already in recess, he had responded to an urgent call from Austria for help against the French in Italy with a secret loan of £1,200,000. When the House reassembled in the autumn Fox used the occasion to put forward a motion for a vote of censure against him for granting a loan without Parliament's consent. Sheridan supported him. Pitt's ministerial conduct, he said, had been one continued attack upon the liberties of his country.

What, he demanded, would be the feelings of his father, the illustrious Chatham, if he could look down on the history of the last three years, 'to see him covering the whole face of the country with barracks and bastilles . . . to see the whole country under military government, and the people placed under the subjection of the bayonet; while, as if this were not sufficient, their mouths were shut up, and themselves prevented from meeting to discuss their grievances; and proceeding in his climax of constitutional violence, wresting from them, one after another, all their rights, till he came at last to take out of the hands of their representatives the guardian disposal of their money?'

It was fine rhetorical stuff, but the house was in no mood to censure Pitt and Fox's motion was defeated. But the government's loans to Austria had helped to precipitate a financial crisis which came to a head when, in February 1797, the Bank of England was forced to suspend cash payments. Two months earlier, a French expeditionary force under Hoche had sailed for Ireland; it was only thanks to bad weather and bad seamanship that they were prevented from landing in Bantry Bay. The threat of invasion had led to a run on the bank, further weakening its position. It took all Pitt's financial skill to avert a collapse, but not without violent criticism from the Foxite opposition who accused him of bringing the country to the brink of bankruptcy by his policies. Sheridan took a prominent part in the debates on the subject, and, in one of his most memorable passages, compared the bank to an elderly lady in the city, of great credit and long standing, who had recently committed a *faux pas*.

'She had unfortunately fallen into bad company, and had contracted too great an intimacy and connection at the St James's end of the town. The young gentleman, however, who had employed all his "arts of soft persuasion" to seduce this old lady, had so far shewn his designs, that, by timely cutting and breaking off the connection, there might be hopes for the old gentlewoman once more regaining her credit and injured reputation.'

The image was picked up in Gillray's cartoon: 'Political Ravishment, or The Old Lady of Threadneedle Street in Danger'.

The financial crisis had scarcely been resolved when a mutiny of the Channel fleet at Spithead on 15 April provided a new cause for dismay. There was no doubt that the sailors had genuine grievances; their rate of pay had not been increased since the time of Charles II, the conditions on board were appalling, the discipline was ferocious. They refused to lift anchor till their demands for improved wages and conditions, with better treatment for the sick and wounded, had been met. After some delays, much criticised by Sheridan and Fox, the majority of their demands were agreed.

On 17 May the Spithead fleet set out to sea. But the infection of mutiny was catching; the terms of the government's agreement had not at first been fully understood. Even before the Spithead affair had been settled, a fresh and more serious mutiny, led by a malcontent named Parker, broke out on the Nore; it was joined by thirteen ships which, under the command of Admiral Duncan, had been setting out for Texel, where a Dutch fleet was preparing to embark for a renewed attempt on Ireland. Duncan, with only two remaining ships, contrived to hold the Dutch in harbour till help arrived but for a time the danger was acute.

At this moment of national crisis Sheridan rallied to the government's side. He had been all for concessions to the seamen, but when, despite a royal proclamation offering them the same terms as at Spithead and the promise of a pardon to all who returned to their duty, they persisted in their insurrection he was the first to recommend prompt action. While the ministry were still hesitating as to what steps to take he called on Dundas, Pitt's Secretary for War. 'My advice,' he said, 'is that you cut the buoys on the river – send Sir Charles Grey [a popular general recently returned from the West Indies] down to the coast, and set a price on Parker's head. If the Administration take this advice instantly, they will save the country – if not they will lose it.'

His 'patriotic promptitude', as Moore describes it, was matched by his attitude in Parliament. 'If there was indeed a rot in the wooden walls of England,' he said in a speech on 2 June, 'our decay could not be very distant. The question ... was not about this or that concession, but whether the country should be laid prostrate at the feet of France.' The government, he insisted, deserved the co-operation of every citizen in maintaining the law and bringing the mutiny to an end; at a moment such as this all party considerations were out of the question. Pitt thanked Sheridan publicly for his support. When the mutiny was finally defeated, thanks in part to Sheridan's advice, Dundas expressed the feeling of the ministry in saying that 'the country was highly indebted to Sheridan for his fair and manly conduct' in the whole affair.

Sheridan had shown that he could rise to a national emergency in a generous spirit, his attitude contrasting with that of Fox, who had seen the government's difficulties as an opportunity to make party capital. But he was still bound by ties of loyalty to his leader and when, after the failure of a renewed attempt by Grey to introduce a bill for electoral reform, Fox announced that the opposition would cease to attend Parliament in protest, he felt impelled to follow him.

Fox's secession had an element of pique about it. Pitt's willingness to negotiate for peace had taken the wind out of the opposition's sails; France's refusal to give up her conquests made it impossible to go on arguing that the government was deliberately prolonging the war. Grey's motion for reform, which Fox had supported, had been defeated so convincingly that the subject would not be raised again for many years. For the moment the opposition seemed without a role, though whether this in itself was an excuse for refusing to take part in parliamentary life was perhaps another matter.

Fox returned to his villa in Surrey, Sheridan to the affairs of Drury Lane. The opposition's self-denying ordinance was not total; one member, indeed, the belligerent George Tierney, ignored it altogether and in consequence stole much of Sheridan's thunder in attacking the government. His exchanges with Pitt culminated in a duel in May 1798, when Pitt, after denouncing him for sabotaging the country's defences, refused to withdraw his accusation. Both men, to the country's great relief, escaped unscathed.

It must have been hard for Sheridan to stand aside; he is recorded as speaking only twelve times in 1798 and 1799, as opposed to fifty in the previous two years. He attacked Pitt on his proposals to raise revenue by taxing income and he renewed his objections to the suspension of the Habeas Corpus Act. But his most important interventions were on the subject of Ireland, which in 1798, encouraged by the prospect of support from France, broke into open rebellion. No subject could be closer to Sheridan's heart. He had shown his patriotism and his determination to resist the enemy in his support for the government over the mutiny at the Nore; he knew that Ireland, if invaded, would bring the rest of Britain into mortal danger. But his sympathies were with the oppressed Catholic peasantry for whom, in the phrase of Lecky, 'a scene of horrors hardly surpassed in the history of modern Europe' was opening up.

# XXI

———⚮———

The failure of the French expeditionary force to land at Bantry Bay in December 1796 had dramatically pointed up Ireland's vulnerability to invasion. Had it succeeded, the whole country might have fallen into French hands and the Directory's aim of setting up an independent Irish republic, with the help of the Irish revolutionary party, might well have been achieved. Thanks to the hurricane, the 'Protestant wind' that had scattered Hoche's fleet, the situation had been saved. But with the Dutch fleet gathered at Texel and a new expeditionary force preparing at Toulon, there was little room for complacency in Dublin.

As always in time of war, England's difficulty had been Ireland's opportunity, and Pitt had done his best in the years immediately after 1789 to redress some of the worst Irish grievances. Despite opposition from the Irish parliament, dominated by a narrowly Protestant oligarchy, he had managed to push through legislation enfranchising Catholic freeholders and relaxing some of the penal laws. He had stopped short of granting full emancipation – the right of Catholics to sit in Parliament – though the appointment of the liberal Lord Fitzwilliam, one of the Portland Whigs who had recently rallied to the government, as Viceroy in 1795 had raised hopes that this last step would be taken. Fitzwilliam's recall, after only two months, made it clear that neither the Irish nor the English parliament were yet prepared to go so far. With the constitutional road to reform now blocked, the aims of the 'United Irishmen', an underground organisation formed to combine all creeds in the fight to achieve Irish independence, became increasingly attractive to Catholic opinion.

The danger of invasion following Hoche's failed attempt spurred the government to drastic action. Their policy of disarming potentially disaffected areas, in particular in the north, led to widespread abuses and atrocities. Unable to provide sufficient regular troops to carry out the searches, they gave the task to the local yeomanry, Protestant volunteers who misused their powers outrageously, increasing sectarian bitterness by their ruthless treatment of the local people. Houses were burnt down, floggings and half hangings inflicted on the flimsiest excuse, their victims responding with violence and assassinations in their turn.

By the beginning of 1798 the country was drifting into anarchy; the breach between the two creeds, which the United Irishmen had hoped to close, was widening daily. The leaders of the United Irishmen, mostly Protestant, were divided on their tactics, the more cautious wishing to wait for help from France before any uprising, the bolder spirits, amongst them Lord Edward Fitzgerald and a young adventurer, Arthur O'Connor, prepared to go ahead alone.

The debate was still undecided when Arthur O'Connor, with four companions, was arrested at Margate. One member of the party, a Catholic priest named Quigley, was carrying a letter addressed to the Directory in France, inviting an invasion of England by Bonaparte. O'Connor himself carried a coded letter to Lord Edward Fitzgerald, to which, amazingly, the cipher was still attached, announcing his intention of going to France, where he intended to be 'very active' on the United Irishmen's behalf.

The trial of the five men, together with O'Connor's brother Roger, who had been arrested when he came to England to arrange for his brother's defence, took place in Maidstone on 21 May. Sheridan, with other leaders of the opposition including Erskine, Fox and Grey, came forward to give evidence for Arthur O'Connor, of whose innocence they were convinced. It is hard to see exactly why they thought so, considering the coded letter to Fitzgerald, but their testimonials won the day. O'Connor was acquitted; a contemporary squib, satirising his defenders under the names of Foxton, Sherryman, and so on, described their evidence as 'giving him, as they thought, the highest character in the world (though many thought they were unsaying all that they had said before), by declaring that *his principles were exactly the same as their own*'.

Quigley, the Irish priest, was sentenced to death for high treason; the other four prisoners were acquitted. The government, however, had not done with O'Connor, for no sooner had he been acquitted than he was rearrested on an Irish warrant. The arrest took place amidst violent scenes in court, for some of his friends, including his counsel and Lord Thanet, had urged him to escape before the warrant could be served. O'Connor leapt over the bar of the dock and in the scuffle that ensued swords were drawn, blows exchanged and soldiers had to be called in. Sheridan did his best to calm the situation, for which he was later thanked by the judge, but he and Fox, as he told Hecca, were 'in sufficient indignation at this horrible Persecution'.

O'Connor's arrest and trial were only a minor incident in the drama that was now unfolding. On 19 May Lord Edward Fitzgerald, who had been in hiding since March, when sixteen leading members of the United Irishmen had been arrested, was captured in Dublin. His arrest threw the revolutionaries into confusion, hurrying on their plans for an uprising despite the lack of French support. Four days later the rebellion began, at first with scattered and ill co-ordinated outbreaks round Dublin, then far more seriously in Wexford, where a force of largely Catholic insurgents, peasants, tradesmen and small farmers, captured the town. From then on the revolution snow-balled; for a few days the fate of Ireland hung in the balance as the rebels advanced towards Dublin. Meanwhile, news had come from France that Bonaparte, with a huge armada, had set sail from Toulon for an unknown destination. His goal in fact was Egypt, from whence he hoped to strike at Britain's possessions in India. Had it been Ireland, as was feared at the time, the rebellion would have had a very different ending. As it was, the desperate courage of the Catholic peasantry, armed only with pikes and pitchforks, was no match in the long run for the better arms and discipline of the government troops. By the end of the summer, though the violence simmered on in pockets, the countryside had been subdued; the only successful French landing, a small expedition which had landed at Killala in August, had been defeated after fierce resistance. But the costs had been appalling: more than 30,000 people had been killed, thousands more transported or driven to emigrate by poverty. The atrocities committed on both sides left a legacy of bitterness which has lasted to this day.

On 19 June, when the rebellion was only a few weeks old, Sheridan spoke in the House of Commons in answer to a loyal address deploring what was happening in Ireland. Though he was unwilling, he said, to refer to the particular events of the moment, he was ready to declare that every effort must be made to prevent Ireland from falling into the power of France. But this was very different from saying, as the previous speaker (Dundas) had said, that the rebellion had been unprovoked, that every attempt at conciliation had been made.

'It was, indeed, with the utmost wonder and surprise that I heard this assertion advanced. What, when conciliation was held out to the people of Ireland, was there any discontent? When the government of Ireland was agreeable to the wishes of the people, was there any discontent? After the prospect of that conciliation was taken away – after Lord Fitzwilliam was recalled – when the hopes that had been raised were blasted – when the spirit of the people was beaten down, insulted, despised, I will ask any gentleman to point out a single act of conciliation which has emanated from the government of Ireland. On the contrary, has not that country exhibited one continuous scene of the most grievous oppression, of the most vexatious proceedings; arbitrary punishments inflicted; torture declared necessary by the highest authority in the sister kingdom next to that of the legislature. And do gentlemen say that the indignant spirit which is roused by such exercise of government is unprovoked? Is this conciliation? Is this liberty? Has every thing been done to avert the evils of rebellion? It is the fashion to say, and the address holds the same language, that the rebellion which now rages in the sister kingdom has been owing to the machinations of "wicked men" . . . It was my first intention to move that these words should be omitted. But no, Sir, the fact they assert is true. It is indeed to the machinations of wicked men that the deplorable state of Ireland is to be imputed. It is to those wicked ministers who have broken the promises they held out; who betrayed the party they seduced into their views, to be the instruments of the foulest treachery that ever was practised against any people. It is to those wicked ministers who have given up that devoted country to plunder; resigned it a prey to this faction, by which it has so long been trampled upon, and abandoned it to every species of insult by which a country was ever overwhelmed, or the spirit of a people insulted, that we owe the miseries into which Ireland is plunged, and the dangers by which England is threatened.'

The loyal address, inevitably, was carried by a government majority, but who is to say that Sheridan did not have the right of the matter? His speech had reverberations far beyond the voting in the House. 'You have *begum-ed* the Chancellor-governor of Ireland', wrote a Whig friend, Sir John Macpherson. 'I heard your speech. If it is printed and published like his own, he must end in impeachment. I conjure you to print it for the sake of a million people.'

For rest of the year, true to his party's self-denying ordinance, Sheridan made no further appearances in the House of Commons. He would return there the following January, when the subject of Ireland was once more to the fore. In the interval the tide of war had turned. On 2 October the news of Nelson's victory at the Battle of the Nile reached London amidst wild rejoicing. Britain now controlled the Mediterranean, and Bonaparte's army was trapped in Egypt. Two weeks later a squadron of French warships on its way to Ireland was intercepted and defeated; 2,500 prisoners, including the Irish revolutionary leader Wolf Tone, were taken and seven of its nine ships captured.

In the wake of these naval triumphs a wave of patriotism and renewed self-confidence swept the country. Russia was limbering up for war with France and in December made an alliance with Britain; Austria joined them in a second coalition four months later. Sheridan, temporarily withdrawn from politics, was able to turn his talents to the theatre, capturing the national mood of defiance and determination in the first play he had written since *The Critic*. His bombastic tragedy *Pizarro*, adapted from Kotzebue's play *Die Spanier in Peru*, was the most sensational success of the decade.

Kotzebue, as *The Stranger* had already shown, had the gift of wringing the hearts of his contemporaries. The combination of heavy German sentiment, inflated language, and what someone called 'slop morality' was something that Sheridan could have mocked as brilliantly as he had heroic tragedy in *The Critic*. But times were different: in Britain's embattled state the patriotism of the Peruvian prince Rolla, rallying his people against the cruel and plundering Pizarro, had an emotional appeal to which Sheridan, as much as any of his audience, could respond.

Sheridan's version of Kotzebue's play, which he had taken from an English translation, was virtually a new work – it was later translated back into German. Sheridan certainly regarded it as his own, and, with his usual habits of procrastination, had still not finished writing the fourth act by the time the play was advertised and every box already taken.

Kelly, who was composing the music, was in despair. Not one line of poetry for the songs had been written, and his daily applications to the author were met with the promise, always unfulfilled, that he would have his text the following day. Finally, one evening when Kelly was entertaining friends Sheridan appeared to carry him off to Drury Lane, where the painters and scene builders were preparing the set for the Temple of the Sun. Settling down on a bench in the empty pit, with a bowl of negus before him, he invited him to admire the scene where the principal choruses would take place and promised him the words next day. 'My dear Mick,' he said, 'you know you can depend on me and I know that I can depend on you; but these bunglers of carpenters need looking after.'

To Kelly's surprise he turned up next day as promised, and after dinner they set to work. 'I sang two or three bars of music to him,' wrote Kelly, 'which I thought corresponded with what he wished and marked them down. He then made a sort of rumbling noise with his voice (for he had not the slightest idea of turning a tune) resembling a deep gruff bow, wow, wow.' This was all Kelly had to work with, for, though Sheridan explained the various situations in which music would be needed, the words for only two songs ever materialised, and Kelly, perceiving that 'it was perfectly ridiculous to expect the poetry of the choruses from the author of the play', found an impoverished writer to provide them.

Kelly's situation was nothing to that of the actors, for, according to his memoirs, while the house was filling for the first performance the fifth act had still not been completed, and Sheridan, upstairs in the prompter's room, was writing the last act of the play while the rest was being acted. Not till the end of the fourth act did Mrs Siddons, Charles Kemble and Barrymore receive their speeches for the fifth. But Sheridan, said Kelly, was 'careful in his carelessness'. He was aware of his power over the actors and the veneration in which they held his talents; moreover he knew that they were all 'quick studies' and that he could trust them to be word perfect, even at half an hour's notice. (At the worst they had the literal translation to fall back on.)

The play was an immediate triumph. Kemble, as the heroic Rolla – a part in which he is immortalised by Lawrence's painting of him, sword in one hand, the child he is rescuing from a raging torrent in the other – won more popular, as opposed to critical, acclaim than in any other part. His speech to the Peruvian soldiers on the eve of battle, easily applicable to the contemporary situation, brought patriotic cheers as he compared the Spaniards' motives to their own: 'THEY, by a strange frenzy driven, fight for power, for plunder and extended rule – WE for our country, our altars and our homes – THEY follow an Adventurer whom they fear and obey a power which they hate – WE serve a Monarch whom we love – a God whom we adore.'

Pitt described Kemble in the role as the noblest actor he had ever seen. He was less impressed by the play. 'If you mean what Sheridan has written,' he remarked, 'there's nothing new in it, for I heard it long ago at Hastings' trial.' Fox went even further; Congreve's *Mourning Bride*, he told Samuel Rogers, was execrable, but *Pizarro* was the worst thing ever.

Sheridan, however, was delighted with both Kemble and the play. He had been intensely nervous about the casting. He was confident of Kemble from the first, but he had had grave doubts whether Mrs Siddons as Elvira, the revengeful mistress of Pizarro, would fall into the part. As for Mrs Jordan, had it not been for the attraction of her name, he would never have chosen her. He had no opinion of her powers in tragedy and her manner, always natural and spontaneous, was ill suited to the declamatory cadences of the play.

The first night saw him too busy behind scenes to give his full attention to the acting, but Boaden who watched it from his box on the third described Sheridan's nervous agitation:

'He repeated every syllable after each performer, counting poetically the measure on his fingers, and sounding his voice like a music master, with a degree of earnestness beyond my power to describe. He was in the utmost ill humour, shocked, almost stamping with anger at everything Mrs Jordan said. With everything Kemble uttered he was invariably delighted; clapping his hands with pleasure like a child. With some passages by Mrs Siddons he was charmed; at others he was shocked, frequently stating to Richardson and me that "*This* was the way the passage should be spoken" and then repeating it in his own way. Upon his sometimes referring to Mrs Siddons, Richardson said to him with his Newcastle burr, "Well, well, Sheridan, you should not be so impatient! You know Kemble told you, that after some time she would fall into the part." '

Mrs Siddons, once accustomed to the part, did indeed fall into it. Decked out in a plumed Amazonian helmet, she made a proud and passionate Elvira and Kemble, when praised for his playing of Rolla, claimed the greater glory for his sister. 'Nay, nay, I have everything to aid me; it is a noble character. Carry your wonder to Mrs Siddons; she has made a heroine of a soldier's trull.'

The success of *Pizarro* was phenomenal. It ran for thirty-one nights (excluding Sundays) in succession, an unprecedented run for a tragedy. Thirty thousand copies of the play were sold, and thousands of people who had never thought of the matter before plunged deep into Peruvian history. A cartoon by Gillray entitled 'Pizarro contemplating the product of his new Peruvian gold mine' showed Sheridan exulting over his new-found riches. The Tories, not pleased at having their patriotic thunder stolen by a former supporter of the French Revolution, ascribed his success to Kemble's acting; a caricature in the *Anti-Jacobin Review* showed Sheridan borne heavenward on Kemble's head.

The tub-thumping so evident in *Pizarro* had been notably absent in Sheridan's interventions in the House of Commons some months earlier on the proposed parliamentary union of Ireland and Great Britain. He had shared whole-heartedly in the patriotic fervour of the play. But though, like George III, he gloried in the name of Briton, he never forgot his debts to Ireland too. 'My country,' he said, when the question was first raised in Parliament in January 1799, 'has claims upon me that I am not more proud to acknowledge than ready to liquidate, to the full measure of my ability.'

Pitt's proposed solution to the Irish situation, the reunion of Ireland with Great Britain after seventeen years of notional independence, had much to recommend it at first sight. The Irish parliament had signally failed to address the Catholic population's grievances, culminating in the disastrous insurrection of the previous year. By bringing its members into the larger context of the British parliament Pitt hoped to restrict their power; at the same time, the proportion of Protestants to Catholics in the two united kingdoms would have shifted. With the Irish Protestants no longer a beleaguered minority, the question of Catholic emancipation would, he hoped, be more acceptable. He had wished, at first, to make Catholic emancipation one of the keystones of the new act of union, but seeing difficulties ahead had decided to take the two questions one at a time.

In the short run, Pitt's solution had all the virtues of expediency. In the long run it was Sheridan who saw more clearly. To force through a union when Ireland was still suffering from the ravages of the rebellion and there were forty thousand troops in occupation was an act of annexation and intimidation. But at no time, he declared, could such a union be desirable; it would not increase the happiness of either and in the end would endanger the constitutional liberties of both: 'It is impossible to conceive that the measure is palatable in Ireland, unless we can suppose that having for three hundred years endured the most inhuman insults, that at last, when they had wrung from this country that which it was a shame to deprive them of, they would freely, and without bias, give it up sixteen years afterwards; that they would surrender their rights, because it was the pleasure of a British minister to propose, that the Irish Parliament should no longer exist.'

Between 22 January 1799, when the subject was first raised in the House of Commons, and 12 February, when the House went into committee to discuss the union, Sheridan made five major speeches on the Irish question, fighting a hopeless battle, as Lecky put it, 'with conspicuous earnestness and courage'.

He dismissed the argument that Ireland, by being formally united to Great Britain, would be less susceptible to French subversion. Great Britain's chief enemies in Ireland were not French principles, but ignorance and poverty. There was doubtless much to be reformed in Ireland, but whatever its faults a parliament sitting in Dublin was more likely to be responsive to Irish opinion than one in London. It had long been accepted that absenteeism was one of the causes of Ireland's miseries; it could hardly be expected that landlords would be kinder to their tenants when further removed from them by their legislative duties. Pitt had held out the stick of imposing commercial restrictions if the union were not carried through, and the carrot of Catholic emancipation if it were. But why should parliamentary union be necessary for free trade between the two countries, or Catholic emancipation delayed till it had taken place? If the government were really sincere they should first end religious discrimination in Britain; their example would be the strongest possible incentive for the Irish parliament to do the same.

In each debate Sheridan's arguments against the union, and his call for at least a breathing space before so important a question was decided, were defeated. He never carried more than twenty-four votes with him. Burke, who might just possibly have supported him, had died the previous year; Fox, in retirement at his villa at St Anne's Hill, did not come to his aid. For most of his contemporaries, his objections appeared to be deliberately obstructive. From a wider perspective his instincts were sounder than theirs. But his was a Cassandra voice and doomed not to be listened to.

The subject of Ireland arose once more that year, when Sheridan was summoned to give evidence at the trial of Fergusson and Lord Thanet for their role in assisting O'Connor's attempt to escape at the end of his trial at Maidstone. (To the embarrassment of his Whig supporters, O'Connor had confessed to his part in the '98 conspiracy and was now in prison at Fort George.) Fergusson and Thanet were left to bear the consequences of helping him, and it must be admitted that Sheridan's evidence, intended to clear them, seems to have done more harm than good. According to Lady Holland, since Horne Tooke's trial, in which he had gained great credit for his wit and repartee, he could never give a direct answer in court and was always 'more occupied to gain applause by his reply than to serve those in favour of whom he is called'.

The nub of her charge against him was that when asked by Law, the prosecuting counsel, whether he believed that Lord Thanet and Fergusson intended to assist O'Connor's escape, he paused for some moments before answering. He later insisted that he had seen nothing to make him believe that either had done so, but his hesitation, at least in Lady Holland's view, had sown doubt in the jury's minds and both men were found guilty. Thanet was sentenced to a year's imprisonment, Fergusson to six months.

Lady Holland went further, suggesting that Sheridan himself had incited O'Connor to escape, but Lord Thanet, in talking to Moore in later years, never questioned Sheridan's good faith in the matter. What is clear, however, is that in contrast to his appearances in the Commons during his speeches on the union, Sheridan was considerably the worse for wear when he gave evidence. He had not been called for till nine in the evening, by which time, according to one reporter, he was well into his second bottle at Bellamy's. His prevarications may or may not have injured the defendants, but they certainly infuriated Law. He had long borne a grudge against Sheridan for treating him roughly in the course of the Warren Hastings trial, and examined him with the 'utmost acrimony'. 'Do answer my questions, Mr Sheridan,' he said, after Sheridan had entertained the court with various sallies, 'without point or epigram'. 'Very true, sir,' replied Sheridan, 'your questions are without point or epigram.' It was the kind of schoolboy retort that gives pleasure at the time, but it helps to explain why Sheridan was not always taken seriously.

# XXII

—⟞⟡⟝—

Sheridan dedicated the printed copy of *Pizarro* to his wife:

> TO HER, whose approbation of this Drama, and whose peculiar delight in the applause it has received from the Public, have been to *me* the highest gratification its success has produced, I dedicate this play.

Hecca, according to Mrs Bouverie, had suffered agonies of mind over the play and remained as violently attached to Sheridan as ever. Its success, and the welcome relief to the theatre's finances, made that summer of 1799 a particularly happy one. They spent much of it at Polesden Lacey.

'He is just come from "Peruvianising", that is from the country', noted Lady Holland in her journal that July. 'He is so delighted with *Pizarro* that his allusions are taken from it in everything he says. He said ye 10th of July was so delicious, something in the temperature so bewitching and tempting to go astray . . . that if he were to sit in judgement upon a cause of gallantry, if the indictment stated it as committed on ye 10th of July, he would go into the evidence, but instantly bring in *Guilty by the visitation of God*.'

Just as his father had done at Quilca, Sheridan took enormous pleasure in his country estate. The property, however, was on a very different scale, a seventeenth-century manor house, somewhat dilapidated when he bought it, but a far cry from the tumbledown farmhouse Swift had derided in his verses. There were 341 acres of land and, though the estate was held as part of Hecca's marriage

233

settlement, Sheridan spent freely on it, adding considerably to its acreage over the years. The theatre suffered accordingly. In 1798, when the purchase was first made, the playwright Thomas Holcroft already found James Aickin, the stage manager at Drury Lane, on the brink of resignation: 'forebodings of bankruptcy, such things as wood and canvas not to be had, yet three thousand guineas given for an estate'.

Sheridan was a generous landlord, immensely popular with his tenants and a firm supporter of their rights. He took their side in the matter of common land enclosure in 1804 and 1805, determined, as he said, to 'see real justice done to the cottages and poorest claimants', and was always ready to help those in trouble. He was an enthusiastic if inexperienced farmer, worrying about his crops like any country squire. 'Rain made my bones ach[e] for my Harvest', he wrote to Hecca soon after they acquired the house. 'O! ye Gods, that my ricks had been thatch'd even with Fern and green boughs!' There were celebrations when things went well.

'Mr Sheridan gave a grand harvest home on Tuesday, to the neighbouring people in the neighbourhood of his beautiful seat at Polesden', the papers reported in October 1802. 'A large tent was erected on the lawn, capable of accommodating three hundred persons, who were treated with English cheer and ancient hospitality, and the industrious and deserving girls of character were rewarded each by an harvest present from their amiable hostess. A select party dined at the mansion house, which was enlivened by the vivacity and gaiety of Mr Sheridan, and the peasantry departed, after preserving the utmost regularity, order and decorum, at a proper hour, all filled with gratitude for their hospitable and kind reception.'

No trace of the Carolean house which Sheridan bought is now left; the 'Sheridan walk', a long terraced avenue of beeches which he laid out, lost its fine trees in 1978, but remains as the sole memorial of his occupancy. (The new house, begun in 1820, and extended by the Edwardian hostess Mrs Ronald Greville, now belongs to the National Trust.)

From his letters, and the memoirs of the time, we catch glimpses of Sheridan in the role of host, inviting friends to fish or shoot – according to Moore he was a hopeless shot – or showing a young lady round his garden: 'Won't you come into the garden? I would like my roses to see you.'

Sometimes there were house parties, lavish if slapdash over details. Reminiscing with Creevey, Sydney Smith described one such gathering. No expense had been spared, there was a magnificent dinner, excellent wines, but when they came to go to bed there was not a single candle to light the way and the guests had to undress in the dark; apparently Sheridan thought that in the circumstances candles would only have confused their blindness. At breakfast, though the table groaned with delicacies, there was not a pat of butter to be seen, their host explaining blandly that it was not a butter county.

Polesden Lacey added a new dimension to Sheridan's life. He yearned for it in London, when the town was a burning furnace in summer; he loved to think of Hecca growing 'fat as a little pig' in the country air. It is pleasant to picture him writing to Whitbread only a year before he died, with 'a hatful of Polesden violets on the Table . . . and three samples of Lambs wool'.

The summer of 1799 which passed so delightfully at Polesden Lacey saw the end of Bonaparte's campaign in the east. On 23 August, leaving his army marooned in Egypt, Napoleon set sail for France. He arrived there six weeks later. On 9 November, with the coup of the 18 Brumaire, the 'foggy month' of the revolutionary calendar, the Directory toppled at his touch. With his appointment as First Consul, he became the effective dictator of France.

For Sheridan, Napoleon's rise to power put a new complexion on the war. It brought a promise of stable government in France, and an end to the Jacobin principles, against which, ostensibly, the war had been waged. The government thought otherwise, and when, in December 1799, Napoleon made overtures for peace, he was rebuffed. It was no longer a time for Sheridan to shun the House of Commons and his speeches calling for peace the following year showed him at the summit of his powers.

Speaking on 17 February 1800, he argued against the prolongation of the war and the system of alliances and subsidies that maintained it. France had renounced the excesses of the revolution which had created so many enemies for her. Jacobinism, the chief threat, was virtually extinct there, destroyed by its own poison. As a republic France might be a bad neighbour; 'but than monarchical France a more foul and treacherous a neighbour never was'. He dismissed the government's apparent policy of making the restoration of the Bourbons a precondition for peace. Bonaparte, he maintained, would be as good a friend and neighbour to Great Britain as the Bourbons ever were; there was no time when they could hope to make better terms.

Sheridan's arguments were rejected. His belief in Napoleon's good faith was optimistic, but on the question of timing he may well have been right. At the beginning of 1800 the second coalition held the advantage. The French had been driven out of northern Italy; the army of Egypt was still stranded in the east. Rebuffed in his overtures for peace by Austria and Britain, Napoleon moved rapidly to the offensive. In a few months the situation was reversed. Italy was reconquered, Austria defeated in the dazzling victory of Marengo. Russia had already given up the struggle. By the end of the year the second coalition was in tatters and with Austria's capitulation at the Treaty of Luneville in 1801 it ceased to exist.

Throughout the previous year Sheridan had continued to argue that Britain should make peace with France. He did not deny that Bonaparte was a usurper, or that he ruled France with a stronger hand than was necessary to protect it from its enemies.

'But, Sir, we have seen religion obtain a tolerant exemption in her favour under the government of this atheist; we have seen the faith of treaties observed under the government of this perfidious adventurer – the arts and sciences find protection under the government of this plunderer; the sufferings of humanity have been alleviated under this ferocious usurper; the arms of France have been led to victory by this Tyro in the arts of peace and war! . . . Buonaparte has shewn his country, that his object is to maintain the power he has attained by the moderation of his government; and I must hope, that when he has achieved the liberty of France, and his enemies have afforded him the opportunity of turning his attention to its internal regulations, he will . . . impart to it all the blessings and happiness of civilised peace.'

His speech, delivered on 27 June, only a month after the victory of Marengo, had an immense effect in France, where it was twice reprinted under the title '*Bulletin officiel de la séance des Communes d'Angleterre. Tableau presenté par le Lord Sheridan. Discours sur la nécessité de négocier la paix.*'

Despite his opposition to the war, which in fact was growing increasingly unpopular, Sheridan's patriotism was no longer in doubt. Even Pitt, with unexpected generosity, paid him the compliment of saying, in the midst of a debate that session, that Sheridan had more than once shown a 'noble disposition' in coming forward to support the government in moments of great national danger. Fox, in retirement, took a more jaundiced view; Sheridan, he once complained, 'itched to be different', and though Sheridan in a further speech that year declared that solid peace could be obtained on the principles of only one man, i.e. Fox, it did not altogether reconcile them.

On 24 May 1800, Sheridan had had a dramatic opportunity to show his patriotic zeal. Earlier that day, whilst attending a military review, the king had been shot at from the crowd. That evening, on one of his rare visits to Drury Lane (for he still detested Sheridan's politics) there was a further attempt on his life, when a madman from the audience fired at him as he entered the royal box. At the sound of the report the king stepped back, then with great sang-froid came forward to the front of the box and, putting his glass to his eye, looked calmly round the house. Sheridan, hurrying to the back of the box, where the queen and princesses were about to come in, managed to delay them with an excuse; it was only when the would-be assassin had been seized by the performers in the orchestra and dragged into the music-room for questioning that they learned what had happened. During the whole of the comedy that followed the royal ladies were bathed in tears, a focus of far greater interest than the stage. At the end of the play, when 'God Save the King', at the audience's demand, was being sung again, Mrs Jordan handed Michael Kelly an impromptu verse which Sheridan had written:

> From every latent foe,
> From the assassin's blow,
> God save the King.
> O'er him thine arm extend,
> For Britain's sake defend
> Our father, prince and friend,
> God save the King.

So successful was this extra verse that Kelly repeated it three times amid 'the most rapturous approbation', and the king left the theatre to the sound of loyal cheers.

From then on the king was more gracious towards Sheridan and visited Drury Lane more often. We hear of him, in a letter from Sheridan to his wife, discussing dancing and the difficulties of learning the new steps; fortunately, he said, the queen's corns had prevented her from wishing to become proficient herself. More memorably, one evening, when emerging from a performance of *The School for Scandal*, he turned to Sheridan who was handing him into his carriage and said, 'I am much pleased with your comedy of the "School for Scandal"; but I am still more so, with your play of the "Rivals"; – that is my favourite, and I will never give it up.' There will always be those who share his view.

In the spring of 1800, encouraged by a substantial distribution of patronage and places and with the implicit promise of Catholic emancipation, the Irish parliament voted for union with the British parliament. The decision was ratified with the Act of Union in January 1801. Pitt planned to bring in Catholic emancipation as a natural sequel to the union. He knew that the opposition of the king, who believed that in admitting Catholics to parliament he would be breaking his coronation oath, would be a major stumbling-block, but he hoped by gaining the support of the Cabinet beforehand he could persuade him to change his mind. The unexpected hostility of the Lord Chancellor, Lord Loughborough, who felt that Catholic emancipation was a breach of the constitutional settlement of 1688, made it impossible to get the Cabinet's agreement. Worse still, while the matter was being discussed, Loughborough alerted the king to what was happening. Furious at not being consulted, and convinced by Loughborough's arguments that his coronation oath forbade any question of Catholic emancipation, the king made it clear that in no circumstances would he agree to the proposal. The House of Commons, for the most part lukewarm or even opposed to the measure, was not prepared to challenge the king. Unable to carry out his implied promise, Pitt felt morally bound to resign. On 5 February 1801, after nearly nineteen years in office, he was replaced as First Lord of the Treasury (or effectively Prime Minister) by Henry Addington, the Speaker of the House of Commons.

Pitt's government had never been more than a heterogeneous collection of groups, held together by his leadership and by the fact that he had the confidence of the king. The party system still barely existed, and Addington, in forming his ministry, was able to draw on all sections of the House. The Foxite opposition, and those in favour of Catholic emancipation, were naturally excluded though Sheridan, to the disgust of his fellow Whigs, was soon on good terms with the Prime Minister. His dislike of Pitt, going back for over twenty years, went far beyond mere politics. In any case, he found Addington far preferable to Pitt, and, though he described the new administration as a ship that was incapable of defending itself, having thrown its great guns (Pitt and Dundas) over, he was more sympathetic than otherwise towards it.

On the question of Catholic emancipation he remained firm. Pitt's honourable stance had been largely vitiated when the king that summer, following a brief recurrence of his illness, told him that it had been caused by the worry of the Catholic question. Pitt, genuinely devoted to the king, and shattered by the thought that he had been responsible for his breakdown, made him a promise that he would never renew the subject in his lifetime. In a way the promise was unnecessary, for it was obvious that whatever the circumstances the king would never agree to Catholic relief. Nonetheless it was not a promise that Sheridan would have made.

Addington, with none of Pitt's stature or charisma, proved unexpectedly successful in cutting taxes and managing the economy. More importantly, he was able to guide the war-weary country towards peace. The signing of the Treaty of Amiens in March 1802 was greeted with general jubilation, though its terms were highly advantageous to the French, and it was soon obvious that it would not last. It was, said Sheridan, in an epigram that Lord Holland accused him of having heard two hours before and borrowed without leave, 'a peace which every man ought to be glad of but no man can be proud of'.

Fox, with a host of other English aristocrats, long starved of travel on the Continent, made their way to Paris to see France's new dictator for themselves and to gaze in wonder at the military pomps of his regime. Sheridan did not accompany them. His faith in Napoleon's good intentions was waning. Unlike Fox, who was eager to meet the First Consul, he abstained from going to Paris on grounds that he would accept 'no civility which might interfere with his manner of speaking of Bonaparte'.

Meanwhile the affairs of Drury Lane were reaching crisis point. The windfall of *Pizarro* had brought a welcome respite, but the theatre was still massively in debt. The burden of expenses and interest payments not only swallowed up the income but often exceeded the receipts. Matters were made worse when Sheridan, in order to raise ready money, sold a number of so-called renters' (or preference) shares at £3,000 each. The capital had been quickly spent, but the renters' entitlement to £1 on each night of performance was a further charge on the theatre's already overloaded income. Sheridan's own raids on the treasury only added to the problem.

There was an urgent need for further capital. In 1800, Joseph Richardson, an old friend and the author of a successful comedy, *The Fugitive*, was persuaded to buy a quarter share in the concern for £25,000. At the same time Sheridan made approaches to Kemble, who, after four years out of office, had begun to turn his thoughts to the management of the theatre again, this time with a view to becoming part proprietor as well.

Despite considerable arrears of salary, carefully noted in his journal, Kemble had amassed a substantial fortune over the years. On this fortune, safely invested in consols, Sheridan had fixed his eye. His proposals were seductive; in a long and skilfully worded letter, buoyant with financial optimism, he set out the advantages of taking a share in the theatre and the dangers, if Kemble did not do so, of its falling into 'vulgar or illiberal hands' who would not respect his theatrical ideals.

Why Kemble, financially and professionally secure, and knowing the embarrassments which beset the theatre, should allow himself to be tempted by Sheridan's proposals is a question which cannot be answered in purely worldly terms. He was, in the words of Walter Scott, a sworn votary to the drama, and this devotion was the over-ruling passion of his life. Moreover, he was convinced that if only the necessary reforms were made, the theatre could once more be a paying proposition. In the autumn of 1800, pending negotiations, he agreed to reassume the management.

It soon became clear that nothing had changed, or if so only for the worst, since he had left in dudgeon four years earlier. The autumn programme, which began with his own appearance in *Hamlet*, was dogged with financial problems from the first. Poor Peake, the treasurer, was besieged from day to day with letters such as this:

My dear Peake,
    Let me remind you that you are to send the fifty pounds for Mrs Siddons today, or we shall have no King John on Saturday . . .
    They are standing still in Greenwood's Room for Want of a little Canvas – Unless you can help us there, we can have no Cymbeline, nor no Pantomime this Christmas.

Not even his own salary was sacred:

My dear Peake,
    It is now two days since my necessity made me send to you for sixty pounds . . . I shall certainly go, and act my part tonight – but, unless you send me a hundred pounds before Thursday, I will not act on Thursday – and if you make me come a-begging again, it will be two hundred pounds before I set my foot in the theatre.

Kemble's negotiations with Sheridan, under these circumstances, hung fire. He struggled on as manager for two more seasons, achieving two notable Shakespearean productions, the *Cymbeline* referred to, and *A Winter's Tale*, amid increasing difficulties. *Pizarro* continued to draw crowded houses but its takings, along with the rest of the receipts, more often found their way into Sheridan's pockets than the treasury.

In 1801, Sheridan's creditors closed in, and Messrs Hammersley, the theatre's bankers, applied to the Lord Chancellor for first call on the theatre's takings. In the legal case that followed Sheridan pleaded persuasively, if disingenuously, on behalf of the performers and the theatre staff; if they were not paid first, he said, the theatre must close down and the creditors lose all chance of repayment. He admitted his own irregularities, but attributed them largely to the uncertainty of his income: 'It is a great disadvantage, relatively speaking, to any man and especially a very careless and very sanguine man, to have possessed an uncertain and fluctuating income. The disadvantage is

241

greatly increased if the person so circumstanced has conceived himself to be in some degree entitled to presume that, by the exertion of his own talents, he may at pleasure increase that income – thereby becoming induced to make promises to himself which he may afterwards fail to fulfil.'

Almost with pride, he produced an example of his carelessness which from anyone else would have been scarcely believable. Some time before, he had applied to the Duke of Bedford, the landlord of Drury Lane, to consolidate the ground rent at a certain sum. The duke had asked him to put his proposals in writing and, when he had done so, wrote back agreeing to his terms. Twelve months later, Sheridan, surprised at not having heard from him, applied to the duke's solicitor on the subject. The solicitor assured him that an answer had been sent a year before, whereupon Sheridan turned to his table and found the letter lying there unopened.

Sheridan's defence, conducted with his usual eloquence, convinced the court, who found in favour of the performers and the theatre staff, though they insisted on the appointment of a management committee to look after the interests of the creditors. On delivering his verdict the Lord Chancellor did not refrain from censuring Sheridan, quoting the famous closing lines from Johnson's *Life of Savage*: 'Negligence and irregularity, long continued, make knowledge useless, wit ridiculous, and genius contemptible.'

'I thought at the time,' wrote Michael Kelly, 'that the quotation might have been spared.' Sheridan's friends and admirers, however, were loud in their congratulations and even Kemble, who, exasperated by persistent arrears in his salary, had determined to leave the theatre, allowed himself to be seduced once more.

'He has now,' wrote the playwright Mrs Inchbald, describing Sheridan's conduct at the trial, '. . . so infatuated all the Court of Chancery and the whole town along with them, that every one is raging against poor Hammersley, the banker, and compassionating Sheridan; *all*, except his most intimate friends who know all the particulars: *they* shake their heads and sigh! Kemble, unable to get even five hundred out of four thousand pounds, packed up his boxes, made a parting supper to his friends, and ordered his chaise at seven o'clock the next morning. As they were sitting down to supper "Pop! he comes like the catastrophe". Mr Sheridan was announced – Kemble and he withdrew to the study; and the next thing I heard *all was settled.*'

The respite was only temporary. Kemble's attorney, unable to establish Sheridan's clear title to Drury Lane, advised him strongly against investing in it. Mrs Inchbald meanwhile had been negotiating on Kemble's behalf with Harris, the proprietor of Covent Garden, with a view to his becoming manager and part proprietor there. At the end of the summer season of 1802, bearing Mrs Siddons with him, Kemble bade farewell to the theatre which had seen him come to fame and which he had graced for over twenty years.

It was the end of a golden period for Drury Lane. Now only Mrs Jordan remained of the three great stars who had raised its artistic standards to such heights. Her drawing power was undiminished, but constant child bearing – she bore ten children to the Duke of Clarence – had taken its toll of her once slender shape. Her figure, as Hazlitt put it, had become 'large, soft and generous like her soul'; it was time to put aside the 'breeches parts' which had delighted her audiences. For Sheridan, with all his optimism, the loss of Kemble and his sister must have been a crushing blow. To outward appearances, however, he seemed as buoyant as ever. He had plans to write another opera *The Foresters* – a project of which he talked for many years and of which various attempts remained at his death. The autumn of 1802 found him at Polesden Lacey, ostensibly putting the finishing touches to his work, and playing the host, as we have seen, to a harvest home on the estate.

# XXIII

———✦———

The peace of Amiens lasted only fourteen months. Each side mistrusted the other's intentions. The British believed rightly that Napoleon was only looking for a breathing space in which to rebuild his fleet and his economy before attempting to invade once more; meanwhile his expansionist ambitions in Europe showed no signs of abating, as Switzerland and Piedmont were added to his list of puppet states. The French in their turn were convinced that the British did not intend to give up their control of the Mediterranean by surrendering Malta, as had been promised in the treaty, or to abandon their gains in the West Indies.

The issue of Malta, which Britain refused to surrender, was the official reason for the renewal of the war in May 1803. Well before that, almost all sections of opinion in Britain – with the exception of Fox and his followers – were convinced that the conflict was inevitable. On 8 December 1802, Sheridan spoke in favour of a large increase in the army estimates for the following year. Only eighteen months after defending him in the House of Commons his ideas on Bonaparte had changed dramatically. Fox tried in vain to restrain him. 'I am very much against your abusing Bonaparte, because I am sure it is impolitic both for the country and ourselves,' he wrote in a note before the debate. 'But as you please; – only for God's sake Peace.'

Sheridan, however, was not to be persuaded. Little by little he had come to believe that Bonaparte's appetite for power was insatiable and that Britain's best safety lay in being prepared.

'Look at the map of Europe; there where a great man [Burke] (who, however was always wrong on the subject) said he looked for France, and found nothing but a chasm. Look at that map now, and see nothing but France. It is in our power to measure her territory, to reckon her population, but is scarcely within the grasp of any man's mind to measure the ambition of Buonaparte.'

Napoleon's ambitions were progressive; he had far stronger reasons than the Bourbons to invade Great Britain.

'They were ambitious, but it was not so necessary for them to feed their subjects with the spoils and plunder of war; they had the attachment of a long and established family applied to them; they had the effect and advantage of a hereditary succession. But I see in the very situation and composition of Buonaparte a physical necessity to go on with this barter with his subjects, and to promise to make them masters of the world if they will be his slaves . . . If that be the case must not his most anxious looks be directed to Great Britain? Everything else is petty and contemptible compared with it. Russia, if not in his power, is at least in his influence – Prussia is at his beck – Italy is his vassal – Holland is in his grasp – Spain at his nod – Turkey in his toils. When I see this, can I hesitate in stating my feelings, still less in giving a vote that shall put [us] upon our guard against the machinations and workings of such ambition?'

It had been said, he continued, that Bonaparte meant nothing more than a commercial rivalry with Britain. 'Of the commercial talents of Buonaparte I can be supposed to know but little, but bred in camps it cannot be supposed to be very great . . . No, Sir, instead of putting his nation apprentice to commerce, he has other ideas in his head. My humble apprehension is that, though in the tablet and volume of his mind there may be some marginal note about cashiering the King of Etruria; yet that the whole text is occupied with the destruction of this country. This is the first vision that breaks upon him through the gleam of the morning; this is his last prayer at night, to whatever Deity he addresses it, whether to Jupiter or Mahomet; to the Goddess of Battles or the Goddess of Reason.'

He dismissed the idea that only Pitt could save the situation. 'Mr Pitt the only man to save the country! No single man can save the country. If a nation depends only upon one man, it cannot, and I will add, does not deserved to be saved; it can only be done by the Parliament and the people.'

Pitt had supported Addington in negotiating the peace; there was no reason why Addington should now be set aside. There was nothing of substance to be said against him. The vague dislike which he inspired was as capricious as that expressed in Martial's well-known epigram,

> Non amo te, Sabidi, nec possum dicere quare,
> Hoc tantum possum dicere, non amo te!

or, as parodied in English,

> I do not like thee, Dr Fell,
> The reason why I cannot tell;
> But this, I'm sure, I know full well,
> I do not like thee, Dr Fell.

This backhanded compliment rebounded on Addington. The son of a physician, supposedly with something of a bedside manner, he was jokingly known as 'the Doctor' in Whig circles. With Sheridan's speech the nickname became universal. 'None but himself could have called Addington Doctor to his face!' wrote a fellow MP, R. Plumer Ward.

Sheridan ended his speech with a reference to Fox, turning towards him as he said,

'I perfectly agree with my right honourable friend that war ought to be avoided, though he does not agree with me as to the means best calculated to produce that effect. From any opinion he may express, I never differ but with the greatest reluctance. For him my affection, my esteem and my attachment are unbounded, and they will end only with my life. But I think an important lesson is to be learned from the arrogance of Buonaparte. He says he is an instrument in the hands of Providence, an envoy of God . . . Sir, I think he is an instrument in the hands of Providence to make the English love their constitution better; to cling to it with more fondness; to hang round it with truer tenderness . . . I believe too, Sir, that he is an instrument in the hands of Providence, to make us more liberal in our political differences, and to render us more determined, with one hand and heart, to oppose any aggressions that may be made upon us. If that aggression be made, my honourable friend will, I am sure, agree with me, that we ought to meet it with a spirit worthy of these islands; that we ought to meet it with a conviction of the truth of this assertion, that the country which has achieved such greatness, has no retreat in littleness; that if we could be content to abandon everything, we should find no safety in poverty, no security in abject submission. Finally, Sir, that we ought to meet it with a fixed determination to perish in the same grave with the honour and independence of this country.'

Sheridan's speech, a patriotic clarion call, was praised on all sides of the House. Even Watkins, the most hostile of his biographers, describes it as vying with anything ever heard within its walls. But it could not be expected to please Fox. There was no way that he could do without Sheridan; his stature in the House of Commons and his brilliance as a speaker were too important to be dispensed with. But he had grown, Fox considered, 'mad with vanity and folly'. 'Sheridan's speech, (O Lord!!!),' he wrote to Grey, 'gave more concern to his friends and more satisfaction to his enemies, than any he ever made.'

Hecca, dressed up as a man (women were not allowed to enter the Chamber), had been smuggled into the Strangers Gallery by Lord John Townshend to hear her husband's speech. Her pride in her husband's public prowess was undiminished, but in private she had much to bear. Sheridan was drinking more heavily than before; his finances were increasingly chaotic. Since the Lord Chancellor's judgment, he was no longer able to raid the theatre treasury at will. His own salary of £5 a night when the theatre was open amounted to £1,000 a year, but though the 'renters' could no longer make a claim on it, there were many others who could. In 1802 and 1803 his position seems to have been particularly bad.

'Words cannot tell you the situation of this House as there is not even a candle in it – or a little tea for Mrs S.,' he wrote to Peake in May 1802. '. . . If I am not assisted with £20 tonight Mrs S. will be distracted.'

Poor Hecca was beginning to experience the realities of life with Sheridan. It was not that his debts were unusual by the standards of the time. Fox's debts were so colossal that in 1793 his friends raised a subscription to clear them and provide him with an annuity. He had no scruples in accepting such largess. When someone expressed a doubt about how he would take it, a friend who knew him well replied: 'Take it? why quarterly to be sure.' Pitt, too, allowed his friends to clear his debts by private subscription, and died owing £40,000. Sheridan's debts were scarcely on such an aristocratic scale, a niggling matter of tradesmen's bills, of wages in London and the country, and above all of interest payments on the accumulated mortgages and loans with which his share in Drury Lane was loaded. It was not likely that anyone would raise a subscription to ease him; even if they had, his touchy pride would not have allowed him to accept it. He made it a matter of honour never to borrow from a private friend.

Unlike the first Mrs Sheridan, Hecca had not been brought up to habits of economy. She was naturally extravagant and thoughtless. She had married Sheridan, she confessed to Granville Leveson Gower in 1807, in a mood of youthful idealism.

'I do not think that any young thing ever enter'd the world with a more enthusiastic admiration for every thing that was great and good than I did or a more romantic indifference to all those advantages that are with very few exceptions so highly prized. Sheridan saw my weak side, & set, not, not my *blood* but my *head* on fire by making me believe that his talents were poor compared with his soul.'

Hecca's confessions, part of a long and hitherto unpublished letter in the Granville papers, paint a sorry picture of her marriage. For the first three years, she wrote, her passion for Sheridan had not lessened, though his drinking had often thrown her into despair. It was not until after seven years, thus in 1802, that she became completely disillusioned. His drinking had come to disgust her, and her health was affected by the nights she passed, for '*never*, on any occasion would S. consent to a separate bed'. Worse still, she had begun to feel herself abused, betrayed and ridiculed by Lady Bessborough (formerly Duncannon), whom Sheridan was once more pursuing. It was at this moment, she wrote, that she was thrown into the company of her cousin Charles Grey.

'I confided my griefs to him – he pitied me and blamed himself for having given S. rather a helping hand with my father [by agreeing to become her trustee], and in short an intimacy arose between us beyond whatever existed but not till I beheld him under the influence of passion for me did I in thought ever deviate from what was right.'

248

The handsome Grey, whose affair with the duchess of Devonshire had ended with his marriage eight years before, had always been Hecca's favourite cousin. 'From the age of fourteen when I first saw him I decidedly thought him the most captivating person in appearance (I do not by that mean person only) I had ever beheld.' Sheridan's aberrations had made her, as she said, a 'dangerous object', but she held out for nearly a year after Grey first declared his passion before she 'passed those bounds which leave a woman no comfort but in the excess of her love'.

It was a complicated sexual minuet, of whose permutations Hecca was probably not altogether aware. Her confidant Granville Leveson Gower, later the first Earl Granville, had been the lover of Lady Bessborough for some years. Unknown to her husband or her mother, she had two children by him, who were later brought up as Granville's wards. Twelve years her junior, Granville would eventually marry the Duchess of Devonshire's daughter, Lady Harriet Cavendish; Lady Bessborough relinquishing him to her niece, we may imagine, with some of the same regrets as the Marschallin in the *Rosenkavalier*. The Duchess of Devonshire, as already mentioned, had been the mistress of Grey, by whom she had had a daughter in 1793. The following year he had married Mary Ponsonby, a cousin of the Bessboroughs, and thereafter met the duchess only on formal occasions. The child, named Eliza Courtney, was brought up by Grey's mother at his family home in Northumberland.

Some of the duchess's story must have been familiar to Hecca, though, as she insisted, she had learned it not from Sheridan, but from Grey. But it is unlikely that she realised the full extent of Sheridan's earlier involvement with Lady Bessborough. Lady Bessborough, naturally, was not going to reveal to Granville that Sheridan had been her lover – she writes of him disingenuously as having 'lik'd me formerly but without success'. She was still on friendly terms with Sheridan, seeing him frequently at Devonshire House and elsewhere. But of late he had begun to annoy her with fine speeches, though his infatuation, she was sure, owed more to obstinacy than love. Her letters to Granville at this time give numerous instances of his so-called persecutions. At one point he appears in her box at the theatre, retiring to the corner and pretending to cry when she takes no notice of him; at another she suspects him of writing anonymous paragraphs about her in the papers; at another he assures her, between pauses in the music at the opera, that her lover is unfaithful and that if she had any spirit she would fly him. He follows her round like a shadow at a ball, behaving so embarrassingly that she is forced to explain, which is true, that he is drunk. On several occasions she refuses to admit him when he calls, but when once he inveigles himself in she finds him 'so abominably entertaining' that she ends by being glad he came.

All this must have been annoying enough for Hecca, who, as her letter to Granville reveals, felt that Lady Bessborough was making fun of her or, worse still, carrying on with Sheridan behind her back. Sheridan's drunkenness, the financial straits to which they were reduced – 'not a silver fork or teaspoon left', noted Grey – were further incitements to be unfaithful. She had fallen for Grey whole-heartedly, with 'such love as . . . under the existing circumstances was irresistible, that love which informs every faculty of our soul, and lays its most inmost feeling open to the object of it'; though her remorse at deceiving Mrs Grey, who had always treated her with special kindness, drove her almost to distraction. Later, when Mrs Grey had become angry and unjust towards her – 'and who that is smarting under the pangs of jealousy is not unjust' – she confessed that her remorse had largely vanished. (Since Mrs Grey eventually bore her husband fifteen children, it seems the episode did no lasting damage to their marriage.)

The outside world knew nothing of Hecca's affair with Grey, though Lady Bessborough told her later that she and Lady Elizabeth Foster had been convinced of it. So, too, had the duchess. She had accepted Grey's marriage as inevitable, but had always believed herself the one great love of his life. She was now in ill health, racked by headaches and with failing eyesight; the thought that he had, as it were, betrayed her must have added greatly to her sufferings.

How much Sheridan himself was aware of what was happening is not certain, but given Hecca's uninhibited character it is unlikely that she concealed it from him for long. It is clear that their marriage reached some kind of crisis point in the summer of 1803 and that Sheridan was desperate at the thought of losing her. 'By my Life and Soul,' he wrote to her on 30 June, 'if you talk of leaving me now you will destroy me. I am wholly unwell – I neither sleep nor eat. You are before my eyes Night and Day. I will contrive that you shall go to the North at all events, but don't leave me to myself . . . Dear Charles kiss your mother for me, for [if] I live 'till you have mind to know me you will not cease to love me.'

In a letter to Lord Holland about the same time, Lady Bessborough told him: 'S. is never sober for a moment and his affairs worse than ever. *Pour comble* he has quarreled with Mrs S. A sort of separation took place, but I believe it is partly made up again – at least they live in the same house again, but not very good friends.'

Somehow the marriage lurched on, though Hecca spent increasingly long periods away from home, staying with her various relations in the country. Interestingly, Sheridan always spoke well of Grey to Hecca; according to Moore, however, Grey hated Sheridan 'because he intrigued with Sheridan's last wife'.

Sheridan suffered a new blow that summer with the death of his old friend Joseph Richardson. Richardson, whom he had talked into buying a quarter share in Drury Lane, had had nothing but trouble from his investment. It was only thanks to the generosity of various noblemen, among them the Duke of Bedford, that his debts were written off and his family was saved from ruin. For Sheridan another link with the past was broken. He had been a friend of Richardson's since his early days in London, when the two of them, with Tickell, had been inseparable companions. He lamented him especially since Richardson, who knew his domestic situation better than anyone else, had often acted as a go-between in his disputes with Hecca.

It was typical of Sheridan that, though he wept bitterly at the news of Richardson's death, he arrived so late for the funeral that the service was already over and the undertaker had left for another funeral elsewhere. The vicar, however, was persuaded to allow his son, the curate, to repeat the service in the church and by the graveside. Sheridan, said John Taylor, who had travelled down with him, showed 'a sort of mournful exultation' that he had been able to show due honour to his friend.

In the autumn of 1803, after a sabbatical year spent travelling abroad, Kemble made his first appearance at Covent Garden, in which he had purchased a one-sixth share. Kemble and the chief proprietor Harris, as new allies, invited Sheridan to dine; there were always matters of mutual interest for the proprietors of the patent theatres to discuss. Sheridan grew bitter, as the wine began to flow, at the cordiality which Kemble and Harris displayed towards each other, and reproached them sarcastically for their hypocrisy. 'Two fellows,' said he, 'that have hated each other deadly all their lives.' 'False,' said Harris cheerfully; 'we have not hated each other these *six* weeks – have we, Kemble?'

Kemble and his sister were sorely missed at Drury Lane but the autumn of 1803 brought one of those reprieves which so often rescued Sheridan at the eleventh hour. This time his saviour was a performing dog, a Newfoundland called Carlo, who, in a musical afterpiece, *The Caravan*, plunged into real water to rescue a child. The exploit, accompanied by an audible splash, was received with riotous applause and repeated nightly to enthusiastic crowds. Well might Sheridan, sensing profit, rush into the green-room after the first performance with a cry of 'Where is my preserver?' – dismissing the author, when he modestly presented himself, with a cry of 'Pooh, I mean the dog!'

In the midst of these theatrical and matrimonial distractions, the peace of Amiens had come to an end. Bonaparte began to assemble a new army of invasion on the cliffs near Boulogne; for the next two years Britain would be France's only enemy. On 23 May 1803, five days after war had been declared, Sheridan listened to Pitt, standing three rows behind the government front bench, make one of his most memorable speeches, supporting the Cabinet's decision to fight.

'Pitt raised the War [w]hoop most vehemently and eloquently,' wrote Sheridan to Lady Bessborough that evening. He described the speech as 'one of the most brilliant and magnificent pieces of declamation that ever fell from that rascal Pitt's lips. Detesting the Dog as I do, I cannot withdraw this just tribute to the Scoundrel's talents.'

In an equally memorable speech the following day, Fox, consistent as ever in his hatred of war, put the case for restoring the peace if 'any just arrangement' could be found.

'I have done what I would do for no one breathing but you,' reported Sheridan to Lady Bessborough, '– Left the House while Fox was speaking to answer your note . . . He has spoken not only wonderfully well, but with the greatest possible dexterity, prudence, management, etc., qualities he has not always at command.'

For all his eloquence, Sheridan was not prepared to vote with Fox; he no longer believed that peace was possible. Six weeks later he spoke strongly in support of a government plan to raise a corps of volunteers, suiting the action to the word by joining up himself. 'Richard is Lieutenant Colonel of the St James's Volunteers', noted his brother on a visit to London that autumn, '. . . so he will be obliged to keep early hours in spite of himself.'

There was much merriment at the idea of Sheridan in this belligerent guise. Gillray summed up his differences with Fox in one of his funniest caricatures. Published under the title 'Physical Aid, or Britannia recovered from a Trance: – also the Patriotic Courage of Sherry Andrew, and a peep thro' the Fog', it shows Fox, with his hat pulled over his eyes, peering vainly in the direction of the French boats which are to carry their army to England. Meanwhile Sheridan, in a tattered harlequin dress, flourishes a cudgel inscribed 'Dramatic Loyalty' and shouts his defiance at the oncoming fleet: 'Let 'em all come, damme! – where are the French bugaboos? – Single handed, I'll beat forty of 'em!! damme, I'll pay 'em off like renter's shares, sconce off their half Crowns, mulct them out of their Benefits and come the Drury Lane Slang over them!'

# XXIV

In May 1804, the Addington administration fell and Pitt was recalled to power. There had been much plotting behind scenes beforehand, with no one group possessing an obvious majority. It was a time when Sheridan, had he wished, might have had a place or even a title under Addington. But he disdained, in his own phrase, to 'hide his head in a coronet' or to accept any offers for himself or his son. In this, thought Lady Bessborough, he behaved very handsomely. Even Fox had said that since Sheridan was obviously sincere in supporting the ministry he saw no reason why he should not accept some post of responsibility with them, and if not for himself, for Tom. Sheridan, however, refused everything, explaining to the Prince of Wales when he remonstrated with him 'that his situation was peculiar, and that his receiving anything like emolument for himself or family from Ministers would *contaminate the purity* of his support and dishonour him for ever'. In any case, he declared, he would never desert Fox.

Sheridan's pride in his 'unpurchaseable mind' had sustained him through long years in political wilderness. Devious in other parts of his life, his insistence on following his own line in politics had something almost naive about it, that simplicity which the prince regent noted. In differing with Fox about the the war, he had lost the confidence of his colleagues without gaining any corresponding advantages elsewhere. He was regarded as unreliable and inconsistent by his former friends. Fox doubted if he even knew what he wanted.

To make matters worse he was damning Fox in his cups, as though to reinforce his own opinions. On one occasion, whilst staying with the Duke of Bedford at Woburn, he spoke so abusively about Fox that he was challenged to a duel by a fellow MP, and would have taken up the challenge had not Whitbread managed to restrain them. Renewing his abuse at Whitbread's house soon after, the argument became so heated that Whitbread thumped the table and looked as though he was going to strike Sheridan, who called out, 'My boisterous landlord [a dig at Whitbread's brewing interests] means to silence me by the weight of his arm, as he cannot by that of his arguments.' Matters might have ended seriously if Sheridan, who had started sober, had not become so drunk that he fell asleep.

Such episodes were common gossip at Devonshire House and Holland House, those two great centres of Foxite loyalty. Feeling himself in disfavour, Sheridan tried to make his peace. He confessed to the Prince of Wales that he had embarrassed himself in such a manner that he did not know how to extricate himself, and that he believed, after all, that it was better to stick to one's old friends, even if they were a little wrong. Fox was too good-natured, and perhaps too lazy, to quarrel with him seriously. It was hard to be angry with Sheridan for long. Even the partisan Lady Holland admitted that after five minutes in his company 'a sort of cheerful frankness and pleasant wittiness' put all her prejudices against him to flight.

Sheridan claimed that he supported Addington not because he approved of him but in order to keep out Pitt. He was horrified at the suggestion that Fox and Pitt should join forces in order to form a truly national government. It was a suggestion which Pitt would have welcomed, but foundered on the opposition of the king, who refused to accept Fox under any circumstances. Fox was ready to stand aside and let his friends take office, but none of them would agree. Sheridan, of course, was among them, though Fox told Grey that he no longer had much confidence in him. Meanwhile, Addington was being attacked on all sides, accused of mismanaging the war, and the call for Pitt was growing. In April 1804, Fox's followers joined with those of Pitt and Grenville, the former Foreign Secretary, to vote against Addington and his majority was reduced to only eleven. Too discouraged to continue, he resigned and Pitt took up office the following month. Unable to form a broad-based government, since neither the Whigs nor Grenville would join him without Fox, he was forced to include six members from the former Cabinet, as well as six new ones, in his new Cabinet. 'The six new nags,' said Sheridan, 'will have to draw not only the carriage, but those six heavy cast-off blacks along with it.'

Once again Sheridan found himself opposing Pitt. On 6 March the following year, in a debate on the Additional Forces Bill, he launched a major attack on the Prime Minister, taxing him amongst other things with his betrayal of the Catholics. Having resigned because he could not carry Catholic emancipation, he had now come back to office with colleagues determined to resist it and 'a character degraded by the violation of a solemn pledge'.

Going on to denounce the incompetence of his various ministers, he reserved the full power of his sarcasm for Lord Melville (formerly Dundas), who, having been Secretary for War in Pitt's previous administration, had now been appointed First Lord of the Admiralty: 'I do not know of any particular qualications the noble lord has to preside over the admiralty; but I do know, that if I were to judge of him from the kind of capacity he evinced while minister of war, I should entertain little hopes of him . . . It may be said, that as the noble lord was so unfit for the military department the naval was the proper place for him.'

He was reminded, he said, of the story of Garrick and a Scotchman called Johnny McCree. Johnny wrote four acts of a tragedy, which he showed to Garrick, who dissuaded him from finishing it, saying his talents did not lie that way. Johnny then set about writing a comedy, which Garrick, when he read it, found even less acceptable. This surprised poor Johnny, who remonstrated:

' "Nay, now David," said Johnny, "did you not tell me that my talents did not lie in tragedy?"

' "Yes," replied Garrick, "but I did not tell you that they lay in comedy."

' "Then," exclaimed Johnny, "gin they dinna lie there, where the de'il dittha lie mon?" '

After indulging in this digression, which raised a loud laugh, Sheridan drew attention once again to the way that patronage had been misused. During the seventeen years that Pitt had been in office, almost half the members of the peerage had been of his creating, for the most part not for any great services to the country but for their usefulness to the ministry. 'It is impossible,' he said, 'that these things can go on much longer without danger to the constitution.'

Pitt gave as good as he got in his reply. He turned on Sheridan for his insincerity in having supported the previous administration, then went on to blast his methods as a speaker with a withering critique.

'The honourable gentleman,' he said, 'seldom condescends to favour us with a display of his extraordinary powers of imagination and fancy, but, when he does come forward, we are prepared for a grand performance. No subject comes amiss to him, however remote from the question before the House. All that his fancy suggests at the time, or that he has collected from others; all that he can utter in the ebullition of the moment; all that he has slept on and bottled up, are combined and introduced for our entertainment. All his hoarded repartees – all his matured jests – the full contents of his common-place book – all his severe invectives – all his bold and hardy assertions – all that he has been treasuring up for days and months – he collects into one mass, which he kindles into a blaze of eloquence, and out it comes altogether, whether it has any relation to the subject of the debate or not.'

There was more than a grain of truth in Pitt's portrait, which prompted Gillray's famous cartoon 'Uncorking Old Sherry' four days later. Sheridan was stung to an immediate reply, hastening to a nearby coffee-house to dash down its main outlines. When the next speaker, Castlereagh, had finished, he rose to answer the Prime Minister.

'The right honourable gentleman,' he said, 'had stated that he (Sheridan) had wandered entirely from the subject; that he appeared to know nothing about the bill, except its title; and that he appeared to have hoarded up a collection of jests and sarcasms to throw upon him. If his speech, however, had been so very ignorant and unworthy of the serious attention of the House, there was no occasion for the right honourable gentleman to jump up immediately to reply to it himself.'

He went on to defend himself against the accusation of insincerity in supporting Addington. He had done so in good faith, he said, because he approved of his measures and because he regarded his continuance in office as a security against Pitt's return to power, which he had always thought the greatest possible calamity. But even if he had not done so, what then? Unlike Pitt, he had never professed to support him.

'If, indeed, I had, like him, recommended Mr Addington to his Majesty and the public, as the fittest person to fill his high station, because it was a convenient step to my own safety, in retiring from a station which I . . . could no longer fill with honour or security; if, having done so from such unwarrantable motives, I should have tapered off by degrees, from a promised support, when I saw the minister of my own choice was acquiring a greater stability and popularity than I wished for: and if, when I saw an opening to my return to power at a safer period than when I had left it, I had entered into a combination with others [Fox and Grenville] whom I meant to betray, from the sole lust of power and office, in order to remove him; and if, under the domination of these base appetites, I had then treated with ridicule and contempt the very man whom I just before held up to the choice of my Sovereign and the approbation of this House and the public; I should, indeed, have deserved the contempt of all sound politicians and the execration of every honest private man; I should, indeed, have deserved to be told not merely that I was hollow and insincere in my support, but that I was base, mean and perfidious.'

More than four hundred members were present during these exchanges, some of the most savage ever heard within the House of Commons. 'Sherry's speech and reply were excellent,' wrote Creevey, who had recently joined the House of Commons as a Foxite Whig. 'When he fired on Pitt for his treachery to the Catholics, Pitt's eyes started with defiance from their sockets, and seemed to tell him if he advanced an atom further he would have his life. Never has it fallen to my lot to hear such words before in publick or in private used by man to man.'

It was the last great confrontation between Sheridan and Pitt. Neither had ever spared the other, but there was nothing petty or small-minded in their antagonism. For all their enmity, Sheridan was never jealous of Pitt's success, nor was Pitt contemptuous of his failure. According to Tierney, Pitt's erstwhile duelling opponent, Pitt thought him a far greater man than Fox.

The sands were now running out for Pitt. Already he was showing signs of the illness which would kill him less than a year later. His face had grown yellow and emaciated and he was suffering from a hollow cough. In April, Lord Melville, who had been his closest political friend, was accused of misapplying public money, and when, by a majority of only one, the House voted to consider proceedings to impeach him, Pitt was seen to press his cocked hat over his eyes to hide his tears.

Sheridan did not join the Whigs in harrying Melville, though some manuscript notes for a speech show that he contemplated doing so. He was still an unpredictable ally but he had once more shown his value to his party as a speaker. He had as well one major trump card, his friendship with the Prince of Wales. Ever since the regency crisis fourteen years before, he had remained one of the prince's closest political advisers. Their views were sometimes at variance, but his advice had always been disinterested and based on a sincere desire to serve him. In 1804, when the king had had a brief recurrence of his illness, raising new hopes of a regency, Sheridan had been the prince's go-between with Addington, deferred to even by Fox in the discussions of the new arrangements. The king's recovery had ended their negotiations, but, though the prospect of the regency receded, it had shown the importance of his influence.

There was a strain of chivalry and quixotry, mixed with a certain harmless vanity, in Sheridan's devotion to the prince. He had defended him in the House of Commons, most notably over his debts, but he prided himself that he had never received or solicited the slightest favour from him. In 1804, however, the post of Receiver General to the Duchy of Cornwall became vacant after forty-five years. It was the only position, apart from those in his own household, which the prince had in his gift. He offered it to Sheridan as a 'trifling proof' of his friendship for him over many years. 'I wish to God,' he added, 'that it was better worth your acceptance.' This time Sheridan accepted – he told Addington that he felt it would be false pride to refuse – only to find that the prince, with typical insouciance, had already promised the reversion of the post to one of his former equerries, Major-General Lake, now commanding the armed forces in India. Lake pressed his claim and Sheridan, protesting that he would do nothing to embarrass the prince, agreed to give up the income as soon as he returned to England. Fortunately this did not cost him too much; Lake did not return to England till 1807 and he died the following year, when the place became Sheridan's for life.

Sheridan's friendship with the prince went well beyond his usefulness in politics. He had been his companion in many youthful escapades. He had helped him in his tangled love affairs, for the prince, as he once remarked, was 'too much every lady's man to be the man of any lady'. He had saved him, memorably, by defending the honour of Mrs Fitzherbert; he had also, regrettably, been his go-between in setting up a brief affair with the beautiful singer Mrs Crouch. (Michael Kelly, to whom she returned after satisfactory financial arrangements had been made, was delighted at this seal of royal approval.) His traducers once suggested that the prince had offered him £20,000 if he could have his way with Elizabeth Sheridan, but it is impossible to take this seriously. Above all, he was matchlessly good company. The prince, deprived of any useful occupation by his father, was always ready to be amused and whether at Carlton House or the Pavilion in Brighton, where a room was always kept for him, Sheridan was one of his most welcome visitors.

Creevey, who spent the autumn of 1805 in Brighton, where Sheridan was staying at the Pavilion, was able to observe his relations with the prince at close quarters. Nothing, he wrote, could be more creditable to both parties than their conduct. 'I never saw Sheridan during the period of three weeks (I think it was) take the least more liberty in the Prince's presence than if it had been the first day he had ever seen him. On the other hand, the Prince showed by his manner that he thought Sheridan a man that any prince might be proud of as a friend.'

Creevey, as an ardent Foxite, had begun by disapproving of Sheridan. There was too much of the scene-shifter about his politics, he thought, and his vanity in trying to be first in the prince's counsels was insufferable. Recently, however, they had grown 'pretty intimate' and in their walks in Brighton Sheridan told him much about his early life. Creevey's recollections of their conversations, written down nearly half a century later, are amongst the most vivid records of Sheridan's youth.

At the Pavilion, wrote Creevey, Sheridan entered into whatever fun was going on as if he had been a boy instead of nearly fifty-five. On one occasion he came into the drawing-room disguised as a police officer to take the Dowager Lady Sefton for playing some illegal game. Another time, when they were having a phantasmagoria and were all shut up in perfect darkness, he continued to sit on the lap of Madame Grebotzoff, a haughty Russian lady, 'who made enough row for the whole town to hear her'.

The prince, of course, was delighted with all this, but eventually Sheridan made himself so ill with drinking that he came to the Creeveys' lodgings one morning, saying that he was in a perfect fever and would spend the day quietly with them, sending his excuses for not dining to the prince. In the evening, when the Creeveys left for the Pavilion, where there was to be a ball, Sheridan said he would go back with them, and asked them to tell the prince, if he enquired for him, that he was far from well and had gone to bed.

At midnight, when supper was being served, the prince came up to Creevey and said, 'What the devil have you done with Sheridan today, Creevey? I know he has been dining with you, and I have not seen him the whole day.' Creevey explained that Sheridan was ill, but the prince, laughing heartily, 'as if he thought it all fudge', took a bottle of claret and a glass and put it in his hands. 'Now, Creevey,' he said, 'go to his bedside and tell him I'll drink a glass of wine with him, and if he refuses, I admit he must be damned bad indeed.'

Creevey, rather unwillingly, went up to Sheridan's room with the message. Sheridan was in bed, and, fixing his 'great fine eyes' on Creevey, said, 'Come, I see this is some joke of the Prince, and I am not in a state for it.' Creevey excused himself as best he could and, as Sheridan would not touch the wine, the prince seemed satisfied that he was really ill.

About two in the morning, when supper was long over and everyone was dancing, who should appear at the door but Sheridan, 'powdered white as snow, as smartly dressed as ever he could be from top to toe'. Creevey went down with him to find some supper in the kitchen. 'Once he arrived there,' he wrote, 'he began to play off his cajolery upon the servants, saying that if he was the Prince they should have much better accommodation, &c., &c., so that he

261

was surrounded by supper on all sides, every one waiting upon him. He ate away and drank a bottle of claret in a minute, returned to the ball room, and when I left it between three or four he was dancing.'

On 6 November, while the prince was still at the Pavilion, the news of Nelson's death at Trafalgar reached England. The whole nation joined in mourning the hero, sorrow at his loss overriding the rejoicing at his destruction of the French and Spanish fleets. So overcome was the prince that he refused to see anyone at the Pavilion, or to attend a ball which was being given in his honour that evening. 'Very shocking,' said the host to Mrs Creevey, when she lamented Nelson's death; 'and to come at such an unlucky time!'

Three days later Pitt was toasted at the Lord Mayor's banquet as the 'saviour of Europe' and answered in the memorable words: 'Europe is not to be saved by any single man. England has saved herself by her exertions and will, I trust, save Europe by her example.' It is not too fanciful to suggest that his first sentence, consciously or unconsciously, was an echo of Sheridan's 'No single man can save the country' in his speech two years before.

Trafalgar changed the course of the war decisively. From now on England was invincible at sea and the threat of invasion was at an end. But the situation in Europe was disastrous. By the end of December the short-lived third coalition (Britain, Austria, Russia and Sweden), which Pitt had struggled to bring together, had virtually collapsed beneath the devastating blows of Napoleon's victories at Ulm and Austerlitz. Austria had capitulated; the Russian and Swedish troops had withdrawn to their own borders. Napoleon's dominance in Europe seemed unassailable.

The news of Austerlitz, by general agreement, sounded Pitt's death knell. Fighting against increasing weakness, he lingered on till 22 January 1806. He left behind him many questions unresolved, Catholic emancipation still denied to Ireland, civil liberties weakened, the hopes of parliamentary reform in ruins. But no one, not even his most extreme opponents, could deny his greatness or his patriotism.

'As for me,' said Sheridan in a speech soon after, 'there were many who flattered him more than I, and some who feared him more; but there was no man who had a higher respect for his transcendent talents, his matchless eloquence, and the greatness of his soul; and yet it has often been my fate to have opposed his measures. I may have considered that there was somewhat too much of loftiness in his mind which could not bend to advice, or scarcely bear co-operation. I might have considered, that as a statesman his measures were not adequate to the situation of the country in the present times, but I always thought his purpose and his hope was for the greatness and security of the empire.'

Pitt's death at last brought Fox back into office, and the king, overcoming his deep-seated abhorrence of his character and politics, was forced to accept him as Foreign Secretary. Grenville, as strong an advocate of war in the past as Fox had been of peace, was First Lord of the Treasury and nominal Prime Minister, and Addington, now Lord Sidmouth, was Lord Privy Seal. The new administration, christened by Sheridan the Ministry of All the Talents, was certainly (with the exception of the Pittites) one of all opinions.

Now was the time when Sheridan might have expected his reward for his long years in opposition. Perhaps, writes Moore, if Fox had been in sole command, he would have done his best to include him in the Cabinet. But Sheridan had been against the union of Fox and Grenville, and Grenville felt no obligations to him. In the end he was made a member of the Privy Council and appointed Treasurer of the Navy, the same post he would have taken seventeen years before at the time of the first regency crisis.

Some of his friends felt that he should refuse it and retain his independence as a speaker, but Sheridan, though mortified at being passed over, was not prepared to carry self-sacrifice so far. But he accepted it, he wrote bitterly to Fox, 'without the slightest feeling of obligation to any one living . . . it is seventeen years since when you professed to me that I should not be content to accept that alone'.

He soon contrived to irritate his new colleagues by opposing a government motion on recruiting, which, if the Addingtonians had supported him, would have led to a government defeat. Creevey, as a good party man, thought his behaviour infamous. Sheridan, however, compounded his offences with a lofty declaration. 'He was sure the Cabinet would never look to him for the subserviency of sacrificing his independence of opinion to any consideration of office; at least, if they should ever so expect, they would be disappointed.'

# XXV

Sheridan's new office as Treasurer of the Navy brought him a salary of £4,000 a year and apartments in Somerset House. It was part of his duty, he considered, to use his position to entertain Members of Parliament whose support might be needed by the government, and he immediately set about doing so. The apartments were redecorated, there were dinners and receptions on a splendid scale, and a magnificent christening party for his first grandchild at which the Prince of Wales and the leading members of the government were present. Tom, after various vicissitudes that included an action for 'crim. con.' from which his father had had to extricate him with a payment of £1,500, had made a runaway marriage with a young Scottish heiress, Caroline Callendar, the previous year. Sheridan, who thought the marriage imprudent, had threatened to cut his son off with a shilling when he first heard of it. 'You haven't got it about you, have you, sir?' was the irrepressible Tom's reply.

As it turned out, Sheridan was delighted with his daughter-in-law, who was pretty and clever, but, alas, not such an heiress that the couple could survive without his help. Three years earlier, Sheridan had refused a sinecure from Addington for Tom, for fear of compromising his political independence. With his friends now in power he hoped that something would be done for Tom. He reminded Fox that he had promised that Tom should be taken care of when the Whigs returned to office but Fox would only answer that he had 'no hopes of doing it instantaneously'. In the end he was appointed Joint Muster Master-General in Ireland, a comparatively minor post, which he held for only a few months before the ministry fell. Sheridan had done what he could for him meanwhile by making him assistant manager at Drury Lane – a role in which, said Kelly, he was 'punctuality personified' – and handing him a quarter of his shares.

Tom had done his best in an increasingly hopeless situation. Since the departure of Kemble and Mrs Siddons receipts had gone down at Drury Lane. There had been occasional flashes in the pan. The success of Carlo, the dog, had been one; the season of 1804–5 had brought another in the shape of the child actor Master Betty.

William Henry Betty, the 'Young Roscius', was the son of a former prompter of the Belfast theatre. An exceptionally beautiful and precocious thirteen-year-old, he had already acquired an enormous following in the provinces when he arrived in London in December 1804. His first appearance at Covent Garden, as Achmet in a forgotten tragedy called *Barbarossa*, created a near riot. 'The Crowd tonight at C. G. was beyond anything ever known,' Sheridan told Hecca. 'They say a man or two has been kill'd . . . The whole talk of the Town nothing but Young Roscius Young Roscius Young Roscius.'

Sheridan had been furious that Covent Garden had been the first with Master Betty, but after 'great bickerings and discussions' with Harris it was agreed that he should appear alternately at the two main theatres, playing in almost all the leading classical roles. (Though *Hamlet*, said Kemble, he should *not* have attempted.) Drury Lane drew in its share of crowds, but though the box-office takings were enormous the demands of Master Betty's father – £50, more than Kemble earned in a week, for each appearance – were so exorbitant that the profits did not match receipts.

Master Betty's heyday, though glorious, was short-lived. By the end of the season the intense enthusiasm which he had generated had begun to die down and the public, rather shamefacedly, withdrew from its infatuation. His second season was not a success and he was not re-engaged for a third. Meanwhile, among the spate of 'prodigies' who sprang up in his wake, a Master Wigley, aged four and a half, was engaged to play the bugle at Drury Lane; Mrs Jordan, on entering the green-room one evening, was said to have remarked, 'Oh, for the days of King Herod!'

Sheridan's appointment as Treasurer of the Navy had been greeted with amusement, even in the gravest circles. 'I heard of Sheridan's appearing before the bank directors to open his Navy Office Account,' wrote the Earl of Essex to Lord Lowther. 'The joke is that they all ran out of the room, carrying away their books and papers.' But no one was more high-minded than Sheridan when it came to public money, and once in office he seems to have carried out his duties conscientiously. We catch a genial picture of him in the papers of a Herefordshire clergyman, the Reverend Archer Clive. One of Clive's parishioners, a Mr Williams, had a son who had been trying to join the Royal Navy, but had fallen into the hands of a 'crimp', or press-gang agent, and was about to be carried off on board a merchant ship. The father, in great anxiety, hurried up to London, where he had never been before and where the only man he knew was his local MP, Robert Biddulph. Biddulph told him that he could not help him, but that if he would care to dine with him that evening, he would introduce him to Fox and Sheridan and other leading members of the government. On hearing Williams's story, Sheridan invited him to call at the Admiralty next morning; he did so and the son was duly given a commission in the Royal Navy, where he later became a lieutenant. Williams remembered his visit to London and his dinner with the great men to the end of his life.

After so long a period in the wilderness, Sheridan might reasonably have expected to remain in office for several years. His reckless extravagance on arriving at Somerset House, if not excusable, was at least understandable in this light. He had always been one, as Hecca said, for eating the calf in the cow's belly. But the Ministry of All the Talents stayed in power for only thirteen months, and Fox, its dominating figure, died in September 1806.

From the spring of that year it had been clear that Fox was very ill. He was suffering from dropsy, probably due to cancer of the liver, which several operations had failed to relieve. His friends urged him to retire, but Fox, as he told Grey, had two 'glorious things' to achieve, peace and the abolition of the slave trade before he did so. He failed in the first, finding, as the Pittites had done before him, that it was impossible to negotiate a secure peace while Napoleon continued to be bent on further conquests. But he had the satisfaction, in his last speech in the House of Commons, of successfully proposing a motion in favour of the abolition of the slave trade. The resolution was carried by both Houses, and, though the bill was not passed till the following year, he knew that it was safely set in train.

Fox's work was now done. He died at Chiswick House, the Duke of Devonshire's country villa, on 13 September 1806. Sheridan was one of those who called to see him in his final days, though according to Moore, Fox was not eager to receive him. 'I *must* see him, I suppose,' said Fox, and when Sheridan came in put out his hand to him. Sheridan later told Samuel Rogers, who was present, that when Fox took his hand, he said in a low voice, 'My dear Sheridan, I love you; you are indeed my friend; as for those others, I merely, etc.' 'This,' said Rogers, 'was an excellent invention of Sheridan, who knew no one would contradict him.'

It is impossible to know the truth of this last interview. Rogers, as an *habitué* of Holland House, was likely to be biased against Sheridan. Certainly, during the previous few years, Fox had been increasingly exasperated by Sheridan; according to Philip Francis, another biased witness, he sometimes spoke to him as though he were talking to a swindler. But Sheridan's friendship with Fox, stretching back for more than a quarter of a century, had far more to it than these last misunderstandings. It had been Fox who had sponsored Sheridan's first entry into politics and the brilliant world of Whig society. They had sat up late so often at Brooks's or the Beefsteak Club, with Sheridan 'firing and blazing away for the evening like an inexhaustible battery', as on a memorable occasion described by the actor John Bernard, when 'Fox was seated between Sheridan and Bannister, and did nothing but fill their glasses and listen to their conversation; whilst they, making his head a kind of shuttlecock, hit it on each side with such admirable repartees, that he roared aloud like a bull.' Beneath the gaiety and good fellowship had lain a common purpose which at the time of the French Revolution had made them the great champions of civil liberties at home. Fox's legacy to English politics was a tradition of aristocratic liberalism which long after his death made it possible to carry through reform without a revolution. Sheridan had been his right-hand man throughout the 1790s, when the threat of reaction was at its height, and without his eloquence and passion the opposition's contribution would been far less. Later differences had soured their relations, but for all their reservations about him it was to Sheridan that Fox's family turned to organise his funeral procession, and he followed him as one of the chief mourners to his grave among the country's statesmen in Westminster Abbey.

Any hopes Sheridan might have had of inheriting Fox's mantle as leader of his party were quickly dispelled. Grey became leader of the House and Foreign Secretary, while Sheridan retained his old post of Treasurer to the Navy. But Fox's death left a vacancy at Westminster and Sheridan had always expected to succeed him in that celebrated constituency. He had abstained from formally presenting himself till Fox had breathed his last, only to find that the grandees of his party had made other plans and that the Duke of Northumberland's son, Lord Percy, had already been chosen as the government's candidate for the post. There may have been some element of misunderstanding – Grenville, apparently, had been told that Sheridan did not wish to stand – but Sheridan was understandably bitter at the way he had been treated. He agreed to withdraw his candidature, however, and Lord Percy was duly elected. Shortly after, Parliament was dissolved and since the second member, Gardner, who had been promised a peerage, was not standing for re-election, Sheridan announced his intention of contesting the seat. Lord Holland accused him of forcing himself on the constitutency, and the Duke of Northumberland, who disapproved of Sheridan, withdrew his son's candidature in disgust. Sheridan, however, was determined not to give way. Another candidate, Sir Samuel Hood, a naval hero and relation of Fox's old opponent Lord Hood, took up the second place and he and Sheridan would have been returned unopposed had not a radical candidate, James Paull, presented himself at the last moment.

The election that followed was as hard fought and violent as Fox's great contest in 1784. This time there were no fine ladies to canvass for votes. The Duchess of Devonshire, who had flung herself into the fray for Fox, had died five months before him. The old light-hearted days were over. Sheridan's opponents spared him nothing on the hustings or in print. 'Nature,' read one pamphlet, 'never cast the image of man in a more unlovely mould than when she formed Bardolpho; his countenance possesses all the characteristics of ugliness and bestial sensuality; in figure he is more ungraceful than a hog, and in his whole appearance scarcely less filthy and disgusting.'

Sheridan did not descend to this level, though his supporters were rough and rowdy enough. He appeared at the hustings on the first day of voting 'escorted by a parcel of men armed with bludgeons', their numbers swelled by the scene-shifters from Drury Lane. He was greeted by such a clamour from the mob already gathered there that his first audible words from the platform were to ask whether they wanted a riot or an election. Over the fifteen days of voting, he faced the invective of the crowd with unruffled coolness and good humour, turning back their insults with his usual readiness. When Paull, the son of a tailor, who prided himself on his humble origins, mocked at Hood's splendid uniform and decorations, remarking that he too could have had such a coat, Sheridan is said to have answered, 'Yes, and you might have made it too.'

At one point in the proceedings a drunken butcher aimed a blow at Sheridan's head with a marrow bone, which would probably have killed him if his weapon had not been deflected. The man was arrested, but on petitioning Sheridan for forgiveness, explaining that he was very much intoxicated at the time and that his wife and family would starve without his support, Sheridan immediately agreed to let him off.

Sheridan and Hood, the government candidates, were returned, though the battle had been a close one. Paull, backed by such radical figures as Cobbett and Horne Tooke, was an unexpectedly effective candidate; furthermore, Sheridan, though brilliant on the hustings, had been negligent of his supporting organisers. 'Such was his confidence in his own personal popularity and management,' wrote Lord Holland disapprovingly, 'that he not only neglected, but derided and insulted the clubs and committees through whose agency Mr Fox's elections had been generally secured.'

Sheridan had come second to Hood in the poll. His election to Westminster, only reluctantly supported by the government, had been less than triumphant. Meanwhile he had alienated the electors of Stafford, who had loyally supported him for twenty-six years. He had hoped that his son Tom would take his place in his old constituency, but the electors were angry at being thrown over and Tom was defeated. It was the third seat for which his father had put him up and he had been unsuccessful in all of them. With a great deal of his father's charm, but less of his ability, Tom would always be a lightweight.

The excitement of the Westminster election had scarcely died down when the Ministry of All the Talents fell. Its last act had been to pass the bill for the abolition of the slave trade, a measure Sheridan had always supported and wished to see carried to its logical conclusion. In a brief but memorable speech the following day, 19 March 1807, he spoke in favour of a motion for the gradual abolition of slavery itself in the West Indies, concluding by quoting the lines,

> I would not have a slave to till my ground,
> To fan me when I sleep, and tremble when
> I wake, for all that human sinews bought
> And sold, have ever earned.

The House was so thinly attended on this occasion that no vote was taken; it would be twenty-six years before the abolition of slavery, as opposed to the slave trade, was made law. Meanwhile, the old issue of Catholic relief, which Fox had felt it wiser to leave in abeyance, had brought about the downfall of the Ministry. This time they had sought nothing so drastic as emancipation, merely a measure to conciliate the Irish by allowing Catholics, already permitted to be officers up to the rank of colonel in the Irish army, to hold the same rank in the British army. It was only a tiny move forward but it was enough to alert the worst fears of the king. At first, he reluctantly agreed to the bill, only to dig in his heels when he discovered that the Ministry intended to widen its terms by allowing Catholics to hold staff appointments and to be eligible for promotion up to the rank of admiral and general. The Cabinet then offered to withdraw the bill, insisting, however, on reserving their right to put forward other measures for Ireland in the future should they be necessary. This act of semi-defiance was too much for the king. He demanded a formal pledge from Grenville that the Cabinet (as opposed to individual ministers) would never reopen the Catholic question again. Grenville firmly but courteously refused. For nine days the situation remained uncertain while the king sought to find a new administration. Eventually, the ageing Duke of Portland was prevailed on to form a new government, and on 24 March the Ministry of All the Talents was dismissed.

To some extent they had dug their own grave. 'He had often heard,' said Sheridan in a much quoted *bon mot*, 'of people knocking out their brains against a wall, but never before knew of anyone building a wall expressly for that purpose.' Surprisingly, for one so committed to the Irish cause, he had not spoken in favour of the measure. He felt the issue had been mishandled and that it had been unnecessary to pin the Ministry's existence to it; he may also have been influenced by the fact that the Prince of Wales had been against it. But he went out loyally with his colleagues, taking with him, had he known it, his last chance of ever holding office.

'The time will come,' writes Macaulay, admittedly a Whig historian, 'when posterity will do justice to the Whigs of England and will faithfully relate how much they did and suffered for Ireland; how, for the sake of Ireland, they quitted office in 1807; how, for the sake of Ireland, they remained out of office more than twenty years, braving the frowns of the Court, braving the hisses of the multitude,. renouncing power and patronage, and salaries, and peerages, and garters, and yet not receiving in return even a little fleeting popularity.'

Sheridan, whatever his reservations at the time, could be counted among this honourable band. The wits of the day, however, saw him in a less heroic light. Catholic emancipation was still an unpopular issue in the country and the king's prejudices were reflected by most of his countrymen. Sheridan's debts and his drinking were of greater interest than his principles. A rhyming letter, supposedly written by Sheridan, in a satirical paper, the 'All the Talents Garland', painted a cruelly witty picture of his plight:

> Alas, I cannot write or speak
> My tears run hissing down my cheek,
> My burning bosom vomits sighs
> Like fumes that from Vesuvius rise.
> Boiled by the flames of face and nose,
> My brain a melted lava grows . . .
> What shall I do? My cash is gone,
> And credit I – alas – have none.
> My wits may furnish me again
> With Burgundy and rich Champagne,
> But driven out of Place and Court,
> Ah! where shall *Sherry* look for *Port*?

# XXVI

—⟨≈⟩—

With the downfall of the Ministry of All the Talents it seemed that the luck on which Sheridan had always relied had deserted him. The change of government meant a new election at Westminster, and this time there were five candidates for the two places. Without the Ministry behind him, Sheridan's chances were considerably diminished and, though he took on his opponents with the same energy and spirit as before, he failed to be re-elected. It was a bitter disappointment. A place was eventually found for him at Ilchester, thanks to the Prince of Wales's influence, but it had none of the prestige of Westminster, or even of his old constituency of Stafford, where Tom, when he presented himself once more, was ignominiously rejected.

In many ways, however, Sheridan was better in opposition than in government. Sharing Fox's feeling that it was unwise to raise the Catholic question prematurely, he had been cautious on the subject of Catholic promotions in the army. But once out of office he had nothing to lose and in a major speech that summer he spoke at length on Ireland's grievances, referring in the course of it to the failure of the bill.

'I think,' he said, 'they began at the wrong end. They should have commenced the measure of redress in Ireland at the cottage, instead of at the park and mansion. To have gone first to the higher order of the Catholics; to have sought to make them judges, and peers, and commoners; I do not know that such a proceeding, had it taken place, would not rather have served to aggravate discontent, as it might have been construed into a design to divide the interests of Catholics. Sure I am, that with a view to conciliate the Catholic population, I mean the poor, the peasantry, its effect would be nothing; indeed it would be quite a mockery. It would be like dressing or decorating the top masts of a ship when there were ten feet [of] water in the hold, or putting a laced hat on a man who had not a shoe to his feet.'

The fact was, he insisted, that the tyranny practised on the Irish had been unremitting. At a time when the country had never been in greater peril, when Napoleon was surrounding France with kingdoms of his own creation, viewing Britain as the only remaining object of his ambition to destroy, was it not time to think of conciliating her own subjects?

'I have heard of subsidies. Your subsidies to Prussia were considerable in amount, and yet quite unproductive in effect. Why don't you subsidise Ireland? And all the subsidies I ask for her is your confidence, affection and justice for her people. These I call on you to grant before it is too late . . . If you want the attachment of the Irish, begin by giving them some reason to love you. If you want them to fight your battles, give them something to fight for . . . Charles the First asked Selden, "what was the best way to put down a rebellion?" to which Selden answered, "remove the cause". He begged of the government to apply this answer to Ireland.'

Sheridan's speech, delivered 'with an animation and vigour worthy of the best period of his eloquence', showed him still at the height of his powers as a speaker. But he relied increasingly on alcohol to see him through. It may have been of this or a later occasion that Watkins gives the following anecdote. 'A person going to hear the debates in the House of Commons, called at the Exchequer Coffee-House, where his attention was fixed by a gentleman taking tea with a parcel of papers before him. Afterwards he called for a decanter of brandy, which he poured into a large glass, and drank off without diluting it in the least, and then walked away. The spectator soon followed, and went into the gallery of the House, where, to his astonishment, he heard one of the longest and most brilliant speeches he had ever heard delivered by this votary of Bacchus, who was no other than Mr Sheridan.'

273

Sheridan's drinking, once an element of high spirits and bonhomie, was more and more becoming a symptom of depression. His financial troubles were crowding in on him. Foolishly or quixotically, he had insisted on repaying a debt of honour to the 'renters' of the theatre on becoming Treasurer of the Navy, though four years earlier he had been specifically absolved from doing so by the Lord Chancellor. The sum, amounting to £5,600, together with his rash expenses while in office, had left him so crippled that only his position as a Member of Parliament saved him from being arrested for debt. He had had to leave one London house after another, driven away for non-payment of rent. Polesden Lacey had been let, and he was currently staying at the house of a friend, Peter Moore, in order to escape his creditors. Hecca was close to despair. 'I am by far the most ill used person in the world & I don't know why I am to bear it – I *won't*,' she wrote to Granville Leveson Gower. She complained that she never had any pleasures in life. She could not command a single thing for herself, or even take what other people offered her – in this case the loan of a horse to go riding with Granville – without causing the most violent offence.

Perhaps Sheridan was jealous of her friendship with Granville, whom she had first approached, she wrote, in order to divert the suspicions of Grey's wife. 'I had no hope of allaying her jealousy,' she told him, 'but by making her suspect a third person, & I knew that you alone could excite those suspicions.' Since then she had made him her confidant, as her letter revealing her affair with Grey had shown. Granville, of course, had passed it on to Lady Bessborough, who, her heart still aching at the Duchess of Devonshire's death, had been furious when she heard of Grey's 'abominable conduct'. Grey, unexpectedly emotional, had sobbed aloud and flung himself at her feet, calling himself by a thousand harsh names, when she reproached him for his treachery to her sister.

Hecca had certainly set the cat among the pigeons. Meanwhile, Sheridan, still vowing love to his wife, was continuing his infatuated pursuit of Lady Bessborough. In a letter to Granville that summer she describes how at Hecca's request she went round to see her late one night. (Hecca, no doubt, was longing to discuss the Grey drama.) She had not sat long in her bedroom when a violent burst at the door announced the arrival of Sheridan, not perfectly sober.

The most ridiculous scene ensued. Sheridan began by begging Lady Bessborough's pardon and entreating her mercy and compassion, saying that he was a wretch and that even now he was more in love with her than any woman he had ever met with, on which Hecca exclaimed, 'Not excepting me? Why you always tell me *I* am the only woman you ever were in love with.' 'So you are to be sure, my dear Hecca; you know *that*, of course – *you know* I love you better than any thing on earth.' 'Except *her*?' 'Pish, pish, child! Do not talk nonsense.' He began upbraiding Lady Bessborough again for her cruelty and for setting Hecca against him, Hecca every now and then coming in with, 'Why, Sheridan, I though Lady B. pursued you, and that you reviled all her violence like a second Joseph? So you used to tell me.'

'I cannot give you all the conversation,' concluded Lady Bessborough, 'for it lasted till near three in the Morning . . . Getting away was the difficulty; he wanted to come down with me, and seized my arm with such violence once before Hecca that I was obliged to call her Maid to help me, and at last only escap'd by locking him in.'

When one thinks that this was the period when Lawrence told Farington that no woman of character dared be left alone in a room with Sheridan, it is no wonder that Hecca sought sympathy where she could. Talking to Thomas Moore after both Sheridan and her sister had died, Sukey Ogle remarked that it was melancholy to compare the letters of Sheridan's two wives (which she had seen amongst his papers), both beginning in the same strain of love and worship and both gradually alienated by his extravagance and vainglorious infidelities, till they ended in disliking and, 'she might have added', wrote Moore, in being unfaithful to him.

In November 1807, Grey's father, the first Earl Grey, died, and Grey, who had been sitting in the House of Commons as Lord Howick, was forced to remove to the House of Lords. Sheridan might reasonably have expected to take his place in the Commons as the leader of the opposition. But he was no longer considered a reliable figure. In a letter to Granville, Lady Bessborough gave the party line. 'With talents and Eloquence to entitle him to any thing had he chose it, he has so degraded his Mind and character that there is scarce any one sunk so low as to look up to Sheridan as his chief.'

The leadership was given to another man, George Ponsonby, a cousin of the Bessboroughs and the Devonshires and Lord Chancellor of Ireland under Fox and Grenville.

For all his disappointments Sheridan remained a formidable figure in the House of Commons. When the British fleet bombarded Copenhagen and seized the Danish fleet in September 1807, as a preemptive strike against Napoleon, Sheridan was vehement in condemning the illegality of the action. 'British rulers,' he declared, 'have lost all character for humanity or national honour by the attack on a peaceful and defenceless nation . . . It is said, forsooth, that by this capture of the Danish fleet you have prevented the invasion of Ireland. In God's name if you would make peace with Buonaparte first make peace with Ireland by conciliating the affection of the Irish people.' He implored ministers to give up 'the detestable system . . . of fighting Bonaparte with his own weapons'.

In condemning the seizure of the Danish fleet Sheridan was taking the opposition line, expressed with equal force by Grey in the House of Lords. In June the following year, however, when the Spanish revolt against the French was just beginning, he struck out on his own by hailing the new movement as England's greatest chance of championing freedom since the outset of the French Revolution.

The rising in Spain, as Sheridan was swift to grasp, opened a new era in the war. The Treaty of Tilsit, at which France and Russia had made peace the previous year, had closed all northern Europe's ports to British trade, but Napoleon's attempts to do the same in the south by seizing control of the Iberian peninsula and putting his brother on the Spanish throne had sparked off a national rebellion.

'If the flame were once fairly caught,' said Sheridan, 'our success was certain. Buonaparte has hitherto run a most victorious race. Hitherto he has had to contend against princes without dignity and ministers without wisdom. He has fought against countries where people have been indifferent as to his success, he has yet to learn what it is to fight against a country in which the people are animated with one spirit to resist him . . . I solemnly declare that if the opportunity . . . of a vigorous interference on the part of England should arise, the present administration shall have from me as cordial and sincere a support as if the man I most loved [Fox] was restored to life and power.'

That Sheridan, speaking from the opposition benches, should pledge his support to the government, invoking Fox's name while doing so, was one more irritation to his colleagues. On 16 June, the day after Sheridan's speech, Whitbread wrote to Grey,

'Sheridan in concert with Canning [the Foreign Secretary], and against the wish and advice of all his Friends has been making a bother about Spain. He did all he could to create a Cry for himself as distinguished from all of us, but he was so exceedingly drunk he could scarce articulate.'

Sheridan's speech may well have been slurred, but in what he was saying he showed a vision and a grasp of great occasions which his colleagues lacked. 'Had his political associates,' wrote Moore, 'but learned from his example thus to place themselves in advance of the procession of events, they would not have had the triumphal wheels pass by them, and over them, so frequently.'

Eighteenth-century theatres, lit by candles and oil lights, and heated by coal stoves, had always been at risk from fire. On the night of 20 September 1808, Covent Garden was burnt to the ground. Thirty people died in the conflagration, which was started, it was said, by a piece of wadding fired from a musket in *Pizarro* which had lodged unnoticed in the scenery. Just over five months later, on the night of 24 February 1809, the skies of London were lit up by a second tremendous blaze. Sheridan was in the House of Commons, where a debate on the Spanish war was taking place, when he received the news that Drury Lane was on fire. It was suggested that the debate should be adjourned out of sympathy for his misfortune but Sheridan, who was reported not to be entirely sober, answered in a low voice that whatever might be the extent of the private calamity, he hoped that it would not interfere with the public business of the country.

Nine members of the House of Commons went with him as he left for Drury Lane. It was obvious that there was nothing to be done. The theatre had been empty when the fire – probably caused by a coal fire that had been left smouldering – broke out. The iron curtain and the tanks of water, so proudly displayed when the new theatre had opened, had been useless; the tanks had not even been filled with water. As the fire spread, Peake and Dunn, the treasurers, had made a heroic dash into the burning building to rescue an iron box in which the most vital documents were stored, but little else was saved. Before long, the fire had spread to the whole structure, so that the entire façade from Drury Lane to Bridges Street was a pillar of flame 450 feet in breadth. 'Never before,' wrote Boaden, 'did I behold so immense a body of flame; and the occasional explosions that took place were awful beyond description.'

Sheridan sat drinking with his friends in the Piazza Coffee House watching the destruction of his property with stoic fortitude. One of them remarked on his calm and Sheridan, witty even in calamity, made his famous reply: 'A man may surely be allowed to take a glass of wine beside his own fireside.' To another who was commiserating with him he replied with equal calmness that 'there were three things which alone could sensibly affect a mind properly constituted. The first was the loss of a woman beloved; the second bodily pain; the third self reproach; – the first he had suffered and felt, – the second he had been happily spared from,' laying a hand on his breast, '– self reproach he had none, having never injured any one.'

If a long line of unpaid creditors, theatre staff and tradesmen were excepted, this astonishing claim, delivered in all sincerity, was not without an element of truth. Sheridan had never deliberately injured anyone. Joseph Richardson, who himself had lost his money in the bottomless pit of Drury Lane, once remarked that if only some enchanter could have given Sheridan the possession of a fortune, he would immediately have been converted into a being of the nicest honour and the most unimpeachable moral excellence. Even those to whom he owed most were inclined to give him the benefit of the doubt; he never really meant to cheat them, he always imagined he would be able to pay his debts, but new embarrassments kept banishing the old ones from his head.

The full extent of the catastrophe took some time to sink in. Sheridan still held a valuable asset in the theatre's patent; meeting with his principal actors on the day after the fire he said that his first concern was to find a theatre where they could use the patent to put on performances pending the rebuilding of the theatre. His only request was that they should stand together for the benefit of the poorer members of the staff. 'Let us make a long pull, a strong pull, and a pull together,' he told them; 'and above all, make the general good our sole consideration!'

After various negotiations establishing the validity of the patent, the company was given permission to perform at the Lyceum Theatre in the Strand, normally used for pantomime and opera. But the question of rebuilding was not to be solved so easily. The management of Covent Garden, in similar circumstances, had been able to raise enough by public subscription to start rebuilding almost immediately; the Prince of Wales had laid the foundation stone only three months after the old theatre had been destroyed. Drury Lane was a very different proposition. Not only had it been disastrously underinsured – the insurance payment, which was immediately attached by the ground landlords, was £35,000 against an estimated loss of £300,000 – but it was encumbered with debts amounting to nearly half a million pounds. The theatre had been teetering on the brink of ruin even before the fire. However valuable the patent, few investors would be likely to put money in an enterprise which still had Sheridan at its head. In a letter to his brother-in-law, George Callendar, a few weeks after the fire, Tom Sheridan summed up the difficulties of the situation.

'As to old Drury the truth is this: – I swear we are utterly ruined but if things are well managed it may turn out one of the best things to have happened. It was a bankruptcy as it stood. It is no more now it is down, with this advantage, that the creditors must compromise to have it built up again, & without it is built (under our Patent too, for that is their security) they can never get anything . . . The danger is delay. The town must have a second theatre, and if we do not build one a struggle will be made, and very foolishly too, for another Patent, which would throw us all on our backs. If my father would withdraw himself from the undertaking, and allow it to be vested in other hands, – or in other words if he would assign the property bona fide over to me, I could do the thing at once, for there are plenty of friends ready to step forward in that case; but they will not trust my father again. That is the truth, and unfortunately he is so tenacious & self-willed that he shuts his eyes and ears to everything. Still he is such a long headed chap when put to a push, that there is no saying what he will do.'

If Sheridan had been ten years younger he might, as Tom suggested, have won through after all. But he was now in his late fifties and not in good health – his letters speak of a severe cold in

March and an unspecified illness in May, which led to a report he had died. (He turned up deliberately at the House of Commons to disprove the rumour.) He was, moreover, stunned by the sheer magnitude of his disaster and the humiliations of trying to survive when his only source of credit had been destroyed. So desperate was his need for ready money that he had taken some workmen to the ruins of the theatre, where, after searching among the ashes, they found the remains of some theatre bells, which they dug out and sold for £90. After several months of turning vainly to and fro, he was forced to seek for help, not from Tom, who lacked the necessary public stature, but from his wife's trustee and parliamentary colleague, Samuel Whitbread.

On 29 May, in a letter which took him several drafts, he wrote to Whitbread asking him to join a committee to rebuild Drury Lane and promising to lay a full statement of the theatre's affairs – 'disordered and ill managed, but by no means desperate' – before him. Whitbread, with some misgivings, agreed to take on the onerous task, first joining and then heading a committee to rebuild the theatre. It was an act of real friendship, for he knew Sheridan's ways, though he little realised what an appallingly labyrinthine web of claims and counter-claims there was to be untangled.

Son of a wealthy brewer, and brother-in-law of Grey, Whitbread had entered Parliament as a radical Whig in 1790. Like Fox, he was a believer in peace at almost any price and had consistently argued against the continuation of the war, differing in this from Sheridan's more belligerent attitude. He had every sympathy for Sheridan in his disaster, but it soon became clear that if any money were to be raised for the rebuilding it was essential that Sheridan should have no part in it. 'It is unquestionably hard and galling,' he wrote to Tom, 'that you should be in the sort of prescription there is on the name of Sheridan, as connected with the New Theatre . . . The Question asked before any Man or Woman will put down their Names is this "Has Mr Sheridan anything to do with it?" a direct negative suffices.'

Later, Sheridan would come to resent his exclusion bitterly, but at the time he welcomed Whitbread's intervention and was consoled by the prospect of receiving ready money for his shares. He insisted, however, that he would claim nothing till the theatre was rebuilt, a self-denying ordinance that Whitbread, alas, took all too literally.

Meanwhile, the danger of a third patent, which was being backed by the Lord Mayor and other moneyed figures in the City, had been averted. Sheridan argued the case against it before the Privy Council in March 1810 and, on the 28th of that month, was able to write in triumph to Hecca from the House of Commons. 'I have but one moment to tell you in one word the good news that the Council have unanimously decided in our Favor on the Patent right Question and now I shall get my affairs right and you shall never know a plague again ... it was going against us till I spoke on monday, and is decided entirely on the ground I put the Question on.'

Sheridan's ready optimism was not shared by his wife, who wrote to him soon after complaining of his indifference to her welfare and suggesting a separation if it would make him happier. Sheridan's answer, a long and moving letter of self-justification, went into the details of his present finances – apart from his salary from the Duchy of Cornwall, amounting that year to £940, and Hecca's income of £200, he had nothing more to live on. 'If from this you take £500 to be paid weekly £200 Pin money and £250 for a carriage which you shall certainly have there will remain only £200 for every other expense, – House Rent, Charles's schooling or to get me even shoes to my Feet which God knows I have often wanted!'

He freely admitted his faults, his negligence, procrastination and forgetfulness in daily matters, combined with a 'most unfortunately sanguine temper' and a rash self-confidence that made him feel that he was capable of dealing with any extremity. But he insisted that she did not understand him. 'I have said before that you do not know me – in truth you do not in the least – you should judge of my conduct character and principles upon a larger scale of observation and not from the defects of daily Life which arise from the Failings I acknowledge.'

He reminded her of the sacrifices he had made in setting up her marriage settlement, and how, even against her father's advice, he had agreed not to touch the income; of the honourable but mistaken pride which had made him repay the renters and plunge himself further into debt; of his worries over Tom, who was showing signs of the tuberculosis which had killed his mother and now had six children to support; and finally of his own health.

'As for my own Life, tho' I feel neither dismay'd nor dispirited at this moment of Time and exertion on my Part, I can safely swear that I never pass a Day or an hour almost without having present to my mind the probability of one's last hour being nearer than the accomplishment of the most immediate object of our hope and pursuit. That disorder which I have lately had some return of and from which I have been more than once in greater Danger than you have imagined may at any time return and quickly end me – the same may occur from the condition of my veins – for no operation for Life's sake will I ever undergo. Thus circumstanced when you say, as you have . . . that you are ready to separate if I think it for *my happiness* I plainly answer that such an act would be follow'd on my Part by my instantly taking my Boy with me to some corner of the earth and be no more heard of till my Death should by him be announced to you, after I should think no very protracted Period, and you should find yourself at least relieved from the embarrass-ments which had caused our separation.'

Hecca was much tried; she was scatty, pleasure-loving and impractical; but she was not unkind or ungenerous, and she had not the heart to abandon her husband in distress. Thereafter they remained together for the rest of Sheridan's life, and though there were quarrels there was no further talk of separation.

The summer of 1810 brought Sheridan a new humiliation when the inauguration of Lord Grenville as Chancellor of Oxford took place. Sheridan was among the distinguished visitors invited to attend, and it was naturally expected that he should receive an honorary degree. In a meeting beforehand, however, two members refused to agree to the proposal, despite an eloquent speech in Latin from one of Sheridan's supporters, pointing out the shame that it would bring upon the university if he was excluded. But the objectors were adamant and Sheridan was forced to write to the Vice-Chancellor asking for his name to be withdrawn. Fortunately, the story had a happy ending, for when he appeared at the inauguration a burst of acclamation broke forth from the audience, with a general cry of 'Mr Sheridan among the Doctors! Sheridan among the Doctors!' and he was pushed up to the seats reserved for the honorary doctors, where he sat, 'in unrobed distinction', for the whole ceremony. Few occurrences, of a public nature, wrote Moore, ever gave him greater pleasure.

Perhaps the episode was a good omen, for very shortly afterwards he received an unexpected windfall from the Duchy of Cornwall. Creevey, with whom he and Hecca were staying for the night, tells the story.

'There being no other person present after dinner, when the ladies had left the room, Sheridan said:-

' "A damned odd thing happened to me this morning, and Hester and I have agreed in coming down here today that no human being shall ever know of it as long as we live; so that nothing but my firm conviction that Hester is at this moment telling it to Mrs Creevey could induce me to tell you."

'Then he said that the money belonging to this office of his in the Duchy being paid into Biddulph's or Cox's bank (I think it was) at Charing Cross, it was always his habit to look in there. There was one particular clerk who seemed always so fond of him, and so proud of his acquaintance, that he every now and then cajoled him into advancing him £10 or £20 more than his account entitled him to ... That morning he thought his friend looked particularly smiling upon him, so he said:

' "I looked in to see if you could let me have ten pounds."

' "Ten pounds!" replied the clerk; "to be sure I can, Mr Sheridan. You've got my letter, sir, have you not?"

' "No," said Sheridan, "what letter?"

'It is literally true that at this time and for many, many years Sheridan never got two-penny post letters, because there was no money to pay for them, and the postman would not leave them without payment.

' "Why, don't you know what has happened, sir?" said the clerk. "There is £1300 paid into your account. There has been a very great fine paid for one of the Duchy estates, and this £1300 is your percentage as auditor."

'Sheridan was, of course, very much set up with this £1300, and, on the very next day upon leaving us, he took a house in Barnes Terrace, where he spent all his £1300. At the end of two or three months at most, the tradespeople would no longer supply him without being paid, so he was obliged to remove. What made this folly more striking was that Sheridan had occupied five or six different houses in this neighbourhood at different periods of his life,

283

and on each occasion had been driven literally away by non-payment of his bills . . . Yet he was as full of his fun during these two months as ever he could be – gave dinners perpetually and was always on the road between Barnes and London, or Barnes and Oatlands (the Duke of York's), in a large job coach upon which he would have his family arms painted.'

It was plain that Sheridan was incorrigible and that for all his protestations he would never change. The dark clouds were gathering round him, but it is good to think of him that summer giving dinners perpetually and as 'full of his fun . . . as ever he could be'.

# XXVII

———————⌐◦⌐———————

S heridan made few appearances in the House of Commons during
1809 and 1810. The Duke of Portland had died in October 1809,
and Spencer Perceval, a determined but colourless politician whom
Sheridan disliked, had taken over as Prime Minister. A certain inertia
seemed to have come over him, and even when Windham and
Grattan in two separate motions raised the question of civic rights for
Catholics in England and Ireland he did not speak on their behalf.
But in December 1810 the political situation changed dramatically
when, following the death of his beloved youngest child Amelia, the
king's health finally gave way and he was declared to be insane.

The whole question of the regency was raised once more, and,
since the king's recovery was still possible, Perceval, as Prime
Minister, proposed that the prince's powers should be restricted for a
year along much the same lines as Pitt had done in 1789. This time,
Sheridan was roused to speak, in a speech which was almost worthy
of his old self – 'Sheridanus Redivus', said a fellow MP – and which
ended in a stirring peroration against this encroachment on the
prince's rights.

'I say now as I have ever said, that we are struggling to preserve a
condition of society far above that to which the civilised nations of
the world have attained. Is this the moment to fetter or restrict the
constitutional powers of him whom the public voice has unanimously called to preside over our destiny, during the indisposition of
his Sovereign and father! Shall we send him forth with a broken

shield and half a spear to that contest on the issue of which depends not only the safety of Great Britain but . . . the happiness of mankind.'

He sat down to cries of 'Hear, hear!' that lasted for some minutes, applause which was always dearer to him than any from a theatre audience.

For the opposition the prospect of a regency opened new horizons, and Grey and Grenville already saw themselves heading a new government. Since Fox's death the prince had distanced himself from the opposition. He disliked Grey, partly from jealousy over his love affair with the Duchess of Devonshire, and he did not forget that at the time of the previous regency negotiations Grenville had supported Pitt in seeking to restrict his powers. But he still saw the Whigs as his natural allies and it was to Grey and Grenville that he turned to draft an answer to the government's proposals for a regency.

Grenville, however, did not wish to appear inconsistent by pressing the prince's claims and Grey, who had taken the opposite view in 1789, was forced to compromise. Their joint composition, prepared in some haste the day before the prince was due to answer, made only the mildest protest at the proposed limitation of his powers. 'Very flimsy', noted Sheridan on the back of his copy of the draft, and the prince himself objected to it strongly. He turned to Sheridan and Adam, his attorney-general, to sketch out another which could be taken round to Grey, who was dining with Lord Holland in Pall Mall. An angry scene took place, Grey indignant that Sheridan, as he saw it, should be intriguing with the prince to override him and Lord Grenville, Sheridan, 'flushed with wine and irritated by dispute', arguing that as they were not yet ministers they had no monopoly of advising the prince. Grey, with some hauteur, refused to comment on a document in which he and Grenville had no hand, and Sheridan and Adam returned to Carlton House.

By now it was well after midnight, and 'those damned fellows', as the prince described the parliamentary deputation, were due to arrive in the morning. At three o'clock the draft was ready for transcribing and Michael Angelo Taylor, who had been summoned to make fair copies, arrived at Carlton House, where the prince was still in consultation with Sheridan and Adam. The prince eventually went to bed, but Adam and Sheridan remained there pacing up and down while Taylor wrote, Adam occasionally stooping to whisper to Taylor that Sheridan was 'the damnedest rascal alive', Sheridan muttering 'Damn them all!' from time to time.

The next morning was a State occasion when the prince, with all his royal brothers in attendance, flanked by his chancellors Adam and Lord Moira on one side, and Sheridan and the Duke of Cumberland on the other, received the proposals of the two Houses in the great saloon of Carlton House. He read out his answer in a cold ceremonious manner, accepting the restrictions, but insisting that his opinion of them had not changed since a 'former and similar distressing occasion', i.e. the regency crisis in 1789. The statement, as Grey and Grenville knew, had been written by Sheridan, a fact which drove them to protest in writing to the prince at his accepting the advice of 'another person' on a matter which had been entrusted to them alone. The high-handed tone of the letter and its arrogant assumption that only they were entitled to dictate the prince's views were duly satirised by Sheridan:

> In all humility we crave
> Our Regent may become our slave;
> And being so, we trust that He
> Will thank us for our loyalty.
> Then, if he'll help us to pull down
> His father's dignity and crown,
> We'll make him, in some time to come,
> The greatest Prince in Christendom.

The sense of being in the midst of great events and of pulling the strings behind scenes was the breath of life to Sheridan. But the episode did him no good, confirming the opposition leaders in their antagonism to him and sowing doubts about him in the prince's mind. The offended aristocrats were out for his blood: Grey even went so far as to insist that he would only accept office if Sheridan and the prince's chancellor, Lord Moira, were excluded from his counsels. The prince liked Sheridan and wished him well, but he liked a quiet life still more. He did his best for Sheridan, suggesting that he should become the Secretary for Ireland, but this, objected Grey, would be like 'sending a man with a lighted torch into a magazine of gunpowder'. For nearly a month the prince, in an agony of vacillation and uncertainty, continued to hold talks with the opposition. In the end, the hectoring tone of Grey and Grenville, the obvious dissensions in the opposition ranks, and the very real possibility that his father might recover, made him decide to continue with the status quo. On 4 February 1811, to the surprise and fury of the opposition, the prince called on Perceval to continue as Prime Minister.

Sheridan, of course, could not be held responsible for the downfall of the Whigs. But he had helped to tip the balance against them, ridiculing their arrogance, and seeking, as ever, to be first in the counsels of the prince. He owed no loyalty to Grenville, who had always treated him with ill-disguised contempt, and, though he was still attached to Grey, the feeling was not reciprocated. But his own chances of office had been destroyed with theirs and this time he must have realised that the game was over.

With the severing of the prince's time-honoured association with the Foxite Whigs, first forged in Devonshire House, went a weakening of his old friendships. The vision of a liberal prince, devoted to Fox's ideals, had long given place to a more sordid reality. The charming Florizel could now be described, in Leigh Hunt's cruel words, as 'a corpulent gentleman of fifty . . . a libertine over head and ears in disgrace, a despiser of domestic ties, the companion of gamblers and demi-reps, a man who has just closed half a century without one single claim on the gratitude of his country or the respect of posterity'.

For Sheridan, the break was gradual. He could still be useful to the prince; he had even composed his letter inviting Perceval to stay in office (although it sealed his party's downfall) and he remained an unofficial adviser behind scenes. But the prince was now regent, Sheridan was a member of the opposition and his influence was bound to be reduced. In private, however, he clung to his friendship, finding a welcome in the rackety society of Carlton House long after other doors had closed to him. The prince's favour was a sign that he still mattered in the world.

In February 1812, the restrictions on the prince's powers expired; his father's recovery seemed increasingly unlikely and he was now the sovereign in all but name. He made one last gesture to the opposition by offering Grey and Grenville places in a coalition government, but they refused to join unless there was an understanding that Catholic emancipation would be granted. The prince, despite his earlier sympathy for the Catholics, was no longer prepared to give this pledge; he let them go with few regrets and Perceval was confirmed in office. The following month, at the St Patrick's Day dinner at the Freemason's Tavern, where the prince was normally the reigning toast, his name was loudly hissed. Sheridan loyally stood up to defend him, but his protests were drowned with cries of 'Change the subject!' and louder hisses than before.

Sheridan might well have had a position in the proposed coalition, but he had always made his views on Catholic emancipation clear and supported Grey and Grenville's stand. But for Sheridan, harassed and at bay, the cost was high. At a dinner some time afterwards, when the Whigs were being praised for their sturdiness in resisting office and sticking to their principles, he was seen to shed tears as he said,

'Sir – it is easy for my Lord G[renville], – or Earl G[rey] – or Marquis B[of Bath] – or Lord H[olland], with thousands upon thousands a year – some of it either *presently* derived or *inherited* in Sinecures or acquisitions from the public money – to boast of their patriotism – & keep aloof from temptation – but they do not know from what temptations those have kept aloof who had equal pride – at least equal talents, & not unequal passions – & nonetheless – knew not in the course of their lives – what it was to have a shilling of their own.'

'To be sure,' said Byron, who recorded the conversation, 'he contrived to exact a good many of other people's.'

On 11 May 1812, Spencer Perceval was assassinated by a madman in the lobby of the House of Commons, and the regent was plunged into a new parliamentary crisis. The Earl of Liverpool, Secretary of War under Perceval and leader of the House of Lords, succeeded as Prime Minister, but before he could establish his administration a back-bench vote of 'no confidence' put the whole situation into flux once more. Liverpool resigned and for two weeks the prince negotiated with the various factions to form a broad-based government capable of carrying on the war. There were still no rigid party labels, though the heirs of the Pittite tradition were beginning to be known as Tories, those of the Foxite persuasion, committed to Catholic emancipation, keeping the name of Whigs.

Throughout the negotiations the prince, according to Sheridan, was in a 'state of perturbation of mind beyond anything he had ever seen'. He hated Grey and Grenville, whom he described as 'a couple of scoundrels', and he dreaded the reopening of the Catholic question. But he felt bound to offer them places in a new administration, and Grey and Grenville, though angry that they had not been asked to lead it, did not refuse outright at first. This time they took their stand, not on the Catholic question, but on the lesser matter of the regent's household, which they insisted should resign. Since the household included the Marquis of Hertford, whose wife Lady Hertford was the regent's current mistress, and whose son Lord Yarmouth was Vice-Chamberlain, the regent at first indignantly refused. The Hertford faction was strongly anti-Catholic, and Grey and Grenville had already broken off negotiations when the regent suddenly changed his mind. Lord Yarmouth was deputed to tell Sheridan, who had been in the thick of the discussions at Carlton House, that the Household would resign once Grey and Grenville had taken office. This was not quite the same as what Grey and Grenville had demanded, but it certainly might have influenced their decision had they known it. Sheridan, however, not only did not pass on the information, but even laid a bet with the Whig MP George Tierney that the Household would not resign. As a result, the regent was able 'to fall back on his old government', and in the absence of any better alternative, Lord Liverpool became Prime Minister once more.

The prince was delighted to be rid of the Whigs, but there was a howl of protest when Sheridan's behaviour was known. Twice, Creevey wrote, he had kept them out of office. Moore, who described the episode as the only indefensible part of his public life, suspected that he had been secretly carrying out the prince's wishes in withholding the information, but it was Sheridan who got the blame, accused at once of indiscretion and underhand intrigue. 'The actors in the plot,' wrote the *Morning Chronicle*, 'have been various, and those who have played the most prominent parts have been farthest from the real secret of the drama, the manager and contriver of which has hitherto kept himself in the background; and if his vanity would have allowed him to be silent, the piece might have gone off successfully, without any one suspecting who was its author. SLY BOOTS is a notable contriver, but he has the misfortune to be leaky in his cups.'

On 17 June, obviously unwell, Sheridan attempted to justify himself in the House of Commons. The information, he said, had been given to him confidentially and not as 'a Channel which was to convey the intelligence to the noble lords'; he insisted that there had been no thought of double-dealing. Half-way through the speech he became so distressed and exhausted that he broke down and the debate was postponed. Two days later, he spoke again, but in such a wandering and painful manner that even the outraged Whigs had not the heart to press him.

'His whole speech was most doting,' wrote a spectator, 'and showed hardly any remains of what he was . . . Tierney told me that he thinks him quite gone; that once during the speech his jaw became locked so that he could not utter. I never witnessed a sight more distressing. I have no doubt he will never speak again.'

Sheridan did speak again, on six occasions. There was something melancholy in the contrast between his earlier brilliance and the ramblings and forced jokes of his final utterances. But on almost the last of of them, on 15 July 1812, he spoke on the Irish question in words which could be regarded as both a vindication of his conduct and his swan song.

'My objection to the present Ministry is, that they are avowedly arrayed and embodied against a principle, – that of concession to the Catholics of Ireland – which I think, and must always think, essential to the safety of this empire. I will never give my vote to any Administration that opposes the question of Catholic Emancipation. I will not consent to receive a furlough upon that particular question, even though the Ministry were carrying every other that I wished. In fine, I think the situation of Ireland a paramount consideration. If they were the last words I should ever utter in this House, I should say, "Be just to Ireland as you value your own honour; – be just to Ireland as you value your own peace." '

On 12 October 1812, the new theatre at Drury Lane was opened. Sheridan was not present at the opening ceremonies. The hope of salvation which Whitbread had seemed to hold out when he first took over the responsibility for the new theatre had become a source of bitterness and vexation. It is possible to see both sides of the question. The financial miseries for which Sheridan blamed Whitbread blighted his last years; on the other hand, the appalling strain and worry of dealing with the theatre undoubtedly played its part in Whitbread's suicide three years later.

Whitbread had been drawn, as he said, into a whirlpool. The task of sorting out the theatre's finances was enough to daunt the stoutest heart. Slowly, methodically, he picked his way through the tangle of Sheridan's liabilities and the millstone of debt with which, by selling off boxes and debenture shares for ready money, he had loaded the theatre. At the end of his calculations Sheridan still had one asset of real value, his share of the patent, which was independently valued at £48,000, of which Sheridan's share was half, his son's a quarter. On this sum at least he had based his hopes, but Whitbread, as trustee of a public fund, was not prepared to advance him the money till the claims on it had been satisfied. Sheridan himself had agreed to leave the matter to Whitbread's judgement, but with his usual airy attitude to money had not expected to be taken at his word. The miseries and frustrations to which he was exposed formed a running background to the various political crises of the previous eighteen months.

It was probably true that Whitbread was being over-cautious and Hecca, forgetting her own grievances, was warm-hearted in her husband's defence.

'Whatever reasons I may have had to complain of Sheridan,' she wrote to Lady Holland, 'and however my comfort and happiness may have been thrown away, I can never see him as *deeply wounded*, as I have seen him lately, without feeling the full extent of my regard for him. The disagreement hurts me more than I can express, though I was from the first but too well aware it must happen. What is most distressing to me is that Whitbread has urged me to employ all my influence to bring S. "to reason", when I confess that on the subject of debate yesterday my whole heart and soul is *with* Sheridan.'

Whitbread, on behalf of the theatre's trustees, wrote offering her a box in the new theatre. It was a gracious gesture, and worth a considerable amount of money, but Hecca would have nothing to do with it. Like her husband, she refused to attend the opening celebrations, for which the young Lord Byron, who had become a member of the Drury Lane committee, wrote the prologue.

Byron, who had already shown his approval of Sheridan as one of the few writers worth praising in his satire 'English Bards and Scots Reviewers', made a graceful reference in his prologue to the golden days of Drury Lane, 'Ere Garrick died or Brinsley ceased to write.' The wits of the day, making fun of Whitbread's brewing interests, wrote their own spoof versions. Sheridan, of course, was a natural target, and one of the longest and most elaborate, to be delivered by one 'Peter Puncheon', dismissed him thus:

'Well, Gentry, welcome to our new-old Inn;
Well stock'd our cellars, full is ev'ry bin;
Old port, old hock, old cider and old perry;
But none of that neat article, *Old Sherry*!
Although well cork'd, and seal'd in quarts and pottles,
It bounc'd, too frisky, and broke all the bottles.

It was thirty-five years since Sheridan, with his father-in-law, had launched himself into the adventure of Drury Lane, and since the falling of the screen in the fourth act of *The School for Scandal* had made the young Frederick Reynolds take to his heels for fear that the theatre was falling down. But it is doubtful whether the loss of the theatre, with all its fatal consequences financially, would hit Sheridan as much the next great loss which now awaited him, the loss of his seat in Parliament and with it the only arena in which he had truly wished to shine. The last act of life, as Swift had told Sheridan's grandfather, is always a tragedy at best and for Sheridan it was now beginning.

# XXVIII

———— ❧ ————

Ever since Perceval's confirmation in power by the prince regent, Sheridan had felt the awkwardness of being in Parliament under his patronage. The prince had always insisted that Sheridan was free to vote as he wished, but Sheridan, with that quixotic sense of honour which ran through even his most devious dealings, was determined that his loyalty to the Catholic cause should be demonstrated by his standing for an independent borough. With a new election pending, he had been to Stafford to gather support for a return to his old constituency.

'I pant for my old *independent* seat . . .' he told a supporter, Thomas Perkins. 'You are a Sportsman and as all lovers of Field Sports must be more or less friendly to Poetry I may refer you to Gouldsmith for my Feelings on the present occasion –

> And as a Hare whom Hounds and Horns pursue
> Pants to the Goal from whence at first she flew
> I still have hopes my long vexations past
> There to return – and die at *home* at last.

Political Death, I mean – but even before that I trust that we and the few surviving old Friends may yet spend some pleasant Days together.'

When it came to the time, however, he procrastinated in London, perhaps hoping that he would be invited to stand for Westminster. The local Catholic grandee Edward Jerningham, whose family had a

294

parliamentary 'interest' in Stafford, described himself as 'straining every nerve for him. I have declared open hostility against every tenant who holds, and every man who expects to hold land, and who opposes Sheridan.' But Sheridan arrived too late to canvass effectively and spent the election loitering at the inn. To his fury and surprise he was defeated, a fact he later blamed on Whitbread, 'that scoundrel' as he called him, for failing to advance him the money he needed to fight the election. He held the electors equally to blame; having promised him their support that summer, they had broken their word. In a furious address, of which the draft exists in Stafford, but which may not have been printed, he described them as wretches and reptiles. 'A correct alphabetical list of the Turncoats is in Preparation,' he ended, 'and will be distributed through every part of the united Kingdom as a caution to all honest men to have nothing to do with this rotten Borough.'

It was a bitter ending to his parliamentary career, not the less so that it was largely his own fault. The first and most immediate consequence of his rejection was that he no longer had parliamentary immunity to arrest for debt. The regent generously offered him a safe haven in 'an apartment in his own Palace', presumably Carlton House. 'I can only say that *Gratitude* is too weak a word to express the feelings which that offer has indelibly planted in my mind,' wrote Sheridan to the prince's private secretary, Colonel Macmahon, but either from pride, or because he still believed that Whitbread was about to settle his affairs, he insisted that the offer was not necessary.

The prince is generally depicted as a faithless friend, but he still felt kindly towards Sheridan. When Lord Moira, who was leaving to be the Governor-General of India, came to him saying that 'it was a pity that poor Sheridan at the close of such a life as his had been, should be out of Parliament', he remarked that Sheridan's own indolence and indecision and his being neither on one side or the other were chiefly to blame. But he had always been ready, and still was, to help bring him into Parliament, without expecting him to sacrifice his independence. The Duke of Norfolk had a seat to dispose of, for which he expected £4,000, but he offered to waive £1,000 of it for Sheridan, leaving £3,000, which the prince agreed to find. For some reason the offer fell through, but Sheridan soon after came up with a second suggestion, for a seat in Wootton Bassett, whose owner, a Mr

Attersol, was prepared to give it up for £3,000. The prince again agreed to find the money, 'not that we advanced the sum to Sheridan himself; we knew him too well for that', he told Croker. The money was to be lodged by Colonel Macmahon with a Mr Cocker, a solicitor named by Sheridan, until the negotiations were completed.

Macmahon left Sheridan, with a travelling carriage outside the door, apparently just about to leave for Wootton Bassett. Three days later, when the prince was riding in Oxford Road, he saw someone who looked very like Sheridan in the distance, who turned off into a side street as if anxious to avoid him. Sheridan was obviously caught out. The next day he called on Macmahon to explain that he had been delayed in town, but was setting out for Wootton Bassett first thing next morning. Two more days passed, then a note from Sheridan arrived, saying that the negotiations had failed, but that he had another, still better arrangement in hand. Macmahon, now seriously alarmed about the money, wrote to Cocker asking for it back as it was no longer needed for the seat. The lawyer replied that he knew nothing of any parliamentary seat, that Sheridan had instructed him to settle various urgent debts, including one to himself. The £3,000 had gone. After this, said the prince, he never saw Sheridan to speak to again; not that it was worse in principle than other things he had done, or that he had ordered him to be excluded, but that Sheridan himself felt it 'so gross a violation of confidence – such a want of respect and such a series of lies and fraud' that he never came near him again.

Such was the prince's story, told to Croker fourteen years later, when Moore's life of Sheridan, criticising him for his neglect of Sheridan, came out. Sheridan attempted to explain himself to Macmahon, at first blaming Whitbread, who, he said, had agreed to pay him £2,000 he owed him on condition he stayed out of Parliament; he had therefore gone to the lawyer to get back the £3,000, only to find that 'that fellow' had applied it all to the repayment of a debt of his own and that consequently the money was not to be had. Macmahon, naturally, did not take this explanation kindly. The truth in fact was probably something closer to the version given by Lord Holland, to whom Sheridan had said that he had refused to accept the prince's offer to help him to a seat 'because . . . he had no idea of risking the high independence of character which he had always sustained', but boasted at the same time of an intrigue by which the prince would be induced to lend him the money. 'From his habit of considering money as nothing, he considered his *owing* the Prince £4,000 [in fact £3,000] as no slavery whatever. "I shall then" he said, "only owe him £4,000, which will leave me as free as air".'

This was typical, said Lord Holland, of one remarkable characteristic of Sheridan's, which accounted for many of his inconsistencies, 'the high ideal system he had formed of a sort of impracticable perfection in honour, virtue &c. – anything short of which he seemed to think not worth aiming at – and thus consoled himself for the extreme laxity of his practice by the impossibility of satisfying or coming up to the sublime theory he had formed – hence the most romantic professions of honour and independence were coupled with conduct of the meanest and most swindling kind.'

It was a cruel judgement, which had more than a little truth in it, but the fact was that Sheridan in his last years was so beaten down by poverty, drink and ill health that he was scarcely responsible for his actions. Despite the prince's statement to Croker, it is clear from Sheridan's letters that he was still received occasionally at Carlton House. But the old familiarity and confidence had gone. The prince now presided over a Tory government; even if Sheridan had been his former self, he could no longer be of use to him. The last time he saw Sheridan, the prince told Croker, was just under a year before his death, on 17 August 1815, when he had gone to visit the Duke of York at Oatlands on his birthday.

'Next day as I was crossing over to Brighton, I saw in the road near Leatherhead old Sheridan coming down the pathway. I can see him now in the black stockings and blue coat with metal buttons. I said to Blomfield [the prince's secretary], "There is Sheridan"; but as I spoke, he turned off into a lane when we were about thirty yards behind him, and walked off without looking round him.'

Deprived of the prince's favour, excluded from Parliament and Drury Lane, harassed by his creditors and in failing health, Sheridan had still not reached the end of his troubles. Hecca had become ill, at times alarmingly so; she was suffering from weakness, exhaustion and continual colds, which she put down to worry, but in fact may have been the first symptoms of the cancer of the womb from which she would die a year after her husband. Charles, his younger son, having left Winchester, where he won the gold medal for English verse, was now at Cambridge. He was a good-looking, good-hearted boy – 'I never saw anything approaching to malice in our dear Beastie,' Sheridan once wrote to Hecca – with nothing more to worry his parents than a tendency to idleness. But Tom's condition was desperate and Sheridan, remembering the course of Elizabeth's illness, had begun to realise there was little hope for him.

More than Charles, whose financial future was assured through his mother's marriage settlement, Tom had suffered from Sheridan's irresponsibility. His father had always meant to do the best for him – when Sheridan was appointed Auditor to the Duchy of Cornwall, he had begged the Prince of Wales to transfer the appointment to Tom, and Creevey, who was present at the time, saw him cry bitterly when the prince refused. (Whether, however, Sheridan's object was affection for Tom or to keep the profit of the office out of the reach of his creditors, Creevey was not sure.) But he had done him no service by involving him in the ruinous affairs of the theatre, and the quarter share he had given him was so encumbered by liabilities that it was almost worthless. Now, he was so ill that his only chance of survival lay in going to a warm climate. Thanks to the Duke of York, with whom Sheridan had remained on good terms, he was given the post of Paymaster General at the Cape of Good Hope, for which he left with his family in September 1813. He had been miserably ill the previous summer.

'It would half break your heart to see how he is changed,' wrote Sheridan to Hecca. 'I spend all the time with him as he seems to wish it, but he so reminds me of his mother, and his feeble, gasping way of speaking affects and deprives me of all hope. He tries to suppress the irritability of his temper in a very amiable way which makes me fear he thinks ill of himself.'

William Linley, Sheridan's brother-in-law, dined with Sheridan and his son shortly before Tom went abroad. The servant, in passing, dropped the platewarmer with a crash that startled poor Tom's nerves a good deal. Sheridan scolded the servant furiously, at last exclaiming, 'And how many plates have you broke?' 'Oh, not one, Sir,' answered the servant, delighted to vindicate himself. 'You damned fool,' said Sheridan, 'have you made all that noise for nothing?'

There were always stories to be told of Sheridan, a good humour that burst through the gloom even when, as now, his heart was breaking for his son. Their farewells must have been especially painful, since neither expected to see the other again. 'Angelo, my old friend,' said Tom to Henry Angelo, who saw him just before he left, 'I shall have but twenty months to live!' In fact he survived till September 1817, outliving his father by just over a year.

Harassed as he was by duns – he once reproved his servant for lighting a fire in the room where they were waiting, because it encouraged them to stay – Sheridan had escaped the indignity of arrest for debt for two years after leaving Parliament. In the spring of 1814 the blow fell and he was carried off to a sponging house for a debt of £600. It was Drury Lane that lay at the root of the trouble, for Whitbread was still holding back the money for his shares to meet possible claims. Writing from prison, Sheridan blamed him bitterly for this last humiliation:

'Whitbread, putting all false professions of Friendship and feeling out of the Question, you have no right to keep me here. For it is in truth *your* act. If you had not forcibly withheld from me £12,000 in consequence of a threatening Letter from a miserable swindler whose claim *you* in particular knew to be *a lie* – I should at least have been out of the reach of *this* state of miserable insult . . . O God! with what mad confidence have I trusted your word – I ask justice from you and no boon – I enclosed you yesterday three different securities which had you been disposed to have acted even as a private Friend would have made it certain you might have done so without the smallest risk . . . I shall only add that, I think, if I know myself, had our Lotts been reversed, and I had seen you in my situation, and had left Lady E[lizabeth Whitbread] in that of my wife I would have risk'd £600 rather than have left you so altho' I had been in no way accessory in bringing you into that condition.'

On receiving this letter, Whitbread immediately left his dinner table to go to Sheridan, only to find that he had already been released thanks to the 'unsolicited interference' of the prince regent. He found Sheridan apparently in a sanguine mood, confidently speculating on making a comeback at Westminster, where a vacant seat was coming up. When he got home, however, he broke down completely, bursting into 'a long and passionate fit of weeping at the profanation, as he put it, which his person had suffered'.

Sheridan was arrested at least two more times, though never for more than a day or two. The friends, from whom he had always refused to borrow, now came to his aid. He was lent a house, 17 Savile Row, by Lord Wellesley. Another friend, Richard Iremonger, gave him the use of a farmhouse, Randalls, near Leatherhead, from which he could visit the estate and its tenants at Polesden Lacey; it must have been here that the prince regent caught his last sight of him on the way to Brighton.

Even in his decline Sheridan remained marvellous company. 'His very dregs,' wrote Byron, 'are better than the "first sprightly runnings" of others.' Much tried though they were, his friends were remarkably faithful to him. He was not an easy guest to have to stay; Haydon, the painter, was told how he would stay up drinking claret till midnight and rum punch till five in the morning, 'ringing up the servants by night' and disturbing all the household. Lady Holland told Moore that he always took a bottle of wine and a book to bed with him, 'the *former* alone intended for use', when he stayed at Holland House. In the mornings he breakfasted in bed, made his appearance at one or two, and, pretending important business, set out for town, stopping for a dram at the Adam and Eve public house at the foot of the park. 'There was indeed a long bill run up by him at the "Adam and Eve", which Lord Holland had to pay.'

It may well have been with Lady Holland that Sheridan first met Byron. Precipitated into celebrity by the publication of the first two cantos of *Childe Harold*, Byron had arrived in London in the spring of 1812 to find himself the lion of Whig society. Sheridan was one of the dramatists he most admired – his letters are scattered with quotations from his plays – and, though he heard him only once in Parliament, he was the only orator, he said, that he ever wished to hear at greater length. The two men, one at the outset of his fame, the other already a figure of the past, saw each other frequently during the four years Byron stayed in London, before departing for Italy in a blaze of scandal not long before Sheridan's death.

'He was superb!' wrote Byron later, '– he had a sort of liking for me – and never attacked me – at least to my face, and he did everybody else – high names & wits and orators some of them poets also – I have seen [him] cut up Whitbread – quiz Mᵉ de Staël – annihilate Colman – and do little less by some others – (whose names as friends I set not down) of good fame and abilities – Poor fellow! he got drunk very thoroughly and very soon – It occasionally fell to my lot to convey him home – no sinecure – for he was so tipsy that I was obliged to put on his cocked hat for him – to be sure it tumbled off again and I was not myself so sober as to be able to pick it up again.'

It is to Byron that we owe the story of Sheridan being taken up by the watchman, who found him in the street, fuddled and bewildered and almost insensible. ' "Who are you, sir?" – no answer. "What's your name?" – a hiccup. "What's your name?" – answer, in a slow, deliberate and impassive tone – "Wilberforce!!!" '

'Is not that Sherry all over?' wrote Byron to Moore, 'and, to my mind excellent.'

Thomas Moore was another of Sheridan's friends of later years. They had first met in 1807, probably with Samuel Rogers, at whose famous literary breakfasts Sheridan was one of the stars. It was the year that the first of Moore's 'Irish Melodies' were published, their lyrical tone owing much to Sheridan's songs for *The Duenna*. Flattered to know Sheridan at first, Moore would be one of his most loyal friends in the miseries of his last months. In his life of Sheridan, he quotes an extract from Byron's journal for 1812–13, which was then in his possession.

Saturday, December 18, 1813

Lord Holland told me a curious piece of *sentimentality* in Sheridan. The other night we were all delivering our respective and various opinions on him and other *'hommes marquans'*, and mine was this: – 'Whatever Sheridan has done or has chosen to do has been, *par excellence*, always the *best* of its kind. He has written the *best* comedy (School for Scandal) the *best* drama [The Duenna] in my mind far better than that St Giles's lampoon, the Beggar's Opera, the *best* farce (*The Critic* – it is only too good for a farce), and the *best* Address (Monologue on Garrick), and, to crown all, delivered the very *best* oration (the famous Begum Speech) ever conceived or heard in this country.'

Somebody told Sheridan this the next day, and on hearing it, he burst into tears! – Poor Brinsley! If they were tears of pleasure, I

301

would rather have said those few, but sincere, words, than have written the Iliad, or made his own celebrated Philippic. Nay, his own comedy never gratified me more than to hear he had derived a minute's gratification from any praise of mine – humble as it must appear to 'my elders and betters'.

There have been few more moving tributes from one great writer to another, and it is interesting in this context to read some of Sheridan's opinions of his literary contemporaries. Johnson's dictionary he regarded as a work of great and commendable labour – 'the labour of a mill horse' – but he detested his moralising, his bearish manners and his Tory prejudices. He greatly admired Walter Scott, describing himself in a letter to Hecca as spending 'near three hours this blessed morning, for mind I don't hop, skip and jump thro' a book as some certain people do, in reading the third volume of Waverley . . . I am enchanted with the work.' He gave enthusiastic praise to Sydney Smith's anonymously published 'Peter Plymley's Letters' on Catholic emancipation, so wittily written that many suspected him to be the author. And in 1813, the year that *Pride and Prejudice* appeared, he told the lady he was sitting next to at dinner at Whitbread's, 'to buy it immediately for it was one of the cleverest things he had ever read'. Since the links with Carlton House were not entirely broken, it is tempting to think that the prince regent, who kept a set of Jane Austen's novels in each of his houses, was introduced to them by Sheridan.

In July 1815, Whitbread committed suicide by cutting his throat. It was generally thought that his anxieties over Drury Lane were one of the contributary factors, but Sheridan, in a letter to his son Charles, told him that on his head being opened by a surgeon, 'part of the Skull and brain were found in such a state that it is impossible he could have kept his senses, or indeed have retain'd a painful existence but for a very short time.' Whitbread had resigned from the theatre committee in May, without having settled Sheridan's claims, but though Sheridan had complained of him bitterly he had never altogether fallen out with him and was genuinely shocked by 'the deplorable end of our poor friend'.

A few months after Whitbread's death, Sheridan entered Drury Lane for the first time since the theatre had been rebuilt. The occasion was a performance of *Sir Giles Overreach*, in which Edmund

Kean was playing the leading role. Since his first appearance as Richard III two years before, Kean had taken London by storm. Mrs Siddons had retired and, faced with Kean's tempestuous energy, the stately Kemble had faded 'like a tragedy ghost'. Sheridan had allowed himself to be persuaded to see the new phenomenon by a friend, Lord Essex. Between the acts, he was found to be missing from the box and was discovered installed in the green-room, with all the actors round him, welcoming him back to the scenes of his old glory. Wine was immediately ordered and Sheridan's health was drunk by everyone present, with the wish that he would 'often, very often, re-appear among them'.

'This scene, as was natural, exhilarated his spirits,' wrote Moore, 'and on parting with Lord Essex that night, at his own door in Savile Row, he said triumphantly that the world would soon hear of him, for the Duke of Norfolk was actually about to bring him into Parliament. This, it appears, was actually the case; but Death stood near as he spoke. In a few days after, his last fatal illness began.'

From December 1815 onwards Sheridan scarcely left his room. Varicose veins, causing severe swelling in his legs, and an abscess in 'a distressing place', had already been a trouble for some time. To them was now added a racking cough, making it almost impossible to sleep, and a total loss of appetite. His digestion had at last been destroyed by years of excess and he could scarcely touch solid food. He knew that his days were numbered. To Hecca, herself now very ill, he wrote.

'Never again let one harsh word pass between us during the period, which may not be long, that we are in this world together, and life, however clouded in me, is mutually spared to us. I have expressed the same sentiment to my son [Charles], in a letter I wrote to him a few days since, and I had his answer – a most affecting one – and, I am sure, very sincere and have since embraced him. Don't imagine I am expressing an interesting apprehension I do not feel.'

There was little chance that Sheridan could die in peace. The Duke of Norfolk, who had promised to find him a seat, died at the end of January 1816. Sheridan would not have been well enough to take up his offer, but his death removed a last hope of freedom from his embarrassments. Sensing that their prey might escape them, his creditors now closed in. All his possessions that could be sold were sold: furniture, pictures, books, and a gold cup presented to him by the burgesses of Stafford, belatedly repentant for their rejection of him in 1812. Bailiffs crowded the house, where Hecca, too ill to move, lay in one room, Sheridan in another. The threat of arrest was a terror. Moore returned home with Samuel Rogers late one evening in May, to find a desperate note from Sheridan on the hall table.

'I find things settled so that £150 will remove all difficulties. I am absolutely undone and broken hearted. I shall negotiate for the Plays successfully in the course of a week, when all shall be returned. I have desired Fairbrother [a servant] to get back the Guarantee for thirty.

'They are going to take the carpets out of the window and break into Mrs S.'s room and *take me* – for God's sake let me see you. R.B.S.'

Although it was after midnight Moore and Rogers hurried round to Savile Row, where they learned from a servant that the arrest had not yet taken place, but that bills would be pasted on the house the next day. Moore returned in the morning with a draft for £150 from Rogers, to find Sheridan talking with his usual optimism of publishing his dramatic works and settling all his affairs if only he could leave his bed.

It was typical of Sheridan that even *in extremis* he still hoped to extricate himself from his embarrassments. But he was now too ill to deal with any practical matters. Dr Bain, who had attended Elizabeth in her last illness, fought off a further attempt by the bailiffs, who tried to carry him off in his blankets, on the grounds that they would kill him if they moved him. The prince regent, hearing of his plight, sent round a certain Mr Vaughan, 'Hat' Vaughan as he was known, with £200 to help him and the promise of more if necessary. Since he knew, as he said, that Sheridan's debts were '*la mer à boire*', he asked only that the source of it should not be known, as it would merely have brought more claimants on him.

Vaughan returned with a most shocking story. He found Sheridan and Mrs Sheridan, he told Macmahon, both in bed and apparently starving. There was hardly a servant left, only a maid for Mrs Sheridan, who had stayed because she was waiting for her wages to be paid. All the reception rooms were bare, and the whole house was

304

in a state of filth and stench that was quite intolerable. Sheridan himself was lying in a garret in a truckle bed, with a coarse red and blue coverlet, like those used for horse cloths, over him. Out of this bed, said Vaughan, he had not moved for a week, and in this state the unhappy man had been allowed to wallow, nor could he discover that anyone had taken any notice of him, except Lady Bessborough, who had sent him £20, and the Hollands, who had sent ice and currant water.

Notwithstanding all this misery, Sheridan, on seeing Vaughan, appeared to revive, said he was quite well, talked of paying off all his debts, and, though he had not eaten a morsel for a week, spoke with a certain degree of alacrity and hope. Vaughan, however, saw that this was a kind of bravado and that he was really in a fainting condition. He sent for spiced wine and toast, bought a new bed, sheets and shirts, and had Sheridan washed and put into the new bed. At the same time he arranged for the house to be cleaned and fumigated, did what he could for Mrs Sheridan, and having spent £150 left the remainder to be used by them. Three days later, however, to Macmahon's amazement, Vaughan came back with the £200, which had been returned, together with a message that '*Mrs* Sheridan's friends had taken care that Mr Sheridan wanted for nothing'. Evidently they suspected the money came from the prince. Their assistance, thought Vaughan, came rather late, since only three days ago he had been enabled by his royal highness's bounty to relieve them both from the lowest state of misery and debasement in which he had ever seen human beings.

This was the prince regent's account, told to Croker some years later. Sheridan's family would deny that he was ever in such poverty, but what probably happened was that the prince's offer alerted his friends to his distresses. The tutor William Smyth, who came to call about this time, gives an equally sad picture of the house, dirty and empty of furniture, with Sheridan lying upstairs, too ill to receive him, and a number of strange men, evidently bailiffs, standing round.

Towards the middle of June an article appeared in the *Morning Post*, in which for the first time the public learned of Sheridan's situation. 'Oh delay not,' said the writer, 'delay not to draw aside the curtain within which that proud spirit hides its sufferings . . . Prefer ministering in the chamber of sickness to mustering at "The splendid sorrows that adorn the hearse"; I say *Life* and Succour against Westminster Abbey and a Funeral.'

Now at last the world rallied round. The Duke of York and other noble acquaintances left their cards, Lady Bessborough, his old love, came to see him three days before he died. He asked her what she thought of his looks, and she told him that his eyes were brilliant still. He took her hand and gripped it hard, telling her that if possible he would come to see her after he was dead. He was resolved, he said, that she should remember him. He said more frightful things, according to Lord Broughton, to whom she described the scene, and she finally withdrew from him in terror.

Soon after this he drifted into semi-consciousness. Hecca, who, though in great pain, had left her bed to look after him in his final days, went into his room, where he lay propped up on pillows, to say goodbye alone. The doors were closed on them, and when she came out she was swollen-eyed and crying. The Bishop of London was sent for and read prayers by his bedside, but though he told Charles and Hecca that Sheridan had joined in reverently, he confessed to Lord Holland that he had been too far gone to understand. On the morning of Sunday, 7 July 1816, the MP Peter Moore, one of Sheridan's most faithful friends, called at Savile Row, to be told that he was dying. Half an hour later, as the clock of St George's, Hanover Square, was striking twelve, Sheridan slipped peacefully away. It seemed, wrote Charles, breaking the news to Tom at the Cape, 'that he almost slumbered into death'.

# XXIX

―――――――――――⚬―――――――――――

S heridan was buried in Westminster Abbey. Years before, when
his sister-in-law Jane had been buried quietly in the country, he
had said that he hoped that his passage to the grave would be the
same; the 'gaudy parade' of Elizabeth's funeral in Wells Cathedral
had always been a painful memory. But the world, which had
neglected him in his last illness, now awoke to the fact that an era
had come to an end. His career had begun when America was
fighting for her independence; he had died the year after Waterloo.
'He is the last of the giants,' wrote the MP H. G. Bennett to
Creevey, 'and there is no one to take the chair he leaves.' A
magnificent funeral was staged for him. Seldom, wrote Moore, had
there been such a display of rank as that which graced his last
procession.

The pallbearers were the Duke of Bedford, the Earl of Lauderdale
(a joke on whose lips, Sheridan once said, was no laughing matter),
Earl Mulgrave, the Bishop of London, Lord Holland and Earl
Spencer. The mourners included two royal dukes, the Dukes of
York and Sussex, the Duke of Argyll, and a phalanx of marquesses,
earls, viscounts and barons in descending order of nobility. So great
was the procession, which began at the house of Sheridan's friend
Peter Moore in Great George Street, that the coffin had reached the
Abbey before all the mourners had moved from the starting point.
The contrast with the scenes that had gone before was striking and
Moore, in a generous burst of verse, put his feelings into print.

307

O it sickens the heart to see bosoms so hollow,
    And friendships so false in the great and high-born; –
To think what a long line of titles may follow
    The relics of him who lay friendless and lorn!

How proud they can press to the funeral array
    Of him whom they shunn'd, in his sickness and sorrow –
How bailiffs may seize his last blanket to-day,
    Whose pall may be held up by Nobles tomorrow!

Richard Peake, the treasurer of Drury Lane, expressed somewhat the same sentiments in a letter to Thomas Perkins, Sheridan's supporter at Stafford, that evening. 'A few lines to say that I have just follow'd my old Master to his last Home seen him to his grave in Poet's Corner Westminster Abbey so much for this World. You will see in the Newspapers that the account of the Funeral which was most awfull the Procession walk'd and the Pall was supported by six Dukes [sic] two of them Royal . . . there were a number of Lords and titles of all descriptions who followed the *poor* old Gentleman to his grave (for there was an execution in his House at the time he died).'

Sheridan's grave in Poet's Corner, with the statue of Garrick nearby, was marked by a simple tablet, placed there by Peter Moore,

Richard Brinsley Sheridan
Born 1751
Died 7th July, 1816
This marble is the tribute
of an attached
Friend
Peter Moore

Had Sheridan had any say in the matter, said his friend Lord Thanet, he would have protested loudly against this final resting place. 'Poet's Corner was his aversion – [he] would have liked to have been placed near Fox &c.' For Sheridan, his successes in politics had always been more important than his triumphs in the theatre. Not long before he died, he was visited by a former political associate, John Graham, who in the margin of a volume of Sheridan's *Speeches* wrote the following note against his speech on the Begums in the House of Lords:

'While reading one of the 12 Quarto volumes containing this

Speech about 6 weeks previous to his decease, he said to me taking a few steps across the Drawing room in Savile Row – "There are certain periods of a Man's life when the horizon looks clear and beautiful, and the grass beneath him assumes a brighter green; at such a time I made use of five words which I will show you." Then turning to the last volume, he put his finger to the concluding sentence, "My Lords, I have done." '

Sheridan had enriched the parliamentary history of his period, leaving behind him a legend of eloquence and wit. At the time of the French Revolution he had gone against the current of public opinion by his championship of civil liberties; later, he had estranged himself from his own party by supporting the government's conduct of the war. But though he fought his battles valiantly and though his judgement was almost invariably sane and sound, he never made a real mark as a statesman. In part this was due to the circumstances of the time and the disadvantages of his background. His talents alone were not enough. Creevey once wrote that neither he nor Burke were considered elevated enough in rank to be admitted into the Cabinet, and perhaps this reason, though unstated, lay behind his exclusion in 1806. Viewed politically, Sheridan's career can be regarded as a splendid failure. The causes he espoused, parliamentary reform, Catholic emancipation, came to fruition long after his death; his political integrity was scarcely appreciated at a time when the scramble for places and sinecures was almost universal. The speeches, on which he devoted so much time and labour, are scarcely read; the plays are as fresh and magical as ever. Posterity has justified his place in Poet's Corner.

Hecca survived her husband for little more than a year. She died of cancer of the womb on 27 October 1817 aged forty-one. Tom had preceded her by only a few weeks; he died at the Cape on 12 September. The news did not reach Charles till November. 'I have again to address you on these sad and heart rending subjects!' he wrote to his cousin, the Reverend T. P. LeFanu. 'I have lost my brother too. A letter, which I have received today from his unhappy widow brought me the sad news ... She is coming home immediately in the *Albion Transport* ... A thousand thanks for your kind, your very kind letter. I only got it on my return here Monday. How sincerely I wish we were together. I am sure you would teach me better and more persuasively than any one how all these things coming in such sad succession *ought* to be borne.'

Charles was a devoted brother-in-law, and uncle to Tom's children. His mother's death and the release of her marriage settlement had left him comfortably off, with a fortune of £40,000. His financial independence, joined to 'some want of steady application, stifled all exertion' and he never married or followed a serious career. Ironically, his father's debts had amounted to little more than £5,000 when they were added up after his death, though this may have been because many of them had been written off as hopeless. Peake noted mournfully that Sheridan had owed him £1,500 which he had no hope of obtaining.

Byron was in Italy when he heard of Sheridan's death, and perhaps it is he who should have the final word. His 'Monody on the death of the Right Hon. Richard Brinsley Sheridan', delivered at Drury Lane at the beginning of the following season, was written as it were to order, and though inspired by genuine feeling was not one of his most successful poems. He gave a more spontaneous judgement in a letter singled out by Ruskin, in his autobiography *Praeterita*, as a supreme example of how Byron wrote 'as easily as a hawk flies, and as clearly as a lake reflects, the exact truth in the precisely narrowest terms'. He was writing to Moore from Venice about his projected life of Sheridan on 1 June 1818:

'The Whigs abuse him; however, he never left them, and such blunderers deserve neither credit nor compassion. As for his creditors – remember Sheridan never had a shilling, and was thrown, with great powers and passions, into the thick of the world, and placed upon the pinnacle of success, with no other external means to support him in his elevation. Did Fox pay *his* debts? or did Sheridan take a subscription? Was —'s drunkenness more excusable than his? Were his intrigues more notorious than those of all his contemporaries? and is his memory to be blasted and theirs respected? Don't let yourself be led away by clamour, but compare him with the coalitioner Fox, and the pensioner Burke, as a man of principle; and with ten hundred thousand in personal views; and with none in talent, for he beat them all out and out. Without means, without connection, without character (which might be false at first, and drive him mad afterwards from desperation), he beat them all, in all he ever attempted. But, alas poor human nature! Good-night, or rather morning. It is four, and the dawn gleams over the Grand Canal and unshadows the Rialto.'

# Notes

There was no official reporting of debates during the period that Sheridan was a Member of Parliament. Both Cobbett's *Parliamentary History* from 1780 1803 and Hansard's *Parliamentary Debates* thereafter were based on newspaper reports, often incomplete and usually written from memory. (No note-taking was allowed in the House of Commons until 1795.) The same applies to the speeches in the five-volume edition of *Speeches of the late Right Honourable Richard Brinsley Sheridan edited by a Constitutional Friend*, covering the period 1780 1808, though some of the most important had been corrected by Sheridan himself. Unless otherwise noted, I have used this edition for his speeches up to 1808, and the reports in Hansard's *Parliamentary Debates* for his speeches from 1809 to 1812.

Quotations from Sheridan's poems are taken from *Plays and Poems*, edited by R. Compton Rhodes, and those from his plays come from *Plays*, edited by Cecil Price.

Quotations from his letters, unless otherwise noted, are taken from *The Letters of Richard Brinsley Sheridan*, edited by Cecil Price.

Full details of books are given in the bibliography; where only one work by an author is listed, the name of the author is given as the reference.

# Introduction

# Chapter I

11 nearly all that the metropolis . . . Alicia LeFanu, 51
11 I leave you to act . . . Sheldon, 203
13 Thomas Sheridan would have been . . . ibid., 253


## Chapter II

14 He wakes as from a dream . . . Rae, I, 25
15 How are my dear little ones . . . Watkins, I, 159
15 can't afford to do a dirty action . . . *The Rivals*, III, i
15 There rises up the cabin small . . . Dufferin Archive, D.1071B/D2/1
16 Mr Sheridan's well informed . . . Boswell, 132
17 my mentor, my Socrates . . . Pottle, 9
17 Sir, your accent is not offensive . . . Boswell, 232
17 Sheridan rang the bell . . . Sichel, I, 249
17 What! Have they given *him* a pension . . . Boswell, 131
17 some damn'd good-natured friend or other . . . *The Critic*, I, i
17 Sir, it is burning a farthing candle . . . Boswell, 154
17 Why Sir, Sherry is dull . . . ibid., 154
17 impressed upon the mind . . . ibid., 133
17 I know not, Madam . . . LeFanu, 113
18 Dick has been at Harrow . . . *Speeches*, V, iv
19 that he was a very low spirited boy . . . Gore, 33
19 Dear Uncle – As it is not . . . *Letters*, I, 1
19 She stopped short . . . Alicia LeFanu, 293
20 I have lost, what the world cannot repair . . . Watkins, I, 134
20 Dear Uncle – It is now almost a week . . . *Letters*, I, 3
21 All the while . . . Sumner and myself . . . Moore, I, 8
21 we used to show his name . . . Marchand, VI, 68
22 I saw him; and my childish attachment . . . Moore, I, 15
22 With the elder Sheridan . . . Angelo, I, 299
23 in which he acquired . . . Gore, 33
23 We have lost all knowledge . . . Moore, I, 268
23 I have some time had full belief . . . Rae, I, 113
23 Now for a phoenix of a song . . . ibid., 111
24 The thoughts of £200 between us . . . ibid., 99
24 Why, Sir, consider how much easier . . . Boswell, 232
25 presently laughed off the stage . . . Gore, 33


## Chapter III

26 a very neat house . . . *Letters*, I, 18
26 May it please your Majesty . . . ibid.
28 'Tis a good lounge . . . *The Rivals*, I, i
28 a fine voice and considerable taste . . . Alicia LeFanu, 246
28 opened a new world of harmony . . . ibid.

42 Most people are (notwithstanding the general tendency ... Rae, I, 185

43 Uncouth is this moss covered grotto ... ibid., 187

43 I will call you Horatio ... Black, 59

43 My mother and me ... ibid., 60

43 How shall I account ... ibid., 62

44 The crowd was so great ... ibid.

44 This raised no small bustle ... ibid., 63

44 filled with the most scurrilous abuse ... Rae, I, 203

45 No, by God I won't ... Moore, I, 65

45 uttering horrid curses ... Rae, I, 204

45 I have done for him ... ibid.

45 But all these precautions ... Rae, I, 201

46 Never was more concern ... Black, 70

46 an oath equivocal ... Rae, I, 206

46 declared he would sooner follow ... ibid., 208

46 Oh! my Horatio ... Black, 72

47 Let me see what they report of me ... Alicia LeFanu, 406

47 I am exceedingly unhappy ... Moore, I, 101

47 contracted later than they should have been ... *Letters*, I, 35

47 particular friends ... Rae, I, 210


## Chapter V

48 excessive melancholy ... *Letters*, I, 40

48 on this subject you shall never again ... ibid., 35

48 I am perfectly convinced ... ibid., 40

48 I have received a letter from her ... Sotheby's catalogue (variations in punctuation from *Letters*, I, 46)

48 How strange is my situation ... *Letters*, I, 46

49 I have here at least one great inducement ... ibid., 35

49 Mechanicks, Mensuration, Astronomy etc ... ibid., 60

49 I wish you could on any pretence ... Sotheby's catalogue (variations in punctuation from *Letters*, I, 66)

49 I think ... as she has acquired a reputation ... Percy Fitzgerald, I, 82

49 The applause and admiration ... Bor and Cleeland, 66

49 Eliza is within an hour's ride ... *Letters*, I, 78

50 which I take to be the great Gate of Power ... ibid., 73

50 It has been an everlasting Fashion ... ibid., 71

50 – Ask the Fond Youth ... ibid., 72

50 It hopes most ... ibid.

50 I would have every man ... ibid., 64

51 A Lover (a true one) ... ibid., 65

51 the basest, meanest and most ungrateful ... ibid., 68

51 Let them go . . . ibid., 71
51 I have so been deceived . . . Black, 87
51 Miss C., I own I pity . . . ibid., 92
52 Believe me . . . I am incapable . . . ibid., 90
52 If not, I cannot compel you . . . ibid., 92
52 serious misunderstanding . . . Moore, I, 110
52 series of stratagems and schemes . . . ibid., 111
53 The King admires the last . . . Lewis, 106
53 He resolved wisely and nobly . . . Boswell, 453
53 After the ceremony . . . *Morning Chronicle*, 16 April 1773
53 I have given orders . . . MS letter, 15 May 1773, Harvard Theatre Collection
53 Had I hunted . . . *Letters*, 82
54 a strumpet . . . Dowden, V, 1964
54 without an atom of principle . . . ibid.
54 I consider myself now as having no other Son . . . Rae, I, 68
54 Who is to settle the precedence . . . Angelo, I, 86
54 captivating manners and superior address . . . ibid.
54 Nor . . . can you . . . *Letters*, I, 80
55 About 3,500 persons were present . . . Walker, 69
55 in the full lustre of unrivalled talents . . . Bor and Cleeland, 73
55 I found him very warm . . . MS letter, 10 Dec 1774, Harvard Theatre Collection
55 We kept it up to a late hour . . . Angelo, I, 87
56 The highest circles of society . . . Bor and Cleeland, 75
56 My dear friend, it is my means . . . Earle, I, 103
56 What reason could they think . . . Morwood, 30
56 the best picture I ever painted . . . Sichel, I, 463
57 the wild Huron . . . *Letters*, I, 49
57 Lord C.'s whole system . . . Moore, I, 134
58 you must absolutely keep from her . . . Bor and Cleeland, 80
58 I must premise to you . . . *Letters*, I, 84
58 There will be a *Comedy* . . . ibid., 85

## Chapter VI

59 scarce equals the picture . . . *Morning Chronicle*, 18 Jan 1775
59 By the powers . . . Linda Kelly, 33
60 My dear Dick . . . I am delighted . . . Creevey, 35
60 I see this play will creep . . . *Morning Post*, 31 Jan 1775
60 In the first . . . you are always at the toilette . . . quoted in Davison, 86
61 including a perspective view . . . *Morning Post*, 18 Jan 1775

63 He was the furthest possible . . . quoted in Davison, 89
63 I have now got the last . . . *Plays*, x
64 As all are born the subjects . . . Moore, I, 152
64 This is the worst doctrine that can be . . . ibid., 153
65 to think that there sat his father . . . ibid., 167
65 My father was astonishingly well received . . . *Letters*, I, 91
65 I would not have been concerned . . . Percy Fitzgerald, I, 135
66 I think he [Sheridan] . . . ibid., 134
66 The inclosed are the words . . . *Letters*, I, 91
67 In days of Gay . . . Rhodes, *Harlequin Sheridan*, 58
68 the old woman . . . will be the death . . . Moore, I, 169
69 the American War, founded in injustice . . . Sichel, I, 625
69 I made the first dinner party . . . *Speeches*, V, xiv
69 I'll answer for it . . . *Letters*, I, 98


## Chapter VII

70 the quicksands of loans . . . Sichel, I, 525
71 while this is *cleared* . . . *Letters*, I, 95
71 I shall shake off my chains . . . Oman, 343
71 The theatre engrossed the minds of men . . . Murphy, II, 201
72 Ye belles and ye beaux . . . quoted in Leech and Craik, 6
72 The drama's laws . . . Murphy, I, 135
73 Indeed . . . there never was known . . . *Letters*, I, 107
73 His plays are, I own . . . Michael Kelly, 339
74 The comedy of *The Relapse* . . . *Morning Chronicle*, 25 February 1775
74 I stood for some moments . . . Percy Fitzgerald, *Sheridans*, I, 147
74 could not fail to be very pleasing . . . Boswell, 532
74 He who has written the two best comedies . . . ibid.
75 astonishes everybody by his vivacity . . . *Letters*, I, 101
75 she uglifies everything near her . . . Barrett, V, 312
75 No state has *Amoret*! . . . *Plays*, 'A Portrait' (Prologue to *The School for Scandal*)
76 But where does Laura pass her lonely hours . . . Sichel, I, 520
76 Ah, Laura, no . . . ibid.
77 It was the fate of Mr Sheridan . . . Moore, I, 241
77 Finished at last. Thank God . . . ibid., 242
77 Amidst the mortifying circumstances . . . 'On the Artificial Comedy of the last Century', quoted in Davison, 137
78 the wasp and the butterfly . . . ibid., 139
78 the prince of pink heels . . . Boaden, *Kemble*, I, 55
78 the perfect gentlewoman . . . quoted in Davison, 139
78 left a taste on the palate . . . Hazlitt, *London Magazine*, 1820

79 With what an air he trod the stage . . . Hazlitt, *The Examiner*, 15 October 1815

80 That will not do . . . Sichel, I, 580

80 Mr Garrick's best wishes . . . Percy Fitzgerald, *Sheridans* . . . I, 161

80 Sheridan wrote for the actor . . . *Saturday Review*, 27 June, 1896, quoted in Shaw, 101

80 all-important lantern . . . 'On the 1948 Production and Others', Introduction to the Folio Society edition of *The School for Scandal*, 1949, quoted in Davison, 153

81 the inexpressible feeling of fulfilment . . . ibid., 157

81 I am prepared to swear . . . ibid., 151

81 *Thee* my Inspirer . . . *Plays*, 'A Portrait' (Prologue to *The School for Scandal*)

81 S. is in Town . . . MS letter, Bath Central Library, ALB 1553

## Chapter VIII

82 Talk of the merit of Dick's play . . . Dowden, II, 756

82 Before dinner Dr Johnson seized . . . Boswell, 591

83 damnatus obstinatus mulio . . . Sherwin, 99

83 Oh, how I long . . . ibid., 217

83 the sister of my heart . . . Rae, II, 26

83 very handsome but nothing like her sister . . . Barrett, I, 162

83 with the most unbounded applause . . . Dulwich Picture Gallery, *A Nest of Nightingales*, 83

83 one of the finest specimens . . . Black, 118

83 true genius . . . Michael Kelly, 112

84 Sweet instrument of him for whom I mourn . . . *Annual Register*, 1784 5

84 The feelings of Mr Linley . . . Percy Fitzgerald, *Sheridans*, II, 51

85 To you, Mr Garrick . . . Murphy, II, 145

85 Every one is raving . . . Oman, 360

86 I read the tragedy . . . Mikhail, 29

86 a thumper! . . . Rhodes, *Harlequin Sheridan*, 78

86 At length a scene opened . . . Rae, II, 4

87 Pray assure your father . . . Oman, 363

88 eclipsed the gaiety of nations . . . quoted in Lee, entry for Garrick

88 had raised the character of his profession . . . ibid.

88 damned canting bitch . . . Marchand, IX, 15

88 Talents in literature . . . Moore, 73

89 I knew what would come of it . . . Sherwin, 137

89 It was very ungrateful of Cumberland . . . Richard Sheridan, *Sheridaniana*, 67

89 *No one* could mistake the Character . . . Susan Burney, Egerton

3691, Department of Manuscripts, British Library

90 A Talent for ridicule ... *Letters*, III, 122

90 Lord, Sir ... that was owing to a joke ... *Morning Chronicle*, 15
December 1779

91 I have repeatedly enjoyed this rich treat ... Boaden, *Kemble*, I, 36

93 It is vastly good ... Bessborough, *Georgiana*, 44

93 The elegance of Mrs Sheridan's beauty (*et seq.*) ... Barrett, I, 153


## Chapter IX

96 Whenever any one proposes ... Moore, I, 301

97 I am glad you did not fall on me ... quoted in Lee, entry for
Fox

98 would hardly survive serious scrutiny ... Edwardes, 14

98 they are damn'd Fellows ... *Letters*, I, 132

99 We have found you men of your words ... ibid., 134

99 when he stole away by himself ... Gore, 36

99 I am entirely at a loss ... *Letters*, I, 135

100 with particular attention ... Moore, I, 347

100 who felt properly the nature of the trust ... ibid., 348

100 It is in me, however ... ibid.

101 His bristly black person ... Ayling, *Fox*, 104

101 I have always thought that the great merit ... Bessborough,
*Georgiana*, 32

101 effaces all without being a beauty ... Leveson Gower, 34

101 Sheridan goes tomorrow ... Bessborough, *Georgiana*, 124

102 like a Leviathan ... Sichel, II, 32

102 Sheridan was a great man ... Earle, II, 316

103 It is not a chip off the old block ... quoted in Lee, entry for
William Pitt the Younger

103 What! was his Majesty's power ... *Speeches*, I, 15 March 1781, 13

104 By constant practice in small matters ... Brougham, 213

104 The Right Hon. Gentleman had acted ... Moore, I, 360

105 No application to be received ... Rae, I, 380

105 Dear Charles ... Tho' I have time only ... *Letters*, I, 138

105 If the business of an American treaty ... ibid., 148

105 Surely, whatever the preliminaries ... ibid., 149

107 It is impossible for me ... Rowland, 180

107 It is not my nature ... Rae, I, 405

107 as fixed as the Hanover succession ... Moore, I, 381

107 Sheridan ... instead of being averse ... Percy Fitzgerald, *Sheridans*,
I, 284

107 would infallibly produce ... Gibbs, 104

107 rejoiced at it ... ibid.

108 turned back his ears and eyes ... Ayling, *Fox*, 111

## Chapter X

109 For God's sake ... improve the opportunity ... Moore, I, 370
109 They talk of avarice, lust, ambition ... Dowden, II, 757
109 indicative at once of intellect ... Wraxall, III, 368
110 No man ... admired more than he did ... Moore, I, 388
110 But ... let me assure the Right Honourable Gentleman ... ibid., 369
111 A correct pronunciation ... *Critical Review*, 1780, quoted in Benzie, 103
111 that wretch ... Rae, II, 5
112 where *alone* ... she could shew him ... Boaden, *Mrs Siddons*, 218
112 At length I was called ... Campbell, 89
113 O glorious constellation! ... ibid., 134
113 it was indeed too disagreable ... ibid., 128
113 because he saw the ghost of a shilling ... Chatel de Briancon, 38
113 a very pretty place ... Bor and Cleeland, 108
113 When you were oblig'd to be in Town ... Black, 149
114 good deal of scurvy ... Betsy Sheridan, 25
114 I see you are ever so affronted with me ... Rae, II, 128
114 Thank'e Dearest Love ... MS letter, Dufferin archive, 1071B/D1/3
115 I forgot to tell you ... Black, 151
115 Tickel[l] had more of vanity ... John Taylor, I, 143
115 In the midst of the scuffle ... Dowden, V, 2022
115 I heard every cruel Pop ... Black, 134
116 like two Tritons in a Sea piece ... MS letter, Bath Reference Library, ALB 1540
116 He [Tickell] found my mother ... Black, 142
116 I wish his great wooden head ... ibid.
117 The manager has got it up ... Rae, II, 6
117 young ladies of the quality ... Weller and Glover, VI, 349
118 Your admiration for Mrs Siddons ... Richard Sheridan, *Sheridaniana*, 283
118 Just as I had finished my toilette ... Campbell, 186
118 Lady Macbeth is supposed to be *asleep* ... quoted in Linda Kelly, 48
119 Here's the smell of blood still ... Campbell, 187

## Chapter XI

121 better than any other man ... Ayling, *Fox*, 117
121 There is good reason to believe ... Wraxall, III, 374
121 It is said that Sheridan ... Dowden, I, 61
121 my son's ministers ... Ayling, *Fox*, 167

122 In answering this strange sally . . . Moore, I, 400

123 whoever voted for the India bill . . . Ayling, *Fox*, 122

123 I am told . . . that his countenance . . . L. G. Mitchell, 65

123 as Audiences on such occasions . . . Ayling, *Fox*, 123

123 A sight to make surrounding nations stare . . . 'The Rolliad', quoted in Trevelyan, *British History*, 45

123 mince pie administration . . . Sherwin, 169

123 When a member is employed to corrupt everybody . . . Rae, II, 342

125 Buff and blue and Mrs Crewe . . . Hibbert, 60

125 It was clear . . . there was no surplus . . . Moore, I, 438

127 All had been delusion . . . ibid., 427

127 We hear astonishing accounts . . . ibid., 432

127 They tell me Sheridan has made the best speech . . . Sichel, II, 82

128 very desperate step . . . Ayling, *Fox*, 156

128 Make yourself easy, my dear friend . . . ibid., 157

129 a question which went immediately . . . Hibbert, 95

129 It not only never could have happened . . . Sichel, II, 111

129 in the kennel like a street walker . . . Hibbert, 98

129 Well, if nobody else will . . . Holland, II, 140

130 But whilst his Royal Highness's feelings . . . Watkins, I, 478

130 unintelligible sentimental trash . . . Holland, II, 140

## Chapter XII

131 It could not happen in any country but England . . . Watkins, I, 308

132 God bless thee my Dear Soul . . . Black, 150

132 shed blubbering tears . . . Hunt, *Autobiography*, 149

132 When we got to the House . . . Betsy Sheridan, 77

133 which made me smile (*et seq.*) . . . ibid., 25

133 The system, the circumstances and the manners . . . Moore, I, 410

134 gave us a bad dinner . . . Betsy Sheridan, 25

134 an unexpected and momentary animation . . . Alicia LeFanu, 417

134 when he saw the formidable Grizzle . . . Black, 161

134 Indeed . . . the life she leads . . . Betsy Sheridan, 49

134 that gives a check to my most pleasurable ideas . . . *Letters*, I, 185

135 I saw many carry off the . . . prizes . . . Sichel, I, 95

135 I wonder I don't sprout at my finger-ends . . . Black, 158

135 In February 1787 my Dear Sister . . . Rae, II, 26

136 he is sadly taken up with managing us all . . . Black, 165

136 I in particular . . . Rae, II, 9

136 a beautiful young woman of eighteen . . . ibid., 27

137 After a profound bow . . . Boaden, *Kemble*, I, 394

182 There never was in the World . . . ibid., 242
183 I can put nothing in competition . . . ibid., 241
183 amazingly well . . . ibid., 244
183 I do not feel (*et seq.*) . . . ibid., 244
183 Ever since she has been brought to bed . . . ibid., 246
184 The women bore it very well . . . Moore, II, 162
184 Your brother behaved most wonderfully . . . ibid., 164
185 the gaudy parade and show (*et seq.*) . . . *Letters*, II, 257
185 The loss of the breath . . . Moore, II, 164
186 richer purses and more contracted minds . . . Sichel, II, 391
186 constant and tender affection . . . Moore, II, 166
186 Poor man, he has gone through a good deal . . . Brian Fitzgerald, II, 68 69
187 When I am dead . . . Moore, II, 189
188 so much in love . . . Ida Taylor, 172
188 touched by his reputation . . . Ellis and Turquan, 240
188 He had a steady, wide . . . ibid., 239
189 But however he may assume . . . Moore, II, 174
189 For instance . . . it was a severe frost (*et seq.*) . . . Smyth, 22

## Chapter XVIII

191 *First*. To restore the freedom of election . . . Trevelyan, *Lord Grey*, 48
192 the preliminary to the overthrow . . . ibid.
193 it was not understood (*et seq.*) . . . *Parliamentary History*, XXX, 13 December 1792
194 God keep us all safe and quiet! . . . Barrett, V, 363
194 It is my object to keep the French . . . Magnus, 259
194 that the age of chivalry . . . *Speeches*, III, 30 December 1792
195 what Pitt saved . . . Cobban, 31
196 the most daring, the most abominable (*et seq.*) . . . ibid., 352
196 I wish . . . that he . . . Watkins, II, 204
196 What! in such an hour as this . . . *Speeches*, III, 21 January 1794, 213
196 the surrounding States . . . ibid., 186
197 The Throne is in danger . . . ibid., 214
198 I suppose . . . she means . . . Balderton, 876
198 The very ravages of fire we scout . . . Linda Kelly, 99
198 theatres for spectators . . . Cumberland, II, 212
199 I am glad you are come . . . Percy Fitzgerald, *The Kembles*, I, 309
199 Why do they take my horses . . . Percy Fitzgerald, *A New History*, II, 351
200 Mr Sheridan came to sup . . . Michael Kelly, 209

## Chapter XIX

201 Not you . . . you will never . . . Michael Kelly, 295

202 It is not to be expressed . . . Smyth, 40

203 If Hardy is hanged . . . Brown, 127

203 On the first trial . . . *Speeches*, IV, 5 January 1795

204 suspending this chief bulwark . . . ibid.

204 To have recourse to such laws . . . ibid., 23 November 1795

205 there has been nothing like it . . . Marchand, IX, 57

206 In the close covert of a grove . . . Washington, 237

206 Keep away, you fright . . . Percy Fitzgerald, *Sheridans*, I, 408

206 He resolved that she should feel his power . . . Smyth, 45

206 the handsomest and honestest man . . . Rae, II, 208

207 She is not very pretty (*et seq.*) . . . Canning, 260

207 I am not handsome . . . Rae, II, 358

208 Take a wife . . . Smyth, 46

208 Here I am and have been . . . ibid.

208 It is not I that is to be married . . . ibid., 47

209 I trust you will be able . . . Moore, II, 314

209 Smooth went our boat . . . ibid., 254

209 ought to be paid immediately . . . *Speeches*, IV, 1 June 1795, 74

210 must take the liberty . . . ibid., 75

210 It was unnecessary . . . ibid.

## Chapter XX

211 *groaning* against each other . . . Dulwich Picture Gallery, *A Nest of Nightingales*, 54

212 a child even in the forms of business . . . Boaden, *Kemble*, I, 186

212 I now kiss the invaluable relics . . . Ireland, 96

213 There are certainly some bold ideas . . . Grebanier, 212

213 you know . . . every Englishman . . . Ireland, 139

214 so placed his unfortunate carcass (*et seq.*) . . . ibid., 153

215 The distracted state of the concern . . . Boaden, *Kemble*, II, 186

215 It is a vile thing . . . Kemble's MS journal, quoted by Linda Kelly, 121

215 But I'll tell you what . . . Boaden, *Mrs Jordan*, I, 35

215 streaked with vivid streams of Blood . . . Linda Kelly, 121

215 The eager fancy for German sentiment . . . Percy Fitzgerald, *Kembles*, II, 1

216 not a child in England . . . ibid., 3

216 He brooded over the recollection . . . *The Times*, 25 June 1817

217 I have a silent bottle here . . . Linda Kelly, 124

217 calamitous waste of treasure . . . *Speeches*, IV, 9 December 1795

218 to see him covering the whole face . . . ibid., 14 December 1796

218 She had unfortunately fallen ... Watkins, II, 356
219 My advice ... is that you cut the buoys ... Moore, II, 271
220 If there was indeed a rot ... *Speeches*, IV, 2 June 1797
220 the country was highly indebted ... Rae, II, 199
221 a scene of horrors ... Lecky, *History of England*, quoted by Pakenham, *The Year of Liberty*, 73


## Chapter XXI

223 giving him, as they thought ... quoted by Ida Taylor, 254
224 in sufficient indignation ... *Letters*, II, 94
225 It was, indeed, with the utmost wonder ... *Speeches*, V, 19 June 1798
226 You have *begum-ed* the Chancellor-governor ... Sichel, II, 282
227 My dear Mick ... Michael Kelly, 254
227 I sang two or three bars of music ... ibid.
228 If you mean what Sheridan has written ... Boaden, *Kemble*, II, 243
229 He repeated every syllable ... Boaden, *Mrs Jordan*, II, 16
229 Nay, nay, I have everything ... Boaden, *Kemble*, II, 239
229 My country ... has claims upon me ... *Speeches*, V, 23 January 1799
230 It is impossible to conceive ... ibid., 34
230 with conspicuous earnestness and courage ... Lee, entry for Richard Brinsley Sheridan
231 more occupied to gain applause ... Lady Holland, I, 270
232 Do answer my questions ... Dufferin archive, D1071B/D2/4


## Chapter XXII

233 He is just come from 'Peruvianising' ... Ilchester, I, 278
234 forebodings of bankruptcy ... Rhodes, *Harlequin Sheridan*, 173
234 Rain made my bones ach[e] ... *Letters*, II, 138
234 Mr Sheridan gave a grand harvest home ... quoted in The National Trust, *Polesden Lacey*, 29
235 Won't you come into the garden ... attributed to Sheridan in the *Oxford Dictionary of Quotations*
235 fat as a little pig ... *Letters*, II, 44
235 a hatful of Polesden violets ... ibid., III, 220
236 but than monarchical France ... *Speeches*, V, 17 February 1800, 133
236 But, Sir, we have seen religion ... ibid., 27 June 1800, 164
237 From every latent foe ... Michael Kelly, 260
238 I am much pleased with your comedy ... ibid., 295
240 no civility which might interfere ... William Windham's diary,

quoted by Sichel, I, 45

240 vulgar or illiberal hands ... Moore, II, 304
241 My dear Peake, Let me remind you ... Boaden, *Kemble*, II, 28
241 It is now two days ... ibid.
241 It is a great disadvantage ... Rhodes, *Harlequin Sheridan*, 188
242 Negligence and irregularity ... Michael Kelly, 267
242 I thought at the time ... ibid.
242 He has now ... so infatuated ... Boaden, *Mrs Inchbald*, II, 47
243 large, soft and generous like her soul ... Linda Kelly, 166


## Chapter XXIII

244 I am very much against your abusing Bonaparte ... Moore, II, 312
245 Look at the map of Europe (*et seq.*) ... *Speeches*, V, 8 December 1802ff
246 None but himself ... Plumer Ward, 103
247 mad with vanity and folly ... Rhodes, *Harlequin Sheridan*, 193
247 Words cannot tell you the situation of this House ... *Letters*, II, 176
248 Take it? why quarterly ... Ayling, *Fox*, 187
248 I do not think that any young thing (*et seq.*) ... MS letter, Granville Papers, PRO 30/29/6/2
249 lik'd me formerly but without success ... Granville, I, 352
250 so abominably entertaining ... ibid., I, 162
250 not a silver fork or teaspoon left ... Ayling, *Sheridan*, 173
250 such love as ... MS letter, Granville Papers, PRO 30/29/6/2
250 By my Life and Soul ... *Letters*, II, 199
251 S. is never sober for a moment ... Sichel, II, 270
251 because he intrigued with Sheridan's last wife ... Dowden, I, 61
251 a sort of mournful exultation ... John Taylor, II, 171
252 Two fellows ... that have hated ... Boaden, *Kemble*, II, 380
252 Pooh, I mean the dog! ... Boaden, *Mrs Jordan*, II, 151
252 Pitt raised the War [w]hoop ... *Letters*, II, 196
252 one of the most brilliant and magnificent pieces ... ibid.
252 I have done what I would do ... ibid., 197
253 Richard is Lieutenant Colonel ... Rae, II, 346


## Chapter XXIV

254 hide his head in a coronet ... Dowden, II, 812
254 that his situation was peculiar ... Granville, I, 431
254 unpurchaseable mind ... Sheridan to Addington, quoted in *Parliamentary History*, V, 150
255 My boisterous landlord ... Granville, I, 432
255 a sort of cheerful frankness ... Ilchester, I, 255

## Chapter XXV

## Chapter XXVI

273 A person going to hear the debates ... Watkins, II, 526
274 I am by far the most ... MS letter, Granville papers PRO 30/29/6/1
274 I had no hope of allaying her jealousy ... ibid., PRO 30/29/6/2
274 abominable conduct ... Granville, II, 274
275 Not excepting me? (*et seq.*) ... ibid., 93
275 she might have added ... Dowden, I, 166
275 With talents and Eloquence ... Granville, II, 307
276 British rulers ... have lost all character ... *Parliamentary Debates*, X, 25 February 1808
276 If the flame were once fairly caught ... *Speeches*, V, 15 June 1808
277 Sheridan in concert with Canning ... *Letters*, III, 38n.
277 Had his political associates ... Moore, II, 356
278 Never before ... did I behold ... Boaden, *Kemble*, II, 481
278 A man may surely be allowed ... Moore, II, 368
278 there were three things ... Grieg, V, 142
278 Let us make a long pull ... Michael Kelly, 310
279 As to old Drury ... MS letter, Dufferin archive, D 107/1B/B3/1
280 disordered and ill-managed ... *Letters*, III, 61
280 It is unquestionably hard ... ibid., 131n.
281 I have but one moment ... ibid., 74
281 If from this you take £500 ... ibid., 82
281 most unfortunately sanguine temper ... ibid., 77
281 I have said before that you do not know me ... ibid., 78
282 As for my own Life ... ibid., 85
282 Mr Sheridan among the Doctors! ... Moore, II, 379
283 There being no other person present ... Gore, 32


## Chapter XXVII

285 Sheridanus Redivus ... Plumer Ward, I, 307
285 I say now as I have ever said ... *Parliamentary Debates*, XVIII, 2 January 1811
286 Very flimsy ... Moore, II, 388
286 flushed with wine ... Sichel, II, 341
286 those damned fellows (*et seq.*) ... Dowden, II, 813
287 In all humility we crave ... Moore, II, 393
287 sending a man with a lighted torch ... Hibbert, 358
288 a corpulent gentleman of fifty ... *The Examiner*, 22 March 1812
289 Sir – it is easy for my Lord G ... Marchand, IX, 32
290 state of perturbation of mind ... Hibbert, 393
290 a couple of scoundrels ... Sichel, II, 352
290 The actors in the plot ... Watkins, II, 521
291 His whole speech was most doting ... Percy Fitzgerald, *The*

*Sheridans*, II, 175

291 My objection to the present Ministry ... Moore, *Life*, II, 430
292 Whatever reasons I may have had ... Sichel, II, 359
293 Well, Gentry, welcome ... Macqueen Pope, 120


## Chapter XXVIII

294 I pant for my old *independent* seat ... *Letters*, III, 137
295 straining every nerve ... Bence Jones, 111
295 A correct alphabetical list ... MS Draft, William Salt Collection
295 an apartment in his own Palace ... *Letters*, III, 165
295 I can only say that *Gratitude* ... ibid.
295 it was a pity that poor Sheridan (*et seq.*) ... Jennings, I, 307ff.
296 because ... he had no idea of risking (*et seq.*) ... Dowden, I, 61
297 Next day as I was crossing over to Brighton ... Jennings, I, 310
298 I never saw anything approaching to malice ... *Letters*, III, 122
298 It would half break your heart ... ibid., 177
298 And how many plates have you broke ... Dowden, I, 53
299 Angelo, my old friend ... Angelo, II, 175
299 Whitbread, putting all false professions ... *Letters*, III, 188
299 unsolicited interference ... ibid., 189n.
300 a long and passionate fit of weeping ... Moore, II, 444
300 His very dregs ... Marchand, IV, 327
300 ringing up the servants by night ... Percy Fitzgerald, *The Sheridans*, II, 246
300 the *former* alone intended for use (*et seq.*) ... Dowden, I, 62
300 He was superb! ... Marchand, IX, 14
301 Who are you, sir? ... ibid., IV, 327
301 Lord Holland told me ... ibid., III, 329
302 the labour of a mill horse ... Earle, II, 298
302 near three hours this blessed morning ... *Letters*, III, 223
302 to buy it immediately ... MS, British Library, Department of Manuscripts, 41253 (B), f. 17
302 part of the Skull ... *Letters*, III, 226
302 the deplorable end ... ibid.
303 like a tragedy ghost ... Leigh Hunt, quoted by Linda Kelly, 195
303 often, very often, re-appear among them (*et seq.*) ... Moore, II, 446
303 a distressing place ... ibid., 449
303 Never again let one harsh word ... *Letters*, III, 242
304 I find things settled so that £150 ... Moore, II, 454
304 *la mer à boire* (*et seq.*) ... Jennings, I, 311ff.
305 Oh delay not ... Moore, II, 459
306 that he almost slumbered into death ... Rae, II, 286

## Chapter XXIX

307 He is the last of the giants . . . Gore, 155

308 O it sickens the heart . . . Moore, II, 462

308 A few lines to say . . . MS letter, William Salt Collection

308 Poet's Corner was his aversion . . . Dowden, II, 452

309 While reading one of the 12 Quarto Volumes . . . Rhodes, *Harlequin Sheridan*, 247

309 I have again to address you . . . Rae, II, 358

310 some want of steady application . . . Percy Fitzgerald, *The Sheridans*, II, 350

310 as easily as a hawk flies (*et seq.*) . . . Ruskin, 134ff.

# Bibliography

## Books

All titles were published in London unless otherwise stated.

Angelo, Henry, *Reminiscences*, Henry Colburn & Richard Bentley, 1830

Aspinall, A. (ed.), *The Correspondence of George, Prince of Wales*, Oxford University Press, 1963 71

Ayling, Stanley, *Sheridan: A Portrait*, John Murray, 1985
*Edmund Burke*, John Murray, 1988
*Fox*, John Murray, 1991

Balderton, Katherine C. (ed.), *Thraliana, 1784 1809* by Hester Piozzi, Clarendon Press, 1942

Barbeau, A., *Une ville d'eaux anglaise au XVIIIe siècle: La société élégante et littéraire à Bath*, Picard, Paris, 1904

Barrett, Charlotte (ed.), *Diary and Letters of Frances d'Arblay*, Henry Colburn, 1842

Bence Jones, Mark, *The Catholic Families*, Constable, 1992

Benzie, W., *The Dublin Orator, Thomas Sheridan*, Leeds, 1972

Bernard, John, *Retrospections of the Stage*, Henry Colburn & Richard Bentley, 1830

Bessborough, Earl of, *Lady Bessborough and her Family Circle*, John Murray, 1940
*Georgiana: Extracts from the Correspondence of Georgiana, Duchess of Devonshire*, John Murray, 1955

Bingham, Madelaine, *Sheridan: The Track of a Comet*, Allen & Unwin, 1972

Black, Clementina, *The Linleys of Bath*, Frederick Muller, 1971

Boaden, James, *Memoirs of the Life of John Philip Kemble*, Longman, Hurst, Rees, Orme, Brown & Green, 1825
*The Life of Mrs Jordan*, Edward Bull, 1831
*Memoirs of Mrs Siddons*, Henry Colburn, 1839
*The Life of Mrs Inchbald*, Richard Bentley, 1883

Bor, Margaret and Cleeland, Lamond, *Still the Lark: A Biography of Elizabeth Linley*, Merlin Press, 1962

Boswell, James, *Life of Johnson*, John Murray, 1890

Briggs, Asa, *The Age of Improvement, 1783–1867*, Longmans, 1979

Brooke, John, *King George III*, Constable, 1972

Brougham, Lord, *Historical Sketches of Statesmen Who Flourished in the Time of George III*, Charles Knight, 1839

Brown, Philip, *The French Revolution in English History*, Allen & Unwin, 1923

Bryant, Arthur, *The Years of Endurance*, Collins, 1942
    *The Years of Victory*, Collins, 1944

Burke, Edmund, *Reflections on the Revolution in France*, Everyman, 1912

Butler, E. M., *Sheridan: A Ghost Story*, Constable, 1931

Butt, John, *The Age of Johnson*, Clarendon Press, 1979

Byron, Lord, *Poetical Works*, John Murray, 1863

Calder Marshall, Arthur, *The Two Duchesses*, Hutchinson, 1978

Campbell, Thomas, *Life of Mrs Siddons*, Edward Moxon, 1839

Chatel de Briancon, Françoise, *R. B. Sheridan: personnalité, carrière politique*, Didier, Paris, 1974

Cobban, Alfred, *The Debate on the French Revolution*, Nicholas Kaye, 1950

Cumberland, Richard, *Memoirs*, Cadell & Davis, 1807

Darlington, W. A., *Sheridan*, Duckworth, 1933

Davison, Peter (ed.), *Sheridan: Comedies, A Collection of Critical Essays*, Macmillan, 1986

Derry, John W., *Politics in the Age of Fox, Pitt and Liverpool*, Macmillan Education, 1990

Dowden, Wilfred S. (ed.), *Thomas Moore: Journal*, Associated University Press, 1983–91

Earle, William, *Sheridan and his Times by an Octogenarian who Stood by his Knee in Youth and Sat at his Table in Manhood*, J. F. Hope, 1859

Edwardes, Michael, *The Nabobs at Home*, Constable, 1991

Ehrman, John, *The Younger Pitt: The Reluctant Transition*, Constable, 1983

Ellis, Lucy, and Turquan, Joseph, *La Belle Pamela*, Herbert Jenkins, 1924

Fitzgerald, Brian (ed.), *Emily, Duchess of Leinster: Correspondence*, Irish Manuscripts Commission, Dublin, 1953

Fitzgerald, Percy, *The Kembles*, Tinsley Bros, 1871
    *A New History of the English Stage*, Tinsley Bros, 1882
    *Lives of the Sheridans*, Richard Bentley, 1886

Foote, Samuel, *The Maid of Bath*, 1778

Foss, Kenelm, *Here Lies Richard Brinsley Sheridan*, Secker & Warburg, 1939

Foster, R. F., *Modern Ireland: 1600–1972*, Penguin, 1989

Furber, H., and Marshall, P. J. (eds), Edmund Burke, *Correspondence (Vol. V), July 1782–June 1789*, Cambridge University Press, 1967

Gibbon, Edward, *Autobiography*, J. M. Dent, 1923

Gibbs, Lewis, *Sheridan*, J. M. Dent, 1947

Gore, John (ed.), *Creevey*, John Murray, 1949

Granville, Countess Castalia (ed.), *Private Correspondence of the First Earl of Granville: 1781 1821*, John Murray, 1916

Grebanier, Bernard, *The Great Shakespeare Forgery*, Heinemann, 1966

Grieg, James (ed.), *The Farington Diaries*, Hutchinson, 1922

Hibbert, Christopher, *George IV*, Penguin, 1976

Hill, Draper, *Mr Gillray: The Caricaturist*, Phaidon, 1965

Hobhouse, Christopher, *Fox*, John Murray, 1934

Hogan, Charles Beecher (ed.), *The London Stage: 1660 1800*, Part 5, Vols. 1 and 2, Southern Illinois University Press, 1967 8

Holland, Lord (ed.), *Memoirs of the Whig Party during my Time*, Brown, Green & Longmans, 1852

Howell, W. S., *Eighteenth Century British Logic and Rhetoric*, Princeton University Press, 1972

Ilchester, the Earl of (ed.), *The Journal of Elizabeth, Lady Holland*, Longman Green, 1908

Ingpen, R. (ed.), *Leigh Hunt: Autobiography*, Constable, 1903

Ireland, W. H., *Confessions*, Thomas Goddard, 1805

Jennings, Louis J. (ed.), *John Wilson Croker, Correspondence and Diaries*, 1884

Johnson, Paul (ed.), *The Oxford Book of Political Anecdotes*, Oxford University Press, 1975

Jupp, Peter (ed.), *George Canning, The Letter-Journal: 1793 1795*, Royal Historical Journal, 1991

Lee, Sidney (ed.), *Dictionary of National Biography*, Smith, Elder & Co., 1897

Leech, Clifford, and Craik, T. W. (eds), *The Revels History of Drama in English*, vol. VI, 1750 1880, Methuen, 1975

LeFanu, Alicia, *Memoirs of the Life and Writings of Mrs Frances Sheridan*, G. and W. B. Whitaker, 1824

LeFanu, William (ed.), *Betsy Sheridan: Journal, 1774 76 and 1788 90*, Eyre & Spottiswoode, 1960

Leslie, Shane, *George IV*, Ernest Benn, 1922

Leveson Gower, Iris, *The Face Without a Frown: Georgiana, Duchess of Devonshire*, Frederick Muller, 1944

Lewis, W. S. (ed.), *Horace Walpole: Correspondence with the Countess of Upper Ossory*, Oxford University Press, 1965

Macaulay, Lord, *Essays*, Longmans, Green & Co., 1886

Macqueen Pope, W., *Pillars of Drury Lane*, Hutchinson, 1975

Magnus, Philip, *Edmund Burke*, John Murray, 1939

Marchand, Leslie A. (ed.), *Lord Byron, Letters and Journals*, John

Murray, 1979

Markham, Felix, *Napoleon*, The New English Library, 1966

Marshall, P. J., *The Impeachment of Warren Hastings*, Oxford University Press, 1965

Masters, Brian, *Georgiana: Duchess of Devonshire*, Hamish Hamilton, 1981

Maxwell, Constantia, *Dublin Under the Georges*, Harrap, 1946

Mikhail, E. H. (ed.), *Sheridan: Interviews and Recollections*, Macmillan, 1989

Minto, First Earl of, *Life and Letters of Sir Gilbert Elliot*, Longman, 1874

Mitchell, Brigitte, and Penrose, Hubert (eds), *Rev. John Penrose: Letters from Bath: 1766–1767*, Alan Sutton, 1983

Mitchell, L. G., *Charles James Fox*, Oxford University Press, 1992

Moore, Thomas, *Memoirs of the Life of the Right Honourable Richard Brinsley Sheridan*, Longman, Hurst, Rees, Orme, Brown & Green, 1825

Moorehead, Lucy (ed.), *Freya Stark: Letters*, Vol. VI, 1947–52, Michael Russell, 1981

Morwood, James, *The Life and Works of Richard Brinsley Sheridan*, Scottish Academic Press, 1985

Morwood, James, and Crane, David (eds), *Sheridan Studies*, Cambridge University Press, 1995

Murphy, Arthur, *The Life of David Garrick, Esq.*, J. Wright, 1801

Nicolson, Harold, *Helen's Tower*, Constable, 1937

O'Brien, Conor Cruise, *The Great Melody: A Thematic Biography of Edmund Burke*, Sinclair-Stevenson, 1992

Oliphant, Margaret, *Sheridan*, Macmillan, 1883

Oman, Carola, *David Garrick*, Hodder & Stoughton, 1958

*Oxford Dictionary of Quotations*, Oxford University Press, 1962

Paine, Thomas, *The Rights of Man*, Penguin, 1987

Pakenham, Thomas, *The Year of Liberty*, Hodder & Stoughton, 1969

Pakenham, Thomas and Valerie (eds), *Dublin: A Traveller's Companion*, Constable, 1988

Pares, Richard, and Taylor, A. J. P. (eds), *Essays Presented to Sir Lewis Namier*, Macmillan, 1956

*Parliamentary Debates, The*, Hansard, 1803–12

*Parliamentary History of England: 1780–1803, The*, Cobbett, 1780–1803

Pearson, Hesketh, *Lives of the Wits*, Heinemann, 1962

    *The Smith of Smiths*, Hogarth Press, 1984

Phipps, the Hon. Edward, *Memoirs of the Political and Literary Life of Robert Plumer Ward*, John Murray, 1850

Plumb, J. H., *The First Four Georges*, Collins Fontana, 1966

Pottle, Frederick A. (ed.), James Boswell, *London Journal*, Heinemann, 1950

Price, Cecil (ed.), *The Letters of Richard Brinsley Sheridan*, Oxford University Press, 1966

    *Richard Brinsley Sheridan: Plays*, Oxford University Press, 1975

Quennell, Peter, *The Years of Fame: Byron in Italy*, Collins, 1976

Rae, W. Fraser, *Sheridan*, Richard Bentley, 1896

Rhodes, R. Crompton, *Harlequin Sheridan*, Blackwell, 1933

    (ed.), *Richard Brinsley Sheridan: Plays and Poems*, Basil Blackwell, 1928

Richardson, Samuel, *Correspondence*, Richard Phillips, 1804

Rogers, Samuel, *Recollections of the Table Talk of Samuel Rogers*, D. Appleton, New York, 1856

Rose, J. Holland, *William Pitt and the Great War*, G. Bell, 1911

Rowland, Peter (ed.), *Lord Macaulay's History of England in the 18th Century*, The Folio Society, 1980

Ruskin, John, *Praeterita*, Oxford University Press, 1990

Russell, Lord (ed.), *Memoirs, Journal and Correspondence of Thomas Moore*, Longmans, 1852–6

Sadler, Michael T. H., *The Political Career of Richard Brinsley Sheridan*, Basil Blackwell, 1912

Sheldon, Esther K., *Thomas Sheridan of Smock Alley*, Princeton University Press, Princeton, 1967

Sheridan, Frances, *Memoirs of Miss Sydney Biddulph*, 1761

    *The Discovery*, 1763

    *Eugenia and Adelaide*, 1791

Sheridan, Richard Brinsley, *Sheridaniana*, Henry Colborn, 1826

    *Speeches of the Late Right Honourable Richard Brinsley Sheridan, edited by a Constitutional Friend*, Patrick Martin, 1816

Sheridan, Thomas, *British Education*, 1756

    *A Plan of Education for the Young Nobility and Gentry of Great Britain*, 1769

    *A General Dictionary of the English Lanuage*, 1780

    *The Life of the Reverend Dr Jonathan Swift*, Bathurst, Strachan, Collins, Rivington, Davis, Dodsley, Longman, Baldwin, Cadell, Egerton & Bent, 1784

Sherwin, Oscar, *Uncorking Old Sherry*, Vision, 1960

Sichel, Walter, *Sheridan*, Constable, 1909

Smith, E. A., *Whig Principles and Party Politics: Earl Fitzwilliam and the Whig Party*, Manchester University Press, 1975

Smyth, William, *Memoir of Mr Sheridan*, Leeds, 1840

Stokes, Hugh, *The Devonshire House Circle*, Herbert Jenkins, 1917

Taylor, Ida M., *The Life of Lord Edward Fitzgerald*, 1903

Taylor, John, *Records of My Life*, Edward Bull, 1832

Taylor, T. (ed.), *Benjamin Robert Haydon: Autobiography and Memoirs*, Peter Davies, 1926

Thorne, R. G. (ed.), *The History of Parliament, The House of Commons, 1790–1820*, Vol. V, Secker & Warburg, 1986

Trevelyan, G. M., *Lord Grey of the Reform Bill*, Longmans, Green, 1920

    *British History in the Nineteenth Century and After*, Longmans, Green, 1944

Turnbull, Patrick, *Warren Hastings*, New English Library, 1975

Walker, R. S. (ed.), James Beattie, *London Diary, 1773*, Aberdeen, 1946

Ward, A. C. (ed.), *Bernard Shaw: Plays and Players*, Oxford University Press, 1958

Washington, Peter (ed.), *Erotic Poems*, Everyman, 1994

Watkins, John, *Memoirs of the Public and Private Life of the Right Honourable R. B. Sheridan*, Henry Colburn, 1817

Watson, J. Steven, *The Reign of George III*, Clarendon Press, 1992

Weller, A. R., and Glover, Arnold (eds), *William Hazlitt: Collected Works*, Dent, 1903

Wheatley, H. B. (ed.), *The Historical and Posthumous Memoirs of Sir N. W. Wraxall*, Bickers & Sons, 1884

White, R. J., *The Age of George III*, The Historical Book Club, 1968

Worth, Katharine, *Sheridan and Goldsmith*, Macmillan English Dramatists, 1992

Ziegler, Philip, *Addington*, Collins, 1965

## Archives

*Bath Reference Library*
Set of Autograph Letters, eighteen complete and one imperfect, from Elizabeth Ann Linley to her closest friend, Mrs Mehitabel Canning

*British Library, Department of Manuscripts*
Letters and papers of the Sheridan family, chiefly on theatrical matters, 1757 1843, 29, 764, Egerton 1975; 1976
Letter-Journal of Susan Burney, Egerton 3691
Praise for Jane Austen's *Pride and Prejudice*, 41253 (B), f. 17
Notes on plays *c.* 1790 1800; 25, 933; 25, 989; 25, 993; 25, 994

*Harvard Theatre Collection, Houghton Library*
The Sheridan papers; 166 letters and documents by various hands, mostly addressed to Richard Brinsley Sheridan, 2 vols. Pf MS Thr. 7
*Mr S—n's Apology to the Town with the Reasons which unfortunately induced him to his late Misconduct, written by Himself* (in fact an anonymous attack against Thomas Sheridan), pamphlet, 1754
*The Imposter Unmasked; or the New Man of the People, with Anecdotes never before Published, Illustrative of the Character of the renowned and immaculate Bardolpho* (attack on Richard Brinsley Sheridan at the time of the Westminster Election), pamphlet, 1806
Sheridan, Thomas, *A Full Vindication of the Conduct of the Manager of the Theatre Royal*, Dublin, 1747

*Office of the Chief Herald, Genealogical Office, State Heraldic Museum, Dublin*
Genealogy of the O'Sheridans, G. O. 297, pp. 17 18

*Public Record Office*

Three letters of Esther Jane (Ogle) Sheridan to Granville Leveson Gower (First Earl Granville), Granville Papers, PRO 30/29/6/1, 30/29/6/2

*Public Record Office of Northern Ireland*

Dufferin Archive, D 1071B/D, D1071B/L: collection of letters, newspaper cuttings, engravings and notes on the Sheridans and Dufferins

*Whitfield Papers, Whitfield, Herefordshire*

Recollections of the Reverend Archer Clive

*William Salt Library, Stafford*

Papers of Richard Brinsley Sheridan: theatrical, personal, financial and political; cuttings, broadsheets, pamphlets and speeches. SMS 343


## Guides, Catalogues and Leaflets

Dulwich Picture Gallery, *A Nest of Nightingales*, 1988

Holburne Museum and Crafts Study Centre, Bath, *A Nest of Nightingales: The Linley Family and Musical Life in Bath*, 1995

The National Trust, *Guide to Polesden Lacey* (introduced by Robin Fedden)

Sotheby's, catalogue for sale of manuscripts, 29 November 1971


## Articles

Price, Cecil, 'Hymen and Hirco: A Vision', *Times Literary Supplement*, 11 July 1958

Pritchett, V. S. 'Anglo–Irish', review of Cecil Price's *The Letters of Richard Brinsley Sheridan*, *New Statesman*, 12 August 1966

# Index

———— ❧ ————

coalition, 262
Austrian Netherlands, 217

younger, 103; in Rockingham ministry, 104; Commons performances, 109, 141; sees Sarah Siddons act, 113; manner in Commons, 120; proposes reform of East India Company, 120–1; crusade against Warren Hastings, 121, 137–8, 140–1, 147, 150, 172;

and Irish question, 126; opposes Pitt, 127; Rolle attempts to silence, 129; praises RBS's speech on Begums of Oudh, 141; on Commons Committee for trial of Hastings, 145–7; writing style, 148; and RBS's speech against Hastings, 149–50; on Thurlow, 157; excluded by Prince of Wales, 158; and regency question, 159, 172; denounces French Revolution, 171–3, 192; hostility to RBS, 172–3, 175; political stance, 173–4; rift with Fox, 175–6; supports Alien Bill, 194; death, 231; on France, 245; humble rank, 309; *Reflections on the Revolution in France*, 173, 175

Burke, Richard, 108
Burney, Charles, 29, 94
Burney, Fanny (Madame d'Arblay): on Elizabeth's singing, 49, 56; on Mrs Crewe, 75; on Mary Linley, 83; meets Sheridans, 93–4; supports Warren Hastings, 146; on French Revolution, 194; *Evelina*, 94
Burney, Susan, 89, 93–4
Byron, George Gordon, 6th Baron: at Harrow, 21; and success of *The School for Scandal*, 77; praises RBS's 'Verses on the Memory of Garrick', 88; praises RBS's speech on Begums of Oudh, 151; on Harriet Duncannon (Bessborough), 167; on RBS's charm, 205; on RBS's finances,

289; praises RBS's company, 300–1; RBS meets, 300; *Childe Harold*, 300; *English Bards and Scots Reviewers*, 293; 'Monody on the Death of . . . Sheridan, 151, 310

Callendar, George, 279
Campo Formio, treaty of (1797), 217
Canning, George, 207, 277
Canning, Mehitabel: friendship with Elizabeth, 127, 135, 159, 165–6, 168–9; estrangement from
Elizabeth, 171; reconciliation at Elizabeth's illness, 181–4; cares for Elizabeth's daughter Mary, 184, 188; at Elizabeth's funeral, 185; and death of Mary, 189
Canning, Stratford, 127
*Caravan* (musical show), 252
Carlo (Newfoundland dog), 152, 265
Caroline of Brunswick, Princess of Wales (*later* Queen), 209
Castlereagh, Robert Stewart, Viscount, 257
Catherine II (the Great), Empress of Russia, 81, 177
Catholic emancipation: RBS's early interest in, 15; RBS's advocacy of, 126, 202, 239, 256, 271, 272–3, 291; Pitt favours in Ireland, 230–1, 238; and fall of Ministry of All the Talents, 270; Windham and Grattan support, 285; prince regent withdraws support for, 289
Catholics: discrimination against, 174; position in Ireland, 221, 230, 238, 270, 272–3, 291
Cavendish, Lady Harriet *see* Granville, Harriet, Countess
Chait Singh, 138–9, 143
Chamberlaine family, 9

345

relations, 166

Croker, John Wilson, 129, 296–7, 305

Crouch, Anna Maria, 84, 179–80, 200, 260

Cumberland, Richard: complains to Garrick of RBS, 85–6; RBS lampoons in *The Critic*, 89, 91; on theatre design, 198; *The Battle of Hastings*, 85

Cumberland, Prince William Augustus, Duke of, 74, 287

Declaratory Act (Irish, 1719): repealed (1782), 126

Devonshire, Elizabeth, Duchess of *see* Foster, Lady Elizabeth

Devonshire, Georgiana, Duchess of: entertains Sheridans, 56, 75; attends first night of *The School for Scandal*, 77; attends first night of *The Critic*, 93; supports RBS's election to Parliament, 98–9; qualities, 101; social–political life, 101; and Prince of Wales, 102; supports Fox, 124; and Mrs Fitzherbert, 128; on RBS and trial of Hastings, 150; on RBS's political ambitions and activities, 156, 158; and regency question, 159–60; relations with Grey, 165, 249–50, 286; sexual freedom, 165; gambling losses, 170; and Elizabeth's final illness, 183; friendship with RBS, 200; sets RBS song to music, 216; and Hecca's affair with Grey, 250; death, 268

Devonshire, William Cavendish, 5th Duke of, 87, 101, 165, 168

Digges, West, 11

Dignum, Charles, 214

Dorset, Charles Sackville, 2nd Duke of, 12

Dowton, William, 199

Drury Lane Theatre, London: Elizabeth performs at, 49, 53; Garrick invites RBS to share in management, 68–9; RBS's management of, 68–73, 85–6, 111, 113, 155, 178–9, 201; patent, 70, 136, 279, 281; RBS buys and holds shares in, 70–1, 85, 155, 292; audience, 72; repertoire, 72; and success of *The School for Scandal*, 81, 85; difficulties and changing fortunes, 85, 132; closes on Garrick's death, 88; as RBS's main source of income, 110; Thomas Sheridan resigns from management, 111; Sarah Siddons at, 112–13; financial problems, 113, 199, 212, 234, 240–3, 279; Tickell helps manage, 116; crowd behaviour, 132–3; Queen Charlotte shuns, 161; closed and rebuilt (1791), 177–8, 198–9; musical successes, 179; reopens (1794), 198; lighter entertainments, 199–200; Kemble resigns managerial post at, 212, 214–15; and *Vortigern* fiasco, 212–14; 1796–7 season successes, 215–17; assassination attempt on George III at, 237–8; Kemble reassumes management, 240; Kemble and Mrs Siddons leave for Covent Garden, 243; Master Betty at, 265; Tom Sheridan appointed assistant manager, 265; fire (1809), 277–80; company plays at Lyceum, 279; post-fire restoration, 279–80, 292; reopens (1812), 291–2; Tom Sheridan holds shares in, 292, 298; RBS revisits after reopening, 302–3

Dryden, John: *King Arthur*, 116

Dublin: character, 1; theatre in, 6–7, 10, 12–13, 33–4; Thomas Sheridan returns to, 33, 47

148; relations with Mrs Armistead, 157, 165; returns to London on illness of George III, 157; supposed rift with RBS, 157-8; supports Prince of Wales for regency, 158-61; Betsy Sheridan on, 162; gambling, 169; intervenes between Clarence and Elizabeth, 169; welcomes French Revolution, 171-2, 175; on Burke's hardening conservatism, 174; opposed by Tooke in 1790 election, 174-5; rift with Burke, 175-6; disbelieves Russian threat, 176-7; and parliamentary reform proposals, 192, 204, 220; opposes increased defence estimates, 193; opposes wars with France, 195, 218, 237, 244, 246, 252-3; condemns sentences on Muir and Palmer, 196; deserted by Party followers, 196; caricatured, 205; and RBS's second marriage, 207; withdraws opposition from Parliament, 220, 231; defends O'Connor, 223-4; visits France, 239; criticises RBS's patriotic speech, 247; debts cleared by friends, 247; on RBS's political aims, 254-5; RBS abuses, 255; suggested alliance with Pitt, 255; appointed Foreign Secretary on Pitt's death (1806), 263; and abolition of slave trade, 266; death and funeral, 266-8; relations with RBS, 267-8

France: declares war on Britain (1778), 87; Fox seeks treaty with (1782), 105-6; 1783 treaty with, 121; internal turmoil, 192; wars in Europe, 192-3; declares war on Britain and Holland (1793), 194-5; dominance in Europe, 197; as enemy of Britain, 205, 217; shift of power in, 205; enforces frontiers, 217; attempts landings in Ireland, 218, 222, 224, 226; and Irish rebellion (1798), 223-4; peace overtures to Britain (1799), 235-6; British visitors to, 239; war with Britain renewed (1803), 244; Sheridan mistrusts, 245; threatens invasion of Britain, 252; Spain revolts against (1808), 276; see also French Revolution; Napoleon I

Francis, Charlotte (née Burney), 146
Francis, Clement, 146
Francis, Philip, 137, 140, 145, 267
Franklin, Benjamin, 105
French Revolution: effect in Britain, 171-2, 175; RBS praises, 173, 309; fervour declines, 205; see also France

Gainsborough, Thomas, 37
Gardner, Admiral Alan, 1st Baron, 268
Garrick, David: in Dublin, 6-7; in London, 12, 14; praises Frances Sheridan's *The Discovery*, 18; RBS and Halhed offer *Jupiter* to, 24; on *The Rivals*, 60; and Linley's music for *The Duenna*, 65-6; plays in revival of Frances Sheridan's *The Discovery*, 68; manages and half-owns Drury Lane theatre, 70, 113; sells Drury Lane shares, 70, 73; final performance, 71; and Drury Lane audience, 72, 199; writes prologue to *A Trip to Scarborough*, 74; at first night of *The School for Scandal*, 77; rehearses *The School for Scandal*, 77, 79-80; and Mrs Abington, 78; and RBS's management of Drury Lane, 85-6; death, 87-8; Thomas Sheridan insults, 87; and Sarah Siddons, 112; idolises Shakespeare, 117; and Johnny

McCree, 256; *The Country Girl*
(based on Wycherley's *Country
Wife*), 132; *Isabella* (adaptation of
Southerne's *The Fatal Marriage*),
112
Genlis, Pamela de (*later* Fitzgerald),
187–8
Genlis, Stéphanie-Félicité Ducrest
de Saint-Aubin, Comtesse de,
187
George III, King: admires Elizabeth,
53; and Gordon riots, 98; and
Prince of Wales's lifestyle, 102,
121, 124; and loss of American
colonies, 104; RBS casts as 'Surly'
(from *The Alchemist*), 110;
discontent with Fox–North
coalition, 121; opposes 1783
India Bill, 121–3; hostility to Fox,
124, 255; expected demise, 132;
illness (1788–9), 155–6; recovery,
160–1, 172; announces increase
in defence estimates, 193; carriage
mobbed, 204; assassination
attempts on, 237; visits Drury
Lane, 237–8; opposes Catholic
emancipation, 238, 239, 270;
illness recurs, 239, 259; declared
insane (1810), 285
George IV, King *see* George, Prince
of Wales
George, Prince of Wales (*later* King
George IV): lifestyle, 101–2;
qualities, 102; independence, 121;
supports Fox, 124–5;
extravagance and debts, 127, 129,
158, 209; love affairs, 127–8;
marriage to Mrs Fitzherbert,
128–30; Whigs depend on, 132;
at Hastings's trial, 146; and first
regency crisis (1788–9), 156,
158–60; RBS's friendship and
influence with, 156–8, 162,
259–61, 264, 288; offered Irish
regency, 161; unpopularity, 161,

288; Betsy Sheridan on, 163–4;
intervenes between Clarence and
Elizabeth, 169; marriage to
Caroline, 209; and RBS's refusal
of honours, 254; RBS confides
in, 255; offers Receiver
Generalship of Duchy of
Cornwall to RBS, 259; affair
with Mrs Crouch, 260; opposes
Catholic emancipation, 271; finds
Ilchester seat for RBS, 272; lays
foundation stone for new Covent
Garden theatre, 279; regency
granted (1811), 285–8; severs
connection with Whigs, 288;
negotiates to form government,
289–90, 294; household, 290;
offers help to RBS after loss of
parliamentary seat, 295–7; last
sight of RBS, 297, 300; has RBS
released from debtors' prison,
299; reads Jane Austen, 302; helps
RBS in final illness, 304–5
Giardini, Felice de, 55
Gibbon, Edward, 75, 113, 148–9
Gillray, James, 205, 219, 229, 253,
257
*Glorious First of June, The* (show),
201
Glorious Revolution (1688), 2, 173
*Gloucester Journal*, 55
Goldsmith, Oliver, 294; *The Vicar of
Wakefield*, 23
Gordon, Lord George: 'No Popery'
riots (1780), 97–8, 100, 103
Graham, John, 308
Granville, 1st Earl *see* Leveson
Gower, Granville
Granville, Harriet, Countess (*née*
Cavendish), 249
Grattan, Henry, 127, 285
Grebotzoff, Madame, 261
Grenville, George *see* Buckingham,
1st Marquis of
Grenville, Thomas: on Elizabeth's

singing after RBS's second duel, 45; RBS confides in, 47–8, 50, 53; and RBS in Waltham Abbey, 49; correspondence and relations with RBS, 50–1, 288; in Westminster Committee, 96; Fox sends as envoy to Paris, 105; and first regency crisis (1788–9), 160; breaks with Fox, 196; and fall of Addington, 255; heads Ministry of All the Talents, 263, 270; and RBS's hopes of Westminster seat, 268; and George III's opposition to Catholic emancipation, 270; Chancellorship of Oxford University, 282; and grant of regency (1811), 286–8; refuses Prince Regent's offer of coalition post, 288–9; Prince Regent dislikes, 290

Grenville, William Wyndham Grenville, Baron, 96, 204

Greville, Frances (later Lady; née Macartney), 75

Greville, Mrs Ronald, 234

Grey, General Sir Charles (later 1st Earl), 219

Grey, Charles (later 2nd Earl): and Prince of Wales's marriage to Mrs Fitzherbert, 129; and Duchess of Devonshire, 165, 249, 286; disbelieves Russian threat, 176; reform proposals, 192, 203, 220; opposes war with France, 195; and Hardy's trial, 203; and RBS's second marriage settlement, 207; defends O'Connor, 223; Fox criticises RBS's patriotic speech to, 247; relations with Esther Sheridan, 248–50, 274; marriage, 249; and Fox's political ambitions, 266; succeeds Fox as leader, 268; succeeds to earldom, 275; and RBS's advocacy of war in Spain, 277; and grant of

regency (1811), 286–8; Prince of Wales dislikes, 286, 290; hostility to RBS, 287–8; refuses Prince Regent's offer of coalition post, 288–9

Grey, Mary, Countess (née Ponsonby), 149, 249–50, 274

Grosvenor Street, London, 202

Habeas Corpus Act: suspended (1794), 196, 203–4, 221

Haidar Ali, 139

Halhed, Nathaniel Brassey, 23–4, 33

Hammersley, Messrs (bankers), 241–2

Hardy, Thomas (shoemaker), 191; trial and acquittal, 203

Hare, James, 69, 175

Harris, Thomas: and RBS's The Rivals, 58–9; owns theatre patent, 178; Kemble joins, 243, 252; invites RBS to dine, 252; and Master Betty, 265

Harrow school, 18, 20–1

Hastings, Warren: Burke's hatred of, 121, 137–8, 140–1, 147, 150, 172; impeachment, 137–9, 143–5; achievements in India, 138; and Begums of Oudh, 138–40, 142; Indian revenues, 142; trial proceedings, 145–51, 172, 195; acquitted, 150; meets RBS, 150

Haydon, Benjamin Robert, 300

Haymarket theatre, 70, 161, 178

Hazlitt William, 60, 63, 78–9, 216, 243

Hecca (RBS's second wife) see Sheridan, Esther

Hernan's Miscellany (satirical newspaper), 23

Hertford, Francis Ingram Seymour, 2nd Marquis of, 290

Hertford, Isabella, Marchioness of, 290

Hibernian Academy, 14

351

Hobhouse, John Cam *see*
Broughton de Gyfford, Baron
Hoche, General Lazare, 218, 222–3
Holcroft, Thomas, 234
Holland: and French threat, 193,
195; France declares war on, 194;
treaty with France (1796), 217
Holland, Elizabeth, Lady (*earlier*
Lady Webster), 98, 165–6, 231–3,
255, 292, 300, 305
Holland, Henry (architect), 177
Holland, Henry Fox, 1st Baron:
origins, 98; and RBS's attitude to
Fox–North alliance, 107; RBS
confesses vanity to, 109;
condemns RBS's speech on
Prince of Wales's marriage, 130;
accuses RBS of stealing epigram,
239; and RBS's drinking, 251; on
RBS's election to Westminster
seat, 268–9; and Grey, 286;
wealth, 289; and Prince Regent's
help for RBS, 296–7; settles
RBS's public house bill, 300;
helps dying RBS, 305; and RBS's
death, 306; as pall bearer at RBS's
funeral, 307
Hood, Admiral Samuel, 1st
Viscount, 124, 174, 268–9
Hopkins, Priscilla, 78
Hopkins, W. (prompter), 77
Howe, Admiral Richard, Earl, 201
Howley, William *see* London,
Bishop of
Hunt, Leigh, 132, 288

Ilchester: RBS elected MP for, 272
Impey, Sir Elijah, 142–3
Inchbald, Elizabeth, 216, 242–3
India: British commercial motives
in, 142–3; *see also* Oudh
Ireland: RBS's interest in, 125–6,
221, 229, 271, 272–3, 291; and
free trade with England, 126–7,
231; French attempt invasion of,

218, 222–3, 226; position of
Catholics in, 221, 230–1, 238,
270, 272–3, 291; rebellion (1798),
221, 222, 224–6; repression and
atrocities in, 223, 225; reunion
with Britain (1801), 230–1, 238;
Whig support for, 271
Ireland, William Henry: and
*Vortigern* deception, 212–14
Iremonger, Richard, 300
Irish Parliament: independence,
126; offers regency to Prince of
Wales, 161; opposes Catholic
concessions, 222, 230; accepts
union with Britain, 238
Irish Volunteer army, 126
Isleworth, 187, 202
Italy: Napoleon reconquers, 236

Jackson, William, 66
Jacobite rebellion (1745), 145
James II, King, 2
Jarvis, Dr Daniel, 153
Jerningham, Edward, 294
Johnson, Esther (Swift's 'Stella'),
3–4
Johnson, Samuel: and Thomas
Sheridan, 16–17, 22, 24, 74, 154;
cows Samuel Foote, 32; on
theatre audience, 72; friendship
with Savage, 74; proposes RBS's
election to Literary Club, 74–5;
reads Charles Sheridan's account
of Sweden, 82; on Garrick's
death, 88; death, 154; RBS's view
of, 302; *Life of Savage*, 242;
*Taxation No Tyranny*, 64
Jonson, Ben: *The Alchemist*, 110
Jordan, Dorothea: at Drury Lane,
132, 179; relations with Duke of
Clarence, 169, 201, 243; attends
first night of *Vortigern*, 214; in
*Pizarro*, 228–9; and assassination
attempt on George III, 237;
remains at Drury Lane, 243; on

Bor, Margaret and Cleeland, Lamond, *Still the Lark: A Biography of Elizabeth Linley*, Merlin Press, 1962

Boswell, James, *Life of Johnson*, John Murray, 1890

Briggs, Asa, *The Age of Improvement, 1783–1867*, Longmans, 1979

Brooke, John, *King George III*, Constable, 1972

Brougham, Lord, *Historical Sketches of Statesmen Who Flourished in the Time of George III*, Charles Knight, 1839

Brown, Philip, *The French Revolution in English History*, Allen & Unwin, 1923

Bryant, Arthur, *The Years of Endurance*, Collins, 1942
    *The Years of Victory*, Collins, 1944

Burke, Edmund, *Reflections on the Revolution in France*, Everyman, 1912

Butler, E. M., *Sheridan: A Ghost Story*, Constable, 1931

Butt, John, *The Age of Johnson*, Clarendon Press, 1979

Byron, Lord, *Poetical Works*, John Murray, 1863

Calder Marshall, Arthur, *The Two Duchesses*, Hutchinson, 1978

Campbell, Thomas, *Life of Mrs Siddons*, Edward Moxon, 1839

Chatel de Briancon, Françoise, *R. B. Sheridan: personnalité, carrière politique*, Didier, Paris, 1974

Cobban, Alfred, *The Debate on the French Revolution*, Nicholas Kaye, 1950

Cumberland, Richard, *Memoirs*, Cadell & Davis, 1807

Darlington, W. A., *Sheridan*, Duckworth, 1933

Davison, Peter (ed.), *Sheridan: Comedies, A Collection of Critical Essays*, Macmillan, 1986

Derry, John W., *Politics in the Age of Fox, Pitt and Liverpool*, Macmillan Education, 1990

Dowden, Wilfred S. (ed.), *Thomas Moore: Journal*, Associated University Press, 1983–91

Earle, William, *Sheridan and his Times by an Octogenarian who Stood by his Knee in Youth and Sat at his Table in Manhood*, J. F. Hope, 1859

Edwardes, Michael, *The Nabobs at Home*, Constable, 1991

Ehrman, John, *The Younger Pitt: The Reluctant Transition*, Constable, 1983

Ellis, Lucy, and Turquan, Joseph, *La Belle Pamela*, Herbert Jenkins, 1924

Fitzgerald, Brian (ed.), *Emily, Duchess of Leinster: Correspondence*, Irish Manuscripts Commission, Dublin, 1953

Fitzgerald, Percy, *The Kembles*, Tinsley Bros, 1871
    *A New History of the English Stage*, Tinsley Bros, 1882
    *Lives of the Sheridans*, Richard Bentley, 1886

Foote, Samuel, *The Maid of Bath*, 1778

Foss, Kenelm, *Here Lies Richard Brinsley Sheridan*, Secker & Warburg, 1939

Foster, R. F., *Modern Ireland: 1600–1972*, Penguin, 1989

O'Keeffe, John, 87
Olivier, Laurence, 80–1, 90
Orde, Thomas, 123, 153
Orléans, Adèle d', 187–8
O'Sheridan family, 2
O'Sheridan, Ostar, 2
Ossory, Anne, Countess of, 144
Ottomans *see* Turkish Empire
Oudh (India): East India Company
actions against Begums of,
138–40; RBS's speech on, 141–5,
149, 308–9; and trial of Warren
Hastings, 148
Oxford University, 54–5, 282

Paine, Tom, 192, 195; *Rights of
Man*, 175
Palmer, John ('Plausible Jack'), 79,
136–7
Palmer, Revd Thomas, 195
Panton (clergyman), 45
Parker, Mr and Mrs Edward, 47
Parker, Richard (mutineer), 219
Parliament: reform proposals, 125,
191–2
Parr, Dr Samuel, 20, 23, 166, 183,
186
Parson, William, 91
Paull, James, 268–9
Paumier, Captain, 46, 51
Peake, Richard, 241, 247, 277, 308,
310
Perceval, Spencer: premiership, 285,
288–9, 294; assassinated, 289
Percy, Hugh, Earl (*later* 3rd Duke of
Northumberland), 268
Perkins, Thomas, 294, 308
*Phaedria* (boat), 209
Philippe Egalité (*earlier* Duc
d'Orléans), 187–8
Piedmont, 244
Pitt, Thomas, 98
Pitt, William, the younger: enters
Parliament, 98; maiden speech,

103; as Chancellor of Exchequer,
106; seeks coalition with Fox,
106–7; declines to form
government (1783), 107; and
RBS's performances in
Commons, 109–10; as 'the
Angry Boy', 110; drinking, 114;
spoof assault on, 115; first
ministry (1783), 123; 1784
election victory, 124–5; and Irish
question, 125–6; reform
proposals (1785), 125, 191;
supported by George III, 127;
and Parliament's settling Prince
of Wales's debts, 129, 210; and
impeachment of Hastings, 138,
145; and Thurlow, 157; and first
regency bill (1788–9), 158–9,
162; Whig hostility to, 162; and
French Revolution, 172; requests
increase in Army estimates, 172;
political stance, 173; defeated
over ultimatum to Russia, 176–7;
and Fox–Burke rift, 176; and
French threat, 192–4, 197;
opposes Grey's reform proposals,
192; on suspension of civil
liberties, 196; fear of RBS, 197;
and Habeas Corpus Act, 204;
introduces Seditious Meetings
Bill, 204; accused of impotence,
210; subsidises Allies in wars with
France, 217–18; duel with
Tierney, 220; seeks peace
negotiations, 220; thanks RBS for
support over fleet, 220; and Irish
grievances, 222; on Kemble and
*Pizarro*, 228; proposes reunion of
Ireland, 230–1; supports Catholic
emancipation, 230–1, 238, 256,
258; praises RBS's patriotism,
237; resigns (1801), 238 9;
RBS's hostility to, 239, 252,
256–8; RBS dismisses as sole
saviour, 245; supports Peace of

357

359

portrait of, 37; marriage, 115–16;
children, 116; helps father, 116;
on Elizabeth's verses to Maria,
134; Weymouth holiday, 134;
death from consumption, 135–6;
burial, 184
Tickell, Richard ('Anticipation'):
friendship with RBS, 115–16,
251; marriage to Mary Linley,
115; songwriting, 117;
Weymouth holiday, 134;
remarries after Mary's death, 136;
at Thomas Sheridan's funeral,
154; political expectations, 160;
falls to death, 211
Tierney, George, 220, 258, 290–1
Tilsit, Treaty of (1807), 276
Tone, Wolfe, 226
Tooke, John Horne: contests
Westminster seat with Fox,
174–5; revives Constitutional
Society, 191; trial and acquittal,
203, 231; backs Paull in
Westminster election, 269
Tories: development as party, 290
Town and Country Magazine, 59
Townshend, Charles, 69
Townshend, Lord John, 35, 69, 96,
107, 147
Trafalgar, Battle of (1805), 262
Treasonable Practices Bill (1795),
204
Turkish Empire (Ottoman): and
Russian threat, 176–7

Ulm, Battle of (1805), 262
Union, Act of (1801), 238
United Irishmen, 222–4
United States of America see
America

Valentia, Arthur Annesley, 9th
Viscount, 140
Vanbrugh, Sir John, The Relapse
(renamed A Trip to Scarborough),

73–4, 132
Vaughan, John Taylor ('Hat'),
304–5
Voltaire, François Marie Arouet de:
Mahomet, 11, 87
Vortigern (forged Shakespeare play),
212–14

Walpole, Horace, 53, 101, 144
Waltham Abbey, Essex, 47–50
Wanstead, 202
Ward, R. Plumer, 246
Washington, George, 81
Watkins, John, 40, 131, 247, 273
Webster, Sir Geoffrey, 165
Wedderburn, Alexander see
Loughborough, 1st Baron
Wellesley, Richard Colley
Wellesley, Marquis (earlier 2nd
Earl of Mornington), 196–7, 300
West Indies: in French wars, 217,
244
Westminster: Fox stands for, 174–5;
RBS elected MP for, 268–9;
RBS loses seat, 272
Westminster Committee, 89, 96–7
Weymouth, 134
Whateley, William, 55
Whigs: development as party, 290
Whitbread, Lady Elizabeth, 299
Whitbread, Samuel: as trustee for
Hecca's marriage settlement, 207;
RBS writes to from Polesden
Lacey, 235; prevents duel, 255;
on RBS's speech on Spain, 277;
background, 280; supervises
restoration of Drury Lane, 280,
292–3; suicide, 292, 302; RBS
blames for losing parliamentary
seat, 295–6; RBS blames for
imprisonment for debt, 299; RBS
criticises, 301
White, Miss (of Bath), 35–6
White's Club, 162
Whyte, Samuel, 15, 16, 18